Deep Mediatization: Concepts and Transformations in Communication

Deep Mediatization: Concepts and Transformations in Communication

Loren Sullivan

CLANRYE INTERNATIONAL
www.clanryeinternational.com

Clanrye International,
750 Third Avenue, 9th Floor,
New York, NY 10017, USA

ISBN: 978-1-64726-613-4

Cataloging-in-Publication Data

Deep mediatization : concepts and transformations in communication / Loren Sullivan.
p. cm.
Includes bibliographical references and index.
ISBN 978-1-64726-613-4
1. Digital media. 2. Digital media--Social aspects. 3. Digital communications.
4. Communication. I. Sullivan, Loren.
HM851 .D44 2023
303.483 3--dc23

For information on all Clanrye International publications
visit our website at www.clanryeinternational.com

CLANRYE INTERNATIONAL

Contents

Preface

It is often said that books are a boon to mankind. They document every progress and pass on the knowledge from one generation to the other. They play a crucial role in our lives. Thus I was both excited and nervous while editing this book. I was pleased by the thought of being able to make a mark but I was also nervous to do it right because the future of students depends upon it. Hence, I took a few months to research further into the discipline, revise my knowledge and also explore some more aspects. Post this process, I begun with the editing of this book.

Mediatization refers to a process in which mass media influences other sectors of society such as politics, business, culture, entertainment, sports, religion and education. Development of technologies such as newspapers, radios, televisions, Internet and interactive social media has been instrumental in shaping the process of mediatization. Deep mediatization refers to an advanced stage of mediatization in which all the elements of the social world are deeply related to digital media and related infrastructures. It has the ability to transform communication in the society. Deep mediatization also leads to a sharp increase in the influence of IT companies. This book provides a comprehensive understanding of deep mediatization and its capacity to transform communication. For all those who are interested in media and communications, it can prove to be an essential guide. Coherent flow of topics, student-friendly language and extensive use of examples make this book an invaluable source of knowledge.

I thank my publisher with all my heart for considering me worthy of this unparalleled opportunity and for showing unwavering faith in my skills. I would also like to thank the editorial team who worked closely with me at every step and contributed immensely towards the successful completion of this book. Last but not the least, I wish to thank my friends and colleagues for their support.

Loren Sullivan

PART I

Transforming Communications: An Introduction

1

Revisiting Transforming Communications: An Overview

Andreas Hepp, Andreas Breiter and Uwe Hasebrink

1.1 Transforming Communications in Times of Deep Mediatization

Since the early 2000s mediatization has become a new, anchoring concept in media and communication research. In essence, mediatization is a 'sensitising concept' (Blumer 1954: 7), in other words a concept that makes us sensitive to two kinds of empirical phenomena (Jensen 2013: 206–208).

The first of these, called the 'quantitative aspects' of mediatization (Couldry and Hepp 2013: 197), is the spread of technologically based communication media. There is virtually no domain in society today that does not somehow relate to media (Lunt and Livingstone 2016: 464).

A. Hepp (✉) · A. Breiter
ZeMKI, Centre for Media, Communication and Information Research, University of Bremen, Bremen, Germany
e-mail: ahepp@uni-bremen.de

A. Breiter
e-mail: abreiter@informatik.uni-bremen.de

U. Hasebrink
Hans Bredow Institute for Media Research, University of Hamburg, Hamburg, Germany
e-mail: u.hasebrink@hans-bredow-institut.de

If we reflect on how we maintain our family relationships, friendships and relationships with our colleagues, how learning, work and leisure, how politics, regulation and administration take place, everything is done nowadays with the use and help of technologically based communication media. As a consequence of this spread of media across all domains of society, it would be inappropriate to continue to understand 'media' as a separate sphere of society (Livingstone 2009: 2f.).

Second are the related 'qualitative aspects' of mediatization (Couldry and Hepp 2013: 197), whereby this spread of technical communication media makes a difference to how social reality is constructed. Irrespective of the social domains that we are talking about, their social construction changes when it takes place with the help of media. We maintain our relationships differently via the use of media (Madianou and Miller 2012), just as we construct other domains of society differently when helped by media. This has to do with the particularities and specificities of media; that is, how they change the possibilities of communication (cf. Lundby 2014). For example, media make it possible to extend processes of social construction locally. Moreover, they offer new chances to stabilize processes or bring in new dynamics by speeding up communication. This is what is called the 'shaping role' or 'moulding force' of media within processes of social construction (Hepp 2013: 54).

Such changes are not merely to do with the media as such but about how communication transforms thanks to changing media. It is through changes in human communicative practices together with other social practices that social construction processes change. This is what we call *transforming communications*. Understood in this way, analyzing transforming communications is not a question of media effects; rather it has to do with analyzing a dialectic relation: media shape or mould practices of communication. We communicate differently depending on the media we use because these media differ in their affordances and specificities (Hjarvard 2013: 27–30). At the same time, media come into existence by building up means and infrastructures of enabling and enhancing communication (Hepp 2013: 54–68). From this point of view, media are institutionalizations and materializations of practices of communication. So, while shaping communication when being established, media at the same time are rooted in the social necessity of communication. We are not confronted with a one-way street of media-driven changes but with a complex dialectic in which social construction becomes more and more entangled with media. This dialectic is the starting point for this volume.

However, we must be aware that mediatization has fundamentally changed over the last decades. For a long time, mediatization research had two waves of mediatization in focus: mechanization and electrification. Neither of these relates to the emergence of one single medium but to the qualitative change of the whole media environment. When media became mechanical—a change that is mostly related to the printing press—a 'systematic cultural transformation began to take hold' (Thompson 1995: 46). As John B. Thomson put it in his book on the emergence of modern societies and their relationship with technically based communication media, the mechanization of communication media offered the chance that 'symbolic forms [could be] produced, reproduced, and circulated on a scale that was unprecedented' and 'patterns of communication and interaction began to change in profound and irreversible ways' (Thompson 1995: 46). The institutional basis for this was the development of media organizations as they first appeared in the second half of the fifteenth century. This process intensified with the use of electricity, that is when radio and television developed and when the various mechanical media of print became dependent upon electricity. Especially because of electronic media such as television, the idea of a 'media logic' crystallized, that is the assumption of a unifying logic of certain media (Altheide and Snow 1979; Asp 1990; Schulz 2004; Mazzoleni 2008; Lundby 2009).

But owing to digitalization we are now confronted with a new wave of mediatization (Finnemann 2011, 2014). Again, the significance of this is not the mere invention of a new medium but the qualitative change occurring in the whole media environment: 'New' digital media arose; and the 'old' mechanical and electronic media also became digital. This is, for example, the case for television, which nowadays is digitally produced, transmitted and watched (using digital television sets, tablets or other devices). In addition, the originally mechanically produced book and newspaper were produced digitally, and later on used as digital artefacts (Thompson 2005). This relates to a remarkable shift to 'datafication' (van Dijck 2014): media are not *only* means of technologically based communication any more. Being digital, at the same time and in addition they became means of producing data that can be delinked from the specific acts of communication and can be used for very different purposes. For example, communicating online via digital platforms, we produce 'metadata' of our social networks, and searching or buying online we leave 'digital traces' (Karanasios et al. 2013: 2452). Such data is processed by algorithms in automatized ways. Processes of social construction through media no longer refer only to human communication, but also to the automatized accumulation and calculation of the data we produce while we use digital devices for communication. Or to put it differently, the social world becomes more and more constructed through datafication.

We can understand this as a new stage of mediatization which needs a distinct term to reflect its specificity. We want to call this new stage one of *deep* mediatization (cf. Couldry and Hepp 2017: 7; Hepp and Hasebrink in this volume). Deep, at this point, has at least a double meaning. First, through the advanced spread of media by digitalization, the character of the social world we inhabit very deeply relies on these technologically based communication media. Second, being digital, these media are not only means of social construction through communication but in addition and on a 'deeper' level means of construction through datafication. With deep mediatization, the very elements and building blocks from which a sense of the social is constructed become themselves based on technologically based processes of mediation. In such a sense, deep mediatization is an advanced stage of mediatization. This results in new challenges for research—such as how we can properly analyze transforming communications in times of deep mediatization.

1.2 Taking a Figurational Approach

The origin of this volume is research that is being undertaken in a Creative Research Unit funded by the German Excellence Initiative in order to develop a new approach to research on transforming communications in times of deep mediatization.[1] One important implication of deep mediatization is that research has to take on a cross-media perspective. As already pointed out, the different waves of mediatization do not refer to the emergence of one single kind of new medium which can be analyzed in an isolated way but to changes in the whole media environment. This implies that research has to look at a variety of different media and take their interrelations into account. Taking an actor's point of view—that is, the perspective of humans acting in this changing media environment—there are even more arguments for this cross-media perspective. In times of deep mediatization, what matters is not the way humans act in social domains in respect of any one single medium, but the way in which a whole variety of different media figure in constructing these different social domains. To give some examples. We inform ourselves via online news, news apps, television and weekly papers (Hasebrink and Domeyer 2010). Our learning does not refer to one single kind of medium (i.e. the book), but to a wide variety of different media (Livingstone and Sefton-Green 2016: 107–147). And our work practices exist across a variety of different media as work more and more becomes 'digital labour' (Scholz 2013: 1). Therefore, from the point of view of everyday practice, we have to take this 'polymedia' (Madianou and Miller 2013) or 'transmedia' (Jansson and Lindell 2014) of present processes of communication seriously. However, doing this implies that we can no longer build our analysis around the investigation of any one kind of medium that is considered as having an impact. Instead, a change of perspective towards a cross-media approach is called for; one that analyses how the various media come together in the communicative construction of social domains. Or put differently, the question is how transforming communications takes place across media in each of these domains.

In doing so, it is obvious that a new analytical concept becomes necessary, one which is able to offer the basis for cross-media research on transforming communications. The idea of the Creative Research Unit was to bring researchers from various disciplines together in order to develop this analytical concept jointly. To reflect the technical nature of deep mediatization from various perspectives, besides scholars from media and communication studies, the Creative Research Unit involved researchers from cultural history, informatics, educational sciences, the study of religion as well as sociology and political science. By comparing transforming communications in various social domains, we developed an approach for describing the communicative and therefore social construction as being rooted in various 'communicative figurations' (Hepp and Hasebrink 2014; Hepp and Hasebrink in this volume). The term figuration goes back to Norbert Elias (1978), who used it to describe structured interrelations between humans in situations such as for example families, groups of office colleagues or political parties. The special capacity of Elias's original idea was his consideration that figurations are not 'given' but are (re)produced in an ongoing 'doing'. In this, Elias's idea has a certain closeness to practice theory in its present form (Couldry 2004; Pentzold 2015).

For the analysis in question, we also had to sharpen and extend the original concept when it comes to questions of communication. This is the reason why we speak of *communicative* figurations. We sharpened it by distinguishing three features of communicative figurations (see Hepp and Hasebrink in this volume): first the constellation of actors who are—having characteristic social roles—involved in a figuration. The second feature constitutes the shared orientations that these actors have in practice within a figuration; that is, their frames of relevance. And the third feature comprises the practices of communication by which these figurations are constructed as meaningful. At the same time, we had to extend the idea of figurations compared with the original idea conceived by Elias, who did not further reflect on the role that technologically based communication media play in our present social world of deep mediatization. Therefore, communicative figurations, as we use this term, are fundamentally entangled with the characteristic media ensemble that the communicative practices refer to.

The core idea of our Creative Research Unit was to develop this figurational approach theoretically on the basis of and in close relation to empirical research. To do this practically, the Creative Unit was structured in three groups, each consisting of a number of projects: one group focusing on *individuals*, their habits, learning and everyday coping in a changing media environment; one group focusing on *social relation* by researching localities and social movements, identity constructions and communication networks; and one group dedicated to *social fields*, namely those of economics, religion, education and politics.

To hold this research together and to ensure theoretical discussion and reflection across the different projects, we met regularly to discuss the progressing empirical work. The Creative Unit also held various workshops and conferences, partly in cooperation with other institutions and associations. Topics covered were approaches to investigating media-related changes, rethinking the mediatization of politics (in cooperation with the Section Mediatization of the European Communication Research and Education Association, ECREA), the expertization of amateurs, diversity in inter- and transcultural communication (in cooperation with the International Communication Section of the German Communication Association, DGPuK), a workshop on media, the city and mobility, a workshop on mediatization and social movements (in cooperation with the Media Sociology Section of the German Communication Association, DGPuK) and finally a concluding conference at which the results published in this book were presented and discussed.

All this was done in close cooperation with colleagues at the Hans-Bredow-Institute Hamburg as well as the University of Hamburg, who are part of our Communicative Figurations network. The idea is to continue its work after this Creative Research Unit ceases its activities. As a research network, we hope to be able to provide a basis for cooperative research on transforming communications in times of deep mediatization and to stimulate others who are developing more complex, multi-level approaches to understanding media-related changes in the social world.

1.3 An Overview of This Volume

This volume is structured in four parts. The first part acts as an introduction, the second is dedicated to collectivities and movements, the third to institutions and organizations, and the fourth to methodologies and perspectives of research.

Part I: Introduction consists—besides this introductory chapter—of a chapter by Andreas Hepp and Uwe Hasebrink in which they outline a figurational approach to investigate transforming communications. This chapter explains the concept of deep mediatization, discusses the trends of the present changing media environment and explains our approach to communicative figurations. As this is the underlying concept for all other chapters in this volume, the chapter by Hasebrink and Hepp is an important step for our overall line of thought.

Within *Part II: Collectivities and Movements* the figurations of different collectives are analyzed. The first chapter investigates the complexity of young people's urban communities in the mediatized city. In doing so, Andreas Hepp, Piet Simon and Monika Sowinska have a double focus. On the one hand, they analyze young people's friendship groups. On the other hand, they explore the figurative quality of mediatized locations in the city; that is, how far certain locations support specific methods of community building. The following two chapters focus on the figurations of different social movements. Sebastian Kubitschko analyzes the communicative construction of media technology as a political category within the Chaos Computer Club. He is interested in the (historical) formation of this critical hacker association in Germany and how acting on media technologies and infrastructures becomes a core issue. In her chapter, Sigrid Kannengießer investigates the consumption-critical media practices of the repair café movement. She is especially interested in the specific actor constellations of repair cafés and in the formation of communicative communities in and through repair cafés. The chapter by Karsten Wolf and Urszula Wudarski reflects the expertization within two cultures of amateur learning: do-it-yourself maker and multi-player online gaming. Taking these two cases, the chapter explores how recent technological changes support new forms of amateur learning and expertization. Taking a historical point of view, Yvonne Robel and Inge Marszolek discuss the construction of space-related identities in Hamburg and Leipzig. They can demonstrate the importance of local and global spaces in the construction of imagined identities with relation to these cities. And in the last chapter of Part II, through a network analysis Thomas Friemel and Matthias Bixler approach what they call networked media collectivities: collectivities of adolescents as they are constructed by a joint interest in and by the use of media as contents and technologies. In all, Part II of this volume addresses different figurations of collectivity building, their specificities and transformation in times of deep mediatization.

The following *Part III: Institutions and Organizations* changes the perspective: less informal collectivities and their transformations are of interest but primarily the focus is on formalized institutions and organizations. In the first chapter, Leif Kramp and Wiebke Loosen reflect on the transformation of journalism. Based on various empirical studies, they investigate to what extent newsroom cultures and the communicative orientation of journalists to their audience change. Rebecca Venema and Stefanie Averbeck-Lietz move to another organizational context, that of professional online blogging, and look at the so-called financial crisis in 2008. They ask to what extent financial blogging was a moralizing or a deliberating venture. The organization of interest in the chapter by Kerstin Radde-Antweiler, Sina Gogolok and Hannah Grünenthal is the Catholic Church. With reference to recent media developments, they ask how the construction of religious authority has changed. A further move in the institutional perspective is undertaken in the chapter by Tanja Pritzlaff-Scheele and Frank Nullmeier. Being interested in political institutions, they reflect the remaining importance of face-to-face interactions in figurations of political decision-making. The last chapter in this section is by Andreas Breiter and Arne Hendrik Schulz. They focus on the school as an organization. Comparing England and Germany, Breiter and Schulz reconstruct the changing role of media in these different figurations and reflect on governance to explain differences between both countries.

Part IV of this volume moves to *Methodologies and Perspectives*. The first three chapters discuss the extent to which researching communicative figurations in times of deep mediatization needs new methodological approaches and methods. Taking a more general point of view, Christine Lohmeier reflects on the methodological challenges of researching communicative figurations. Mainly, she argues that they are rooted in the related move to a non-mediacentric and at the same time cross-media perspective. More specific problems for the methods are addressed in the following two chapters. On the basis of various tests, Juliane Klein, Michael Walter and Uwe Schimank ask what kinds of qualitative interview strategies are appropriate for the investigation of individuals' media repertoires and their relation to certain figurations. The interest of Andreas Breiter and Andreas Hepp in their chapter is the technological side of deep mediatization. They discuss the challenge of putting digital traces in context by the triangulation of automatized data analysis with qualitative data. The following two chapters are written by authors who are not part of the Communicative Figurations research network, and therefore they offer an external perspective on the possibilities of this approach. Kim Schrøder takes a methodological point of view and asks about the implications in this respect. And finally, Giselinde Kuipers reflects the theoretical perspectives of such an approach.

In all, the chapters of this volume cannot and are not aimed at offering a final analysis of transforming communications. This is a project which needs much more effort and a much longer perspective than is possible in a three-year Creative Research Unit. Rather, the idea is that the chapters demonstrate how far a figurational approach is able to link empirical research into transforming communications in various areas in a way that comparison across them becomes possible. It is exactly this kind of comparative research that is needed if we want to understand the changes in our social world that are driven by the trends of deep mediatization in a changing media environment. Our hope is that this volume is able to inspire future research with such a perspective.

Note

1. Creative Units are a format in the institutional strategy of the University of Bremen to offer a kind of exploratory funding to research emergent and new areas. Support for these Creative Units is based on the additional research funding accruing to the University of Bremen as a University of Excellence.

References

Altheide, David L., and Robert P. Snow. 1979. *Media logic*. Beverly Hills, CA: Sage.

Asp, Kent. 1990. Medialization, media logic and mediarchy. *Nordicom Review* 11 (2): 47–50.

Blumer, Herbert. 1954. What is wrong with social theory? *American Sociological Review* 19: 3–10.

Couldry, Nick. 2004. Theorising media as practice. *Social Semiotics* 14 (2): 115–132.

Couldry, Nick, and Andreas Hepp. 2013. Conceptualising mediatization: Contexts, traditions, arguments. *Communication Theory* 23 (3): 191–202.

Couldry, Nick, and Andreas Hepp. 2017. *The mediated construction of reality*. Cambridge: Polity Press.

Elias, Norbert. 1978. *What is sociology?* London: Hutchinson.

Finnemann, Niels O. 2011. Mediatization theory and digital media. *European Journal of Communication* 36 (1): 67–89.

Finnemann, Niels O. 2014. Digitalization: New trajectories of mediatization? In *Mediatization of communication*, ed. Knut Lundby, 297–322. Berlin, New York: de Gruyter.

Hasebrink, Uwe, and Hanna Domeyer. 2010. Zum Wandel von Informationsrepertoires in konvergierenden Medienumgebungen. In *Die Mediatisierung der Alltagswelt*, ed. Maren Hartmann and Andreas Hepp, 49–64. Wiesbaden: VS.

Hepp, Andreas. 2013. *Cultures of mediatization*. Cambridge: Polity Press.

Hepp, Andreas, and Uwe Hasebrink. 2014. Human interaction and communicative figurations: The transformation of mediatized cultures and societies. In *Mediatization of communication*, ed. Knut Lundby, 249–272. Berlin, New York: de Gruyter.

Hjarvard, Stig. 2013. *The mediatization of culture and society*. London: Routledge.

Jansson, A., and J. Lindell. 2014. News media consumption in the transmedia age: Amalgamations, orientations and geo-social structuration. *Journalism Studies* 16 (1): 79–96.

Jensen, K.B. 2013. Definitive and sensitizing conceptualizations of mediatization. *Communication Theory* 23 (3): 203–222.

Karanasios, Stan, Dhavalkumar Thakker, Lydia Lau, David Allen, Vania Dimitrova, and Alistair Norman. 2013. Making sense of digital traces: An activity theory driven ontological approach. *Journal of the American Society for Information Science and Technology* 64 (12): 2452–2467.

Livingstone, Sonia, and Julian Sefton-Green. 2016. *The class. living and learning in the digital age*. New York: NYU Press.

Livingstone, Sonia M. 2009. On the mediation of everything. *Journal of Communication* 59 (1): 1–18.

Lundby, Knut. 2009. Media logic: Looking for social interaction. In *Mediatization: Concept, changes, consequences*, ed. Knut Lundby, 101–119. New York: Peter Lang.

Lundby, Knut. 2014. Mediatization of communication. In *Mediatization of communication*, ed. Knut Lundby, 3–35. Berlin, New York: de Gruyter.

Lunt, Peter, and Sonia Livingstone. 2016. Is 'mediatization' the new paradigm for our field? A commentary on Deacon and Stanyer (2014, 2015) and Hepp, Harvard, and Lundby (2015). *Media, Culture and Society* 38 (3): 462–470.

Madianou, Mirca, and Daniel Miller. 2012. *Migration and new media: Transnational families and polymedia*, 1st ed. London: Routledge.

Madianou, Mirca, and Daniel Miller. 2013. Polymedia: Towards a new theory of digital media in interpersonal communication. *International Journal of Cultural Studies* 16 (6): 169–187. doi:10.1177/1367877912452486.

Mazzoleni, Gianpietro. 2008. Mediatization of society. In *The international encyclopedia of communication*, vol. VII, ed. Wolfgang Donsbach, 3052–3055. Oxford: Blackwell Publishing.

Pentzold, Christian. 2015. Praxistheoretische Prinzipien, Traditionen und Perspektiven kulturalistischer Kommunikations- und Medienforschung. *Medien & Kommunikationswissenschaft* 63 (2): 229–245.

Scholz, Trebor. 2013. Introduction: Why does digital labour matter now? In *Digital labor. The internet as playground and factory*, ed. Trebor Scholz, 1–9. New York: Routledge.

Schulz, Winfried. 2004. Reconstructing mediatization as an analytical concept. *European Journal of Communication* 19 (1): 87–101.

Thompson, John B. 1995. *The media and modernity. A social theory of the media.* Cambridge: Cambridge University Press.

Thompson, John B. 2005. *Books in the digital age.* Cambridge, Malden: Polity.

van Dijck, José. 2014. Datafication, dataism and dataveillance: Big Data between scientific paradigm and ideology. *Surveillance and Society* 12 (2): 197–208.

2

A Figurational Perspective on Transforming Communications Research

Andreas Hepp and Uwe Hasebrink

2.1 Introduction

Investigating the influence of changing media and communications on society is a long-term aim of research. With the perspective of media effects, this was grasped to be the influence of a certain media content—media coverage, political campaigns, television shows and so on—on audiences. From the point of view of medium theories, this influence is related to a single kind of medium—books, television, mobile phones and so on—which shape our communication and perception, and by so doing influence our society's characteristics. Both perspectives have a long and rich tradition, and exploring them has resulted in many, partly path-breaking, contributions—far too many to discuss here.

A. Hepp (✉)
ZeMKI, Centre for Media, Communication and Information Research, University of Bremen, Bremen, Germany
e-mail: andreas.hepp@uni-bremen.de

U. Hasebrink
Hans Bredow Institute for Media Research, University of Hamburg, Hamburg, Germany
e-mail: u.hasebrink@hans-bredow-institut.de

However, nowadays the situation has become much more complicated. With a huge variety of different media and their spread across very different domains of society, it no longer seems appropriate to conceptualize any certain kind of media content or medium as *the* 'driving force' that is changing society. We have to accept that any possible influence of media as contents and technologies arises out of 'cross-media' (Bjur et al. 2014) and 'polymedia' (Madianou and Miller 2013) situations, or to be more specific, a 'media manifold' (Couldry and Hepp 2016: 11, 53). By 'manifold', we refer not just to the plurality of today's media channels and interfaces, but their interlinked nature and the many-dimensional order that results from this and encompasses our whole media environment. In addition, we have to consider that what we call 'media' has been changed fundamentally by digitalization and a related datafication. Nowadays, more and more media—'new' as well as 'old'—are becoming digital. This means not just that they rely on a digital infrastructure which is closely related to the internet. At the same time and much more far-reaching, it also means that all media are tending to be based on software, which means algorithms become part of our media-related sense-making. Media, nowadays, are no longer simply means of communication but at the same time and additionally are means of collecting data about us as their users in real time.

With all these changes, the question of 'transforming communications'—that is, how media change communication and by that our social construction of reality—has not lost any of its relevance. In fact, the question has become even more important as media-related influences enter different societal domains. Mediatization research argues that we can notice a 'domain specificity' of mediatization (Hjarvard 2013: 4; Nieminen 2014: 64; Lunt and Livingstone 2016: 1), while remaining rather vague about what 'social domain' precisely means and how we can theorize it properly. The challenge at this point is to clarify how we can conceptualize the very different domains of society so that we are able to undertake comparative research on (deep) mediatization across them.

This chapter aims to outline one possible approach to reattempting the research of transforming communications. We closely relate this to what we call a 'figurational approach'. This is a perspective that moves the figurations of human actors into the foreground and at the same time takes into account how far these figurations are entangled with media as contents and technologies, which on a deeper level refers both to media organizations and infrastructures. Through stepwise and comparative empirical research on media-related changes in certain communicative figurations, we can gain a bigger picture that shows the more complex processes of societal transformations.

In this introductory chapter, we want to outline this figurational perspective and in so doing develop an approach for empirically investigating transforming communications. To do this, we will first reflect on our changing media environment, which we understand as marked by deep mediatization. Second, we will argue that mediatization research is right to emphasize the domain specificity of (deep) mediatization. However, we need to sharpen the idea of social domain. On this basis, we want to argue how far it is helpful to investigate transforming communications by analyzing changing 'communicative figurations'. Finally, in the conclusion we will make some remarks about what this means for practical empirical research.

2.2 The Changing Media Environment in Times of Deep Mediatization

The idea of mediatization is a particularly helpful starting point to describe how changes in the media environment are part of an overall 'meta process' (Krotz 2007: 256).[1] This is related to other meta processes of change: mainly individualization, globalization and commercialization. Mediatization is a long-term and non-linear process traceable back at least to the beginning of various modernities (Thompson 1995; Meyen 2009; Hjarvard 2013; Esser and Strömbäck 2014; Lundby 2014b). In essence, the term mediatization captures on the one hand the increasing spread of technologically based media in society; and on the other hand how different social domains are being more and more shaped by these media. As we have already emphasized, this process has fundamentally intensified over the last decade. To approach this, we wish to use the term *deep mediatization*. By calling the contemporary mediatization *deep*, we want to indicate that with the recent wave of digitalization, mediatization has entered a new stage[2]: it is no longer expedient to grasp the social impact of 'media' merely as the influence of a distinct domain (i.e. journalism) which is separate from other domains of the social world (Livingstone 2009: 2–4). No matter which domain of society we consider, its formation is in one way or another related to the technologically based media of communication, which are all becoming digital.

Deep mediatization is by no means homogeneous or linear. It is highly complicated, contradictory and a conflict-driven process. Nevertheless, in the Western hemisphere, deep mediatization takes place across societies as a whole. Yet even when we strive to escape from this all-encompassing contemporary mediatization—for example, individuals who refuse to use certain (digital) media in an attempt at 'coping' (Schimank 2011: 459–462) with being reachable at all times of the day and night, or organizations that introduce email-free holidays—such behaviour merely constitutes what we can call temporary 'oases of de-mediatization', in loose reference to Hartmut Rosa (2013: 87). In this sense, popular self-help literature on 'mindfulness'—the practice of bringing one's attention to things occurring in the present moment, beyond any mediated communication—is less about any durable containment of mediatization: it is rather an expression that deep mediatization includes spaces of self-reflection and controlled escape in order to remain manageable for us as human beings.

With respect to these arguments, the concept of deep mediatization is neither an attempt at a closed theory nor a limited theoretical approach. There are various traditions of mediatization research, and such a range is needed because of the complexity of the field.[3] However, across these different traditions, we can at *a first level* understand mediatization as a 'sensitising concept' (Jensen 2013: 213–217; Strömbäck and Esser 2014: 4; Lunt and Livingstone 2016: 464); that is, a concept that 'gives the user a general sense of reference and guidance in approaching empirical instances' and that 'merely suggests directions along which to look' (Blumer 1954: 7). This means to look at the overall spread of different media and the related changes in various social domains (Schulz 2014: 58–62). Using the term *deep* mediatization makes us 'sensitive' to how far mediatization nowadays progresses into what has been called 'mediatized worlds' (Hepp and Krotz 2014: 6) and a 'mediatized way of life' (Vorderer et al. 2015: 259).

At a second level, and departing from this, we need further concepts and approaches to describe *in detail* how the transformation that we relate to the term mediatization actually takes place. While we have a rough estimate of the processes and practices that constitute deep mediatization, we still lack thorough empirical investigations.

Reflecting this specificity of different phenomena of media-related changes and their particularities, it is nevertheless striking that they are all confronted with certain *trends* that characterize the change of the present media environment. If we understand the 'media environment' as the entire body of available media at any given time in society (Livingstone 2001: 307; Hasebrink and Hölig 2014: 16; Jensen and Helles 2015: 292), we can initially distinguish at least five such trends: first, a *differentiation* of a vast number of technologically based media of communication; second, an increasing *connectivity* of and through these media, which offers the possibility to individually and collectively 'link' across space and time; third, a rising *omnipresence* of media that creates the possibility to connect permanently and everywhere; fourth, a *rapid pace of innovation*, the emergence of 'new' media and services in ever-shorter periods of time; and fifth, a *datafication*, which is the representation of social life in computerized data via media devices and their underlying software and infrastructure.

None of these trends is to be seen as a separate individual media phenomenon; rather, they are all closely linked with each other, and altogether they are characteristic of the present changes in our media environment (Bjur et al. 2014: 15). We have to be aware that these trends are not 'linear'. It is also uncertain whether these trends will continue or whether other trends will emerge. In addition, they are highly contradictory in themselves. However, altogether they are manifestations of deep mediatization, and distinguishing between such trends provides us with a first understanding of the media-related changes in which we are involved.

The trend for *differentiation* in the media means that the number of media and their functionalities have increased over recent decades. While in the beginning there was a discussion concerning whether digitalization might result in the dominance of the computer as the sole 'metamedium' (Kay and Goldberg 1977; Höflich 2003),[4] it turned out that the result of digitalization was rather the arrival of a variety of very different media, which at the present stage are becoming more and more digital and increasingly based on software (see Manovich 2013). The differentiation of media gives rise to a variety of contradictory impacts. While digital media might support self-paced learning for young people and adults (Wolf 2015; Wolf and Wudarski in this volume), the same media can be used to build up authoritarian relationships in religious organizations (Radde-Antweiler 2015; Radde-Antweiler and Grünenthal and Gogolok in this volume). Reflecting both these aspects, across the variety of possible consequences we can assume that differentiation might result in an *optionality* (Rusch 2006) of ways of use. These can be related to processes of individualization (Hasebrink 1999) and, following from this, *contingency* within and across social domains and related questions of inequality and power. This can have various further influences on the *segmentations*, *exclusions* and *divides* articulated in a specific social domain (van Deursen and Helsper 2015; Nieminen 2016). For example, an increasing number of media as contents and technologies might weaken (as our preliminary research shows) the binding power of communicative practices within communities (Marszolek and Robel 2016), and the variability of possible contacts might increase (Friemel 2013). This may be especially discussed in relation to internet-based contact platforms, which are understood as supporting 'weak ties' instead of 'strong' relations within the direct living environment (Wittel 2008; Rainie and Wellman 2012: 131–134).

The media environment of deep mediatization is characterized by the trends of an intensified *connectivity*. By connectivity, we primarily mean the interconnectedness of various media owing to their digitalization and the infrastructure of the internet. This is the case for 'old' media such as television and the digital press, but increasingly and with reference to personal communication for 'new' media such as online platforms and mobile phone applications. As a consequence, there is a close relationship between more recent processes of mediatization and globalization (Krotz 2008). A characteristic of contemporary everyday life is our ability to socially connect globally, across various media, if we want to. But, '"connectivity" does not necessarily mean "social connectedness"' (van Dijck 2013: 4). Increasing media connectivity can result in a *spatial extension* of processes of construction (Wessler and Brüggemann 2012: 119–136; Hepp 2015: 13–18), and through that social domains can extend and their borders become *blurred*. This might 'disembed' (Giddens 1990: 20) social processes being maintained across large distances. For example, it can become easier to build networks for learning over long distances (Thomas and Brown 2011: 53; Ito et al. 2009: 213), popular cultures can exist transnationally (Buckingham and Kehily 2014) and whole organizations or networks of organizations can be built up across various locations (Breiter 2003; Ribes et al. 2013; Lammers and Jackson 2014: 33–47; Jarke 2015)—all of this held together by technologically based communication. However, we must be careful in assuming any one single set of possible consequences of media's connectivity. In other words, the further consequence of connectivity is very much context dependent.

Besides the increasing differentiation and connectivity, the social, temporal and spatial spread of media relates to their *omnipresence*. Face-to-face meetings, talks or walking and other social situations, which for a long time were not related to media, have nowadays become so in one way or another. These dynamics are especially propelled through the spread of mobile communication technologies (Katz and Aakhus 2002; Ling and Donner 2009; Goggin 2011; Vorderer et al. 2015). It has become possible to be 'always on' (Chen 2011: 63) and 'constantly in touch' (Agar 2003: 22); that is, reachable at any time. This omnipresence of various media can result in an increasing 'acceleration' (Rosa 2013: 41–43) of social processes. We might, for example, expect immediate answers, a quick delivery and a fast response. With reference to this, social domains can be marked by new temporalities, especially with expectations of a new '*immediacy*' (Tomlinson 2007: 72–93) of communicative reaction. Arguably, the result of this is a general *acceleration* of life (Wajcman 2015: 13–35). This can be the case in the sphere of work, and also in our private life. More recent research indicates that the omnipresence of media also stimulates a new appreciation of 'media-free' situations and spaces, in highly institutionalized contexts such as politics (Pritzlaff-Scheele and Nullmeier in this volume) as well as in private life (Roitsch 2017). It is, again, worth noting that substantial differences exist between one social domain and another.

A rapid *pace of innovation* has accompanied recent media developments. This means that the time sequence of more or less fundamental media innovations has—at least in the *perception* of many media users—shortened over the past few decades (Rosa 2013: 71–74).[5] This pace of innovation might result in a constantly perceived *adjustment pressure*, a perceived pressure to 'conform' to these changes with a possible breakdown of the ability to adapt. While various innovations surrounding the smartphone and its apps have become widespread, the most recent assumption is that the 'internet of things' and its 'locations awareness' might once again change 'everything' (Greengard 2015: 60). However, we should generally be cautious about any 'rhetoric of the technological sublime' (Morley 2007: 235) related to the present pace of innovation, because complex articulations of *segmentation* and *exclusion* are evident as they are reflected in such concepts as *divide* (Norris 2001;

van Dijk and Hacker 2005; Zillien 2009; Livingstone and Helsper 2007; Tsatsou 2011). Being able to appropriate and adjust to certain media innovations means to be in a power position, no matter whether this is within the family, a group of friends or in certain organizations, especially when it comes to questions of regulation (Schulz et al. 2011). Even an attitude of openness towards innovations might privilege entire social groups as 'pioneer communities' (Hepp 2016), such as, for example, the Quantified Self movement vis-à-vis other social groups such as excluded homeless people (Koch 2016a). An outcome of all this can be segmentation between different sections of the population (Drgomir and Thompson 2014; Friemel 2016).

The term *datafication* refers to digitalization: a growing number of media are based on software. As a result, through the use of these media we leave 'digital traces' (Karanasios et al. 2013), data that can be aggregated and processed in automated ways on the basis of algorithms. This is the case across the variety of digital media platforms (van Dijck and Poell 2013), which are also understood as 'social software' (Stegbauer and Jäckel 2007: 7–10). In public discourse, this change of the media environment is mainly discussed with reference to the concept of 'big data' (Mayer-Schönberger and Cukier 2013; for a critique see boyd and Crawford 2012; Lohmeier 2014). This means that the representation of social phenomena by quantified data plays an increasing role in societal self-understanding and self-conception, with the result that technical intermediaries (search engines, platforms, etc.) *disguise agency* by 'quantification' (Passoth et al. 2014: 281–283; Pasquale 2015: 32–38). On the other hand, there is the hope of new, technologically based forms of transparency that might support *participation* as it is discussed, for example, with reference to open data and smart cities (Townsend 2013; Koch 2016b: 210, 218). Furthermore, such a datafication can result in a *stabilization* of sociality, which is 'society made durable' (Latour 1991: 103). At the same time, as the public debate following Edward Snowden's revelations has illustrated (Schulz 2013), new possibilities of *surveillance* emerge—for governmental agencies (Fuchs 2013; Lyon 2014) as well as for private actors (Andrejevic and Gates 2014; Christensen and Jansson 2014).

As we have already pointed out, one must be cautious about the trends of deep mediatization we outlined above: these are preliminary interpretations on the basis of the general state of media and communication research. Keeping the uncertainty about their directedness and future stability in mind, these trends offer us guidance in respect of how our media environment is changing with the process of deep mediatization.

2.3 The Domain Specificity of Deep Mediatization

Beyond detailed research results, existing studies on mediatization agree that any process of mediatization is very specific in relation to the social domain under consideration. This term social domain is used by various representatives of mediatization research (amongst others Hjarvard 2013; Ekström et al. 2016; Lunt and Livingstone 2016), while coming close to the everyday understanding of 'spheres' of society. In its widest sense, the term 'social domain' refers to those 'spheres' as being meaningful in everyday practice. The scaling of the different 'meaningful domains' can be very different, reaching from certain social groups or organizations to whole social fields or systems. We can understand this scaling to be a problem of terminological blurriness. However, the main argument being pushed forward in mediatization research is different. By hinting at the domain specificity of mediatization, scholars want to emphasize the variety of mediatization across different spheres of society. Mediatization is not a homogeneous process but very much differs from one area to another. It is a 'domain-specific' phenomenon.

We can understand this as taking up a long tradition in social sciences relating to the idea of 'social' as well as 'cultural' differentiation (Winter and Eckert 1990: 142–151; Hahn 2000: 14–24; Schimank 2013: 37–50; 131–149). Max Weber, for example, used the term *Wertsphären* (Weber 1988 [1919]: 611) to reflect this. Pierre Bourdieu (1993) described processes of differentiation by analyzing differences within and across 'social fields'. Roger Friedland and Robert Alford (1991) preferred the idea of 'institutional fields'. In system theory, we find the concept of 'subsystem' (Luhmann 2012, Vol. 2: 4–27), a term which was also used by Jürgen Habermas (1992) to describe social differentiation. In a similar vein, phenomenology puts emphasis on different (small) 'life-worlds' (Schütz 1967: 139–144; Luckmann 1970: 587), with a certain relationship to the 'social worlds' of symbolic interactionism (Shibutani 1955: 566; Strauss 1978; Clarke 2011: 384–385). More recently, Luc Boltanski and Laurent Thévenot (2006) proposed the idea of different 'orders of justification'.

Mediatization research investigates its 'domain specificity' with reference to such different theoretical conceptualizations and scalings. For example, there is a discussion about the mediatization of different 'social fields' in Bourdieu's understanding (Couldry 2012: 144–153), of different (sub-)systems in the sense of Luhmann (Kunelius and Reunanen 2016: 8–12), or different 'social worlds' in the sense of phenomenology and symbolic interactionism (Hepp and Krotz 2014: 6–9). Therefore, using the term 'social domain' within mediatization research does not have the intention of suggesting that these different theoretical conceptualizations are the same. Rather, using the less theoretically loaded term 'domain', it emphasizes one fundamental empirical result across these theoretical conceptualizations within mediatization research: mediatization takes place very differently in different spheres of society.

To empirically operationalize such a domain specificity, the level of society as such seems to be inappropriate and even the level of whole fields of society seems to be too general. One becomes able to operationalize such a kind of research as soon as one moves to what is called the 'meso-level' (cf. Donges and Jarren 2014: 181–182), that is the level of specific kinds of collectivities (groups, communities, etc.) and specific kinds of organizations (enterprises, schools, etc.). We are able to investigate the domain specificity of (deep) mediatization if we move to a level which is called in actors-centred sociology 'supra-individual actors' (Schimank 2010: 327–329), that is a structured constellation of individual actors: collectivities then become concrete as 'collective actors', whose members share certain practices of meaning construction and reciprocal observation. Organizations become 'corporative actors' whose shared practices are based on binding agreements.

Approaching from such a point of view the 'domain specificity' of (deep) mediatization makes a specific challenge of mediatization research explicit. It is less helpful to understand (mass) media as a domain of their own in the sense of a certain social field or system, and to investigate their influence on other social domains in a way that 'media logic' (Altheide and Snow 1979) would colonize the logics of other domains. For a critique of such an approach see for example (Strömbäck 2008; Esser 2013; Landerer 2013), who all ask for further concretization of 'media logic as a metaphor' (Hjarvard 2017). Beyond such a need to make the idea of media logic more concrete, there is a second problem about theorizing media as a domain of its own that relates closer to the character of present deep mediatization: when digital media permeate the various domains of society (Livingstone 2009: 2f.), it becomes more complicated to see them as a domain of their own.

To substantiate this, we can think about collectivities. To research, for example, the question about how the communicative construction of families transforms with today's media changes, questions arise regarding which representations of the family become communicated by mass media (and if the 'logic' of journalistic coverage has consequences for an everyday construction of the family). In addition, further questions matter: for example, how communicative networking in the family takes place, how unknown or forgotten family members are 'found' by the algorithms of Facebook, how family members construct their family memories by exchanging digital images and so on. Again, we are confronted with the necessity of reflecting the cross-media and technology-related character of present communicative constructions of the family (Hasebrink 2014: 232).

Generalizing this, there is a certain paradox. This is that today's media of communication are not a domain on their own. They are a phenomenon across domains. At the same time the characteristics of the transformations that relate to these media are 'domain specific', and we have to have different levels of scaling in mind. This domain specificity becomes especially concrete at the level of supra-individual actors, that is collectivities and organizations.

2.4 Researching Transforming Communications

Having an understanding of the changing media environment of deep mediatization, and within this the domain specificity of related transformations as outlined so far, it is evident that the possible consequences of a changing media environment can differ depending on context. But how can we research and compare the possible consequences of a changing media environment with reference to very different social domains? Basically, we are confronted with the challenge of firming up the idea of social domains in a conceptual framework. This framework has to be substantiated sufficiently enough to offer a stable design for collaborative empirical research, comparison and theory development; and it has to be flexible enough to reflect the specificity of the social domain under investigation.

This is where an actor's point of view is particularly important, as it is related to the figurational approach we want to outline. From such a point of view, two aspects matter above all. First, a changing media environment can develop only if practices change. When it comes to media, these are predominantly *practices of communication*. Second, such changing practices are not just individual phenomena; they have to be analyzed with respect to the social domains in which humans act. We refer here to the already mentioned concept of *communicative figuration*.

2.4.1 Communicative Practices and Their Entanglement with Media

In media and communication research, approaches that move agency and social practice into the foreground have a long tradition and can be traced back to the beginnings of sociology. This perspective first peaked in the 1970s across different areas, such as audience research (Teichert 1972; Blumler and Katz 1974; Renckstorf and Wester 2001) or cultural studies (Hall 1973; Morley 1980; de Certeau 2002) that no longer considered media users as 'dopes' but as persons acting reflexively with media, being situated in a wider social and cultural surrounding. On such a basis, it became common to consider people as actors who 'deal' with media (Hasebrink 2003; Neumann-Braun 2000; Napoli 2010; Bonfadelli and Friemel 2014)—no matter whether they come from the side of media production, media use or various kinds of hybrids (Bruns and Schmidt 2011).

Based on this tradition, we can witness a recent and more focused move in research towards media practice.[6] This has to be seen in the wider context of a *practice turn* in the social sciences.[7] There are two aspects to be learned from this development: first, to consider every activity as 'embodied', and second, to consider the nexus of practices with 'artefacts, hybrids, and natural objects' (Schatzki 2001: 11).

When it comes to human acting, a practice approach is interested in the 'embodied doing' of an activity as such. This doing is based on 'practical consciousness' (Giddens 1984: xxiii), which is learned in highly contextualized ways. Based on this learning, practices can be realized in a meaningful way *without* being 'discursively' accessible to the actors; that is, they cannot personally explain their doing, and this is also the case for communication.[8] 'Practical consciousness' as embodied capacity is rather understood as know-how, skills, tacit knowledge and dispositions, related to the habitus of a person. Most practices are based on this 'practical knowledge', which has its own potential for situational creativity. Practices are anchored in the body and cannot be described as a mechanical obedience to rules. In this sense, practices of communication—with media but also without—are also embodied and have to be considered in their interrelation to other forms of practice (Bourdieu 1977: 16–22; Reichertz 2009: 118–120).

The argument that we should focus on the entanglement of practices with objects is of special interest, because with deep mediatization communicative practice increasingly turns into a media-entangled and therefore object-related practice. Here, practice theory itself puts emphasis on the media as a specific kind of object when it comes to the production of meaning: 'writing, printing and electronic media mould social (here, above all, discursive) practices' (Reckwitz 2002: 253). This is the reason why many communicative practices are 'media practice[s]' (Couldry 2004: 125); that is to say, they are undertaken in relation to media.

Following this line of reasoning, we can understand *practices of communication* as complex and highly contextualized patterns of doing. Or to put it another way, certain forms of communicative action build up complex practices of communication as they are realized today in the increasingly complex media environment of the media manifold. Communication therefore involves the use of signs that humans learn during their socialization and which, as symbols, are for the most part entirely arbitrary. This means that the meaning of communicative practices depends on social conventions. Practices of communication are fundamental to the human construction of reality: we 'create' the meaning of our social world in multiple processes of communication; we are born into a world in which communication already exists; we learn what is characteristic of this social world (and its society) through the (communicative) process of learning to speak; and when we proceed to act in this social world our practices are always also communicative practices.

This understanding of communication has certain implications for conceptualizing *media*. Putting aside symbolic generalized media of influence such as 'love' or 'money' (Luhmann 2012: 190–238) and focusing on technologically based communication media of 'second order' (Kubicek 1997: 218–220), we can understand them as means of communication, distinguished by specific technologies and their infrastructures, a system of signs and various institutionalizations and organizations that furnish us with services for communicative practice (Beck 2006: 14). Media of communication 'institutionalize' and 'objectify', that is to say 'materialize' symbol systems and practices (Berger and Luckmann 1967: 49–61; Fornäs 2000; Knoblauch 2013: 300f.; Couldry and Hepp 2016: 15–33). This is how they 'mould' (Reckwitz 2002: 253) communication. With deep mediatization, the challenging question is the 'moulding influence' of a medium in its respective typical constellation with other media. We have to address this constellation on at least three levels. These are, firstly, the level of the entire *media environment*. As we have already noted above, what we mean by media environment is the entire body of available media at any given time. Secondly, there is the level of the *media ensemble*. This is the subset of the media in a media environment as it is used in a particular social domain (family, company, etc.) with respect to the available options (Bausinger 1984: 349). Thirdly, there is the level of *media repertoire*. This is the individuals' selection of the media as they use and appropriate them as part of their everyday practices (Hasebrink and Popp 2006).

With deep mediatization, our practices of communication typically reach across media. When we inform ourselves with reference to a certain topic, we talk with people, we email others, read online articles and possibly books, and we might 'ask' Apple's software assistant Siri to search for information on the internet. Therefore, when it comes to the question of how our social domains are moulded by media, we have to consider such cross-media influences with regard to various types of communication.

2.4.2 Social Domains as Communicative Figurations

Investigating transforming communications from a cross-media and therefore 'non-mediacentric' point of view entails defining the starting point of analysis,[9] via the social entity—the 'social domain'—under consideration. But this is exactly the point where we have to become clearer about what we have, up to this point, loosely called the 'meso level' of social domains.

To theorize this further, the process-sociological approach of Norbert Elias (1978) is of great help and importance.[10] Elias identified two problems for any social analysis: the relative autonomy but co-dependence of individuals and society, and the distinction between social change (the fact that each progression of life means variances) and structural transformation (fundamental changes in society). His solution was to argue that structural transformation could be explained in terms of the shifting relation between individuals and society through time. Elias referred to these dynamics as figurations—or as we would put it, as figurations of certain social domains. Figurations are 'networks of individuals' (Elias 1978: 15) or, in more encompassing terms, actors, including collectivities and organizations. These actors constitute, by their interaction, larger social entities. Therefore, figuration is a 'simple conceptual tool' to understand social domains in terms of 'models of processes of interweaving' (Elias 1978: 30, 130).

A development that Elias could hardly reflect, though he had some presentiment of it (Elias 1991: 163), is that today many figurations are made up by the use of media. This is one possible driving force of their transformation: the figurations of individuals, collectivities (families, peer groups, communities, etc.) and organizations (media companies, churches, schools, etc.) change with their media ensembles. In addition, deep mediatization makes new figurations possible, such as online gatherings in chatrooms, on platforms or through apps. But there are even further developments. Nowadays, some figurations are entirely built up by media technologies. One example is the 'collectivities of taste' as they become represented by groups of people with the same shopping interests in online stores such as Amazon (Passoth et al. 2014: 282). Other examples are 'networked media collectivities' (Friemel and Bixler in this volume) that are constituted around certain media events and topics.

From a media and communication research point of view, we can consider each figuration as a *communicative* one: practices of communication are of high importance when it comes to a meaningful construction of the respective figuration. *Communicative figurations* are (typically cross-media) patterns of interweaving through practices of communication. Members of families as collectivities, for example, are possibly separated in space but connected through multi-modal communication such as (mobile) phone calls, emailing, sharing on digital platforms and so on that keep family relationships alive (Madianou and Miller 2012; Hasebrink 2014; Hepp et al. 2015) and allow the construction of family memories (Lohmeier and Pentzold 2014). Or organizations as communicative figurations are kept together with the help of databases and communication across the intranet, as well as printed flyers and other media of internal and external communication. Individuals are involved in such figurations through the roles and positions they have in the respective actor constellations. An approach of media and communication research that starts with figurations, therefore, is able to link perspectives on individuals, collectivities and organizations in a productive way.

Taking such a perspective, there are at least three features that are characteristic of a communicative figuration (see Hepp and Hasebrink 2014: 260–262; Couldry and Hepp 2016: 66f.):

- First, a communicative figuration has a certain *constellation of actors* that can be regarded as its structural basis: a network of individuals who are interrelated and are communicating amongst themselves.
- Second, each communicative figuration has dominating *frames of relevance* that serve to guide its constituting practices. These frames define the 'topic' and therefore the character of a communicative figuration.
- Third, we are dealing with specific *communicative practices* that are interwoven with other social practices. In their composition, these practices typically draw on and are entangled with a *media ensemble.*

Investigating communicative figurations offers us a cross-media and processual meso-level approach to the construction of what are called 'social domains' in mediatization research as well as their transformation through deep mediatization. Today, we are confronted with various dynamically changing media-related figurations. We gain access to them by researching their actor constellations, frames of relevance and communicative practices, all of which are entangled with a media ensemble.

Summing up this understanding of communicative figurations and referring back to the main trends in a changing media environment, we can visualize such an analytical approach as follows (see Fig. 2.1):

A changing media environment moulds the communicative figurations of social domains—their actor constellations, frames of relevance and communicative practices. As outlined above, with deep mediatization we may expect at present five dominant trends in a changing media environment: a differentiation of media, increasing connectivity through various media, their rising omnipresence, a rapid pace of innovation and datafication of human interaction through media. It depends on the social domain under consideration how strongly these trends shape or mould the related figuration. Investigating the transformations of such a domain, the following questions are obvious: To what extent do the actor constellations transform with a changing media ensemble in this

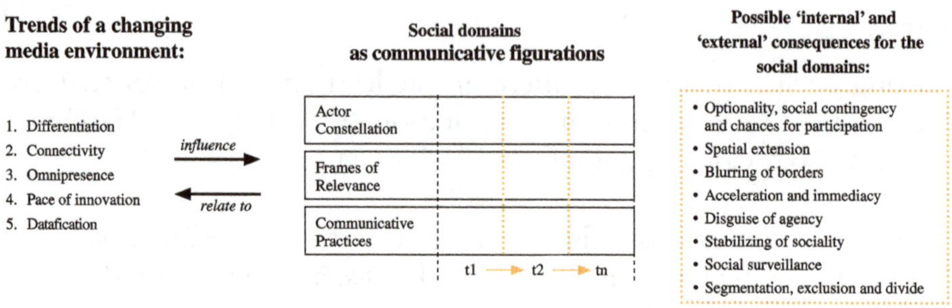

Fig. 2.1 Investigating transforming communications in times of deep mediatization

communicative figuration? How far do practices of communication shift? And what are the consequences of this on a figuration's relevance frames?

Based on the research discussed so far, we can assume a number of possible consequences as a hypothetical set: the optionality, contingency and chances of participation in social domains might increase; social domains' communicative figurations might extend spatially; their borders might blur; there might be an acceleration and increasing immediacy within and across them; a disguise of agency might come about; media technology might stabilize sociality in social domains; social surveillance might take place; or all might result in segmentation, exclusion and division. While these assumed consequences are a starting point for future research, it remains an open question as to which of them is characteristic for which social domain, how these different consequences interfere with each other and even if there might be further consequences we are not aware of at present. In addition, we have to consider the different ways in which social domains relate to these trends in deep mediatization's changing media environment. They can be supportive of such changes, for example by always appropriating the latest media. Alternatively, by rejecting certain media, they can hinder these trends.

For any empirical research, we need to have the dual character of possible consequences in mind. On the one hand, a changing media environment might have 'internal' consequences for a social domain—for example, optionality, disguise of agency or segmentation of figuration might take place. This is the case, for example, when relations in an organization change partly owing to the media that are used for communication, for instance in news rooms (Loosen 2014). The same can be said for families in which the segmentation of knowledge transforms when digital media become part of the family's memory construction (Lohmeier and Pentzold 2014). On the other hand, there might be 'external' consequences: figurations also change in their relation to each other. If journalism organizations change, for example, their relationship with audiences transforms: we are confronted with so-called '"blurring boundaries" of journalism' (Loosen 2014: 68). Detailed comparative empirical research into the communicative figurations of different social domains can offer us the chance to make more general statements about transforming communications, focusing on individuals, collectivities and organizations.

2.5 Communicative Figuration as an Approach for Empirical Research

By investigating communicative figurations, we therefore adopt an *open analytical approach* that gives us the chance to research the transformation of social domains with deep mediatization. This approach is open to various macro-concepts of society such as 'network society' (Castells 2000), 'media society' (Imhof et al. 2004), 'communication society' (Münch 2002), 'next society' (Baecker 2007) or a 're-assembling of the social' (Latour 2007). Such concepts offer more general considerations of how the social world might transform with the changing media environment, and are therefore an important source for posing empirical questions about media-related changes. Yet, as we are living in the middle of the changes we capture with the term deep mediatization, it might be too early to draw conclusions about any particular communication model of media-related transformations of society. Taking into account all of the above, we still need further detailed comparative research on different social domains before we can make general claims.

For this kind of research, communicative figuration constitutes a highly productive 'bridging concept' because of its process perspective on practices and its emphasis on actor constellations.[11] The concept of figurations links a micro-analysis of individual practices with a meso-analysis of certain social domains and thus offers us various possibilities to contextualize this with macro questions about society at the very least (see Ryan 2005: 503). In so doing, it offers an important contribution to the discussion of the 'micro-meso-macro link in communications' (Quandt and Scheufele 2011: 9) that is open to various empirical and theoretical approaches.[12]

To link the detailed analysis of specific figurations with macro ques tions of transformation, it is important to be aware of the fact that figurations of social domains are interrelated in various ways: via their overlapping actor constellations, different figurations can be linked with each other. In addition, figurations of collectivities and organizations can become 'supra-individual actors' (Schimank 2010: 327–342) that are part of the actor constellation of other figurations and thus build 'figurations of figurations' (Couldry and Hepp 2016: 71–78). One example here is constituted by figurations of various organizations acting together in a certain institutional field. Besides that, it is important to take into account that figurations do not simply co-exist side by side, but that they are arranged with each other in a meaningful way. For example, in the majority of Western societies, the family is given some special societal meaning because of recreation and bringing up children; organizations such as schools or adult education centres are constructed with certain responsibilities for educating people; journalism organizations deal with information and entertainment, while as companies they also have the role of generating income and jobs. One could continue with many other examples.

On this basis, it is clear that communicative figurations are hardly 'harmonious' phenomena. In contrast, we have to be aware that certain power relations, inequalities and conflicts characterize many figurations. Therefore, all the criteria which are used to describe social disparities—class, race, gender and others (Norris 2001; Zillien 2009; Stegbauer 2012; Pollock 2013; Klaus 2015; Maier 2015)—matter when it comes to the analysis of figurations. We even go so far as to argue that a figurational analysis has specific capabilities for analyzing such disparities: the origin of the concept is rooted in analyzing the 'power balances' of actor constellations (Elias and Scotson 1994 [1965]).[13] Describing communicative figurations with reference to their actor constellations, frames of relevance and communicative practices always imply that we have to be sensitive to all lines of inequalities and conflicts that are inherent in or characteristic to them. When analyzing communicative figurations, we can expect to be confronted with the entirety of social disparities concerning media use and appropriation that have been researched so far, and possibly also new ones too.

Notes

1. See for a present overview Kaun and Fast (2013); Krotz et al. (2014); Lundby (2014a); Adolf (2015); Eskjær et al. (2015).

2. See on this subject Finnemann (2014: 312–315); Couldry and Hepp (2016: 34–56).

3. For an overview see—among others—Schulz (2004); Mazzoleni (2008); Krotz (2009); Couldry and Hepp (2013); Hjarvard (2013); Lundby (2014b); Meyen et al. (2014); Strömbäck and Esser (2014).

4. Typically, these changes are discussed with reference to what is called 'media convergence', being based on the spread of the computer as a 'hybrid medium' and 'universal machine' (Schröter 2004; K. Beck 2006). See for this discussion especially: Jenkins (2006); Latzer (2009); Hohlfeld (2010); Jensen (2010); Schorb et al. (2013); Meyer (2014).

5. While the assessment of a rapid pace of innovation corresponds with our everyday experience, we must be very careful not to over-emphasize this. Referring to social studies of technology, the challenge is to reflect what actually constitutes an innovation: a so-called 'key innovation' and 'improvement innovation'. Moreover, there are 'recursive innovations' and other complex patterns of innovation processes (see Dosi 1982; Rammert 2007: 28; Häußling 2014: 331–335). Hence, we have to be aware that 'pace of innovation' relates to experiencing an apparent acceleration of minor improvements that are constructed, among others for marketing reasons, as 'ground-breaking'. Examples for this are smartphones or tablets where the latest software only works on the most recent generations.
6. See for this discussion Couldry (2004); Raabe (2008); Postill (2010); Schmidt (2012); Genzel (2015); Pentzold (2015).
7. Compare for this, among others, Giddens (1984); Bourdieu (1992); Schatzki et al. (2001); Reckwitz (2002); Hörning and Reuter (2006); Nicolini (2012).
8. However, methodologically we do not share the position that we could not gain access to practices and their meaning via interviews. Depending on the interview strategy, we can in an indirect way gain access to (media related) practices (of communication), for example by asking questions about specific habits and everyday experiences (Klein et al. in this volume).
9. There is a long discussion in media and communication research about the necessity of such a 'non-mediacentric' perspective on transforming communications that does not always consider media as the angle of change (see recently Couldry 2006; Morley 2009; Moores 2012; Krajina et al. 2014). We refer here to the argument that only research which

takes into account non-media-related changes is able to assess when media as contents and technologies matter.

10. For such a development of process sociology as a basis for media and communications research see Ludes (1995); Krotz (2003); Buschauer (2012); Hepp and Hasebrink (2014); Hepp et al. (2015); Couldry and Hepp (2016); for (con)figurational thinking in general: Schnell (2006: 10); Suchman (2012: 48); Jarke (2014: 43–45); and for general overviews of recent developments in this approach see Treibel (2008a); Baur and Ernst (2011); Willems (2012); Dunning and Hughes (2013).
11. The suitability of 'figurations' as a 'bridging concept' between micro- and macro-question is emphasized by various social scientists: Esser (1984); Emirbayer (1997); Baur and Ernst (2011); Willems (2012).
12. For a general discussion of 'micro-macro links' in social sciences see Alexander et al. (1987); Coleman (1990); Schützeichel et al. (2009); Beamish (2011).
13. Later, this was proved by various analyses in a figurational perspective, for example focusing on gender (Leach 1997; Liston 2007; Mandel 2009) or on migrant groups (Treibel 2008b); for a general discussion of a figurational approach in social sciences see van Krieken (2007), Dunne (2009), Morrow (2009) and Dunning and Hughes (2013).

References

Adolf, Marian. 2015. Unboxing mediatization theory. Status and future directions of mediatization research. Conference: "New Directions in Mediatization Research: Culture, Conflict and Organizations" October 1–2, 2015, University of Copenhagen.

Agar, Jon. 2003. *Constant touch: A brief history of the mobile phone.* Cambridge: Icon Books Ltd.

Alexander, Jeffrey C., Bernhard Giesen, Richard Münch, and Neil J. Smelser. 1987. *The micro-macro link.* Berkeley and Los Angeles: University of California Press.

Altheide, David L., and Robert P. Snow. 1979. *Media logic.* Beverly Hills: Sage.

Andrejevic, Mark, and Kelly Gates. 2014. Big data surveillance: Introduction. *Surveillance & Society* 12 (2): 185–196.

Baecker, Dirk. 2007. *Studien zur nächsten Gesellschaft.* Frankfurt am Main: Suhrkamp.

Baur, Nina, and Stefanie Ernst. 2011. Towards a process–oriented methodology: Modern social science research methods and Norbert Elias's figurational sociology. *The Sociological Review* 59 (1): 117–139.

Bausinger, Hermann. 1984. Media, technology and daily life. *Media, Culture and Society* 6 (4): 343–351.

Beamish, Rob. 2011. Micro-macro links. In *The concise encyclopedia of sociology*, ed. George Ritzer and J. Michael Ryan, 398–400. Malden: Wiley.

Beck, Klaus. 2006. *Computervermittelte Kommunikation im Internet*. München: Oldenbourg.

Berger, Peter L., and Thomas Luckmann. 1967. *The social construction of reality: A treatise in the sociology of knowledge*. London: Penguin.

Bjur, Jakob, Kim C. Schrøder, Uwe Hasebrink, Cédric Courtois, Hanna Adoni, and Hillel Nossek. 2014. Cross-media use: Unfolding complexities in contemporary audiencehood. In *Audience transformations. Shifting audience positions in late modernity*, ed. Nico Carpentier, Kim C. Schrøder, and Lawrie Hallet, 15–29. New York: Routledge.

Blumer, Herbert. 1954. What is wrong with social theory? *American Sociological Review* 19: 3–10.

Blumler, Jay G., and Elihu Katz. 1974. *The uses of mass communications: Current perspectives on gratifications research*. London, Thousand Oaks and New Delhi: Sage.

Boltanski, Luc, and Laurent Thévenot. 2006. *On justification: Economies of worth*. Princeton: Princeton University Press.

Bonfadelli, Heinz, and Thomas N. Friemel. 2014. *Medienwirkungsforschung: Grundlagen und theoretische Perspektiven*, 5th ed. Stuttgart: UTB.

Bourdieu, Pierre. 1977. *Outline of a theory of practice*. Cambridge: Cambridge University Press.

Bourdieu, Pierre. 1992. *The logic of practice*. Cambridge: Polity Press.

Bourdieu, Pierre. 1993. *The field of cultural production: Essays on art and literature*. Cambridge: Polity Press.

boyd, danah, and Kate Crawford. 2012. Critical questions for big data: Provocations for a cultural, technological, and scholarly phenomenon. *Information, Communication & Society* 15 (5): 662–679.

Breiter, Andreas. 2003. Regional learning networks. Building bridges between schools, university and community. In *Informatics and the digital society. Social, ethical and cognitive issues*, ed. Tom J. van Weert and Robert K. Munro, 207–214. Boston: Kluwer Academic.

Bruns, Axel, and Jan Schmidt. 2011. Produsage: A closer look at continuing developments. *New Review of Hypermedia and Multimedia* 17 (1): 3–7.

Buckingham, David, and Mary J. Kehily. 2014. Rethinking youth cultures in the age of global media. In *Youth cultures in the age of global media*, ed. David Buckingham, Sara Bragg, and Mary J. Kehily, 1–18. Basingstoke and New York: Palgrave Macmillan.

Buschauer, Regine. 2012. 1-, Mii & MySpace. Mediale Figurationen des Nächsten. In *Medialität der Nähe*, ed. Pablo Abend, Tobias Haupts, and Claudia Müller, 47–63. Bielefeld: Transcript.

Castells, Manuel. 2000. *The rise of the network society. The information age: Economy, society and culture*, vol. 1, 2nd ed. Oxford: Blackwell.

Chen, Brian X. 2011. *Always on*. Philadelphia: Da Capo Press.

Christensen, Miyase, and André Jansson. 2014. Complicit surveillance, interveillance, and the question of cosmopolitanism: Toward a phenomenological understanding of mediatization. *New Media & Society* 17 (9): 1473–1491.

Clarke, Adele E. 2011. Social worlds. In *The concise encyclopedia of sociology*, ed. George Ritzer and J. Michael Ryan, 384–385. Malden and Oxford: Wiley.

Coleman, James S. 1990. *Foundations of social theory*. Cambridge: Belknap Press.

Couldry, Nick. 2004. Theorising media as practice. *Social Semiotics* 14 (2): 115–132.

Couldry, Nick. 2006. Transvaluing media studies: Or, beyond the myth of the mediated centre. In *Media and cultural theory*, ed. James Curran and David Morley, 177–194. London: Routledge.

Couldry, Nick. 2012. *Media, society, world: Social theory and digital media prac-tice*. Cambridge and Oxford: Polity Press.

Couldry, Nick, and Andreas Hepp. 2013. Conceptualising mediatization: Contexts, traditions, arguments. *Communication Theory* 23 (3): 191–202.

Couldry, Nick, and Andreas Hepp. 2016. *The mediated construction of reality*. Cambridge: Polity Press, submitted.

de Certeau, Michel. 2002. *The practice of everyday life*. Berkeley: California University Press.

Donges, Patrick, and Otfried Jarren. 2014. Mediatization of political organizations: Changing parties and interest groups? In *Mediatization of politics. Understanding the transformation of Western democracies*, ed. Frank Esser and Jesper Strömbäck, 181–199. Houndmills: Palgrave Macmillan.

Dosi, Giovanni. 1982. Technological paradigms and technological trajectories: A suggested interpretation of the determinants and directions of technical change. *Research Policy* 11 (3): 147–162.

Drgomir, Mariius, and Mark Thompson. 2014. *Mapping digital media. Global findings*. New York: Open Society Foundations.

Dunne, Stephen. 2009. The politics of figurational sociology. *Sociological Review* 57 (1): 28–57.

Dunning, Eric, and Jason Hughes. 2013. *Norbert Elias and modern sociology. Knowledge, interdependence, power, process*. London: Bloomsbury.

Ekström, Mats, Johan Fornäs, André Jansson, and Anne Jerslev. 2016. Three tasks for mediatization research: Contributions to an open agenda. *Media, Culture and Society* 38 (7): 1090–1108.

Elias, Norbert. 1978. *What is sociology?* London: Hutchinson.

Elias, Norbert. 1991. *The society of individuals*. London: Continuum.

Elias, Norbert, and John L. Scotson. 1994 [1965]. *The established and the outsiders: A sociological enquiry into community problems*. London: Sage.

Emirbayer, Mustafa. 1997. Manifesto for a relational sociology. *American Journal of Sociology* 103 (2): 281–317.

Eskjær, Mikkel F., Stig Hjarvard, and Mette Mortensen. 2015. *The dynamics of mediatized conflicts.* New York: Peter Lang.

Esser, Frank. 2013. Mediatization as a challenge: Media logics versus political logics. In *Democracy in the age of globalization and mediatization*, ed. Hanspeter Kriesi, Sandra Lavenex, Frank Esser, Jörg Matthes, Marc Bühlmann, and Daniel Bochsler, 155–176. London: Macmillan.

Esser, Frank, and Jesper Strömbäck (eds.). 2014. *Mediatization of politics. Understanding the transformation of Western democracies.* Houndmills: Palgrave Macmillan.

Esser, Hartmut. 1984. Figurationssoziologie und methodologischer Individualismus. *Kölner Zeitschrift für Soziologie und Sozialpsychologie* 36 (4): 667–702.

Finnemann, Niels O. 2014. Digitalization: New trajectories of mediatization? In *Mediatization of communication*, ed. Knut Lundby, 297–322. Berlin and New York: de Gruyter.

Fornäs, Johan. 2000. The crucial in between. The centrality of mediation in cultural studies. *European Journal of Cultural Studies* 3 (1): 45–65.

Friedland, Roger, and Robert R. Alford. 1991. Bringing society back in: Symbols, practices and institutional contradictions. In *The new institutionalism in organizational analysis*, ed. Walter W. Powell and Paul J. DiMaggio, 232–263. Chicago: University of Chicago Press.

Friemel, Thomas N. 2013. *Sozialpsychologie der Mediennutzung: Motive, Charakteristiken und Wirkungen interpersonaler Kommunikation über massenmediale Inhalte.* Konstanz: UVK.

Friemel, Thomas N. 2016. The digital divide has grown old: Determinants of a digital divide among seniors. *New Media & Society* 18 (2): 313–331.

Fuchs, Christian. 2013. Societal and ideological impacts of deep packet inspection internet surveillance. *Information, Communication & Society* 16 (8): 1328–1359.

Genzel, Peter. 2015. *Praxistheorie und Mediatisierung. Grundlagen, Perspektiven und eine Kulturgeschichte der Mobilkommunikation.* Wiesbaden: VS.

Giddens, Anthony. 1984. *The constitution of society. Outline of the theory of structuration.* Cambridge and Oxford: Polity Press.

Giddens, Anthony. 1990. *The consequences of modernity.* London: Polity.

Goggin, Gerard. 2011. *Global mobile media.* London: Routledge.

Greengard, Samuel. 2015. *The internet of things.* Cambridge and London: MIT Press.

Habermas, Jürgen. 1992 [1981]. *The theory of communicative action*, vol. 2. Boston: Beacon Press.

Hahn, Alois. 2000. *Konstruktionen des Selbst, der Welt und der Geschichte.* Frankfurt am Main: Suhrkamp.

Hall, Stuart. 1973. Encoding and decoding in television discourse. *Centre for Contemporary Cultural Studies, Birmingham, Occasional Papers* 7: 1–12.

Hasebrink, Uwe. 1999. Woran lassen sich Individualisierung und Integration in der Medienrezeption erkennen? In *Publikumsbindungen. Medienrezeption zwischen Individualisierung und Integration*, ed. Uwe Hasebrink and Patrick Rössler, 57–72. München: Reinhard Fischer.

Hasebrink, Uwe. 2003. Nutzungsforschung. In *Öffentliche Kommunikation. Handbuch Kommunikations- und Medienwissenschaft*, ed. Günter Bentele, Hans-Bernd Brosius, and Otfried Jarren, 101–127. Wiesbaden: Westdeutscher Verlag.

Hasebrink, Uwe. 2014. Die kommunikative Figuration von Familien: Medien, Kommunikation und Informationstechnologie im Familienalltag. In *Zukunft der Familie – Anforderungen an Familienpolitik und Familienwissenschaft. Tagungsband zum 4. Europäischen Fachkongress Familienforschung*, ed. Marina Rupp, Olaf Kapella, and Norbert F. Schneider, 225–240. Opladen, Berlin and Toronto: Verlag Barbara Budrich.

Hasebrink, Uwe, and Jutta Popp. 2006. Media repertoires as a result of selective media use. A conceptual approach to the analysis of patterns of exposure. *Communications* 31 (2): 369–387.

Hasebrink, Uwe, and Sascha Hölig. 2014. Topografie der Öffentlichkeit. *APuZ* 22–23: 16–22.

Häußling, Roger. 2014. *Techniksoziologie*. Baden-Baden: Nomos (UTB).

Hepp, Andreas. 2015. *Transcultural communication*. Malden: Wiley.

Hepp, Andreas. 2016. Pioneer communities: Collective actors of deep mediatization. *Media, Culture & Society*, accepted with minor revisions.

Hepp, Andreas, and Friedrich Krotz. 2014. Mediatized worlds: Understanding everyday mediatization. In *Mediatized worlds: Culture and society in a media age*, ed. Andreas Hepp and Friedrich Krotz, 1–15. London: Palgrave.

Hepp, Andreas, and Uwe Hasebrink. 2014. Human interaction and communicative figurations: The transformation of mediatized cultures and societies. In *Mediatization of communication*, ed. Knut Lundby, 249–272. Berlin and New York: de Gruyter.

Hepp, Andreas, Peter Lunt, and Maren Hartmann. 2015. Communicative figurations of the good life: Ambivalences surrounding the mediatization of homelessness and the transnational family. In *Communication and "the good life"*, ed. Hua Wang, 181–196. Berlin and New York: Peter Lang.

Hjarvard, Stig. 2013. *The mediatization of culture and society*. London: Routledge.

Hjarvard, Stig. 2017. Mediatization. In *International encyclopedia of media effects*, ed. Cynthia A. Hoffner and Liesbet van Zoonen, in print. New York: Wiley.

Höflich, Joachim R. 2003. *Mensch, Computer und Kommunikation: Theoretische Verortungen und empirische Befunde*. Frankfurt am Main: Lang.

Hohlfeld, Ralf. 2010. *Crossmedia: Wer bleibt auf der Strecke? Beiträge aus Wissenschaft und Praxis.* Münster: Lit.

Hörning, Karl H., and Julia Reuter. 2006. Doing material culture: Soziale Praxis als Ausgangspunkt einer "realistischen" Kulturanalyse. In *Kultur – Medien – Macht. Cultural Studies und Medienanalyse*, 3rd ed., ed. Andreas Hepp and Rainer Winter, 109–124. Wiesbaden: VS.

Imhof, Kurt, Roger Blum, and Heinz Bonfadelli. 2004. *Mediengesellschaft.* Wiesbaden: VS.

Ito, Mizuko, Judd Antin, Megan Finn, Arthur Law, Annie Manion, Sarai Mitnick, David Schlossberg, Sarita Yardi, and Heather A. Horst. 2009. *Hanging out, messing around, and geeking out: Kids living and learning with new media.* Cambridge: MIT Press.

Jarke, Juliane. 2014. Performances of associations: Sociomaterial orderings and configurations of a European egovernment 'community of practice'. Dissertation, Lancaster University.

Jarke, Juliane. 2015. Networking a European community: The case of a European commission eGovernment initiative. ECIS 2015 Completed Research Papers 86.

Jenkins, Henry. 2006. *Convergence culture: Where old and new media collide.* New York: New York University Press.

Jensen, Klaus B. 2010. *Media convergence: The three degrees of network, mass and interpersonal communication.* London: Routledge.

Jensen, Klaus B. 2013. Definitive and sensitizing conceptualizations of mediatization. *Communication Theory* 23 (3): 203–222.

Jensen, Klaus B., and Rasmus Helles. 2015. Audiences across media. A comparative agenda for future research on media audiences. *International Journal of Communication* 9: 291–298.

Karanasios, Stan, Dhavalkumar Thakker, Lydia Lau, David Allen, Vania Dimitrova, and Alistair Norman. 2013. Making sense of digital traces: An activity theory driven ontological approach. *Journal of the American Society for Information Science and Technology* 64 (12): 2452–2467.

Katz, James E., and Mark Aakhus. 2002. *Perpetual contact. Mobile communication, private talk, public performance.* Cambridge: Cambridge University Press.

Kaun, Anne, and Karin Fast. 2013. *Mediatization of culture and everyday life.* Stockholm: Commissioned by the sector committee mediatization of culture and everyday life of the Riksbanken Jubileumsfond.

Kay, Alan, and Adele Goldberg. 1977. Personal dynamic media. *Computers & Education* 10 (3): 31–41.

Klaus, Elisabeth. 2015. Klasse. In *Handbuch cultural studies und medienanalyse*, ed. Andreas Hepp, Friedrich Krotz, Swantje Lingenberg, and Jeffrey Wimmer, 39–47. Wiesbaden: VS.

Knoblauch, Hubert. 2013. Communicative constructivism and mediatization. *Communication Theory* 23 (3): 297–315.

Koch, Gertraud. 2016a. Marginalised groups in the city. *Ethnologia Europaea*, under preparation.

Koch, Gertraud. 2016b. Städte, Regionen und Landschaften als Augmented Realities. In *Zur kommunikativen Konstruktion von Räumen*, ed. Gabriela Christmann, 209–222. Wiesbaden: VS.

Krajina, Zlatan, Shaun Moores, and David Morle. 2014. Non-media-centric media studies: A cross-generational conversation. *European Journal of Cultural Studies* 17 (6): 682–700.

Krotz, Friedrich. 2003. Zivilisationsprozess und Mediatisierung: Zum Zusammenhang von Medien- und Gesellschaftswandel. In *Medienentwicklung und gesellschaftlicher Wandel. Beiträge zu einer theoretischen und empirischen Herausforderung*, ed. Markus Behmer, Friedrich Krotz, Rudolf Stöber, and Carsten Winter, 15–37. Wiesbaden: Westdeutscher.

Krotz, Friedrich. 2007. The meta-process of mediatization as a conceptual frame. *Global Media and Communication* 3 (3): 256–260.

Krotz, Friedrich. 2008. Media connectivity. Concepts, conditions, and consequences. In *Network, connectivity and flow. Conceptualising contemporary communications*, ed. Andreas Hepp, Friedrich Krotz, Shaun Moores, and Carsten Winter, 13–31. New York: Hampton Press.

Krotz, Friedrich. 2009. Mediatization: A concept with which to grasp media and societal change. In *Mediatization: Concept, changes, consequences*, ed. Knut Lundby, 19–38. New York: Peter Lang.

Krotz, Friedrich, Cathrin Despotovic, and Merle Kruse. 2014. *Die Mediatisierung sozialer Welten*. Wiesbaden: VS.

Kubicek, Herbert. 1997. Das Internet auf dem Weg zum Massenmedium? Ein Versuch, Lehren aus der Geschichte alter und neuer Medien zu ziehen. In *Modell Internet? Entwicklungsperspektiven neuer Kommunikationsnetze*, ed. Raymund Werle and Christa Lang, 213–239. Frankfurt am Main and New York: Campus.

Kunelius, Risto, and Esa Reunanen. 2016. Changing power of journalism: The two phases of mediatization. *Communication Theory* 26: 369–388.

Lammers, John C., and Sally A. Jackson. 2014. The institutionality of a mediatized organizational environment. In *Organizations and the media. Organizing in a mediatized world*, ed. Josef Pallas, Lars Strannegard, and Stefan Jonsson, 33–47. London and New York: Routledge.

Landerer, Nino. 2013. Rethinking the logics: A conceptual framework for the mediatization of politics. *Communication Theory* 23 (3): 239–258.

Latour, Bruno. 1991. Technology is society made durable. In *A sociology of monsters. Essays on power, technology and domination*, ed. John Law, 103–131. London: Routledge.

Latour, Bruno. 2007. *Reassembling the social: An introduction to actor-network-theory*. Oxford: Oxford University Press.

Latzer, Michael. 2009. Information and communication technology innovations: Radical and disruptive? *New Media & Society* 11 (4): 599–619.

Leach, Mary. 1997. Feminist figurations: Gossip as a counter discourse. *International Journal of Qualitative Studies in Education* 10 (3): 305–314.

Ling, Rich, and Jonathan Donner. 2009. *Mobile communication*. Cambridge and Malden: Polity Press.

Liston, Katie. 2007. Revisiting the feminist-figurational sociology exchange. *Sport in Society* 10 (4): 623–645.

Livingstone, Sonia M. 2001. Children and their changing media environment. In *Children and their changing media environment. A European comparative study*, ed. Sonia M. Livingstone and Moira Bovill, 307–333. London: Lawrence Erlbaum.

Livingstone, Sonia M. 2009. On the mediation of everything. *Journal of Communication* 59 (1): 1–18.

Livingstone, Sonia M., and Ellen Helsper. 2007. Gradations in digital inclusion: Children, young people and the digital divide. *New Media & Society* 9 (4): 671–696.

Lohmeier, Christine. 2014. The researcher and the never-ending field: Reconsidering big data and digital ethnography. In *Studies in qualitative methodology*, ed. Martin Hand and Sam Hillyard, 75–89. Bingley: Emerald Group Publishing.

Lohmeier, Christine, and Christian Pentzold. 2014. Making mediated memory work: Cuban-Americans, Miami media and the doings of diaspora memories. *Media, Culture and Society* 36 (6): 776–789.

Loosen, Wiebke. 2014. The notion of the "blurring boundaries": Journalism as a (de-)differentiated phenomenon. *Digital Journalism* 3 (1): 68–84.

Luckmann, Benita. 1970. The small life-worlds of modern man. *Social Research* 37 (4): 580–596.

Ludes, Peter. 1995. Langfristige Medienentwicklungen. Zu ihrer Analyse im Lichte der Theorien von Stein Rokkan und Norbert Elias. *Historical Social Research* 20 (2): 55–87.

Luhmann, Niklas. 2012. Theory of society, vol 1. Stanford, CA: Stanford University Press.

Lundby, Knut. 2014a. *Mediatization of communication*. Berlin and New York: de Gruyter.

Lundby, Knut. 2014b. Mediatization of communication. In *Mediatization of communication*, ed. Knut Lundby, 3–35. Berlin and New York: de Gruyter.

Lunt, Peter, and Sonia Livingstone. 2016. Is 'mediatization' the new paradigm for our field? A commentary on Deacon and Stanyer (2014, 2015) and Hepp, Harvard and Lundby (2015). *Media, Culture and Society* 38 (3): 462–470.

Lyon, David. 2014. Surveillance, Snowden, and big data: Capacities, consequences, critique. *Big Data & Society* 1 (2). doi:10.1177/2053951714541861.

Madianou, Mirca, and Daniel Miller. 2012. *Migration and new media: Transnational families and polymedia*. London: Routledge.

Madianou, Mirca, and Daniel Miller. 2013. Polymedia: Towards a new theory of digital media in interpersonal communication. *International Journal of Cultural Studies* 16 (6): 169–187.

Maier, Tanja. 2015. Feminismus, Gender und Queer. In *Handbuch Cultural Studies Und Medienanalyse*, ed. Andreas Hepp, Friedrich Krotz, Swantje Lingenberg, and Jeffrey Wimmer, 49–58. Wiesbaden: VS.

Mandel, Hadas. 2009. Configurations of gender inequality: The consequences of ideology and public policy. *British Journal of Sociology* 60 (4): 693–721.

Manovich, Lev. 2013. *Software takes command*. New York, London, New Delhi and Sydney: Bloomsbury.

Marszolek, Inge, and Yvonne Robel. 2016. The communicative construction of collectivities: An interdisciplinary approach to media history. *Historical Social Research* 41 (1), in print.

Mayer-Schönberger, Viktor, and Kenneth Cukier. 2013. *Big data: A revolution that will transform how we live, work and think*. New York: John Murray.

Mazzoleni, Gianpietro. 2008. Mediatization of society. In *The international encyclopedia of communication*, vol. VII, ed. Wolfgang Donsbach, 3052–3055. Oxford: Blackwell.

Meyen, Michael. 2009. Medialisierung. *Medien & Kommunikationswissenschaft* 57 (1): 23–38.

Meyen, Michael, Markus Thieroff, and Steffi Strenger. 2014. Mass media logic and the mediatization of politics: A theoretical framework. *Journalism Studies* 15 (3): 271–288.

Meyer, Klaus. 2014. Media convergence revisited. Lessons learned on newsroom integration in Austria, Germany and Spain. *Journalism Practice* 8 (5): 573–584.

Moores, Shaun. 2012. *Media, place and mobility*. Houndmills: Palgrave.

Morley, David. 1980. *The nationwide audience: Structure and decoding*. London: British Film Institute.

Morley, David. 2007. *Media, modernity and technology. The geography of the new*. London and New York: Routledge.

Morley, David. 2009. For a materialist, non-media-centric media studies. *Television & New Media* 10 (1): 114–116.

Morrow, Raymond A. 2009. Norbert Elias and figurational sociology: The comeback of the century. *Contemporary Sociology: A Journal of Reviews* 38 (3): 215–219.

Münch, Richard. 2002. *Dynamik der Kommunikationsgesellschaft*. Frankfurt am Main: Suhrkamp.

Napoli, Philip M. 2010. *Audience evolution: New technologies and the transformation of media audiences.* New York: Columbia University Press.

Neumann-Braun, Klaus. 2000. Publikumsforschung – im Spannungsverhaältnis von Quotenmessung und handlungstheoretisch orientierter Rezeptionsforschung. In *Medien- und Kommunikationssoziologie. Eine Einführung in zentrale Begriffe und Theorien*, ed. Klaus Neumann-Braun and Stefan Müller-Doohm, 181–204. Weinheim, München: Juventa Verlag.

Nicolini, Davide. 2012. *Practice theory, work, and organization: An introduction*˙ Oxford: Oxford University Press.

Nieminen, Hannu. 2014. A short history of the epistemic commons critical intellectuals, Europe and the small nations. *Javnost – The Public* 21 (4): 55–76.

Nieminen, Hannu. 2016. Digital divide and beyond: What do we know of Information and Communications Technology's long-term social effects? Some uncomfortable questions. *European Journal of Communication* 31 (1): 19–32.

Norris, Pippa. 2001. *Digital divide. Civic engagement, information poverty and the internet worldwide.* Cambridge: Cambridge University Press.

Pasquale, Frank. 2015. *The black box society: The secret algorithms that control money and information.* Cambridge: Harvard University Press.

Passoth, Jan-Hendrik, Tillmann Sutter, and Josef Wehner. 2014. The quantified listener: Reshaping providers and audiences with calculated measurement. In *Mediatized worlds*, ed. Andreas Hepp and Friedrich Krotz, 271–287. London: Palgrave.

Pentzold, Christian. 2015. Praxistheoretische Prinzipien, Traditionen und Perspektiven kulturalistischer Kommunikations- und Medienforschung. *Medien & Kommunikationswissenschaft* 63 (2): 229–245.

Pollock, John C. 2013. *Media and social inequality. Innovations in community structure research.* London and New York: Routledge.

Postill, John. 2010. Researching the Internet. *Journal of the Royal Anthropological Institute* 16: 646–650.

Quandt, Thorsten, and Bertram Scheufele. 2011. Die Herausforderung einer Modellierung von Mikro-Meso-Makro-Links in der Kommunikationswissenschaft. In *Ebenen der Kommunikation: Mikro-Meso-Makro-Links in der Kommunikationswissenschaft*, ed. Thorsten Quandt and Bertram Scheufele, 9–22. Wiesbaden: VS.

Raabe, Johannes. 2008. Kommunikation und soziale Praxis: Chancen einer praxistheoretischen Perspektive für Kommunikationstheorie und -forschung. In *Theorien der Kommunikationswissenschaft*, ed. Carsten Winter, Andreas Hepp, and Friedrich Krotz, 363–382. Wiesbaden: VS.

Radde-Antweiler, Kerstin. 2015. Das "Medienphänomen Franziskus". Eine mediensoziologische Analyse der deutschen Berichterstattung. *ThPQ* 163: 54–65.

Rainie, Harrison, and Barry Wellman. 2012. *Networked: The new social operating system.* Cambridge, MA: MIT Press.

Rammert, Werner. 2007. *Technik – Handeln – Wissen. Zu einer pragmatistischen Technik- und Sozialtheorie.* Wiesbaden: VS.

Reckwitz, Andreas. 2002. Toward a theory of social practices. A development in culturalist theorizing. *European Journal of Social Theory* 5 (2): 245–265.

Reichertz, Jo. 2009. *Kommunikationsmacht: Was ist Kommunikation und was vermag sie? Und weshalb vermag sie das?* Wiesbaden: VS.

Renckstorf, Karsten, and Fred Wester. 2001. The 'media use as social action' approach: Theory, methodology, and research evidence so far. *Communication* 24 (4): 389–420.

Ribes, David, R. Steve Jackson, Stuart Geiger, Matt C. Burton, and Tom Finholt. 2013. Artifacts that organize: Delegation in the distributed organization. *Information and Organization* 23 (1): 1–14.

Roitsch, Cindy. 2017. Von der "Aversion" zum "Schutzwal": Kommunikative Grenzziehung als gegenläufiges Medienhandeln in mediatisierten Welten. In *De-Mediatisierung. Diskontinuitäten, Non-Linearitäten und Ambivalenzen im Mediatisierungsprozess*, ed. Michaela Pfadenhauer and Tilo Grenz, 207–224. Wiesbaden: Springer VS.

Rosa, Hartmut. 2013. *Social acceleration: A new theory of modernity.* New York: Columbia University Press.

Rusch, Gebhard. 2006. The many mediatic turns. and a significant difference. *Siegener Periodicum zur internationalen empirischen Literaturwissenschaft* 25 (1): 23–34.

Ryan, Michael. 2005. Micro-macro-integration. In *Encyclopedia of social theory*, vol. 1 [A-M], ed. George Ritzer, 501–503. Thousand Oaks: Sage.

Schatzki, Theodore R. 2001. Introduction: Practice theory. In *The practice turn in contemporary theory*, ed. Theodore R. Schatzki, Karin Knorr-Cetina, and Eike von Savigny, 10–23. Hove: Psychology Press.

Schatzki, Theodore R., Karin Knorr-Cetina, and Eike von Savigny. 2001. *The practice turn in contemporary theory.* Hove: Psychology Press.

Schimank, Uwe. 2010. *Handeln und Strukturen. Einführung in die akteurstheoretische Soziologie*, 4th ed. Weinheim, Basel: Juventa.

Schimank, Uwe. 2011. Nur noch Coping: Eine Skizze postheroischer Politik. *Zeitschrift für Politikwissenschaft* 21: 455–463.

Schimank, Uwe. 2013. *Gesellschaft.* Bielefeld: Transcript.

Schmidt, Robert. 2012. *Soziologie der Praktiken: Konzeptionelle Studien und empirische Analysen.* Berlin: Suhrkamp Verlag.

Schnell, Ralf. 2006. "Medienumbrüche" – Konfiguration und Konstellation. In *MedienRevolutionen. Beiträge zur Mediengeschichte der Wahrnehmung*, ed. Ralf Schnell, 7–12. Münster: Transcript.

Schorb, Bernd, Nadine Jünger, and Thomas Rakebrand. 2013. *Die Aneignung konvergenter Medienwelten durch Jugendliche. Das Medienkonvergenz Monitoring.* Berlin: Vistas.

Schröter, Jens. 2004. *Das Netz und die Virtuelle Realität. Zur Selbstprogrammierung der Gesellschaft durch die universelle Maschine.* Bielefeld: Transcript.

Schulz, Winfried. 2004. Reconstructing mediatization as an analytical concept. *European Journal of Communication* 19 (1): 87–101.

Schulz, Winfried. 2014. Mediatization and new media. In *Mediatization of politics. Understanding the transformation of Western democracies*, ed. Frank Esser and Jesper Strömbäck, 57–73. Houndmills: Palgrave Macmillan.

Schulz, Wolfgang. 2013. After Snowden: Toward a global data privacy standard? In *Internet monitor 2013: Reflections on the digital world*, ed. Urs Gasser, R. Faris, and J.R. Heacock, 30–31. Cambridge: Berkman Center for Internet and Society.

Schulz, Wolfgang, Stephan Dreyer, and Stefanie Hagemeier. 2011. *Machtverschiebung in der öffentlichen Kommunikation.* Bonn: FES.

Schütz, Alfred. 1967. *The phenomenology of the social world.* New York: Northwestern University Press.

Schützeichel, Rainer, Jens Greve, and Annette Schnabel. 2009. *Das Makro-Mikro-Makro-Modell der soziologischen Erklärung. Zur Ontologie, Methodologie und Metatheorie eines Forschungsprogramms.* Wiesbaden: VS.

Shibutani, Tamotsu. 1955. Reference groups as perspectives. *American Journal of Sociology* 60: 562–569.

Stegbauer, Christian. 2012. *Medien und Ungleichheit.* Wiesbaden: VS Verlag.

Stegbauer, Christian, and Michael Jäckel. 2007. Social Software – Herausforderungen für die mediensoziologische Forschung. In *Social Software. Formen der Kooperation in computerbasierten Netzwerken*, ed. Christian Stegbauer and Michael Jäckel, 7–10. Wiesbaden: VS.

Strauss, Anselm. 1978. A social world perspective. *Studies in Symbolic Interaction* 1 (1): 119–128.

Strömbäck, Jesper. 2008. Four phases of mediatization: An analysis of the mediatization of politics. *The International Journal of Press/Politics* 13 (3): 228–246.

Strömbäck, Jesper, and Frank Esser. 2014. Mediatization of politics: Towards a theoretical framework. In *Mediatization of politics. Understanding the transformation of Western democracies*, ed. Frank Esser and Jesper Strömbäck, 3–28. Houndmills: Palgrave Macmillan.

Suchman, Lucy. 2012. Configuration. In *Inventive methods. The happening of the social*, ed. Celia Lury and Nina Wakeford, 48–60. Hoboken: Taylor and Francis.

Teichert, Will. 1972. 'Fernsehen' als soziales Handeln. Zur Situation der Rezipientenforschung: Ansätze und Kritik. *Rundfunk und Fernsehen* 4 (20): 421–439.

Thomas, Douglas, and John S. Brown. 2011. *A new culture of learning: Cultivating the imagination for a world of constant change*. Lexington, KY: CreateSpace.

Thompson, John B. 1995. *The media and modernity. A social theory of the media.* Cambridge: Cambridge University Press.

Tomlinson, John. 2007. *The culture of speed: The coming of immediacy.* New Delhi: Sage.

Townsend, Anthony M. 2013. *Smart cities: Big data, civic hackers, and the quest for a new utopia.* New York: W.W. Norton.

Treibel, Annette. 2008a. *Die Soziologie von Norbert Elias: Eine Einführung in ihre Geschichte, Systematik und Perspektiven.* Wiesbaden: VS.

Treibel, Annette. 2008b. *Migration in modernen Gesellschaften.* Weinheim and München: Juventa.

Tsatsou, Panayiota. 2011. Digital divides revisited: What is new about divides and their research? *Media, Culture & Society* 33 (2): 317–331.

van Deursen, Alexander J.A.M., and Ellen J. Helsper. 2015. The third-level digital divide: Who benefits most from being online. In *Communication and information technologies annual: Digital distinctions and inequalities.*, ed. Laura Robinson, Sheila R. Cotten, Jeremy Schulz, Timothy M. Hale, and Apryl Williams, 29–52. Bingley: Emerald Group Publishing.

van Dijck, José. 2013. *The culture of connectivity. A critical history of social media.* Oxford: Oxford University Press.

van Dijck, José, and Thomas Poell. 2013. Understanding social media logic. *Media and Communication* 1 (1): 2–14.

van Dijk, Jan, and Kenneth Hacker. 2005. The digital divide as a complex dynamic phenomenon. *The Information Society* 19: 315–326.

van Krieken, Robert. 2007. *Norbert Elias.* London: Routledge.

Vorderer, Peter, Christoph Klimmt, Diana Rieger, Eva Baumann, Dorothée Hefner, Karin Knop, Nicola Krömer, Jutta Mata, Thilo von Pape, Thorsten Quandt, Sabine Reich, Leonard Reinecke, Sabine Trepte, Sabine Sonnentag, and Hartmut Wessler. 2015. Der mediatisierte Lebenswandel: Permanently online, permanently connected. *Publizistik* 60 (3): 259–276.

Wajcman, Judy. 2015. *Pressed for time. The acceleration of life in digital capitalism.* Chicago and London: University of Chicago Press.

Weber, Max. 1988 [1919]. *Gesammelte Aufsätze zur Wissenschaftslehre*, 7th ed. Tübingen: Mohr Verlag (UTB).

Wessler, Hartmut, and Michael Brüggemann. 2012. *Transnationale Kommunikation.* Wiesbaden: VS.

Willems, Herbert. 2012. *Synthetische Soziologie: Idee, Entwurf und Programm.* Wiesbaden: VS.

Winter, Rainer, and Roland Eckert. 1990. *Mediengeschichte und kulturelle Differenzierung. Zur Entstehung und Funktion von Wahlnachbarschaften.* Opladen: Leske + Budrich.

Wittel, Andreas. 2008. Towards a network sociality. In *Connectivity, network and flow. Conceptualising contemporary communications*, ed. Andreas Hepp, Friedrich Krotz, Shaun Moores, and Carsten Winter, 157–182. New York and Cresskill, NJ: Hampton Press.

Wolf, Karsten D. 2015. Erklärvideos auf YouTube: Produzieren Jugendliche und junge Erwachsene ihr eigenes Bildungsfernsehen? *televIZIon* 28 (1): 35–39.

Zillien, Nicole. 2009. *Digitale Ungleichheit: Neue Technologien und alte Ungleichheiten in der Informations- und Wissensgesellschaft.* Wiesbaden: VS.

PART II

Collectivities and their Figurations

3

Urban Communities and the Youth

Andreas Hepp, Piet Simon and Monika Sowinska

3.1 Introduction

Since 2000, research on media and communications has devoted an increasing amount of attention to the city as an object of study. There are various reasons for this. The city has once more become a topic of great interest for the social sciences, if only because of the increasing tempo or processes of urbanization (United Nations 2015). Here the most important reference points are probably gentrification and segregation (Smith and Williams 2010). Another issue is that of changes to the city resulting from the diffusion of information and communication technologies (Castells 2000: 407–459). Research into communications and media

A. Hepp (✉) · P. Simon · M. Sowinska
ZeMKI, Centre for Media, Communication and Information Research, University of Bremen, Bremen, Germany
e-mail: ahepp@uni-bremen.de

P. Simon
e-mail: piet.simon@uni-bremen.de

M. Sowinska
e-mail: sowinska@uni-bremen.de

has a place within this more general social scientific discussion. Specific research questions have been developed that result in a focus upon the deep mediatization of the city. Topics range from the visions and limits of a 'smart city' (Townsend 2013), to the study of 'locative media' (Evans 2015) and '(hyper)local journalism' (Nielsen 2015), and to the way that media support urban communal living (Georgiou 2013).

This chapter deals with this last thread. We wish to examine the following question: what does deep mediatization mean to young people in their daily urban sense of community? Here 'urban sense of community' is not treated as a given, but rather as an open process that can assume different empirical forms. For instance, we might think of different forms in the city for which the 'urban' environment is the general context. But it can also involve definite urban forms of community experience, an 'urban community' in a more restricted sense of the term. Hence, we shall deal with a spectrum of community in the urban context: the increasing and many-layered dispersion of media within the city has no direct and automatic consequences for the sense of community created by and among young people. Instead, we are faced with the multi-dimensionality of different possible processes, and the way in which they change as media are transformed.

How this multi-dimensionality can be grasped without relapsing into mere description where 'anything goes' is the empirical challenge here. We wish to make clear in this chapter that research based upon a figurational perspective holds great promise for a multi-dimensional analysis of this kind. That is not just because the idea of figuration was first deliberately employed to analyze conflicts arising in one particular urban area (Elias and Scotson 1994 [1965]). It is more that developing figurational analysis within a media and communications framework allows us to grasp the mediatization of different processes of community in the urban space, without at the same time losing sight of their contradictory nature. Here we are not concerned, as Elias and Scotson were, with conflict, but rather with the process of creating and experiencing community.

In the following, we do this by studying young people in Leipzig and Bremen, two German cities each with around 550,000 inhabitants. First of all we will relate our own work to existing research on media, community and the city. Then we will detail our empirical procedure. Using empirical data, we will demonstrate the degree to which for young urban dwellers—besides family, acquaintances and colleagues—it is their network of friends that remains the primary figuration of their experience of community construction. And this has become to a very great degree a mediatized phenomenon. Developing from this analysis, we then turn to what we might call the figurative quality of individual sites of community construction. We are interested in the way that the mediatization of particular locations in the city lends them a particular quality of community construction, and that we can detect segregation processes linked to particular locations. This leads us to the question of the extent to which the city can be, for young people, something like an imagined community.

A study of the type we present here has its limitations. There are at least two obvious ones. First of all, our data relates to two specific cities in Germany, and we do not know how applicable our findings are for others. Secondly, we focus upon young people between the ages of 16 and 30, and we do not know whether our results would apply to people from different age groups. While we acknowledge these limitations, we presume, as did Norbert Elias and John Lloyd Scotson, that the basic features we identify here are to be found in other cities, too, and that they are also characteristic of other age groups. We consider this to be our general contribution to communications and media research into the nature of media in the city.

3.2 Media, the City and Community

Studying the relationship between media, city and community takes us back to the beginnings of work on media and communications. Robert Park's classic paper of 1915/1925 still repays reading for many reasons. Park emphasized that on the one hand, the decay of cities led to a 'mosaic of little worlds' (1967: 40) which, drawing an explicit parallel with Georg Simmel (2006 [1903]), promoted the 'mobilization of the individual' (1967: 40). On the other hand, he saw a clearly defined role for public communication, on the basis of which public opinion in the city developed (1967: 38). This was, he thought, a 'source of social control' (1967: 38) that transcended the various 'little worlds'. Hence, he emphasized, it made no sense to think of the city as a *single* community. Rather, he considered the 'urban environment' (1967: 1) as a more specific context in which different processes of communitization took place that were in part contradictory, and thus also in part the source of conflict. He treated the media above all as a means of mass communication that aided the creation of 'public opinion' and the corresponding 'control' in a thoroughly segregated city.

Park's reflections were first published over 100 years ago. They can therefore help us identify what has changed in the city and what has not.

From today's perspective, we can still agree with Park that we should treat the city more as a specific context for different processes of communitization than necessarily a coherent community; although constructions of the city as a community are of course quite possible. But all the same, they should be treated more at the level of public communication, where their function can range from appeal to 'social control'.

By contrast, what we understand by 'the media' has fundamentally changed in 100 years. Today's urban media environment no longer consists of a few printed media for public communication, plus the letter and the telephone. With the deep mediatization of the city, this environment has become more varied, complex and also contradictory. But this, in turn, takes us back to Park's starting point concerning the role of media in the 'mosaic of little worlds'.

Recent study of the role of media in urban life is likewise concerned with this role. There is particular interest in the analysis of the city as a diverse and transcultural living space that is also in many respects segregated and gentrified. In this context, Myria Georgiou talked of the 'mediated city' (2013: 41). This concept draws attention to the fact that our experience of the city today can no longer be treated as separate from the media of communication. She is likewise interested in seeing the relationship of media and city 'from street level' (2013: 3; see also Lane 2016); substantively, this means in terms of people's 'consumption, identity, community, action'. Shopping malls are in particular locations of urban consumption, locations that are comprehensively saturated medially, while also being an expression of gentrification (cf. Bolin 2004). It can be observed that the medial construction of identity in the city takes place in a relation of tension between very different cultural definitions (Christensen and Jansson 2015: 130–152), given that the city is itself a transcultural space in which people of many different backgrounds live together (cf. Hepp 2015: 120–123). With respect to the formation of community, it follows from this that the city cannot be simply seen as a single community. Instead, we have a variety of diverse and local communities that are in part opposed to each other, as well as diasporas with a very weak sense of community (Georgiou 2013: 92–116). Here, then, media open opportunities for political action in the city, examples being 'urban gardening' or 'reclaim the streets', the organization of both of which is supported via digital media (Bridge 2009; Rauterberg 2013: 97–128). From this perspective, it is also necessary to describe this complexity of the city critically, as a medially saturated space of transcultural human existence. We can also include in this tradition those critical studies that have highlighted the increasing fragmentation of urban public life (Hasebrink and Schmidt 2013; Metag and Donk 2013). From this, we can see a close connection between research into media and communication and more general social science research on urbanism (see, for example, Christmann 2013; Metag and Donk 2013; Zukin et al. 2016) It thus becomes evident that we require multi-layered conceptions if we are to grasp the relationship between media, city and community construction. What would a multi-layered conception look like?

In an analysis of the link between media and the city, we continually encounter two approaches: the concept of network and that of assemblage. Accordingly, different urban social networks are studied, or networks between cities (see among others Neal 2013); or the various assemblages of people in the city are examined (see among others Farías 2010). As we have argued elsewhere (Couldry and Hepp 2017: 60–63), both conceptions do have their strengths, but they are not suited to the contradictoriness of the everyday production of meaning, of grasping existing social differentiation and hierarchization.

Hence, we think that approaching the experience of constructing urban community in the mediatized city from the perspective of figurational analysis is worthwhile, and fits in with the other contributions in this volume. This approach allows us to make use of a differentiated, multi-layered analysis that takes account of actor networks and the materiality of media, while also making possible a connection with a critical, social scientific appraisal of urbanism as initiated by the Chicago School.

If we consider the forms of community construction in the mediatized cities of today, we note that they are *mediatized* processes, since this is comprehensively interwoven with the appropriation of media as content and as technology. Media are important resources as *contents* with which community can be constructed. This is, for example, the case where public viewing contents are available that promote a common identification (Krajina 2014), or if in the communicative construction of community reference is made to particular media contents (Keppler 2014). If communities are maintained through the continual use of mobile phones, digital platforms and other media technologies by community members confirming their close connectedness through their continued communication, media are basic to the formation of community as *technologies* (Baym 2015: 80–111).

With regard to urban community construction, we think it is necessary to distinguish at least three contexts. First of all, we are dealing with particular *figurations of communities in the city*; that is, particular groups of people who see themselves as forming a community. We can identify in these communities a characteristic constellation of actors who share a specific frame of relevance and (communicative) practices.

If these urban communities are considered more closely, one encounters a second phenomenon, something we can describe as the *figurative quality* of individual mediatized communitized locations. These (mediatized) locations in the city—shopping malls, meeting rooms, cinemas and so on—have characteristics that lend them a special potential for individual figurations of community. This does not mean that these qualities are inherent to these particular locations. Rather, these qualities are generated through human practice, but rendered lasting by virtue of the locational materialization. This close coupling of such figurative qualities with the character of these locations seems quite remarkable to us.

Third, the city itself can be a reference point for the construction of an *imagined community*, in the sense proposed by Benedict Anderson (1983). This does not mean that the city as an imagined figuration of a community is a homogeneous construction. But it is a shared connection to the construction of community—even if to different degrees for different people.

On the basis of this distinction, we intend to develop below the argument that these three levels provide an appropriate point of departure to understand the complexity of the process of community construction of young people in the mediatized city.

3.3 The Methodical Approach

The data we use in our analysis come from two sources. The first of these is an investigation funded by the German Research Council into the communicative networking and mediatized community construction of people from different media generations. The second source is linked to a research seminar that conducted a study specifically upon the various urban locations of community construction shared by young people.

Our study of communicative networking and mediatized community construction is based upon a *contextualized communication network analysis* (see Hepp et al. 2016).[1] The selection of interview subjects was made according to 'theoretical sampling' (Strauss and Corbin 1996: 148–65;

Glaser and Strauss 1998: 53–83; Strübing 2008: 29–32). The material analyzed below was collected between November 2010 and September 2011, and includes a total of 60 cases of youths and young adults aged between 16 and 30. The data was collected in Bremen and Leipzig and the surrounding areas. The evaluation of the data was done through qualitative coding aimed at developing empirically founded theory. In coding the material, we focused upon patterns of community formation as well as structures, processes and imputations of meaning to communicative networking, and the associated underlying practices of media appropriation.

While conducting this evaluation, we encountered the phenomenon of individual mediatized community construction locations. These involved locations that had a special sense of community for young people. Between April 2014 and January 2015, we made a special study of these locations in the context of a research seminar.[2] This was done in two stages: first of all, we issued an appeal to young people in Bremen to identify what they considered to be their 'most important' locations for community construction. We explicitly asked them to name places where 'stuff was going on'. These appeals were made in different ways through local media in newspapers, radio, the web—and there were a number of responses. The locations that were identified in this way were then marked on a map of the city. Following this, we studied these locations in greater detail. Observations were made and interviews conducted, following which the material was coded according to Grounded Theory.

This material enabled us to arrive at an understanding of the urban community construction of young people at the three levels outlined above: the figuration of communities in which they live; the mediatized community construction locations and their figurative qualities; and the construction of the city as an imagined community.

3.4 Young People's Friendship Groups in the City

Our study of communicative networking and mediatized community makes clear the varied levels of communal life that are important to young people: they do not feel that they belong simply to one community, but to various communities—even if some are more important than others, according to local distribution, thematic orientation and plurality.[3] What is striking is the high value placed on the local in community processes: even if young people are strongly oriented to particular themes in their community construction (popular culture, a religion), or are instead very plural and so among themselves globally oriented, it is local communities that are important to them. To different degrees this is true for families, members of a school or college class, work colleagues, the community of individual associations and experiences with various acquaintances. However, the immediate group of friends has for young people a special importance, their 'clique' as they often call it. We therefore want to direct our attention to this phenomenon below. We focus upon young people who live in Bremen or Leipzig and the surrounding areas, and who in their experience of community are strongly oriented to these cities.

There are three striking aspects of these friendship groups that emerge from a consideration of their communicative figuration. First of all, the city is an important context for their circle of friends when they want to do something together. Second, this group of friends is the stable framework for community construction. Third, these figurations are supported by a media ensemble that carries with it both a potential for the communicative practices of members of this circle of friends, as well as certain restrictions.

If one considers the actor constellations of this circle of friends, it becomes evident that the core of the circle is formed by friends who 'all come from around here' (Mala Hempel, 21, Bremen area, trainee nurse); and 'with whom one stays in touch regularly' (Konstanze Mitscherlich, 26, Leipzig, printer).[4] This shared space of the local is important for the way in which the friendship circle is experienced, as Mala makes clear when she distinguishes between close and less close relationships. This shared local space allows them above all direct communication:

> ... so, I am fairly thick with her ((laughs)) [...] we don't really speak on the phone, if we do then I write more on Studi [StudiVZ, an online platform]; or maybe text, something like that. So it is with her that I am mostly in contact. And then with other girls, that's OK. So of course, we write now and then, when something comes up. But now I don't think we would phone on my account. (Mareike Bonitz, Leipzig, 19 years old, student)

The circles of friends that we interviewed ranged from two to ten persons. Konstanze said, for instance, that she divided her circle of friends into 'rings', with an 'inner ring' of eight persons which was 'the important' group for her. In this way, she emphasized that the links of persons to each other were not necessarily equal—her friends 'just came together [...] that does *not* mean that the people who I now see as the most important, that they are connected with each other in exactly the same way'. Konstanze sees herself at the centre of a circle of friends and emphasizes that the relationships between these friends themselves vary.

Lara-Marie Michaelis (28, Leipzig, cook) describes her own circle of close friends similarly. This is made up of 'six or seven girls [...] maybe also three other boys'. They tend to meet up separately, 'because working hours always makes things a bit complicated'. To have a solid core to a circle of friends is linked in this case to changing constellations for individual meetings. The friendship groups for those we interviewed tend to fluctuate over time. Mareike, the Leipzig student, exemplifies this:

> Thus, something like a solid clique developed. Over the years, though, more and more drifted off because they moved away or school, work, whatever. So it somehow became a bit fractured. But the core is still there.

Those we interviewed felt it very important to do different things together with their close friends, not least spontaneous meetings: 'Oh what to do this evening, let's open a bottle of Sekt or something, have a nice evening' (Katja Hosner, 21, trainee therapist). Or the way that Henning Rowohlt (16, Bremen, school student) described this kind of spontaneous meetup: 'In the summer we are really always outside, on the Weser [the river] [....], behind the stadium, playing music, drinking some beer.'

Besides these spontaneous events that are arranged quite casually, there are meetings that are organized more in advance. Here, media facilitating mutual communication plays a role. Evenings are planned with mobile calls, the web is used for information and agreement reached in various ways before meeting. In part, this takes place during evenings out. Henning reports, for instance, that his friends often check on different events through the internet 'and then sitting [in the pub], Saturday evening, having a drink, my mates get in touch: hey, want to go there?'.

Arrangements like this do not only occur using mobiles and when going out together. Digital platforms in particular, such as Facebook, are used for the planning. For example, Felicitas Franke (Leipzig, 17, school student) emphasizes that from her point of view Facebook is much better than email for friends to draw each other's attention to events and to arrange to meet: 'so there is always an event and then you know who is going, and then you can go too'. Emails are not practical, since 'a lot of people don't check their mails' (Felicitas). Other interviewees also stress that they use Facebook within their group of friends to find out 'what's going on, what's happening at the weekend, what happened on the weekend [...] and otherwise finding out what's going on' (Mala Hempel, 21, Bremen region, trainee nurse). A digital platform offers young people the possibility to arrange to meet up with friends, draw attention to events or just stay in touch.

In each of the groups of friends formed among those we interviewed there is a particular set of established media that supports communication within the group and for other purposes. This set of media contributes to the maintenance of the groups. By using the same media—mobiles, media content, especially digital platforms—each person is bound into a constant stream of group communication. There is some pressure here to use the right media, so that an individual does not get shut out of communication. This is especially clear with digital platforms, Facebook above all else. For several groups this has become the 'central' (Henning) medium for contact and meeting up. This is felt particularly by those who had not so far joined up. They have to find other ways so that they do not get shut out of group communication. Konstanze describes her experience with this as follows:

> So there are times when it's like 'So you, Wednesday, are you coming?' If I then say 'Wednesday?'—'well I did post about that'—If I say: 'Yes, sorry, don't have it, can't check!'—And then I get a sort of special catchup, what is going on Wednesday and then it's fine.

Nor is Lara-Marie on Facebook, saying that she is 'constantly asked why she isn't on Facebook', that she can't be Googled as a result, and whether 'she can't register'. She responds to this as follows: 'Somehow I don't really listen. Then I decided to definitely do it the day after tomorrow, and then, yes, that is I think really no problem.' So Lara-Marie makes up her mind to give into the pressure and register with Facebook—as many other interviewees report. Mala said in her interview with us that she was only pushed by her friends to join Facebook, 'because they all had it'. And she went on: 'I wasn't on there until a few months ago. But then everybody had Facebook; and then [I] had it as well.' She, too, had to adopt the relevant communication form to prevent being closed out of the circle of friends. Even if the telephone, texting and emails are part of the media set used by the group, they are not really any substitute for digital platforms, since 'why write an email if you can write a lot quicker on Facebook?' (Felicitas).

The pressure articulated here can also be related to produced media contents. Felicitas describes this as follows: 'you mostly [listen to] what friends listen to, and then it is on Facebook, they write the words of the song—oh yes, I love the song! - then you listen to it too and like it too'. Jana Jäger (28, Leipzig, Primary School teacher) describes a similar process, and says that '... if you spend more time with friends [...] you come across new CDs'. This 'social dependence', as Jana calls it, forms the expectations articulated in group communication within the figuration of the group of friends.

The above illustrates the high value placed on friendship groups in the community life of young people. It is evident that the set of media used both stabilizes its figuration, while also creating a degree of pressure on its members.

How does the urban context fit in here for the circle of friends? This question can best be answered if the city is seen as a *space of opportunity* for young people. The following more detailed extract from an interview exemplifies that. Katja Hosner describes an evening spent together with friends:

> Well, first we were in the restaurant, and then we thought, now we can really do something, everyone is in such a good mood. So we went straight to the cocktail bar for their happy hour, and the happy hour was over and then we went to the next cocktail bar's happy hour. And the evening just didn't want to end (smirks). And then we just decided then to go to someone's place, we got on the tram and went to her place, we stopped off here quickly because I've got a hookah. We picked it up and left for her place down the street (smirks). Why didn't we do it here? Well (smirks), and then it went on to two and then I had to get up at six to go to school.

Besides the many things that can be done in a city, the quote emphasizes a second aspect: the locations that are important for sharing such fun with friends are concentrated in the city. Lara-Marie emphasizes this, too; for her, Leipzig is 'the city of short cuts': 'You can really, if all else fails, just walk from A to B. I think that is fantastic. It is sometimes like a village, you always meet someone.'

Lennard Schimmang (18, Leipzig, community service worker) also stresses the way locations to which you go out are concentrated in the city, contrasting this with his home village, where 'nothing ever happens'. In the city you 'just have more possibilities'. There is a 'big cinema and a few nice pubs'. Susanne Mattuschek (23, Leipzig, court clerk) describes the city as a context where 'there is simply more to do', and where you 'have all kinds of possibilities'. She also compares Leipzig, where she now lives, with the small town where she came from, and where 'basically nothing ever happens'. Tim Lautermann (21, Leipzig, student), who also moved to Leipzig from a small town, quickly realized that the city offered a whole range of opportunities to be taken on the spur of the moment, and described it as a 'certain kind of freedom'. For him, this 'freedom' was to do with the spontaneity opened up by the urban context.

The possibilities that the city offers can be used without needing to put much effort into travelling. Lara-Marie stresses that 'here in a big city I don't really need to have a car [...] and so want to live as close as I can to everything and not somewhere where I have to travel for half an hour to my friends'. Jasmin Preußler (25, Bremen, trainee teacher) says much the same thing: 'It is just so important to me that I live in a city where I can get everywhere, where I get to the centre quickly.' The city is a space of opportunity that opens up a wide range of possibilities to a group of friends, and so also the chance of doing things on the spur of the moment. All the same, it is the figuration of the group of friends that is relevant to the way in which the young people we interviewed form communal bonds.

The group of friends has assumed such an importance that some activities are felt to be less attractive if done without friends. Felicitas describes, for example, that she does not go to parties if her 'friends are not going where no-one knows anybody'. It is the 'sense of being together' (Konstanze) itself that is central, not the particular event or activity. The possibilities that are exploited in the city are heavily influenced by the interests of the group as a whole. For instance, Lara-Marie emphasizes that 'my friends like this music [drum'n bass], [...] I can really get into the music for a whole evening, I do that.' Katja describes something similar: she 'looks at new things that would not to begin with have interested me so much, but then I say: perhaps that would be great if I went with two or three people'.

We can summarize what we have established so far on the basis of our interview material. It is plain how important groups of friends are for the young people we interviewed. Besides family, it is the central figuration of community. We can see a certain pattern here, quite independent of educational background or the social position of those we interviewed. In the forefront is having fun with others, taking the form of diverse practices through which the community of the group of friends is created. The set of media employed plays an important strengthening role here for the group of friends. Members of the group feel a certain pressure to use the media that dominate in the group—both as technologies of joint communication and as substantive resources for mutual communication. In this way, the existence of a 'networked collectivism' (Baym 2015: 101) can be seen to typify the group of friends, rather than a 'networked individualism' (Rainie and Wellman 2012: 115). There is intensive communicative networking especially in *local* groups of friends, in which the shared experience of common things and events is very important. The city is consequently a special space of opportunity.

3.5 The Figurative Quality of Mediatized Locations

Our presentation of the friendship group as the central communicative figuration for the urban community construction of young people shows how important individual locations in the city are for this: places to which one goes on a night out, where one meets up, does things together, or experiences things together. Seen from this perspective, a location is a place with a special meaning—not something physically given, but places whose meaning is created by people through repeated and varied interaction (Massey 1994: 39; see also Berg and Roitsch 2015 and the contributions in Christmann 2016). Put another way, localities are, materially and physically, socio-culturally defined places with shared space for human interaction (Hepp 2015: 187). By referring here to *mediatized places of community construction* we seek to emphasize two things. First of all, the places are not simply something that is counterposed to the use of media. Instead, today's localities are largely created through media-related practices, and are in this sense themselves mediatized. Secondly, our interest is directed to those places that for young people have a great potential for creating a sense of community. We are thinking here of semi-public places, places to which young people have general access, depending upon their financial resources.

In the light of such ideas, we published the appeal mentioned above in the Bremen local media, inquiring about those places 'where

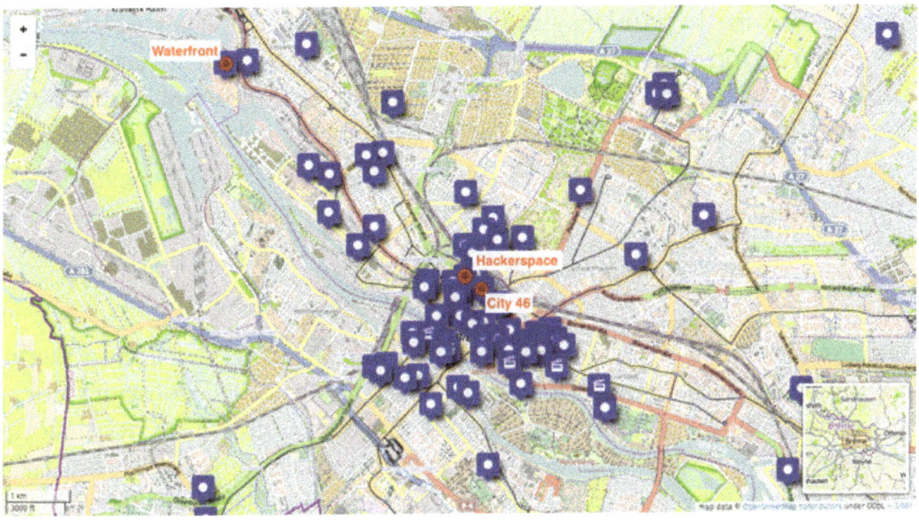

Fig. 3.1 Mediatized public places for community-building in Bremen. This figure presents a section of the map that is available online.

something was going on' and thus had this kind of enhanced potential for community-building. The responses received were marked on an Open Street Map (see Fig. 3.1), in the course of a student research seminar linked to the project.

This map certainly does not exhaust all the mediatized places of com munity construction in Bremen. If the map is examined more closely, it becomes clear that the places identified—from squares and open spaces, to pubs, the stadium, cinemas and other kinds of cultural sites—are localities that hold a special potential for the young people's communities. This is a bias that is given by the way the material was collected and which corresponds to the object of our research. The localities identified, as also particular kinds of localities, are concentrated in specific parts of Bremen. This partly has to do with the segregation of the city: there are well-to-do and partly gentrified areas such as Ostertor and Steintor, where many of the cultural places and also pubs are located; and in contrast, there are other parts of the city, such as Gröpelingen, which are strongly associated with migrants, and where there are only few places for community construction, such as the shopping mall Waterfront. The results of the visualization provided by the above map formed our point of departure in the study of individually mediatized places of community construction through ethnographic observation and interviews. We select three examples here: a shopping mall, a communal cinema and a hackerspace. The idea is to make a comparison between these places, treating them as part of a spectrum of mediatized places of community construction.

3.5.1 Shopping Mall

One example of a mediatized place of community construction is the shopping mall Waterfront. Opened in 2008, it was built on former dockland in the city district of Gröpelingen, once an area where dock workers lived, but whose population is now 40 per cent migrants from over 50 states, but especially Turkey and Bulgaria. In Bremen's deprivation index, Gröpelingen lies in the bottom third (Freie Hansestadt Bremen 2010: 8). Waterfront attracts young people from the neighbouring city districts, and not only for what is sold there. There are large open areas in which different groups of friends meet. They also find the free wi-fi available from the fast food outlets and cafés an additional attraction. Besides that, events are regularly held in the mall: live appearances or particular artists, fashion and car shows, song contests, children's programmes and, above all, public viewing of TV. Waterfront is therefore a commercial space that, besides being a shopping experience, also offers economically disadvantaged young people the opportunity to meet, use the internet together and have fun.

The figurative qualities of this mediatized space of community construction are exemplified by the public viewing of TV. On days when the local football club is playing, amongst others, a screen and seating are set up in the Food Court (see Fig. 3.2).

The circular space of the Food Court has a glass roof and is connected to the shopping mall by two passages (see for the following Andrae et al. 2015). Tables and seating are arranged in circles in the court, surrounded by a variety of cheap food outlets. The 25 m^2 LED screen on which football games are shown is fixed to one of the walls of the Food Court. When public viewings are taking place there are around 500 people of different ages present, judging by the seating. From the interviews that we held during events, it turned out that some of those present made a regular thing of attending. Six of the eight interviewed said that

Fig. 3.2 Public viewing in the Food Court of Bremen's Waterfront Mall

they had been attending live broadcasts at the Waterfront in groups for a long time. Some thought that a live viewing was better than going to the stadium, because of the special qualities of the shopping mall:

> [...] if I'm honest, here you can eat what you like and meet a lot of people and that would be a lot more difficult to do in the stadium with several people. [...] Because you can just do that here with friends. The main thing is, for me that is the thing about football: it is less about the game than, um, to watch it with friends. (Manfred, visitor to public viewing)

From this short passage, it is clear how much watching a big screen in the shopping mall has to do with the sense of being together with friends. This is confirmed by observation of such events. From the way that tables and chairs are arranged (see Fig. 3.2), it is plain that very few of those present are alone. It is much more usual to go as a couple, with friends or with family to a screening. There is seldom direct communication between these groups. The voice of the commentator to the live screening dominates the space, and the audience follow the game closely. If they speak at all, it is within their group or to family members. Only occasionally there is restrained cheering and clapping. In the middle of the Food Court are mostly middle-aged and older people, who concentrate on the transmission. Groups of youths are scattered around the edges; they move around from time to time, and turn now and then from the screen to their smart phones or to conversation with their friends.

The special figurative quality of this shopping mall is to provide a commercial space that, besides providing opportunities for shopping and socializing, also offers events that people on low incomes can share with their families or groups of friends. In this sense, Waterfront is a place providing a reference point for diverse figurations of people who, while not being in direct contact with each other, share experiences with friends and family.

3.5.2 Communal Cinema

In the middle of Bremen city centre, about a five-minute walk from the main railway station, there is the communal cinema, City 46. This has a different figurative quality. The institution goes back over 40 years, having been founded in 1974 in connection with the student movement of the time, seeking to promote a more reflexive approach to the media.[5] In 2011, the communal cinema moved from a working-class district into the city centre, and it has since then shared its space in the former commercial City Kino with an improvisational theatre company, changing its name as a consequence from Kino 46 to City 46 (see Fig. 3.3).

The former City Kino dates from the 1950s, and both interior and exterior have been deliberately preserved and not modernized. Approaching the cinema, a visitor is greeted by the suggestion of nostalgia given by a neon sign. Once inside, there is a very striking stairway with a mirrored wall that likewise dates from the 1950s. The styling of the place reflects a consciousness of tradition on the part of the governing board, marking off the communal cinema aesthetically from the city's commercial multiplexes (cf. Gerhard et al. 2015). As someone who has worked in Bremen's communal cinema for many years emphasized in interview, those running City 46 rate very highly the choice of films shown. They should involve either some element of social criticism or

Fig. 3.3 Communal cinema City 46

have some special aesthetic value. It is a matter of the emphasis adopted, in which 'sometimes […] the emphasis is more on the aesthetic, sometimes […] more on the political side' (Peter Maier, employed at City 46).

If the figurative quality of City 46 is examined more closely, it becomes apparent that particular sets of films address particular groups of people—the cinema does not direct itself to individual cinema-goers. Specifically, cultural programming is practised. Peter Maier noted that 'there are not a lot of members of a proletarian milieu, if there is such a thing anyway. Our audience is bourgeois, that's clear, it is also older.' He did, however, emphasize how the composition of the audience changed from one film theme to another. The shifting emphasis of programming and the associated co-operation with various Bremen cultural and educational groups is designed to address different communities:

> And that is just true of many of the things we show, they are very much to do with the film's theme, or a series of films is oriented to a target group.

> But that is a good thing, because in this way you get a natural palette, we are really I think well linked up with the migrant scene, they are always just pleased to be able to see sometimes stuff from back home. There are always films from Africa, we've got some in November, another series. Or again, this year art and film has been a big thing, the art scene is a bit stronger there than otherwise.

Maier emphasizes that those running the cinema place great store in making the cinema a 'social place' through film programming and related events, making it somewhere special. The communal experience of the cinema audience provided a sense of community of especially 'good quality'. These statements were confirmed by interviews with members of the audience: 'You share impressions, ideas, you comment' said one audience member, and another suggested that 'you have the feeling that everyone feels the same thing, because that is so great'.

Going to the cinema is seen by audience members as something related to their own lives and interests. Examples might be historical or musical interests, or belonging to a particular migrant group, and thus a consequent interest in films in one's own language. In this sense, City 46 is not a place where particular groups meet up. It is a place where shifting constellations of different groups of friends are formed according to the films being screened, all meeting as a communal cinema audience. The special figurative quality of the space is thus derived from the themes of the screenings, which address quite different groups.

3.5.3 Hackerspace

It is already plain from the professional presentation of the home page for Hackerspace Bremen e.V. that this is run by a group of engaged and enthusiastic 'people interested in technology, who have fun with informatics, electronics and mechanics'.[6] Their activities focus on the use and creation of media technologies, open source projects, internet policy and online gaming. In the hobby workshop. it is possible to use tools and equipment together with others. Among the equipment available is a 3D printer, a soldering station, a laser cutter, an electric drill, oscilloscope, a sewing machine, a CNC milling machine and so on.

Hackerspace has premises in the city centre, only a few minutes from the main railway station. Behind a back courtyard, you find a small building with a common room of about 35 square metres. In the middle, a number of tables have been pushed together to create a large work

Fig. 3.4 Interior of Hackerspace

surface liberally supplied with electrical points, and here several people can work together (cf. Baumgarten et al. 2015). At the end of the work surface there is a screen and projector, and in the left-hand corner of the room there is a sofa. Along the sides of the room there are workstations and various technical apparatus, tools, cables, electronic components and other related material (see Fig. 3.4). There is also another room that is used as a store and workroom.

While the accommodation has the atmosphere of a hobbyist's workshop, the location of Hackerspace has no special significance for its users. The chosen location is more functional than anything else: the amount of space, the central location and the possibility of using it as a workshop. From interviews and participant observation, it is evident that Hackerspace is mainly used by men between the ages of 20 and 60 who are interested in technology. They come from many occupational backgrounds, especially technical occupations. School and college students are also active in the association, the most important people here being the committee and association members who are organized into different groups by interest. Apart from external experts who sometimes come and give lectures, there are also visitors to events and workshops. However, Hackerspace remains basically a place 'where you can talk about technology and from time to time use equipment that would really be too expensive to buy yourself' (Janosch, committee member, Hackerspace Bremen e.V.). Members of the Hackerspace governing body see it as sharing in a worldwide network. As Janosch continued: 'there are different networks that you can use, different mailing lists where you can now and then ask for help if [...] if something here does not work or goes wrong[...]. We help each other [...] if there are problems, or if someone wants to do something involving the whole city.'

Among the places for community construction discussed here, Hackerspace is certainly the one most strongly bound up with media technology. Besides their own special app for members and professional involvement with the press, for which all available channels of communication are used, even internal communication is media-based: internal processes are organized by a wiki. Discussion on specific technical topics is available outside the workshop space through online forums and email distribution lists. And even in 'hacking' it is a matter of practices that are in the broadest sense related to media. This includes the re-engineering of 'older' technologies ('hacking' an old sewing machine) as well as experimenting with 'new' technologies, for example, the 3D printer. The figurative quality of Hackerspace is therefore that of a place that is thematically focused, and through its use of technology offers 'alternative' groupings possibilities for working and socializing together. The 'alternative' nature of activities is related to the fact that media technologies are used to design and make individual products or spare parts that are different from standardized mass market goods. If in the places we have studied we might see the beginnings of a 'smart city' and of a 'code/space'

(Kitchin and Dodge 2011)—the linking up of communication technology with the social formation of location—then it is most developed here, within an alternative framework. Hackerspace is a place that one member described as a 'home for nerds', as 'Nerdistan': 'our similar interests mean that at this level we come together after we have finished work' (Bruno, member of Hackerspace Bremen e.V.).

If we review the locations with which we have dealt—the shopping mall, the communal cinema, Hackerspace—then it becomes more clear what we mean by the figurative quality of mediatized places of community construction: whatever the place, access to it or the possibilities for interaction for groups there, these places have differing potential for community in the city. Remarkably, the commercial shopping mall seems to be much more open to friendship groups and cliques of young people from disadvantaged areas of the city than the other spaces.[7] Of course, the communal cinema is in principle open to all, and sees itself as having a particular cultural mission. Its programme does, however, address very specific social and friendship groups. Hackerspace in its courtyard seems to be the most closed. Ultimately, it is for individuals and friends interested in technology who find there an alternative possibility for community construction related to technology. It is not a communal space that has any other attraction.

Further, those three localities can represent a typology of mediatized places for community construction. The shopping mall is a *commercial space for situative community construction*, to which we can add pubs, street festivals and concerts in public spaces. These are mostly patronized by young people with their friendship groups, the orientation to the event being a situative one. The communal cinema is a *cultural and educational space*, along with other cultural establishments. They address very specific and shifting groups, for whom they are a communitized space. Finally, the Hackerspace can be seen as an *alternative space for community construction*. We can add to this urban gardening and places for alternative culture. Common to all of these is their appeal to very clearly defined groups who see themselves as representing an 'alternative'.

From this, there emerges a dual segregation of communal life in the mediatized city. On the one hand the various spaces of community construction address very different individuals and groups of friends, according to their distinct figurative qualities. On the other hand, these spaces are very unevenly distributed around the city. Depending on how one moves as an individual or with friends through the city, and the kind of places visited for community construction, the experience of community in the city can be very different.

3.6 The Mediatized City as an Imagined Community

In conclusion, we want to emphasize a third aspect of the urban communitization of young people: if one considers cities as social constructions, they can acquire the status of an imagined community (Jarren 2013: 53). If we link this argument to our data on the communicative networking and community construction of young people and their friendship groups, we find ourselves facing a paradox: not every young person for whom the city is an important space of opportunity for community thinks the city as imagined community to be very important.

At this point, it is worth coming back to the interviews that we carried out. Juliane Brandt (23, Bremen, trainee instrument maker) stated that 'Bremen is not important for me, my home is important, and my home is [...] where my friends [...] are.' The city is an important space of opportunity that she would not like to do without, but this particular city, as an imagined community, has no great importance to her.

Do statements like this just mean that, for the young people we interviewed, the city as imagined community is insignificant? That would be too easy a conclusion to draw. Tom Friedrich (26, Bremen, policeman) states quite explicitly that the city in which he lives is, besides his relationship and family, emphatically a community. So the city as an imagined community can be found in our data. And to recognize the patterns, it helps to look more closely at the way in which young people view the totality of communities in which they position themselves subjectively (Hepp 2013: 122).

As touched on above, we can identify at least four of these horizons of communitization: localists, centrists, multi-localists and pluralists (see Hepp et al. 2014a, b). To put it simply: localists are people whose communal life takes place mainly at the local level, as manifested in their primarily local communicative networks. The sense of community of centrists comes from a particular issue or concern; for example, a religion or some aspect of popular culture. This provides the dominating orientation of their communicative network and sense of community. Multi-localists favour several particular sites, which is reflected in the way that their communicative network is extensive and translocal. Pluralists, finally, are people who involve themselves in very different and in some cases casually formed communities, and are thus correspondingly extensively networked. Even if some individuals combine elements of these four types, this typology helps us understand the way in which the mediatized city as imagined community plays a role in the life of our interview subjects. It would be too simple to say that the imagined community of the city is only relevant to localists. In our data we can find all four types of young people for whom much the same is true as Tom Friedrich: the city as imagined community has a relevance to them. The connection is instead something rather different: *if* the city has a sense for these young people of being an imagined community, then for each of these four types this manifests itself in a *specific* manner.

We can begin with *localists*, something Konstanze Mitscherlich (26, Lepizig, printer) says is especially significant. Regarding her home city of Leipzig, she notes that 'friends take some part in politics, or make a fuss at city council meetings, and so a Leipziger in this way get to know about important things, sort of through verbal propaganda'. Not only does she feel she belongs to the city as an imagined community, she also keeps in touch, if indirectly, with political events and goings on in the city. She values, as do localists generally, strong local networks and being anchored in the communication space of local media. Not only does she inform herself about local political matters through newspapers, TV and the web, but also from her local friends who take part in city politics.

It is different with *centrists*, who approach the imagined community of the city very much on the basis of their own biography and its associated apprehension of community. One example is Dirk Herrmann (26, Leipzig, independent agent for artists), whose sense of community and also his communicative network is directed towards the music scene. Although he sees himself as a Leipziger, and his attachment to the city's imagined community is of relevance, this is overwhelmingly channelled through the Leipzig music scene. This is the dominant issue that for him opens up the city as an imagined community. As he says himself:

> And this attachment to these artists, that it is the same for everyone, whether you now [have] a band in Hamburg, or in Berlin, or in Cologne, or in Mannheim, or wherever. That is something they all share […] The music is different, [but] but everyone has the same baggage in whichever city.

The city as community therefore plays a role with centrists if their dominant interest has a connection with it. If this is so, then this will be reflected in the communicative network. For Dirk, this last element is the music scene, including related websites and magazines for which he also writes.

Our material shows that even *multi-localists* can feel attached to a particular city. Here we can detect clear parallels with what we have already established with respect to localists. What is special about multi-localists is that their imagined community of a city is experienced in connection with other places. Important here is growing up in one place and then moving away, leaving the original group of friends behind. 'Here are my friends and here are my roots' as one says (Adriana-Luise Kück, Bremen region, community social volunteer). For multi-localists, it is less the city as the imagined community of an immediate environment that is paramount, but rather the region. Sabine Elbe (22, Leipzig, trainee healing practitioner) describes this as follows: 'Really, I am only whole in Saxony.' The city in which she lives is then a subordinate matter.

Pluralists also make comparisons between cities. All the same, insofar as the city plays a role as an imagined community, it is wrapped into a much more varied horizon of community. What is initially striking is the refusal of any imagined fixed geographical or cultural community. Torsten Breisler (21, Leipzig, student), for example, insists that he feels 'basically [...] neither Bavarian, nor as someone from Munich, but just as little [...] German'. Or Claas Kuhnert (29, Bremen, trainee health service manager) says with respect to Bremen that it is the 'centre of his life'. But on the other hand, 'this could really have been any other city'. Apparently in contrast to this, Claas sees the need for the solidarity of local communities. From this arises his interest in engaging with the city in which he lives, especially when it involves the 'development of a district' or 'culture'. Presumably this was the reason for his temporary involvement with the Bremen Left Party, which ended after disagreements in the local party organization.

If we consider these examples of localists, centrists, multilocalists and pluralists, it becomes clear how specific yet precarious the connection to the city as an imagined community can be. All of those we interviewed ranked their group of friends very much above the city.

3.7 Conclusion: Community-Building in the Mediatized City

How can we bring together the different levels of urban communitization that we have discussed in this chapter? We began with a discussion about the role of media in supporting life in the city. On the whole, it is striking how few of what are said to be the current hot topics regarding media-related changes in the city are reflected in the everyday life of the young people we interviewed: ideas of a smart city are far removed from their existence, locative media are something that they use tentatively but whose potential for community construction plays little part, while hyperlocal journalism, as with local journalism, had very little resonance among our interviewees, especially the localists among them.

By contrast, our figurational and analytical perspective on the issue of living in the mediatized city highlights the fact that, beyond the family, it is friends who are important in their experience of community in the city: this experience is undertaken with groups of friends for whom, above all, the city represents a space of possibility. The experience of community is, however, segregated by the way that the figurative quality of the community spaces in the city are very different, and that these places are unevenly distributed across the city. The manner in which one group of friends experiences this quite possibly therefore has little to do with how another one does. In addition to this, the idea of the city as an imagined community had relevance for only some of our interviewees, and what this meant for them tended to vary quite widely. Likewise, local political engagement is more the exception than the rule. All the same, a sense of belonging to the city as an imagined community was related to the use of local media content, or communication about this.

These results echo the argument of Robert E. Park that the city is a 'mosaic of little worlds'. Taking account of this, some points can be raised. For one thing, this mosaic is not experienced by young people negatively, but rather as a space of opportunity through which they move with their friends. Park's reflections are today limited by the way that today's media environment promotes media ensembles that tend to stabilize groups of friends rather than foster a divided city public domain. 'Social control'—if one wishes to use this term—takes place primarily *within groups of friends* as 'interveillance' (Christensen and Jansson 2014: 8); there is a degree of pressure to use the favoured media ensemble, so this is not a form of pressure that originates in a public domain. For many, the city remains a—valued—space of opportunity with diverse locations for community construction that are important to them. Only exceptionally is it experienced as a political space of a particular community.

The deep mediatization of the city thus leaves an ambivalent impression. Ideas about the broad possibilities of digital media for urban living are confronted with a young person's reality, in which such speculations are limited to alternative mediatized spaces such as the Hackerspace dealt with above, or are important for individuals such as the pluralist Claas Kuhnert (locally political). The mediatized city remains segregated, and only reveals itself as a communal structure once one considers the variety of its diverse communicative figurations.

Notes

1. Cindy Roitsch and Matthias Berg collaborated on this project and collected the material that underpins this chapter. See for an outline of the results of this project especially Hepp et al. (2014a, b).
2. The following took part in the research seminar: Felix Andrae, Paul Baumgarten, Ulrike Gerhard, Freya Grundmann, Alexander Keßel, Lei Lu, Lisa Pautsch, Kassandra Puderbach, Milena Schulte, Pawadee Tiphyarug and Jana Wagner. They put together the Open Street Map presented in Sect. 5 below, to which we refer in the analysis conducted in that section (see on this Andrae et al. 2015; Baumgarten et al. 2015; Gerhard et al. 2015).
3. We are referring here to different horizons of communitization and distinguish between localists, centralists, multilocalists and pluralists. See on this Hepp et al. (2014a) as well as our discussion in Sect. 6.
4. All the names here are pseudonyms.
5. On the history of the communal cinema and its governing body see http://www.city46.de. Accessed: 30 March 2017.
6. See http://www.hackerspace-bremen.de. Accessed: 30 March 2017.
7. This coincides with Myria Georgiou's work on a London shopping mall, where she came to similar conclusions—see Georgiou (2013: 51–58).

References

Anderson, Benedict. 1983. *Imagined communities: Reflections on the origins and spread of nationalism*. New York: Verso.

Andrae, Felix, Freya Grundmann, and Pawadee Tiphyarug. 2015. Mediengebrauch bei situativen Eventvergemeinschaftungen. ZeMKI, MA research report.

Baumgarten, Paul, Alexander Keßel, Milena Schulte, and Jana Wagner. 2015. Alternative Vergemeinschaftungsorte in Bremen. ZeMKI, MA research report.

Baym, Nancy K. 2015. *Personal connections in the digital age*, 2nd ed. Cambridge, Malden: Polity.

Berg, Matthias, and Cindy Roitsch. 2015. Lokalität, Heimat, Zuhause und Mobilität. In *Handbuch Cultural Studies und Medienanalyse*, ed. Andreas Hepp, Friedrich Krotz, Swantje Lingenberg, and Jeffrey Wimmer, 147–155. Wiesbaden: VS.

Bolin, Göran. 2004. Spaces of television. The structuring of consumers in a Swedish shopping mall. In *Media space: Place, scale and culture in a media age*, ed. Nick Couldry and Anna McCarthy, 126–144. London: Routledge.

Bridge, Gary. 2009. Reason in the city? Communicative action, media and urban politics. *International Journal of Urban and Regional Research* 33 (1): 237–240.

Castells, Manuel. 2000. *The rise of the network society. The information age: Economy, society and culture*, vol. 1, 2nd ed. Oxford: Blackwell.

Christensen, Miyase, and André Jansson. 2014. Complicit surveillance, interveillance, and the question of cosmopolitanism: Toward a phenomenological understanding of mediatization. *New Media & Society* 17 (9): 1473–1491.

Christensen, Miyase, and André Jansson. 2015. *Cosmopolitanism and the media. Cartographies of change*. London: Palgrave Macmillan.

Christmann, Gabriela B. 2013. Raumpioniere in Stadtquartieren und die kommunikative (Re-)Konstruktion von Räumen. In *Kommunikativer Konstruktivismus*, ed. Reiner Keller, Jo Reichertz, and Hubert Knoblauch, 153–184. Wiesbaden: Springer.

Christmann, Gabriela B. 2016. *Zur kommunikativen Konstruktion von Räumen: Theoretische Konzepte und empirische Analysen*. Wiesbaden: VS.

Couldry, Nick, and Andreas Hepp. 2017. *The mediated construction of reality*. Cambridge: Polity Press.

Elias, Norbert, and John Lloyd Scotson. 1994 [1965]. *The established and the outsiders: A sociological enquiry into community problems*. London: Sage.

Evans, Leighton. 2015. *Locative social media: Place in the digital age*. London: Palgrave Macmillan.

Farías, Ignacio. 2010. Introduction: Decentring the object of urban studies. In *Urban assemblages. How actor-network theory changes urban studies*, ed. Ignacio Farías and Thomas Bender, 1–24. London, New York: Routledge.

Freie Hansestadt Bremen. 2010. Stadtteilbericht Gröpelingen.

Georgiou, Myria. 2013. *Media and the city: Cosmopolitanism and difference*. Cambridge: Polity.

Gerhard, Ulrike, Lei Lu, Lisa Pautsch, and Kassandra Puderbach. 2015. Medien-Stadt-Vergemeinschaftung. Eine Untersuchung zur Mediatisierung urbanen Gemeinschaftslebens an Kultur-, Bildungs—und Freizeit-Orten in Bremen. ZeMKI, MA research report.

Glaser, Barney G., and Anselm L. Strauss. 1998. *Grounded Theory strategien qualitativer forschung*. Bern: Huber.

Hasebrink, Uwe, and Jan-Hinrik Schmidt. 2013. Informationsrepertoires und Medienvielfalt in der Großstadtöffentlichkeit. Eine Untersuchung der Berliner Bevölkerung. In *MediaPolis—Kommunikation zwischen Boulevard und Parlament: Strukturen, Entwicklungen und Probleme von politischer und zivilgesellschaftlicher Öffentlichkeit*, ed. Barbara Pfetsch, Janine Greyer, and Joachim Trebbe, 161–184. Konstanz: UVK.

Hepp, Andreas. 2013. *Cultures of mediatization*. Cambridge: Polity Press.

Hepp, Andreas. 2015. *Transcultural communication*. Malden: Wiley Blackwell.

Hepp, Andreas, Matthias Berg, and Cindy Roitsch. 2014a. *Mediatisierte Welten der Vergemeinschaftung: Kommunikative Vernetzung und das Gemeinschaftsleben junger Menschen*. Wiesbaden: VS.

Hepp, Andreas, Matthias Berg, and Cindy Roitsch. 2014b. Mediatized worlds of communitization: Young people as localists, centrists, multi-localists and pluralists. In *Mediatized worlds: Culture and society in a media age*, ed. Andreas Hepp, and Friedrich Krotz, 174–203. London: Palgrave.

Hepp, Andreas, Cindy Roitsch, and Matthias Berg. 2016. Investigating communication networks contextually. Qualitative network analysis as cross-media research. *MedieKultur* 32 (60): 87–106.

Jarren, Otfried. 2013. MediaPolis oder Monopoly? Stadt und Medien als Gemeinschaftsversprechen. In *MediaPolis—Kommunikation zwischen Boulevard und Parlament: Strukturen, Entwicklungen und Probleme von politischer und zivilgesellschaftlicher Öffentlichkeit*, ed. Barbara Pfetsch, Janine Greyer, and Joachim Trebbe, 51–62. Konstanz: UVK.

Keppler, Angela. 2014. Reichweiten alltäglicher Gespräche. Über den kom-munikativen Gebrauch alter und neuer Medien. In *Unser Alltag ist voll von Gesellschaft*, eds. Alfred Bellebaum and Robert Hettlage, 85–104. Wiesbaden: VS.

Kitchin, Rob, and Martin Dodge. 2011. *Code/space: Software and everyday life*. Cambridge, MA: MIT Press.

Krajina, Zlatan. 2014. *Negotiating the mediated city*. Routledge: Everyday encounters with public screens. London.

Lane, Jeffrey. 2016. The digital street: An ethnographic study of networked street life in Harlem. *American Behavioral Scientist* 60 (1): 43–58.

Massey, Doreen. 1994. *Space, place and gender*. Cambridge: Polity Press.

Metag, Julia, and André Donk. 2013. Fragmentierung städtischer Öffentlichkeit. Integration soziogeografischer und kommunikationswissenschaftlicher Ansätze. In MediaPolis—Kommunikation zwischen Boulevard und Parlament: Strukturen, Entwicklungen und Probleme von politischer und zivilgesellschaftlicher Öffentlichkeit, eds. Barbara Pfetsch, Janine Greyer, and Joachim Trebbe, 63–82. Konstanz: UVK.

Neal, Zachary P. 2013. *The connected city. How networks are shaping the modern metropolis*. London, New York: Routledge.

Nielsen, Rasmus K. 2015. *Local Journalism—The decline of newspapers and the rise of digital media*. London, New York: Tauris.

Park, Robert E. 1967. The city: Suggestions for the investigation of human behaviour in the urban environment. In *The city*, ed. Robert E. Park, Ernest W. Burgess, and Roderick McKenzie, 1–46. Chicago: University of Chicago Press.

Rainie, Harrison, and Barry Wellman. 2012. *Networked: The new social operating system*. Cambridge, MA: MIT Press.
Rauterberg, Hanno. 2013. *Wir sind die Stadt!: Urbanes Leben in der Digitalmoderne*. Berlin: Suhrkamp.
Simmel, Georg. 2006 [1903]. *Die Großstädte und das Geistesleben*. Frankfurt am Main: Suhrkamp.
Smith, Neil, and Peter Williams. 2010. *Gentrification of the city*. London: Routledge.
Strauss, Anselm, and Juliet Corbin. 1996. *Grounded Theory: Grundlagen qualitativer Sozialforschung*. Weinheim: Beltz.
Strübing, Jörg. 2008. *Grounded Theory. Zur sozialtheoretischen und epistemologischen Fundierung des Verfahrens der empirisch begründeten Theoriebildung*, 2nd ed. Wiesbaden: VS Verlag.
Townsend, Anthony M. 2013. *Smart cities: Big data, civic hackers, and the quest for a new utopia*. New York: WW Norton & Company.
United Nations. 2015. *World urbanization prospects. The 2014 revision*. New York: United Nations.
Zukin, Sharon, Philip Kasinitz, and Xiangming Chen. 2016. *Global cities, local streets. Everyday diversity from New York to Shanghai*. New York, London: Routledge.

4

Digital Media, CCC and Political Activism

Sebastian Kubitschko

4.1 Introduction

In recent years, scholars have theorized about and conducted outstanding research on the interrelation between digital media and political activism. The interrelation between digital media and emerging forms of political activism has been investigated in insightful ways especially when it comes to protest, mobilization and other forms of 'contentious' involvement. When it comes to scholarship in the field of media and communication the focus of a number of recent studies has been on movement-based activism and more or less loosely networked collectives (Juris 2012; Theocharis et al. 2015; Mercea et al. 2016). These studies are particularly valuable because they manage to bridge disciplinary boundaries by bringing together analytical and methodological approaches from media studies, anthropology, political science and sociology. Yet, in contrast to the number of writings on networked and movement-based activism, far less work has been undertaken on more

S. Kubitschko (✉)
ZeMKI, Centre for Media, Communication and Information Research, University of Bremen, Bremen, Germany
e-mail: sebastian.kubitschko@uni-bremen.de

concrete entities such as civil society organizations and on the role media technologies and infrastructures play in political engagements other than protest and mobilization (see Karpf 2012). Recent studies on hackers and hacking—understood as one particular set of contemporary political engagement—are no exception in this regard, as they tend to focus on contentious and globally networked forms of activism (Coleman 2014).

By presenting findings from qualitative research on the Chaos Computer Club (CCC), one of the world's oldest and largest hacker organizations, this chapter displays how hackers' political engagement today relies on a wide range of practices related to media technologies and infrastructures and, at the same time, continues to be oriented towards larger publics as well as 'traditional' centres of political power. While we have certain knowledge about hacker collectives at large and singular activities of the CCC in particular (see, for example, Wagenknecht and Korn 2016), we still lack a more detailed understanding of the processes that ultimately enable the Club to thematize and problematize the political qualities of specific media technologies and infrastructures. By employing the concept of communicative figuration—*actor constellations*, *communicative practices* and their *frames of relevance*—the chapter elaborates how the CCC communicatively constructs media technologies and infrastructures as a political category in its own right.

Adopting a figurational approach in this context is particularly helpful as it allows us to take into account the hacker organization's development over a longer period of time. In addition, it enables researchers to employ an inclusive understanding of the contemporary 'media environment' (Hasebrink and Hölig 2014), which includes a wide range of media technologies and infrastructures, instead of restricting the empirical inquiry to the use of a singular medium or the effects of specific media content. Finally, the approach allows us to investigate the relations between the communicative figuration that is internal and the communicative figuration that is external to the organization. To implement this approach, the chapter will proceed in three aligned steps. First, the hacker organization itself is conceptualized as a communicative figuration, which also includes direct political action in the form of hacking. Second, the chapter explains how the CCC positions itself in the public discourse around media technologies. Third, the chapter demonstrates how the Club's internal figuration and its linkages with relevant actors such as journalists, politicians and judges as well as the general public creates a spiral of legitimation that enables the hacker organization to constitute media technologies and infrastructures as publicly recognized political phenomena. What this shows us, ultimately, is how hackers problematize media technologies and infrastructures as a theme and field of political engagement in itself, instead of considering them simply a means to an end.

4.2 Researching Hacker Cultures

Scholars have condensed the far-reaching political relevance of technology by emphasizing that not only the appropriation of individual tools but also access to telecommunications infrastructure such as satellites and internet servers, as well as 'logical' infrastructure such as codes and protocols, are prime points of political engagement (Milan and Hintz 2013; Hunsinger and Schrock forthcoming/2017). In other words, with the increasing relevance of practices related to media technologies and infrastructures for social arrangements in general, and for political engagements in particular, media technologies and infrastructures increasingly become sites of political struggle in their own right (Kubitschko 2017). It is in this context that scholarly interest in 'hacker cultures'—owing to the diversity of hacker collectives the plural is essential—has grown considerably in the past decade. While governmental institutions and mainstream media often use 'hacking' as an umbrella term for computer-related crime, these depictions are contrasted with insightful research that highlights hackers' interaction with contemporary political landscapes.

Chris Kelty (2008) emphasizes that hackers play an important role in society as they argue with and about technology. Tim Jordan (2013) characterizes hacktivism as an explicitly political form of computing. Leah Lievrouw (2011) pictures hacking as 'alternative computing' to describe a range of activities that focus on constructive political, social and cultural purposes. Gabriella Coleman (2012) depicts hacking not only as a technical endeavour but also as an aesthetic and a moral project that converges powerfully with humour, cleverness, craft and politics. John Postill in his writing on protest movements such as the Indignados in Spain refers to hackers who combine technological skills with political acumen as 'freedom technologists' (Postill 2014: 2). There has been growing interest in hackers' collaborations with alternative media networks such as Indymedia (see Giraud 2014). At the same time, the growing approximation of established news outlets and hackers could be witnessed in WikiLeaks' collaboration with a range of mainstream media as well as in Edward Snowden's disclosures that were initially edited by Glenn Greenwald for the *Guardian*. Taken together, recent theorization and research highlights the ever more substantial role hackers play for contemporary social and political arrangements. Overall, it can be said that recent investigations of hacker cultures bring forward a multilayered and revealing characterization of hackers by looking closely at who they are, what they do and why they do it, instead of preserving stereotypes or proclaiming generalizations. It is this latter conceptual positioning of hackers, hacking and hacktivism that this research is drawing on and aims to expand by adapting a figurational approach.

In the context of recent studies on hacker cultures, the CCC is a somewhat particular case. First, in contrast to newer hacker collectives, the Club has been around since the early 1980s—a time before the World Wide Web when the increasing spread of personal computers further stimulated the transition from analogue to digital communication. Second, the CCC is not necessarily a loosely networked collective but rather a concrete entity that is registered as a non-profit organization with around 5,500 members and acts an official advocacy group. Third, for the most part its activities are not destructive or illegal, but best considered constructive and in accordance with the established law. What started in 1981 as an informal gathering of a few 'politically sensitized computer enthusiasts' (Wagenknecht and Korn 2016: 1107) today is a digital rights and civil society organization whose members have advised all major political parties in Germany over the past years, have written expert reports for the German constitutional court on six occasions and have been invited to be part of governmental committees. Organization, in the context of this framework, is not understood as a static phenomenon, but as a 'discursive construction' (Fairhurst and Putnam 2004) produced through an ongoing process of 'organized sense making' (Weick et al. 2005). It is understood that there is both an internal side to this sense-making—members negotiating what the organization is and should be—and an external side—how the surrounding environment relates to the organization.

The qualitative case study research (Yin 2014) presented in this chapter relies on an 'extended case method' (Burawoy 1998) that is based on a mixed method approach. It brings together 40 face-to-face open-ended interviews with Club members (e.g. co-founders, spokespersons, new members), participant observations during public gatherings at hackerspaces across Germany (e.g. Berlin, Hamburg, Stuttgart) and hacker conventions (e.g. Chaos Communication Congress in Berlin, SIGINT in Cologne) as well as during more private get-togethers (e.g. personal meetings with journalists). Based on a constructivist grounded theory approach (Charmaz 2002: 677), the primary data set was supplemented with a contextualizing media analysis: taking into account 'old' and 'new' self-mediation practices (e.g. the Club's *Datenschleuder* magazine, press releases, the official CCC Twitter account @chaosupdates, legal expert reports, Chaosradio), prominent media coverage (e.g. mainstream media after hacks, during annual Congress) as well as different forms and styles of media access (e.g. columns of CCC members in mainstream outlets, participation in political talk shows, interviews with CCC members). The lion's share of the research took place over a three-year period from 2011 to 2014 and the contextualizing media analysis continued until 2016.

4.3 Forming a Coherent Hacker Organization

Let me start by going way back in time to unpack the political development of the CCC. The Club's first activity that attracted attention to the hackers as actors in the field of computing was the so-called Btx hack. Since its nationwide launch in 1983, Btx (abbreviation for *Bildschirmtext*, 'screen text') was an 'interactive' online system that was part of the German Federal Post Office's monopoly on mediated communication—including mail, telephone, computer networks and hardware. Integrating a telephone and a screen in one medium, the main purpose of Btx was to facilitate and promote e-commerce and digital communication. Although the system was far less networked, it can be seen as a precursor of more recent services such as online payment systems and news tickers. In the autumn of 1984, two CCC members exploited a security flaw in Btx, which allowed the hackers to transfer 135,000 Deutschmark (*c.* 68,000 euros) from Hamburg's savings bank to their own donation page. Immediately after the hack, the CCC retransferred the money and reported the incident to the data protection commissioner. The hack not only demonstrated the system's security flaws but also provided evidence of the hackers' technology-related skills and knowledge.

At this time, the network of actors interrelated and communicating with each other was still readily comprehensible and the Club's communicative practices were largely based on face-to-face interaction, as most of its members were based in Hamburg. Yet the increasing spread of personal computers and digital infrastructures such as bulletin board systems at that time went hand in hand with the emergence of local CCC chapters and meet-ups across Germany. In stark contrast to other existing means of communication, the newly developed networks were largely decentralized. This was important in a social and a political sense when it comes to *actor constellations.* As hackers were still a minor sub-cultural phenomenon and people interested in the creative and subversive use of technology were dispersed across the country, the possibility of sharing information and knowledge across time and space was a big step towards building a sense of communality. More concretely, the emerging ability to merge offline and online communication showed the initial Club members that new forms of connectivity were possible, opening up new modes of engagement. The *frames of relevance* that guided the Club's constituting practices were predominantly concerned with the political demand for more open and freely accessible communication and information infrastructures. Overall, the character of the CCC was defined by the objective to form a collective of politically motivated technologists that would not only do things with technology but also act upon it. The Btx hack was exemplary in this context as it explicitly problematized the Post Office's monopoly by showing its limitations and shortcomings. Similarly, the desire to communicate and collaborate and to coordinate activities within and beyond the Club's boundaries through decentralized infrastructures was the driving force behind the hackers' efforts to establish these networks.

Yet, throughout the mid- and late 1980s, the CCC had to acknowledge that to establish and keep up its frames of relevance was anything but an easy task. During that time, the CCC was publicly affiliated with illegal hacks that, amongst other things, involved the Soviet Union's KGB (the Committee for State Security) and hacking into NASA (National Aeronautics and Space Administration) computer systems. As internal communication soured, accusations got out of hand and disputes amongst core members led to controversies that almost saw the Club's dissolution. After reorganizing and re-establishing its own identity over the coming years, the hacker organization got its feet back on the ground by keeping its activities more coherent and better structured. The CCC also reformed its organizational structure. While the Club continued to grow and spread across German-speaking countries and increasingly brought together people who contributed heterogeneous backgrounds, perspectives and experiences, the 1990s saw the re-emergence of a more exclusive core team; which echoed the organization's constitution in its early days. This team of core members effectively coordinated the heterogeneity by merging face-to-face and mediated communication that relied on technologies such as Internet Relay Chats (IRC) and other self-programmed protocols for online messaging and data transfer, allowing one-to-one as well as group communication. Communicative practices were not only critical in the exchange of expertise and the debate of issues across the CCC's members, but also in the formation of a core team of actors who would coordinate the hackers' collective actions and specify its frames of relevance.

In this context, drawing clear boundaries between inward-oriented and outward-oriented communication was essential. One of the main reasons for establishing and upholding internal communication boundaries was the importance of coordinating collective action in ways that didn't allow 'outsiders' such as journalists and other actors interested in the Club's undertakings to gain sensitive information about ongoing or upcoming activities. For this purpose, communication had to be more exclusive and oriented towards individual members and subgroups instead of the Club as a whole. Participants identified several tools as adequate solutions to establish tailored and more efficient modes of communication, with IRC being one of the main channels for elaborating projects amongst a rather exclusive circle of members. In contrast to the more open information environment of internal mailing lists to which large numbers of members could subscribe, IRC was a much more restricted channel: it allowed longer-term, active and trusted members to communicate amongst each other and to form small groups that shared valuable information. Being able to communicate with each other through online systems such as IRC allowed the CCC to create different layers of exclusivity in which members could communicate one to one and amongst a selected few. These layers permitted the hackers to solve most of the issues related to keeping up boundaries between internal and external communication. Likewise, these layers formed and deepened existing organizational structures within the Club by creating exclusive communication environments for the sake of executing political work in more dynamic and secretive ways.

More recently, the spectrum of these tools has, of course, increased beyond IRC. While newer channels were not 'cannibalizing' existing tools, CCC members were employing contemporary digital technologies that played an important role in internal collaboration, coordination of digital direct action and more basic practices such as fine-tuning press releases. Web-based editing tools, for example, allowed a number of individuals to collaboratively edit a file, either simultaneously in real time, or deferred in non-real time. The major asset of these web-based editors, generally referred to as Pads, was seen to be in their ability to enable time-efficient, location-independent collaborations amongst a chosen group of people. Pads were an advancement on wikis, for example, as they brought different technological affordances together and enabled CCC members to act interlinked, multi-locally, and time-efficient. Depending on the particular need of the group, different communicative practices that formed layers of exclusivity fluently merged from one application to another. While the use of particular tools such as IRC and Pads was creating and underlining organizational structures, this was not only done for reasons of secrecy or exclusivity. The fact that only a selected number of individuals were involved in particular activities and included in exclusive communicative practices was to a large degree also down to practicality. Considering the growing size of the CCC, the Club's activities and internal organization would be simply unmanageable without the discussed practices. Bringing together a well-integrated group of people and keeping the number of participants in a given collective action down meant that the communication process could be more direct, productive and effective.

The overall level of connectivity had intensified drastically since the emergence of the Club in the early 1980s—from bulletin boards, through global communication networks, to instantaneous and overlapping web-based interaction. Yet in spite of this ongoing development, one can observe certain forms of continuity. Despite the rapid growth in membership figures, the CCC's communicative practices enabled members to form internal groups and layers of communicative intimacy that created margins between internal and external communication and maintained organizational boundaries within the Club. Communicative practices related to face-to-face communication as well as tools that emerged in the 1990s, and more contemporary technologies allowed a core group of members to stabilize the Club's political engagement successfully over time. On the one hand, restricting the number of actors also helped to maintain the boundary between internal and external communication. On the other hand, it enabled the Club to establish a more constructive communication process, as a lower number of participating members also meant a lower number of differing opinions; which, in turn, enabled the group to keep the frames of relevance more focused and to make decisions in a timely manner. Accordingly, performing direct digital action in the form of hacking was directly related to communicative practices, as they later played an important role in relation to organizing, coordinating and executing the Club's political projects. Despite rapid growth of the organization, communicative practices allow the Club to act on politically controversial issues in timely and discreet ways. Consequently, considering the internal side of sense-making when it comes to the CCC's organizational formation, one can see how communicative practices, a specific actor constellation and establishing frames of relevance go hand in hand. This communicative figuration within the hacker organization formed the Club's basis for executing well-orchestrated hacks, emphasizing that for the hacker organization media technologies and infrastructures are not simply instruments for acting politically but are political matters in themselves.

Only taking into account the past decade, the following hacks are of particular relevance in this context. In October 2006 the CCC, together with the Dutch citizen group Wij Vertrouwen Stemcomputers Niet ('We do not trust voting computers'), hacked a voting computer that was at that time in use in elections in the Netherlands, France, Germany and the United States. By demonstrating that the computers were not forgery-proof and that a fraud would be almost impossible to reconstruct, the hackers convincingly showed that basing elections on the use of these computers would endanger the democratic process. In 2008 Club members obtained fingerprints from the German interior minister at that time, Wolfgang Schäuble, and published them in a format designed to fool passport fingerprint readers. The hack underlined the vulnerability of biometric identity systems at a time when biometric passports were increasingly being introduced on a global scale and fingerprints became obligatory in German passports. The critique of the spread of insecure biometric applications in day-to-day life was recapitulated when in 2013 the Club hacked Apple's Touch ID—a technology that allows users to unlock their iPhone by fingerprint identification—within a week of its release. Another prominent recent collective action was the so-called Staatstrojaner ('Federal Trojan Horse') hack. In 2011, two years before the issue of surveillance gained global currency owing to Edward Snowden's revelations, the CCC disclosed surveillance software used by German police forces that violated the terms set by the constitutional court on this matter. Yet, as will be shown in the following section, to understand the way the Club thematizes and problematizes the political qualities of technology, one also needs to take into account another dimension: besides the aforementioned internal dynamics the Club's activities were, of course, also interrelated to external elements.

4.4 From the Inside to the Outside

Taking the above into account, it might come as no surprise that from day one the Club complemented its hacks with outward-oriented communication aimed to make the hackers' findings comprehensible and its political demands visible to the largest possible public. The Btx hack itself, for example, would not have been overly effectual if news media had not picked up the story. As news media reported widely on the hack and were largely in support of the hackers' criticism, the hack gained an event character. Following the Btx hack, the CCC was recognized as a collective actor that had something relevant to say about the communication and information landscape in Germany. The CCC was invited to speak on the main television news magazine of public broadcaster ZDF, the advice of Club members was frequently sought by national newspapers, they were asked by corporations to speak on data security and were requested by the newly established Green Party to write a report on the Party's potential use of networked computing. One of the important details here is that instead of only being the subject of media coverage, the CCC had the opportunity to communicate its point of view to different audiences.

Related to the relationship of non-state actors and established media outlets, Richard Ericson and his colleagues (1989) make a useful distinction between media access and media coverage. By access, they mean the news space, time and context to reasonably represent one's own perspective, whereas coverage entails news space and time but not necessarily the context for favourable representations (Ericson et al. 1989: 5). This distinction is vital because it demonstrates that media access—as with access to all kinds of resources at institutional levels—remains a political question (Freedman 2014). While media coverage simply denotes the amount and prominence of attention and visibility a group receives, media access indicates that an actor has a particular standing and is treated as an actor with a serious voice in the media. Gaining positive coverage once may not be hard. Sustaining regular access and standing, which enhances the actor's ability to embed its concepts and ideals in public discourse (see Phillips et al. 2004), can be extremely difficult. Seen from this perspective, the Btx hack shows the ways in which the CCC as a non-state actor had to rely on established media outlets to mobilize public support, to increase the validity of their demands and to circulate their messages beyond like-minded people. Established news media were, however, not the only part of the Club's media ensemble; and these are a few examples that date back to the CCC's early days. Right from the start the Club had close affiliations with the then newly founded alternative *tageszeitung* ('daily newspaper'), commonly referred to as *taz*, one of the Club's co-founders (Wau Holland) being a columnist during the mid-1980s. In addition, the hacker organization has published its own *Datenschleuder* magazine since 1984 (still ongoing) and was very active in enlarging bulletin boards systems (BBS) in Germany throughout the 1980s. Consequently, the Club's media ensemble relied on practices related to analogue and digital media and comprised both coverage by and access to news outlets.

At this point it is helpful to make a leap in time and focus on more recent developments. The end of the 1990s and the early 2000s saw a growing pervasiveness of radical and alternative media platforms and online networks that amplified actors' ability to voice the political relevance of their endeavours (see Rodríguez et al. 2014). Along with this development, scholars emphasize that actors increasingly invest human, technological and financial resources in '"being the media" instead of hating it' (Cammaerts 2012: 125). The CCC is no exception in this regard. Over the past two decades, Club members have initiated a regular radio show (Chaosradio), podcasts (e.g. CRE and Alternativlos), accounts on both popular and alternative online platforms such as Twitter, Quitter and personal blogs, to name some of the more prominent examples. Instead of abandoning outward oriented channels such as the Chaosradio show or the *Datenschleuder* magazine, the Club integrates its 'trans-media' (Costanza-Chock 2014) efforts into a 'media manifold' (Couldry 2012), where one communicative practice does not necessarily substitute for the other, but plays a part in the Club's overall media ensemble.

Following this depiction, one might expect that the CCC has detached itself from interactions with mainstream outlets. This is not the case at all. On the contrary, the CCC has in fact intensified its interactions with well-established media. In particular its styles and modes of access to mainstream media have diversified and multiplied (e.g. personal contacts to journalists, writing regular columns for well-established newspapers, being an editorial member of online outlets, acting as informants). Despite the ability to increase its media ensemble, the importance of gaining positive coverage by and access to established media outlets and news channels is essential for the CCC. Mainstream outlets are important sites for the Club to exist in the public mind, make its voices heard and achieve public recognition beyond the circle of like-minded individuals—especially important because of the ongoing fragmentation of the media environment and the competition of different actors for public attention. Being covered by and having access to mainstream media outlets continues to be an effective and possibly necessary route to co-determine public discourse for non-state actors such as the CCC.

For emerging groups such as Anonymous, it has been argued that sat ing the media hunger for spectacle, media attention and column inches has become an end in itself and therefore an obstacle to political movement building (Coleman 2014). In the context of the CCC, it cannot be said that the hacker organization has been captivated by the demands of news media and popular online platforms, which might lead to trivialization and debasement of its aims. Similarly, the Club is not aiming for visibility at any price; which can be seen in the fact that it does not make use of Facebook or many other capital oriented and data hungry infrastructures. In the case of the CCC, publications of particular activities such as the Staatstrojaner hack in the *Frankfurter Allgemeine Zeitung* are the result of elaborated coordination amongst core members of the Club and the newspapers' editors. While mediated visibility does not equal empowerment and is not a political end in itself, access to established news channels appears to be particularly important for 'hackers' also because the term still tends to have a negative connotation.

Based on a multi-layered media ensemble that reaches different audi ences and publics, the CCC is able to communicate its political message to a wide range of actors. As a consequence of this, the hackers' outward-oriented communication establishes and strengthens the Club's position in public discourse. It is important to mention here that the hackers' communicative practices are not limited to mediated communication but, as briefly mentioned above, also strongly rely on face-to-face interactions; which is the case when members are invited to share their expertise in governmental committees and public hearings, and when they advise individual legislators and politicians, as well as when they are invited as experts to advise sections of a parliamentary party in the Bundestag or the constitutional court in Germany. The ability to interact with 'outsiders' largely relies on the fact that a core group of members forms clear and well-recognizable frames of relevance through organizing both inward- and outward-oriented communication. Bringing the previous section together with this line of reasoning, one can remark that the CCC's internal communicative figuration not only enables the Club to execute direct digital action in the form of hacking, but also allows the hacker organization to communicate with a diversity of relevant actors (including the larger public) in coherent ways. In the case of the CCC, the relations between hacking and the communicative figuration within the Club are best understood as interlocking arrangements (Kubitschko 2015). These, as will be argued below, have wider consequences for the Chaos Computer Club's standing as a political actor. To substantiate this line of argument, the final section will put the spotlight on the dynamics that result from the figurational arrangements discussed above, and show how they put the Club into a position to influence larger frames of relevance related to media technologies and infrastructures.

4.5 Spiral of Legitimation

So far this chapter has argued that the hacker organization's internal figuration is closely connected to its way of executing political work. In addition it has been shown that the CCC's direct digital action and its mode of publicizing its activities rely on one another. Interestingly enough, when we look more closely at the way the Club interacts with the media environment and with institutionalized politics, one notices that theses interactions complement one another or are in fact even interdependent. The Club's media ensemble and interactions with relevant actors perpetuate each other and co-determine the Club's ability to politicize media technologies and infrastructures. The dynamic at hand that best describes this process will be referred to as a spiral of legitimation.

According to Mark Suchman, legitimacy is practically the basis of politics as it addresses the forces 'that constrain, construct, and empower organizational actors' (Suchman 1995: 571). In the expanding literature on legitimacy Suchman's definition has been generally accepted as the most suitable: 'Legitimacy is a generalised perception or assumption that the actions of an entity are desirable, proper, or appropriate within some socially constructed system of norms, values, beliefs, and definitions' (Suchman 1995: 574). Overall, legitimacy, to a large degree, rests on being socially 'comprehensible' and 'taken-for-granted' (Suchman 1995). Echoing the notion of taken-for-grantedness, Berger and Luckmann (1967: 94–95) consider legitimation a process whereby comprehensibility deepens and crystallizes. Skill, effort and practice are regarded necessary elements in the process by which an actor becomes taken-for-granted (Bourdieu 2000). Accordingly, legitimacy is not simply out there for the asking, but has to be created as well as exploited by actors who seek to gain legitimation.

Scholars who diagnose correlations between communicative practices and the social standing of political actors have argued for a strong link between media representation and legitimacy (Lazarsfeld and Merton 2004 [1948]; Koopmans 2004). This chapter agrees with these accounts, as far as the media environment serves both as an indicator of legitimacy by society at large and as a source of legitimacy in its own right (Deephouse and Suchman 2008). At the same time, the figurational approach presented here complements and complicates existing lines of reasoning. It does so in two ways. First, as has been underlined above, one needs to take into account both actors' inward oriented and outward oriented communicative practices. In addition, it is understood that media representation today goes far beyond coverage by mainstream media as it relies on actors' multi-layered media ensemble. Second, instead of arguing for a straightforward causal correlation between 'media attention' and social standing, this research reveals a more eclectic process: a spiral of legitimation that is based on the relation between the organization's internal communicative figuration and the communicative figuration related to the public discourse around the political qualities of contemporary media technologies and infrastructures.

At least over the past two decades it has become a dominant *frame of relevance* in public discourse that along with their pervasiveness (or even omnipresence) media technologies and infrastructures are an ever more important part of the social world. More and more people make use of and relate their daily activities to media in one way or another. At the same time legislators, politicians, judges and other actors with decisive power related to policy-making and the law are in need of advice, consulting and grounded recommendations. That is to say, the CCC's ability to manoeuvre their issues into public discourse and to advance their political goals to a great extent relates to prevailing social arrangements. The more media technologies and infrastructures find their way into people's everyday lives, the more attentive citizens, media representatives and decision-makers are to actors who demonstrate and articulate reasonable engagement in relation to technical transformations. Gaining and maintaining legitimacy is something that is framed and conditioned by social realities. While legitimation can be at least partially secured through institutions such as the media, legitimacy is never simply mediated.

In the case of the CCC, institutional politics react, amongst other things, to public pressure that is built up through a multi-layered media ensemble; which confirms that actors who receive preferred standing and are able to stabilize their appearances across the media environment over time tend to be considered trustworthy. Interestingly enough, this relationship also operates the other way round. Media representatives consider CCC members as legitimate voices and provide them access to their outlets owing to their regular interaction with institutional politics. Politicians, legislators and judges learn about the organization's engagement in part through the hackers' outward oriented communication. As a consequence, they invite Club members to articulate their stance in particular contexts, such as committees, consultations and hearings. Owing to the Club's involvement in institutional politics, different media outlets regard the CCC as worth covering as well as worth granting access to. Media environments and institutional politics, each in their own way, mutually signify the CCC's engagement before a wide public. As a consequence its virtuous role as a civil society organization that has something valuable to say about the political relevance of technical developments continues to be acknowledged, inscribed and stabilized. Throughout this process, the Club gains opportunities to illustrate its activities, articulate its objectives and politicize particular themes. This process is accompanied by the Club's regular direct digital actions that constantly demonstrate the hackers' high level of technology-related skills, experience and knowledge. Overall, instead of linearity one needs to stress rotation and reciprocity as the defining processual dynamics that create an attribution process, whereby the narration 'CCC hackers are the good ones' emerges and stabilizes.

This is not to say that this spiral of legitimation cannot go into reverse. Legitimacy is never definitively acquired and remains open to challenge and dependent on social perceptions (Rosanvallon 2011: 7). Similarly, it is understood that no political actor is (il)legitimate for 100%

of the time or across all locations. The Club's de-legitimation during the mid-1980s is a telling example in this context. Accordingly, a spiral of legitimation refers to the growth and spread as well as decline and withdrawal of a given actor's legitimacy and explicitly takes into consideration that organizational legitimacy changes over time. Conceptualizing the processes at hand as a spiral of legitimation takes into account that legitimation is never constructed in a vacuum, but relies on communicative practices and is evolved in relation to concrete actors' constellations within an environment that has specific dominant frames of relevance. While it is impossible to (mathematically) measure legitimation, it is certainly possible to observe a given actor's standing, reputation and taken-for-grantedness. Similarly, by taking into account the figurational arrangements both within and surrounding a given organization it is possible to determine whether the spiral is in an upward or downward dynamic.

Considering that, analytically, one can distinguish between different levels of legitimation, it should be noted that empirically these levels overlap the term spiral of legitimation, which conceptualizes legitimacy as a relational process. Legitimacy is not a matter of singular events but of the relation between different communicative figurations over time. Again, it is necessary to highlight that spirals of legitimation are not self-perpetuating feedback loops. Neither do they rest on figurations that occur overnight. Accordingly, spirals of legitimation point to a process of inscription over time whereby individuals coming together around common ends, objectives or projects develop into meaningful political actors. By doing so, it echoes understandings that see time as a critical component in actors being able to co-determine political settings, as political claims can only be realized over the long term (see Andrews and Edwards 2004). Looking more closely at the Club's legitimation, one notices that the hackers' current ability to practise a demanding vision of politics is strongly affiliated with the organization's history. For more than 30 years, CCC members have been acting on the politicization of media technologies and infrastructures. Only by transporting its activities and voice over time and space did the Club manage to establish itself as a reliable reference point with a lasting resonance to which different actors, publics and audiences can relate.

Sustaining political engagement over time to challenge existing conceptions of what is understood as political and shifting the legitimate boundaries of recognized actors is a demanding task. The CCC continuously actualizes its engagement to avoid it becoming vague through more or less spectacular hacks, and has established mechanisms to survive the ebbs and flows of mass attention. Considering the social standing of the Club as a trusted civil society organization, one needs to take into account distinct temporalities that include the effective publicizing of actions such as the Staatstrojaner hack as well as the hackers' continuous contributions to the public discourse around the political qualities of media technologies and infrastructures since the early 1980s.

4.6 Conclusion

Taking into account both the deep embeddedness of hacker cultures in the evolution of computerized society and the concrete case of the Chaos Computer Club, it becomes clear that acting on media technologies and infrastructures entails a wide set of activities: it manifests itself not only in form of direct engagement with technical devices and systems, but also occurs through interaction with different actors, through articulating viewpoints, through sharing knowledge and experiences in different circumstances. As has been argued in this chapter, to understand the way the Club has gained recognition as a trustful actor that has something valuable to say about the role media technologies and infrastructures play in society, it is beneficial to investigate the communicative figurations within and surrounding the hacker organization. By investigating the *constellation of actors*, the *frames of relevance* and *communicative practices*, the chapter shows how the CCC thematizes media technologies and infrastructures as sites of an active political struggle in their own right. Doing so not only allows conceptualizing the relations between hacking and the communicative figuration within the Club as interlocking arrangements but also points towards a dynamic that has been described as a spiral of legitimation. This denotes the process through which the CCC's engagement is acknowledged and stabilized (or denied and destabilized) over time. While the Club's current role as a trusted civil society organization strongly relates to internal figurations, it is likewise related to the public discourse surrounding media technologies and infrastructures' role as an ever more important part of the social world. By bringing these two dimensions together and by considering time as a critical component, it is possible to further understandings of organizational actors' ability to co-determine political arrangements.

References

Andrews, Kenneth T., and Bob Edwards. 2004. Advocacy organizations in the U.S. political process. *Annual Review of Sociology* 30: 479–506.

Berger, Peter L., and Thomas Luckmann. 1967. *The social construction of reality.* London: Penguin.

Bourdieu, Pierre. 2000. *Pascalian meditations.* Cambridge: Polity.

Burawoy, Michael. 1998. The extended case method. *Sociological Theory* 16 (1): 4–33.

Cammaerts, Bart. 2012. Protest logics and the mediation opportunity structure. *European Journal of Communication* 27 (2): 117–134.

Charmaz, Kathy. 2002. Qualitative interviewing and grounded theory analysis. In *Handbook of interview research: Context and method*, ed. Jaber F. Gubrium, and James A. Holstein, 675–710. London: Sage.

Coleman, Gabriella. 2012. *Coding freedom: The ethics and aesthetics of hacking.* Princeton, NJ: Princeton University Press.

Coleman, Gabriella. 2014. *Hacker, hoaxer, whistleblower, spy: The many faces of Anonymous.* London: Verso.

Costanza-Chock, Sasha. 2014. *Out of the shadows, into the streets!* Cambridge, MA: MIT.

Couldry, Nick. 2012. *Media, society, world: Social theory and digital media practice.* Cambridge: Polity.

Deephouse, David L., and Mark Suchman. 2008. Legitimacy in organizational institutionalism. In *The Sage handbook of organizational institutionalism*, ed. Royston Greenwood, Christine Oliver, Roy Suddaby, and Kerstin Sahlin, 49–77. London: Sage.

Ericson, Richard V., Patricia M. Baranek, and Janet B.L. Chan. 1989. *Negotiating control: A study of news sources.* Toronto: University of Toronto Press.

Fairhurst, Gail T., and Linda L. Putnam. 2004. Organizations as discursive constructions. *Communication Theory* 14 (1): 5–26.

Freedman, Des. 2014. The puzzle of media power: Notes toward a materialist approach. *International Journal of Communication* 8: 319–334.

Giraud, Eva. 2014. Has radical participatory online media really "failed"? Indymedia and Its Legacies. *Convergence* 20 (4): 419–437.

Hasebrink, Uwe, and Sascha Hölig. 2014. Topografie der Öffentlichkeit [Topography of the public sphere]. *Aus Politik und Zeitgeschichte* 22–23: 16–22.

Hunsinger, Jeremy, and Andrew R. Schrock. (eds.) forthcoming/2017. *Making our world: The hacker and maker movements in context.* New York: Peter Lang.

Jordan, Tim. 2013. *Hacking: Digital media and technological determinism.* Cambridge: Polity.

Juris, Jeffrey S. 2012. Reflections on #Occupy everywhere: Social media, public space, and emerging logics of aggregation. *American Ethnologist* 39 (2): 259–279.

Karpf, David. 2012. *The moveon effect: The unexpected transformation of American political advocacy*. Oxford: Oxford University Press.

Kelty, Chris. 2008. *Two bits: The cultural significance of free software*. Durham, NC: Duke University Press.

Koopmans, Ruud. 2004. Movements and media: Selection processes and evolutionary dynamics in the public sphere. *Theory and Society* 33 (3–4): 367–391.

Kubitschko, Sebastian. 2015. Hackers' media practices: Demonstrating and articulating expertise as interlocking arrangements. *Convergence* 21 (3): 388–408.

Kubitschko, Sebastian. 2017. Acting on media technologies and infrastructures: Expanding the media as practice approach. *Media, Culture & Society*. (online first).

Lazarsfeld, Paul F., and Robert K. Merton. 2004 [orig. 1948]. Mass communication, popular taste, and organized social action. In *Mass communication and American social thought: Key texts, 1919–1968*, ed. John D. Peters and Peter Simonson, 230–241. Lanham, MD: Rowman & Littlefield.

Lievrouw, Leah A. 2011. *Alternative and activist new media*. Cambridge: Polity.

Mercea, Dan, Laura Ianelli, and Brian Loader. 2016. Protest communication ecologies. *Information, Communication & Society* 19 (3): 279–289.

Milan, Stefania, and Arne Hintz. 2013. Networked collective action and the institutionalized policy debate: Bringing cyberactivism to the policy arena? *Policy & Internet* 5 (1): 7–26.

Phillips, Nelson, Thomas B. Lawrence, and Cynthia Hardy. 2004. Discourse and institutions. *Academy of Management Review* 29 (4): 635–652.

Postill, John. 2014. Freedom technologists and the new protest movements: A theory of protest formulas. *Convergence* 20 (4): 402–418.

Rodríguez, Clemencia, Benjamin Ferron, and Kristin Shamas. 2014. Four challenges in the field of alternative, radical and citizens' media research. *Media, Culture and Society* 36 (2): 150–166.

Rosanvallon, Pierre. 2011. *Democratic legitimacy: Impartiality, reflexivity, proximity*. Princeton, NJ: Princeton University Press.

Suchman, Mark C. 1995. Managing legitimacy: Strategic and institutional approaches. *Academy of Management Review* 20 (3): 571–610.

Theocharis, Yannis, William E.M. Lowe, Jan W. van Deth, and Gema García-Albacete. 2015. Using Twitter to mobilize protest action. *Information, Communication & Society* 18 (2): 202–220.

Wagenknecht, Susann, and Matthias Korn. 2016. Hacking as transgressive infrastructuring: Mobile phone networks and the German Chaos Computer Club. In *Proceedings of the 19th ACM conference on computer supported cooperative work & social computing*, 1104–1117.

Weick, Karl E., Kathleen M. Sutcliffe K, and David Obstfeld. 2005. Organizing and the process of sense making. *Organization Science* 16(4): 409–421.

Yin, Robert K. 2014. *Case study research: Design and methods*, 5th ed. Los Angeles: Sage.

5

Repair Cafés: A Media and Communication Perspective

Sigrid Kannengießer

5.1 Introduction

Repair Cafés are a new format of events in which people meet to work together on repairing objects of everyday life such as electronic devices, textiles or bicycles—media technologies being among the goods which are brought along most often. While some people offer help voluntarily and without charge, others seek help in undertaking repairs. The idea is to help people to help themselves. The Dutch foundation Stichting Repair Café claims to have invented the concept in 2009 (Stichting Repair Café: no date). Whether this is the origin or not, Repair Cafés have spread all over Western European and North American countries within the past few years.[1] In Germany, the foundation Anstiftung & Ertomis builds a network of repair initiatives by inviting organizers and helpers to face-to-face meetings and offering a website on which Repair

S. Kannengießer (✉)
ZeMKI, Centre for Media, Communication and Information Research, University of Bremen, Bremen, Germany
e-mail: Sigrid.kannengiesser@uni-bremen.de

Cafés can register and become visible through appearing on a map and in a calendar announcing events.[2]

While repairing is an old practice, what is new is that the act of repairing becomes public in Repair Cafés, and the actual repairing as well as the repair events are staged as political actions which strive for cultural transformation aiming at sustainability.

In this chapter, results of a qualitative study are presented in which Repair Cafés in Germany have been analyzed from the perspective of media and communication studies. Choosing this approach, the focus of the study was on the people repairing media technologies as well as the organizers of the events. Why do people participate in Repair Cafés and repair media technologies? What do Repair Cafés and the practice of repairing mean to the participants? And what relevance do the participants see in the Repair Cafés for a (mediatized) society?

A figurational perspective (see Hepp and Hasebrink in this volume) is helpful to structure the findings, to further analyzed Repair Cafés and to answer the research questions.

When analyzing Repair Cafés from a perspective of media and communication studies, the transformation of media and communicative practices becomes visible as do media practices aiming at cultural change. Therefore, on the basis of the study conducted, it can be discussed how media are and can be used for cultural transformation; here, with a view to sustainability. Defining the repairing of media technologies as media practice in this chapter, it is argued that the term media practice has to be understood in a broad sense in media and communication studies, not only taking into account what people do with media content but also what they do with media technologies.

5.2 Research on Repairing and Public Sites of Repair

Repair and Repair Cafés are mainly analyzed in technology and design studies. Here, repair is defined as 'the process of sustaining, managing, and repurposing technology in order to cope with attrition and regressive change.' (Rosner and Turner 2015: 59) Steven J. Jackson 'rethinks repair' and suggests the approach of 'broken world thinking' in media and technology studies, shifting the approach from the new, growth and progress to erosion, breakdown and decay (2014: 221). He sees a necessity for this shift in current crisis and instabilities and perceives repairing as a way to sustain and restore infrastructures and lives (2014: 222). Reflecting on the collaboration with artists and their work of art, Jackson and Kang argue that reuse and creative repurposing of broken technologies does not only enable technologies to *be or become* anything, but rather facilitates 'communication with material objects' (Jackson and Kang 2014: 10): Even though claiming that things act or have agency is too strong for the authors (which would be the argument of the Actor–Network Theory, see e.g. Latour 2007), they stress that ascribing affordances to things might be too weak and require that the human relationship to technologies must be reconsidered (Jackson and Kang 2014: 9).

When analyzing repair initiatives in Paraguay and the USA, Daniela K. Rosner and Morgan G. Ames point to the affordances that technologies imply. They introduce the notion of *negotiated endurance*, which 'refers to the process by which different actors—including consumers, community organizers, and others—drive the ongoing use, maintenance, and repair of a given technology through the sociocultural and socioeconomic infrastructures they inhabit and produce' (Rosner and Ames 2014: 319). With this term, they stress that the lifecycle of things is negotiated by the users in the appropriation process rather than planned ahead by the people who designed such things (Rosner and Ames 2014: 329, see also Rosner and Turner 2015, 63ff.).

Rosner and Ames argue that breakdown and repair of technologies is actively produced through everyday practices, and these practices are shaped by material, infrastructural, gendered, political and socio-economic factors (Rosner and Ames 2014: 328).[3] The latter might make repairing a 'privileged practice, relying on certain kinds of materials (replacement parts, testing equipment) and forms of expertise to be carried out' (Rosner and Ames 2014: 320).

Nevertheless, the repair initiatives that Rosner and Ames analyzed follow the idea of technical empowerment, which they define as 'knowing more about technology and making more informed choices around technology as a result—and sustainability—advancing reuse over recycling and disposal' (Rosner and Ames 2014: 326). But the authors also concede that empowerment rarely emerges in the repair initiatives as often the things are repaired *for* the people seeking help (Rosner and Ames 2014: 327).[4]

However, this technical empowerment has a political character, and repairing can become 'a mode of political action' (Rosner and Turner 2015: 64f.). Repairing can be characterized an act of unconventional political participation as it is not institutionalized but might aim at shaping and transforming society (Kannengießer 2017).[5]

Rosner and Turner call Repair Cafés 'Theaters of alternative industry' (2015), which are 'meant to demonstrate the power of creative remanufacturing to change the world' (Rosner and Turner 2015: 65) and whose participants strive for social change (Rosner and Turner 2015: 67), whereupon the change here is seen in questions of egalitarianism and collectivity.

Charter and Keiller analyze the motivations of 158 volunteers in Repair Cafés in nine countries in a quantitative study: the top three reasons why participants engage in Repair Cafés were encouraging others to live more sustainably, providing a valuable service to the community and being part of the movement to improve product reparability and longevity (2014: 5). The authors draw the conclusion that volunteers act altruistically and that their personal gain is not important to them (Charter and Keiller 2014: 13).

The qualitative study I conducted analyzing Repair Cafés from a perspective of media and communication studies contributes to the research field dealing with public repair sites and points to the meanings people repairing media technologies as well as organizers of these events construct regarding the relevance of Repair Cafés in a mediatized society and the repairing of media devices itself. Moreover, aspects of the current transformation of media practices as well as a broader cultural change regarding media appropriation become apparent.

The results discussed below show that many people repairing media technologies act as critical consumers. Consumer criticism and critical consumer campaigns are analyzed in media content analysis within the field of political communication (e.g. Greenberg and Knight 2004; Micheletti and Stolle 2007; Baringhorst et al. 2010; Gaßner 2014). But the study of repairing media technologies in Repair Cafés also shows that critical consumers' *media practices* have to be acknowledged in media and communication studies, as they are on the one hand a reaction of the transformation of media environments and on the other hand themselves aim at cultural change.

5.3 Methods Used and Figurational Perspective

A qualitative approach is useful when analyzing the aims that people repairing media technologies have and the meanings that participants as well as organizers of Repair Cafés construct regarding the relevance of repairing media devices as well as the relevance of Repair Cafés in a mediatized society. The approach of Grounded Theory (Corbin and Strauss 2008) allows for an open perspective and reconstruction of the perspectives of people involved in Repair Cafés.[6] Using the theory-generating approach of Grounded Theory and based on the empirical findings, the theory of *consumer-critical media practices* was developed (see also Kannengießer 2016). Consumer-critical media practices 'are those practices which either use media to criticize (certain) consumption or which are (conscious) alternatives to the consumption of media technologies' (Kannengießer 2016: 198), repairing media technologies being an example of the latter.

As case studies for the qualitative study, I chose three Repair Cafés in Germany which differ regarding the context in which they were organized and the background of the organizers: one is set in a university context in Oldenburg (a mid-sized city in North-Western Germany), a second is organized by an artist in the quarter of Kreuzberg in Berlin (this was the first Repair Café in Berlin and was awarded a prize for sustainability by the City of Berlin, Berlin Online 2013), and the third is in Garbsen (a small city near Hanover in the north of Germany), organized by a retired teacher in collaboration with the Agency for Volunteers of the City of Garbsen. I chose these different case studies to find out whether there are differences regarding the aims of people involved when they have different backgrounds and when the events take place in different settings.

In these Repair Cafés, I conducted observations in 2014 and 2015 as well as 38 qualitative interviews with the organizers, with people offering help in repairing media technologies and with people seeking help in repairing their devices.[7] The observations followed the (media) practices during the repair events, and interviews took place to reconstruct the perspective of the people involved. Moreover, I conducted an observation in a network meeting of Repair Cafés in Germany which was organized by the foundation Anstiftung & Ertomis in Berlin on 10 October 2015, and interviewed the two employees of the foundation who organized the event.

I coded the interview transcriptions as well as the protocols of the observations in accordance with the coding process of Grounded Theory (Corbin and Strauss 2008). As a key category, the concept of consumer-critical media practices was developed, under which the findings of the analysis can be subsumed.

The main categories developed through the coding process and thereby the findings can be structured and examined on a further level using a figurational perspective (explained in detail in Hepp/Hasebrink in this volume). In Elias's sense, figurations are networks of individuals (Elias 1978: 15). Communicative figurations are characterized by the *constellation of actors*, the *frames of relevance* (which is the thematic topic or theme of that figuration) and the *communicative and media practices* which can be found in communicative figurations (Hepp and Hasebrink in this volume). Each communicative figuration uses a specific *media ensemble* (Hepp and Hasebrink in this volume), which encompasses the entirety of media that can be found in a figuration.

Drawing attention to these key characteristics of communicative figurations allows us to point to the main characteristics of Repair Cafés, as each Repair Café is a communicative figuration. Moreover, the network of Repair Cafés in Germany becomes a communicative figuration itself. But the focus of this chapter is on the former: Repair Cafés as communicative figurations. Moreover, using a figurational perspective, it is possible to discuss the transformation of communicative and media practices which can be perceived in these events as well as the aims of the actors regarding changes in media practices and cultural transformations.

5.4 Actor Constellation in Repair Cafés

Repair Cafés are in Elias's sense figurations, as here networks of individuals are formed (Elias 1978: 15), the individuals taking different roles as organizers, people offering help (the helpers), and others seeking help (the participants) in the repairing process. The *constellation of actors* participating in the communicative figurations in Repair Cafés comprises these different roles. The network comes into being in a certain location at a certain time, as Repair Cafés are usually organized as monthly events. As they are organized repeatedly, the figuration of each Repair Café becomes stable although happening intermittently. Each Repair Café, the repeatedly organized repair events at a certain location, is a communicative figuration whose organizers and helpers become constant actors, while the participants change from time to time (although many participants do visit several times or regularly).

Analyzing the actor constellation in Repair Cafés, the heterogeneity of people involved has to be stressed as well as the different patterns that can be perceived. On the one hand, organizers, helpers and participants differ in gender and age as well as social backgrounds. In the case studies chosen, the organizers' backgrounds differ (which was one intention for the sampling, see above): The organizers of the Repair Café in Oldenburg are working for the university, the one in Garbsen is arranged by a retired woman in collaboration with the Agency for Volunteers of the city, and the events in Kreuzberg, Berlin, are organized by an artist in her studio in collaboration with the non-governmental organization Kunststoffe e.V. Because of this background, the age of the organizers differs: in the organizational group in Oldenburg, students between 25 and 30 years old are involved as well as a female lecturer and a male professor, who are in their early 50s. The retired teacher in Garbsen is 65 years old and the artist in Oldenburg is in her early 30s. Regarding the gender of the organizers, mainly women arrange the events of the three case studies, but the observation in the network meeting of Repair Cafés in Germany hosted by the foundation Anstiftung & Ertomis showed that at least half of the organizers participating in this network event have been men. Regarding gender, the most significant pattern in respect of the actor constellations in the communicative figurations of Repair Cafés can be found in the group of helpers: while nearly exclusively men offer to repair media technologies, women volunteer to repair textiles; this finding goes along with the results of the study Daniela Rosner conducted in the USA (Rosner 2013).

With regard to class and educational background, it has to be noted that the organizers of the case studies chosen all have an academic background. This is clear for the Repair Café that is organized in the university context of Oldenburg, while the artist in Berlin has a university degree and the retired woman organizing the repair events used to be a teacher. But in the network meeting, many organizers of Repair Cafés had a vocational training.

Looking at the group of participants who bring along their broken media technologies (which was the focus of the study presented in this chapter), characteristics in the social categories of gender, class, age and educational background are very heterogeneous. Men as well as women from different age groups and social backgrounds all participate. Regarding class, it has to be stressed that the organizers of the case studies chosen are sensitive to this category. The Repair Café in Oldenburg does not take place at the university but was first hosted in a café. After this, it was organized in cooperation with Oldenburg's theatre (Oldenburgisches Staatstheater), in a building which used to be a shop in the city centre and is rented by the theatre but is not the theatre building itself. This choice of location indicates that the organizers intend the Repair Café to be open to everyone. In Garbsen, the repair events take place in a community centre hosted by the Agency of Volunteers of the city, which is located in a quarter where many socially deprived people, predominantly migrants, live. The intention of the organizers is to approach as many people in the neighbourhood as possible and to construct the repair event as a social event (see below).[8]

5.4.1 *Repairing Media Technologies as Media Practice*

A second characteristic of communicative figurations is communicative practices (see Hepp and Hasebrink in this volume), which are often mediated and are therefore media practices. Analyzing the *communicative and media practices* in the communicative figurations in Repair Cafés, it first has to be described what people actually *do* at these events. In Repair Cafés, people join forces to repair their media technologies (among other things). They bring along new technologies such as laptops and smartphones, and old ones such as slide projectors and old radios. They open the devices, clean them, mend them and screw them back together. Helpers explain the defects the devices have, what could be done, what they can do and what the owners could do in future when similar problems occur. Sometimes the repair is successful—and sometimes not. Moreover, people in Repair Cafés chat together and partake of the beverages and cake which are served during the repair events.

Analyzing the *communicative and media practices* in the communicative figurations in Repair Cafés, it is important to distinguish between the practices in which people communicate (face to face or mediated) and the repair practices. Taking the latter into account—the repairing of media technologies—I will discuss here why the repairing of technologies can be characterized as *media practice*.[9]

Practice theory has a long tradition in media and communication studies (for an overview and the discussion see e.g. Couldry 2012: 33–58, Genzel 2015, Pentzold 2015). Nick Couldry defines media as 'the open set of practices relating to, or oriented around, media' (2004: 117). He stresses that we need the perspective of practice to help us address how media are 'embedded in the interlocking fabric of social and cultural life' (Couldry 2004: 129). A practice perspective helps us to understand how people actually appropriate media (technologies) in everyday life and which meanings they construct regarding media. The central question of the paradigm perceiving media as practice is: 'What, quite simply, are people doing in relation to media across a whole range of situations and contexts?' (Couldry 2004: 119) This question can be answered quite easily when looking at Repair Cafés: people repair media technologies (successfully or not). Depending on the broken media technologies which people bring, participants open the devices with the support of the helpers and the tools offered. New technologies, especially laptops and smartphones, are difficult to open, and special tools are needed, but there are often 'experts' among the helpers who are able to solve these problems. Helpers and participants identify the defects, participants describe the problems which occur during usage, helpers share their knowledge about the devices. Helpers bring with them spare parts, and sometimes they have to improvise or tinker with broken parts. But often simply cleaning is sufficient to get the objects working again.

Defining these processes of repairing media technologies as media practice, I want to stress that we have to understand the term in a broad sense, not only asking what people do with media content but what people in general do in relation to media; that is, with regard to media content *and/or* media technologies. Following such a broad understanding of media practice, the repairing of media technologies is an example of the latter. Defining the repairing of media technologies as media practice, we are able not only to understand what people are actually doing with media technologies when repairing them but we can also acknowledge why they are repairing media technologies, and what kind of sense they ascribe to media technologies. This brings me to the *frame of relevance* of the communicative figuration in Repair Cafés. Regarding this characteristic of communicative figurations, the media practice of repairing can be described as *consumer-critical*, which I will explain here.

5.5 Consumer-Critical Media Practice and Small Media Repertoires

The *frame of relevance* of the communicative figurations in Repair Cafés can be reconstructed by analyzing the aims of the people involved. Why do people come to Repair Cafés and why do they repair their broken media technologies? The meanings people involved in repair events construct regarding the repairing process as well as the Repair Cafés allow us to reason the frame of relevance, or the theme, of communicative figurations in Repair Cafés.

Eight main aims were identified concerning the question why people participate in Repair Cafés and why they repair media technologies and why they organize the repair events: conservation of resources, waste prevention, appreciation for the device, the fun of repairing, meeting and talking to people, sharing knowledge, learning repair skills and economic considerations.

People involved in Repair Cafés are aware of the harmful production processes of media technologies: 'I think especially the repairing of computers is important as they contain resources, because of which people in other countries die. And we should not throw these [technologies] away and buy a new iPhone,' says Simon Meyer,[10] a Repair Café organizer.[11] One participant even calls the people producing media technologies 'slaves'. Many organizers and participants point to the harmful pollution and situations of war under which the resources needed for digital media technologies (such as coltan) are extracted. They try to conserve resources by not buying new technologies but prolonging the lifespan of existing ones.

A second dominant aim for people who are repairing their devices is waste prevention: 'We would have a better world if more people repaired their things [...] because our planet would be less polluted,' says 60-year-old Maria Frey, repairing her broken mobile phone. Participants point to waste dumps, in Ghana for example, where people burn broken media technologies to extract reusable resources while damaging their health and the environment in the process, including through the pollution caused by toxic substances that end up in soil and groundwater.[12]

Therefore, participants try to avoid the production of new media technologies and disposal of existing ones by prolonging the lifespan of their possessions. They stress the value of their existing devices and their personal relationship with the technologies they possess: 'I'm befriended with my smartphone,' says Peter Stephen, who is trying to repair his mobile phone. The 58-year-old participant Manuel Maier underlines the amount of work which goes into each device. The people inventing, developing and designing the products, and those constructing them, are a reason for him to value his goods and try to maintain them.

Another aim for people offering help in the repair process (who were in the case studies chosen only men) is that they enjoy repairing things: Paul Winter, a 55-year-old organizer, describes the volunteers as technophiles. But the pleasure of participants who successfully repair their devices is a reason to arrange these events: 'When the repair was successful, people leave with a smile on their face [...]. It's great to see that people are delighted,' says Paula Klee, a 20-year-old volunteer helping to organize the Repair Café in Berlin.

Actors involved in all three groups interviewed stress the social character of Repair Cafés. They come to these events not only to get things repaired but also to meet people and have a chat. These communicative practices in the figuration in Repair Cafés are analyzed in detail below.

Several people seeking help in the repair events (mainly those receiving welfare, working in jobs in which they earn low wages or students) also seek help in repairing their media technologies as they do not have the financial resources to buy new devices or cannot pay for the repair services of commercial providers.

The repairing of media technologies can be characterized as a consumer-critical media practice, as many actors involved criticize the consumption of media technologies and try to avoid buying new devices by repairing their existing ones. Some participants face financial pressure to repair but many are also critical consumers.

These different aims might be but are not necessarily contradictions. The organizers do not perceive any discrepancy between consumer-critical practices and financial reasons or seeking pleasure. They noticed that many people come to Repair Cafés because they do not know where else to go with their very old radios or mobile phones, as the bigger stores do not repair old devices and just advise people to buy new technologies or offer a rather expensive service.

Therefore, some organizers also advertise smaller service centres and distribute lists with these service centres' addresses, because they support the idea of repairing things and the establishment of a 'culture of repair' is very important to them.[13] *Why* people actually repair—because of consumer-critical aims, pleasure or financial necessity—is of no consequence to them.

The Repair Café in Berlin Kreuzberg also cooperates with a service centre called iDoc. This offers commercial repair services for iPhones but wants to support the idea of repair and to give something back to society, as one employee explains, and therefore sends along a volunteer to help repair mobile phones without charge.

Regarding media repertoires (Hasebrink and Domeyer 2012),[14] attitudes and practices differ among the participants. While some 'consumption-critical people' reduce the number of media technologies they own to only a few devices and/or buy media technologies second hand, technophile people, including many of the volunteers, own many devices and buy innovative technologies regularly.

Some participants explain that they still use quite old devices, such as 12- or even 20-year-old computers. Others have only one device of each type, as 58-year-old Manuel Maier, who is currently unemployed, explains. He could not listen to the radio for three weeks as his only radio was broken and he had to wait until the Repair Café to fix it. Some participants also explain that they buy or acquire used media technologies from people who have bought new devices. Several participants 'resist' technological innovation, for example by not having a smartphone but still using 'old' mobile phones. Others abstain from technologies, with some participants saying they do not own a television or mobile phone, for example. But many volunteers own complex media repertoires, an example being 30-year-old Jan Schmitz, a trained IT technician, who helps to repair smartphones, explains: 'I like technology a lot. I don't need a new mobile phone every year but I want to see what's new and what makes sense. [...] I test [devices] [...], either I like it, or if I don't, I sell it again.'

To sum up, not only do the aims of people participating in Repair Cafés differ (even though the consumer-critical aims were dominant) but also they have a range of media technologies. What unites all of them is the wish to repair their media technologies.

5.6 Communicative Practices in Repair Cafés and the Formation of Communicative Communities

While in the last two sections the repairing of media technologies has been discussed as a consumer-critical media practice, there are other *media and communicative practices* taking place in the communicative figurations in Repair Cafés. These will be analyzed here. The communicative practices in Repair Cafés are intertwined with the process of repairing, as the repairing of media technologies is not only a media practice—as explained above—but also a communicative one: people repair their things *together*. Participants seeking help ask about the defects of their devices or problems in the repairing process. Many are keen to learn how to do repairs on their own in future. Many volunteers offering help like to explain this process and try to teach others how to repair. But people also start talking about their reasons for coming to such events and discuss the consumer-critical aims explained above. Enabling these communicative exchanges is one of the intentions of the organizers of the Repair Cafés, who try to build a network among like-minded people through these events. This network shares a specific practice, repairing things, and many participants also share a common aim and frame of relevance: consumer criticism.

The Repair Cafés are *communicative* figurations in that within the events face-to-face communication takes place and is intentionally wanted. Participants stress the social dimension of Repair Cafés, the event giving people the possibility to get into contact with others, to have a chat and also to discuss the political dimensions of repairing their possessions. Spreading the idea of sustainability and consumer criticism is one of the aims of the actors who organize the Repair Cafés. Paul Winter, one of the organizers of the Repair Café in Oldenburg, for instance, perceives these events as 'subversive communication instruments' to lobby for sustainability and put pressure on the economy and politics.

In Repair Cafés communities—*Vergemeinschaftungen*—are built in Max Weber's sense: people meet because of a shared aim and many develop a feeling of belonging (1972: 21). As 68-year-old Karl Klaus helping to repair computers explains:

> People who are participating in something of this kind [Repair Cafés] have a different social and political attitude. [...] For me, it is much nicer to get involved in something cooperative than in business life, because there is a sense of belonging. I do not belong to Saturn,[15] I purchase from Saturn, but actually I don't give a shit about Saturn.

These communities are communicative (Knoblauch 2008: 74)[16] as they are constructed by face-to-face communication during the event and through mediated communication between the different events. Besides the face-to-face interaction, which is bound to the place and time of the event, mediated communication among the organizers and helpers also takes place between events: The organizers of the Repair Cafés keep in touch with each other and with the helpers via telephone, email and emailing lists. These media as well as flyers or posters, which are used for public relations, form the media ensemble of each Repair Café.[17] Because of the mediated communication between the repair events, their communicative figuration is not only bound to the place and time of the event but also exists in between the occasions, although then the figuration becomes smaller as most of the people only participate during the face-to-face meetings and not in the mediated communication processes between the events.

Those repair initiatives which have registered with the German network of repair initiatives that is coordinated by the German foundation Anstiftung & Ertomis become visible on the online platform for repair initiatives (www.reparatur-initiativen.de). Here, repair initiatives can be found via a map showing all locations in Germany where repair events are organized, as well as a calendar which structures the events according to the dates on which they take place. When registering on the platform, the repair initiatives create a profile in which they also point to their websites, if these exist. The aim of the employees of Anstiftung & Ertomis in establishing this online platform is to create visibility for the repair initiatives: 'repairing does not only happen piecemeal, but nearly every day in many different places in Germany', explains Lisa Wilde, an employee of Anstiftung & Ertomis. She stresses that the foundation strives to build a network among the German repair initiatives, to support them and the establishment of new Repair Cafés, and to lobby for the idea of repairing. Next to the online platform, which creates visibility, Anstiftung & Ertomis uses an email newsletter to inform members about new events or developments. Moreover, the employees are in personal contact via email or telephone with organizers of repair events, helpers or simply interested people. In addition, the foundation organizes annual face-to-face meetings to which all organizers and helpers of repair initiatives in Germany are invited as well as regional meetings, which happen more regularly. While the former function as forums to exchange ideas and experiences, the latter serve as possibilities to develop regional cooperation projects, as several helpers participate in more than one Repair Café.

The online platform as well as the face-to-face meetings facilitate the creation of a 'repair movement' that strives for cultural transformation.

5.7 Repair Movement Striving for Cultural Transformation

The overall aim of the organizers interviewed and many participants in the Repair Cafés is a sustainable society, to which they want to contribute by the practice of repairing. For example, 29-year-old Anna Platt, organizing the Repair Café in Oldenburg, says: 'We make a small contribution to improve the world, to conserve resources. (…) The Repair Café is very important for our culture—(…) from a "throwaway society" to a "culture of repair".' The organizers of the Repair Cafés strive for cultural transformation aimed at sustainability.

'We cannot talk about sustainability without a culture of repairing, and a fundamental extension of the lifespan of technologies.' In this quote 55-year-old organizer Paul Winter stresses that a 'culture of repair' is needed to establish a sustainable society and perceives a need for change regarding identification with technologies. 'We need to have a cultural change, through which it becomes cool again and socially acceptable to walk around with technologies which have signs of use and patina, where the display has scratches or fractures and one says: "This is my good old device, I stand by this, this is my trademark."'

Such a cultural transformation could only happen when there are people who identify with and support these ideas. Currently dominating is a consumer society in which the ownership of goods is important to people, as is the act of purchase itself (Oetzel 2012). This is what many people involved in Repair Cafés want to change, as Manuel Maier, a participant in the Repair Café in Berlin, claims: 'We need to get rid of the consumption mentality.'

The number of Repair Cafés gives us cause to think about a repair movement. In total, 491 repair initiatives are registered on the website supported by Anstiftung & Ertomis (www.reparatur-initiativen.de, 10 February 2017), and on the website supported by Stichting Repair Café, 1211 Repair Cafés are registered worldwide (http://repaircafe.org/en/visit/, 10 February 2017).[18]

Four characteristics of social movements also match a repair movement: shared aims and a shared identity, protest and network character (Ullrich 2015: 9ff.): As the results of the study show, Repair Café stakeholders share the aim of sustainability and a consumer-critical identity, their forms of protest are the repair events and the practice of repairing, and they network not only locally in these events but also translocally on a national level (organized in Germany by Anstiftung & Ertomis). The aim of the repair movement is to transform society into a culture of repair, thereby striving for a sustainable society.

In mediatized societies, where the media environment of the people becomes more and more complex and where media gain in importance in all societal areas (Krotz 2009), the number of media technologies is increasing. By repairing a device and prolonging its lifespan, people avoid the acquisition process of media technologies. They take enjoyment from repairing their media technologies rather than from the act of buying. These are people who say about themselves 'I am not a consumer person', as Nils Werner, a 27-year-old bicycle courier trying to repair his laptop, describes himself. Therefore, the actors involved try to contribute to an alternative to the consumer society. They criticize today's 'deep mediatization' (Couldry and Hepp 2016). But people repairing media technologies do not reject media technologies. Many are 'technophiles', who offer to help to repair media technologies, and many of them use media to communicate with each other or to advertize their events. When asked about the need to repair media technologies, helpers and participants alike stress that the lifespan of media devices should be prolonged by doing repairs and thus promoting sustainability.

5.8 Repair Cafés as Communicative Figurations: Analyzing the Transformation of Communication and Media Practice, and the Struggle for Change

A figurational perspective was used in this chapter for analyzing Repair Cafés from a media and communication perspective. Repair Cafés are in Elias's sense a figuration, as here networks of individuals are formed, the individuals taking different roles as organizers, people offering help (the helpers) and others seeking help (the participants) in the repair process. The *actor constellation* of the communicative figurations in Repair Cafés is composed by these different roles. The network comes into being at a certain location at a certain time. Repair Cafés are usually organized as monthly events. As these events are organized repeatedly, the figuration of each Repair Café becomes stable, although happening intermittently.

Although the motivations of the participants are not homogeneous, the overall *frame of relevance* of the communicative figuration in Repair Cafés can be identified as consumer criticism. This is because many of the participants and all of the organizers interviewed value their existing devices, are trying to avoid the consumption of new media technologies and to avoid polluting production and waste.

The *communicative practices* in Repair Café happen mainly face to face within the events, but organizers and volunteers offering help also connect via email, emailing lists or telephone calls between events. But media are not only relevant for the communication process among the participants but also as objects of repair. Therefore, media practices in Repair Cafés are on the one hand mediated communication practices of the people involved, while on the other hand the repairing of media technologies can be defined as a media practice itself, a practice which is related to media. Conceptualizing the repair of media technologies as media practice shows that in media and communication studies, the concept of media practices has to be understood in a broad sense, not only taking into account what people do with media content but also analyzing what they do with media technologies.

The repairing of media technologies in Repair Cafés can be perceived as a change in media practices in consumer society (which is dominantly characterized by an increasing number of media technologies and regular purchases), which again strives for a cultural transformation aiming at sustainability. Many stakeholders question the present trends of changing media environments, in which the media environments become more and more complex, with the lifespan of media technologies becoming shorter and therefore an increase in production and disposal of media devices. Instead, they aim at maintaining existing media technologies and prolonging the lifespan of devices to avoid the production of new media technologies and the disposal of existing ones.

The participants acknowledge the materiality of media technologies, as they are aware of the problematic effects on the environment regarding the production and disposal of these goods. They draw attention to the negative social and environmental effects of media technologies, which are often not acknowledged in media and communication studies.

With the establishment of more and more Repair Cafés, not only do such communicative figurations emerge, but taken together they become a movement which strives for cultural change as well as the transformation of media practices. As many participants feel a sense of belonging to this repair movement, the Repair Cafés can be described as communities.

Repair Cafés are not the only (rather new) phenomenon criticizing consumer society and striving for cultural transformation. Other projects such as Transition Towns, Urban Gardening projects or exchange circles, share similar goals. In these projects, media also become relevant, for example social networking sites, blogs or online forums which are used to connect and mobilize people, and websites, posters and flyers which are used for public relations. But media are not only relevant for connection and mobilization within consumer-critical action, but in Repair Cafés media technologies themselves move into central focus and become objects of critique and transformation. People try to not only change (their) media practices but also to contribute to a cultural change, towards a 'culture of repair'. As the number of Repair Cafés increases, these events might contribute to cultural transformation and to a more sustainable society, although their influence might not be revolutionary in the context of current consumer cultures.

Notes

1. See a map for locations of registered Repair Cafés at www.repaircafe.org.
2. Visit www.reparatur-initiativen.de for the map and calendar.
3. In public repair events, the repairing of technologies is highly gendered as female participants pass repair work to male volunteers and mainly women do repairs to textiles (Rosner and Ames 2014: 326). I share this finding in the study I conducted, see below. For a detailed analysis of gender roles in public sites of repair (see Rosner 2013).
4. I share this statement in the results of the empirical study I conducted; see below.
5. Unconventional forms of participation are those which are not institutionalized (Nève and Olteanu 2013, Barret and Brunton-Smith 2014, 7).
6. I followed Strauss and Corbin's approach of the Grounded Theory and not Glaser's. For a comparison of the two see, for example Walker and Myrick (2006).
7. Although the interviewees agreed that I use the interviews for my research and publications, all interviews have been made anonymous and pseudonyms are used. All quotes by interview partners have been translated into English by the author.
8. For a detailed analysis of the relevance of the locations of Repair Cafés, see Kannengießer (2018).
9. The communicative practices and media practices through which people communicate in Repair Cafés are analyzed below.
10. Pseudonyms are used for all interview partners.
11. For an analysis of the harmful production processes of technologies see for example, Chan and Ho (2008), Bleischwitz et al. (2012).
12. See for analysis of the effects of e-waste, e.g. Bily (2009), Robinson (2009), Gabrys (2011), Kaitatzi-Whitlock (2015).
13. The popularity of the term 'culture of repair', which many organizers use in the interviews, increased in Germany after the release of the book *Die Kultur der Reparatur* (The culture of repair) by Wolfgang Heckl (2013), who is director of the German Museum in Munich.

14. 'The media repertoire of a person consists of the entirety of media he or she regularly uses' (Hasebrink and Domeyer 2012, 758). In this context, a distinction is made between the media repertoires of individual people and the media ensemble of a communicative figuration, which encompasses the entirety of media that can be found in a figuration (see Hepp and Hasebrink in this volume).
15. Saturn is one of the biggest stores selling electronic goods in Germany.
16. Although Hubert Knoblauch stresses the relevance of mediated communication in today's communities, I argue in respect of Repair Cafés that face-to-face and mediated communication are both relevant for the communities constructed here.
17. The media ensemble of each communicative figuration has to be distinguished from the media repertoires of the individual people (see footnote 14).
18. First Anstiftung & Ertomis cooperated with Stichting Repair Café. But Max Georg, an employee of Anstiftung & Ertomis, explains that they then started working independently, criticizing Stichting Repair Café for using the concept as a commercial idea. For instance, people have to pay to get a 'starter kit', which includes information on how to organize a Repair Café and the right to use the logos (http://repaircafe.org/en/faq/#faq-webwinkel).

References

Baringhorst, Sigrid, Veronika Kneip, Annegret März, and Johanna Niesyto. 2010. *Unternehmenskritische Kampagnen*. Wiesbaden: VS.

Barret, Martyn, and Ian Brunton-Smith. 2014. Political and civic engagement and participation: Towards an integrative perspective. *Journal of Civil Society* 10 (1): 5–28.

Berlin Online. 2013. Reparaturkultur wieder erweckt—Umweltpreis für Repair Café. http://www.berlinonline.de/nachrichten/pankow/reparaturkultur-wieder-erweckt-umweltpreis-fur-repair-cafe-44295. Accessed 12 July 2015.

Bily, Cynthia A. 2009. *What is the impact of e-waste?*. Detroit: Greenhaven Press.

Bleischwitz, Raimund, Monika Dittrich, and Chiara Pierdicca. 2012. Coltan from Central Africa, international trade and implications for any certification. *Resources Policy* 37: 19–29.

Chan, Jenny, and Charles Ho. 2008. The dark side of cyberspace: Inside the sweatshops of China's computer hardware production. Berlin. http://goodelectronics.org/publications-en/Publication_2851. Accessed 30 Mar 2017.

Charter, Martin, and Scott Keiller. 2014. Grassroots innovation and the circular economy. A global survey of Repair Cafés and Hackerspaces. University for the Creative Arts, Farnham, Surrey. http://cfsd.org.uk/site-pdfs/

circular-economy-and-grassroots-innovation/Survey-of-Repair-Cafes-and-Hackerspaces.pdf. Accessed 30 Mar 2017.

Corbin, Juliet, and Anselm Strauss. 2008. *Basics of qualitative research. Techniques and procedures for developing grounded theory*, 3rd ed. Los Angeles: Sage.

Couldry, Nick. 2004. Theorising media as practice. *Social Semiotics* 14 (2): 115–132.

Couldry, Nick. 2012. *Media, society, world: Social theory and digital media practice.* Cambridge: Polity Press.

Couldry, Nick, and Andreas Hepp. 2016. *The mediated construction of reality.* Cambridge: Polity.

de Nève, Dorothée, and Tina Olteanu (eds.). 2013. *Politische Partizipation jenseits der Konventionen.* Opladen.

Elias, Norbert. 1978. *What is sociology?* London: Hutchinson.

Gabrys, Jennifer. 2011. *Digital rubbish: A natural history of electronics.* Ann Arbor: University of Michigan Press.

Gaßner, Volker. 2014. GreenAction—Die Kampagnen-Community. In *Internet & Partizipation. Bottom-up oder Top-down? Politische Beteiligungsmöglichkeiten im Internet*, ed. Kathrin Voß, 129–148. Wiesbaden: Springer VS.

Genzel, Peter. 2015. *Praxistheorie und Mediatisierung. Grundlagen, Perspektiven und eine Kulturgeschichte der Mobilkommunikation.* Wiesbaden: VS.

Greenberg, Josh, and Graham Knight. 2004. Framing sweatshops: Nike, global production and the American news media. *Communication and Critical/Cultural Studies* 1 (2): 151–175.

Hasebrink, Uwe, and Hannah Domeyer. 2012. Media repertoires as patterns of behaviour and as meaningful practices: A multimethod approach to media use in converging media environments. *Participations: Journal of Audience & Reception Studies* 9 (2): 757–783.

Heckl, Wolfgang M. 2013. *Die Kultur der Reparatur.* München: Goldmann.

Jackson, Steve J. 2014. Rethinking repair. In *Media technologies: Essays on communication, materiality, and society*, eds. Tarleton Gillespie, Pablo J. Boczkowski, and Kirsten A. Foot, 221–239. Cambridge: MIT Press.

Jackson, Steve J., and Laewoo Kang. 2014. Breakdown, obsolescence and reuse: HCI and the art of repair. http://sjackson.infosci.cornell.edu/Jackson&Kang_BreakdownObsolescenceReuse%28CHI2014%29.pdf. Accessed 30 Mar 2017.

Kaitatzi-Whitlock, Sophia. 2015. E-waste, human-waste, inflation. In *Media and the ecological crisis*, eds. Richard Maxwell, Jon Raundalen, and Nina Lager, 69–84. Milton Park and New York: Routledge.

Kannengießer, Sigrid. 2016. Conceptualizing consumption-critical media practices as political participation. In *Politics, civil society and participation*, eds. Leif Kramp, Nico Carpentier, Andreas Hepp, Richard Kilborn, Risto Kunelius, Hanno Nieminen, Tobias Olsson, Simone Tosoni, Iija Tomanic Trivundža, and Pille Pruulmann-Vengerfeldt, 193–207. Tartu: Tartu University Press.

Kannengießer, Sigrid. 2017. Repairing media technologies as unconventional political participation. In *(Mis)understanding political participation*, eds. Cornelia Wallner, Jeffrey Wimmer, and Karoline Schulz. London: Routledge.

Kannengießer, Sigrid. 2018. Reparaturcafés—Orte urbaner Transformation. In *Medien, Stadt, Bewegung. Kommunikative Figurationen des Urbanen*, eds. Andreas Hepp, Sebastian Kubitschko, and Inge Marszolek. Wiesbaden: Springer VS.

Knoblauch, Hubert. 2008. Kommunikationsgemeinschaften. Überlegungen zur kommunikativen Konstruktion einer Sozialform. In *Posttraditionale Gemeinschaften. Theoretische und ethnografische Erkundungen*, eds. Ronald Hitzler, Anne Honer, and Michaela Pfadenhauer, 73–88. Wiesbaden: VS.

Krotz, Friedrich. 2009. Mediatization: A concept with which to grasp media and societal change. In *Mediatization: concept, changes, consequences*, ed. Knut Lundby, 21–40. New York: Peter Lang.

Latour, Bruno. 2007. *Reassembling the social. An introduction to actor-network-theory*. Oxford: Oxford University Press.

Micheletti, Michele, and Dietlind Stolle. 2007. Mobilizing consumers to take responsibility for global social justice. *The Annals of the American Academy of Political and Social Science* 611 (157): 157–175.

Oetzel, Günter. 2012. Das globale Müll-System. Vom Verschwinden und Wieder-Auftauchen der Dinge. In *Globale öffentliche Güter in interdisziplinären Perspektiven*, ed. Matthias Maring, 79–98. Karlsruhe: KIT Scientific Publishing.

Pentzold, Christian. 2015. Praxistheoretische Prinzipien, Traditionen und Perspektiven kulturalistischer Kommunikations—und Medienforschung. *Medien & Kommunikationswissenschaft* 63 (2): 229–245.

Robinson, Brett H. 2009. E-waste: An assessment of global production and environmental impacts. *Science of the Total Environment* 408: 183–191.

Rosner, Daniela K. 2013. Making citizens, reassembling devices: On gender and the development of contemporary public sites of repair in Northern California. *Public Culture* 26 (1): 51–77.

Rosner, Daniela K., and Morgan G. Ames. 2014. Designing for repair? Infrastructures and materialities of breakdown. *Proceedings of the Computer Supported Cooperative Work & Social Computing, ACM* 2014: 319–331.

Rosner, Daniela, and Fred Turner. 2015. Theaters of alternative industry: Hrepair collectives and the legacy of the 1960s American counterculture. In *Design thinking research*, eds. Hasso Plattner, Christoph Meinel, and Larry Leifer, 59–69. Heidelberg: Springer International Publishing.

Stichting Repair Café. no date. About repair café. http://repaircafe.org/about-repair-cafe/. Accessed 31 July 2015.

Ullrich, Peter. 2015. Postdemokratische Empörung. Ein Versuch über Demokratie, soziale Bewegungen und gegenwärtige Protestforschung. ipb Working Paper. Berlin. https://protestinstitut.files.wordpress.com/2015/10/postdemokratische-empoerung_ipb-working-paper_aufl2.pdf. Accessed 30 Mar 2017.

Walker, Diane, and Florence Myrick. 2006. Grounded theory: An exploration of process and procedure. *Qualitative Health Research* 16 (4): 547–559.

Weber, Max. 1972. *Wirtschaft und Gesellschaft*, 5th ed. Tübingen: Mohr.

6

A Figurational Approach to Learning Domains

Karsten D. Wolf and Urszula Wudarski

6.1 Introduction: New Cultures of Learning

With the rise of participatory media over the past two decades, a 'new culture of learning' (Gee 2008; Thomas and Brown 2011) has been described, in which younger people especially develop expertise in different domains outside formal education, vocational training or structured apprenticeships. Following the non-media-related work of Hull and Schultz (2002) on 'literacy out of school', Ito et al. (2009: 17) coined the term 'geeking out' for media-rich informal learning processes, in other words the 'intensive and frequent use of new media, high levels of

K.D. Wolf (✉) · U. Wudarski
ZeMKI, Centre for Media, Communication and Information Research, University of Bremen, Bremen, Germany
e-mail: wolf@uni-bremen.de

U. Wudarski
e-mail: wudarski@uni-bremen.de

specialised knowledge attached to alternative models of status and credibility and a willingness to bend or break social and technological rules' (Horst et al. 2009: 66). Thomas and Brown (2011: 104) argue that geeking out 'promotes intense, autonomous, interest driven learning'. In other words, they describe a new level of autodidactical acquisition of expertise in self-chosen learning domains through everyday practices of advanced media appropriation in times of deep mediatization.

This optimistic description of participatory media supporting self-directed learning has been challenged by a more general critical assessment of internet participatory culture.

Keen (2007), for instance, argues that amateurs' contributions are of little value in comparison to experts' opinions. Carr (2010) bemoans the loss of deep reading and a lack of focus induced by heavy multitasking, while Lanier (2013) points out the danger of content created for free distribution by users. All of them have strong concerns that participation on the internet is neither quality enhancing nor open to all. The emergence of critical studies of adult learning theories (Brookfield 2005), social media and the information society question (Fuchs 2013; Fuchs and Sandoval 2013) cast further doubts on a possible empowerment of learners. Educational technology itself is not a neutral tool, but may put across an implicit, hidden, political and economical agenda (Selwyn 2013; Fischer and Wolf 2015), skewing the balance from 'learning by doing' back to instruction (Buckingham 2013: 199). Empirical studies also provoke serious doubts that 'geeking out' is an everyday practice accessible to average people, neither able to transcend the digital disparities (Gibbons 2008; Ragnedda and Muschert 2013) nor break up the educational divide (Lane 2009; Friesen and Lowe 2012).

Therefore, it is an open question as to whether a changing media environment in times of deep mediatization opens up informal expertise development for everyone across all learning domains, or if this process has been overrated and is instead only happening in certain domains and for some elite users. To further investigate this contested field of study, we decided to analyze in detail how amateurs appropriate digital media for expertization. This chapter describes our first steps into analyzing similarities and differences between different learning domains taking a figurational approach (Hepp and Hasebrink 2014).

6.2 Amateurs' Development of Expertise with Media

6.2.1 *Development of Expertise*

A central claim of the 'new learning culture' is that learners can autodidactically develop expertise not only on a beginner's but also on an intermediate to high level. While Ericsson (1996) describes expertise solely as *superior* performance of individuals, Feist (2014) describes expertise as a *stepwise* model of competence development (novice, initiate, apprentice, journeyman, expert, master). To develop expertise, both *intentional learning* processes and *implicit learning* in a stimulating environment is needed to become an expert (Eraut 2000; van de Wiel et al. 2011). In his deliberate practice theory, Ericsson (2008, 2009) argues that a certain *quality* of both practice and experience in a learning domain is needed to achieve true mastery. The *type* of practice that is most effective is domain-specific; for example, chess players have to study differently from piano players or professional athletes (Ericsson 2006). Van de Wiel et al. (2011: 7ff.) emphasize the importance of professional learning support and specific performance contexts (Gruber et al. 2010). It therefore comes as no surprise that most experts have both been formally trained and therefore had access to teachers or coaches with a planned curriculum, as well as working as professionals for several years or even decades with extensive exposure to implicit learning opportunities in the workplace.

At first sight, these findings speak against the concept of a 'new learning culture' described above. Nevertheless, Mieg (2008) reports on amateurs or laypeople who acquire expertise in the absence of a formal education and certification practice, calling them 'relative' experts. According to Mieg, these 'relative' experts can work on a comparable level to 'professional' experts, or even can become such (Mieg 2008: 3266). This is especially the case for new fields of media-related expertise (Thomas and Brown 2011; Wolf 2012).

6.2.2 *Autodidaxy—Everyday Practices of Self-directed Informal Learning*

'Amateur experts' with no access to formal training environments need to be self-directed or self-organized learners (Ponti 2014; Wheeler 2009). Self-directed learning itself is not a new concept, though. In adult education, Malcolm Knowles describes self-directed learning as 'a process in which individuals take the initiative with or without the help of others, in diagnosing their learning needs, formulating learning goals, identifying human and material resources for learning, choosing and implementing appropriate learning strategies, and evaluating outcomes' (Knowles 1975: 18). According to Livingstone (2001: 2), 'other forms of intentional learning in which we engage either individually or collectively without direct reliance on a teacher/mentor and an externally organized curriculum can be termed self-directed or collective informal learning'. Informal learning plays a very large part in adults' process of lifelong learning, both in professional and private contexts (Illich 1971; Sargant 1991, 1993; Marsick and Watkins 2001; Drotner 2009; Marsick et al. 2011).

Significant self-directed learning can be described as a *learning project*, which Tough (1971: 1) defines as 'a major, highly deliberate effort to gain certain knowledge and skill (or to change in some other way)', consisting of several intentional learning *episodes* which add up to at least seven hours. In a fast changing 'knowledge society', both the *necessity* for self-directed informal learning has increased (Livingstone 1999; Hungerland and Overwien 2004), and the *availability* of resources such as digitized, networked and mobile media has grown, forcing a 'mediatic turn' of informal learning options (Tully 2008; Friesen and Hug 2009: 79; Hartung 2010) with 'digital media as transformative resources of learning' (Drotner 2009:16).

In his literature review, Candy (1991) argued that a considerable amount of scientific discussion on 'self-directed learning' revolves around the support or execution *within* formal instructional systems. To differentiate self-directed learning *outside* formal environments, he proposes the term 'autodidaxy' as educational endeavours pursued in non-institutional, 'natural societal settings' (Candy 1991: 404). These learning processes can be intentionally planned by the learners (intentional autodidactical learning) or incidentally happen while solving problems (incidental autodidactical learning; Simons 2000: 28). These can be combined.

Candy (2004: 51) emphasizes that with access to digital media the difference between informal and formal settings becomes more of a *continuum* than a dichotomy, because materials and courses intended for more formal learning can be integrated into intentional self-directed learning. Finally, the autodidactical development of expertise must not only be understood as some kind of accumulative learning, in which to gradually build up knowledge and skills, but also as processes leading to a potential creation of 'new figures of world- and self-relation' (Koller 2011: 377).

6.2.3 *Appropriation of Media to Develop Expertise*

While the field of expertise research is firmly established, especially in competitive domains such as sports, playing chess and musical instruments, there is nearly no research on the role of (instructional/learning/communication/digital) media in processes of expertise acquisition (for an *absence* of discussion of the role of media see Boud and Garrick 1999; Ericsson et al. 2006; Dochy et al. 2012). Even the research on deliberate practice discusses the role of learning media—if at all—only within *formal* learning settings, such as the use of simulations in medical education (McGaghie et al 2011).

The role of media in informal learning processes to develop expertise has been mainly described or touched upon *outside* expertise research in five contexts central for our research project:

1. *Sociocultural studies* focusing on everyday cognition and practices of informal learning (Rogoff and Lave 1984; Lave and Wenger 1991; Rogoff 2008) have examined, 'how people participate in sociocultural activity and how they change their participation' to de-mystify 'the processes of learning and development' (Rogoff 2008: 71). For example, Jean Lave examined cognition and learning processes in the practice of cooking (Lave 1988) and sewing (Lave 2011). Extending this work, especially into professional workplace contexts, Etienne Wenger has analyzed the appropriation of online media in communities of practice (CoP) and has developed a typology of social software tools that can enhance informal learning within CoP (Wenger 2001; Wenger et al. 2009; Wolf 2006). In recent ethnographical analysis of hybrid learning communities, Nalita James and Hugh Busher (2013: 205) describe a 'mediascape', but do not analyze individual processes of media appropriation for learning.
2. In *media research*, Axel Bruns (2008) has coined the term *produsage*, meaning a process where users become producers of shared knowledge in online networks. While not discussing learning or expertise in a deeper way, Bruns describes the mediatized

contribution of amateurs to expert knowledge (Bruns 2011). In 'fandom' research we can find descriptions of fan-group members as self-directed learners appropriating media such as forums, blogs, video portals and wikis (Hills 2002; Jenkins 2006; Jenkins et al. 2009; Ito et al. 2012; Jenkins et al. 2015).

3. *Youth research* in sociology has a long tradition in research of media appropriation (Hasebrink and Lampert 2011; Kammerl 2011). Especially youth scenes are described as non-professional learning communities, in which members attain competences in 'careers' (Schnoor and Pfadenhauer 2009: 302ff.). This research focuses more on phases and positions within scenes (Lachmann 1988) than on individual media usage. Studies about the role of media in scenes so far investigate single communication platforms such as forums or social networking sites (Jörissen 2007; Hugger 2009). The 'media convergence study' in Germany (Schorb et al. 2013) has analyzed young people's searching for information across media forms such as the internet, TV, journals or books (Wagner et al. 2012; Gebel et al. 2014), but not processes of goal-oriented learning to build up expertise.

4. In *media education research*, there is a growing interest in the appropriation of media to understand (young) learners' self-directed learning (Drotner 2008; Wolf 2012; Ranieri and Pachler 2014), but also how to use identified principles of informal learning, such as Kurt Squire's (2011) discussion of 'games for learning' or Ito et al.'s concept of 'connected learning' (Ito et al. 2013), for formal or non-formal education programmes. Learners' informal use of online and social media for learning has mostly been studied in higher education settings (Bernhardt and Wolf 2012; Zawacki-Richter 2015). This line of research clusters usage-types such as advanced media users and recreational media users, but does not analyze individual development of expertise.

5. Research on *personal learning environments* (Downes 2006; Attwell 2007; Fiedler and Väljataga 2013) as well as cMOOCs (Siemens 2005; Kop et al. 2011) focuses on processes such as aggregation, remixing, repurposing and feeding forward, where learners actively appropriate social media to support their own learning processes. A central question in informal learning theory is how learners and their 'ecologies of learning options' (Moravec 2013: 81) can compensate for the lack of a formal learning

> environment. According to Vygotsky, a learner can develop his or her expertise only to an individual maximum level of independent performance (Vygotsky 1980). To widen the 'zone of proximal development', learners need access to a 'more knowledgeable other' (MKO). While Vygotsky thought of the MKO as a human actor, Attwell argues that 'the MKO can also be viewed as a learning object or social software which embodies and mediates learning at higher levels of knowledge about the topic being learned than the learner presently possesses' (Attwell 2011: 89; see also Peña-López 2013). Luckin (2010) has developed an ecology of resources framework extending this understanding of both humans and learning resources as MKOs in self-managed learning settings.

To sum up, a changing media environment seems to provide new opportunities for amateur learners to develop expertise outside formal educational systems and eventually even to become professionals, but it is very unclear what role media repertoires play in individual learning processes and what impact they have on amateurs' (dis-)empowerment and segmentation/participation.

6.3 Research Question and Methods of Data Collection

In this chapter, we want to explore and study amateurs' expertization in a changing media environment. To do this, we are trying to interlace media studies with learning and education studies (Drotner and Erstad 2014). Hepp and Hasebrink (2014: 250) propose communicative figurations as an approach for a 'practical, transmedial analysis of the changing communicative construction of mediated cultures'. Communicative figurations can be described as 'patterns of processes of communicative interweaving that exist across various media and have a "frame of relevance that orients communicative action"' (Hepp 2013: 9).

In the context of informal 'learning projects' (Tough 1971), individual learners become interested in a specific learning domain, which acts as a common frame of relevance. To develop their expertise, learners use certain practices of communication within specific constellations of actors. Practices of communication are complex patterns of communication forms using a subset of the individual's media repertoire (the sum of all media they are using). While communicating, learners eventually discover new media forms, which they may integrate into their own repertoire. The individuals' communicative practices of learning both *shape* and *are shaped by* a specific communicative figuration. Apart from other factors such as different capital sorts (Ziegler 2012), the learners' communicative repertoire affects their level of (possible) participation in a domain's communicative figuration of expertization.

To *reconstruct* communicative figurations of expertise development within and across different learning domains, it is advisable to do multi-site studies. These are especially necessary to discover disconnected parts of a figuration's media ensemble and communication practices. For example, in the learning domain of knitting (a DIY_MAKER subdomain) we identified some older learners who were exclusively using non-digital media such as printed journals and books, advice from family members and friends in private environments or from shop owners in knitting stores, while younger learners in particular often became exposed to knitting on YouTube and did not use any analogue media for their expertization in knitting at all. While there is a vast online culture of knitting, it was important to look for these other analogue places to discover important offline parts of a figuration. Furthermore, when we talked to knitters in knitting stores or at DIY fairs, we also found learners who were using online media solely passively, printing out the information and bringing it into their offline knitting groups. And some younger learners who were active on social media websites such as Pinterest, YouTube and Etsy were actively seeking the knowledge of older 'nonliner' knitters as well as old knitting books, and transferring this knowledge into their online tutorial blogs and videos.

We therefore chose three empirical data access methods for this study: (1) interviews with learners; (2) participant observations within different learning settings; (3) netnographic analysis of learning collectives.

Interviews with learners: the learning practices and media repertoires of learners span from reading analogue media such as printed books and journals or non-networked digital media such as ebooks and pdfs up to online social media sites. Sometimes they participate actively and leave (public) digital traces such as comments, blog entries or YouTube tutorials; sometimes they just read and collect information from websites and forums, operating 'below the radar'. Therefore, interviews are a central data collection method to reconstruct the breadth of learners' communicative practices (Klein, Walter, and Schimank in this volume).

Participant observations: often learning is happening less consciously while solving problems, and learners do not consider their actions to be part of learning, nor do they realize or remember their media use. For example, in our case study of 'bike gearheads', shared workshops or skate parks were very important places for face-to-face learning communication. Moreover, while a lot of bike gearheads were very critical about social media in their interviews, in our observations they were constantly watching and reposting interesting YouTube videos and links to Facebook to share information about new gear, as well as commenting on other's posts.

Netnographic analysis of learning collectives and individuals: traces of learning communication can be found on the internet for every domain of interest. Individuals document their problem-solving processes online, make them searchable for other learners and help each other ('mediatized learning collectives'; Wolf and Breiter 2014). Starting from systematic internet searches and leads from interviews, large online parts of the figuration's shared media ensemble as well as actor constellations can be reconstructed.

Other possible ways of data collection which were not part of this study but which will be considered for further studies are: (1) online surveys in learning collectivities; (2) learning diaries and learning logging; (3) data scraping for both quantitative network analysis and critical discourse analysis.

6.4 Selection of Learning Domains

Thomas and Brown (2011) suggest that in particular new learning domains with no established formal educational structures are open for a 'new culture of learning'. In this study, we therefore selected two emerging learning domain clusters with a large proportion of autodidactical amateur learners and a possible social openness to allow for a more diverse participation.

Multiplayer Online Gaming (MOG): MOG is for most players a recreational (learning) interest. While a professional e-sports scene has been established, most players are hobbyists, and as yet there is no real formal system for professionalization in MOG. MOG encompasses different genres such as First Person Shooters (FPS; e.g. Counter Strike), Massive Open Online Roleplaying Games (MMORPG; e.g. World of Warcraft), Real Time Strategy Games (RTS; e.g. Starcraft), Mobile MOGs (e.g. Clash of Clans) or Multiplayer Online Battle Arenas (MOBA; e.g. DotA2). Playing MOG is a broadly established hobby. Popular MOG-franchises such as Call of Duty sell 30 million copies worldwide (D'Angelo 2016). In Germany, 34% of all teens aged 12–19 play online games daily or several times a week (JIM 2015), although there is a large gender effect, as genres such as FPS are played by approximately 80% or more male players (Yee 2017).

DIY_MAKER: a resurgence of the Do It Yourself movement has resulted in a growing interest of amateurs not only in the crafts, but also in involvement as an artist or creator (Spencer 2008). DIY encompasses a rich diversity of subcultures ranging from feminist craftism (Greer 2014), environmental conscious upcycling (Smith 2010), anti-capitalist bicycle cooperatives and subculture artists to political-neutral hobbyists such as home improvement and apartment therapy, or commercially oriented self-employed crafters selling their products on DIY e-commerce platforms. The Maker culture can be understood as a kind of technology-based extension of DIY culture (JBushnell on Wikipedia 2010), in which 3D printers and the physical-computing platform Arduino especially have made hardware development more accessible for amateurs. As there are many connections between DIY and Maker practices (Tanenbaum et al. 2013), we have chosen to use an underscore gap in DIY_MAKER in our study to emphasize the existing overlaps.

A main distinction between the two learning-domain clusters is the natural inclination of MOG learners to use computers/digital media, because they already use them to play games, while in DIY_MAKER learners are often in a manual process of crafting and making, away from their computing devices. Another difference is that MOG developed in parallel to internet technology and makes heavy use of it, while DIY_MAKER is a new chapter in the century-old history of crafts. Finally, the MAKER movement sits between computer-centred hobbies such as MOG and analogue-focused creation processes of DIY.

As part of the DIY_MAKER complex, we studied bike gearheads in trending bike activities such as bike messaging, dirtbiking and BMX; 3D printing enthusiasts; knitting, tailoring and upcycling crafters; and vegan baking. As part of the MOG complex, we studied First Person Shooter players, Multiplayer Online Battle Arena players; and MMORPG players. In total, we have conducted 42 interviews, collected field notes from participative observations in nine offline sites and studied online learning collectives on more than 40 websites and social media platforms, such as Facebook, Twitter, Instagram and YouTube.

In Table 6.1 the research sites are described in detail.

6.5 Differences in Figurations Between Learning Domains

Building upon the analysis of individual communication repertoires, media biographies, observations of practices and online activities, this section describes the main aspects and differences of the two learning domains' communicative figurations of learning.

For a conceptual overview, Fig. 6.1 shows *schematic* media repertoires of five individuals. All five media repertoires are subsets of the current media environment, which is the sum of all media today. A *learning domain's media ensemble* (LDME) is formed by all individuals' media usage for learning communication within the domain. In reality, thousands or even millions of individuals shape an LDME. Individuals' media repertoires also include other types of media usage that are not part of the

Table 6.1 Description of research sites for data collection

Interviews		
Domain	*Sub-domain*	*Number of Interview Partners*
DIY[a]	Trending Bike Activities	13
DIY	3D Printing Enthusiast	2
DIY	Knitting/Upcycling	5
DIY	Cooking/Baking	5
MOG[a]	FPS	11
MOG[a]	MOBA	3
MOG	MMORPG	3
Observations		
Domain	*Sub-domain*	*Number of Sites/Visits*
DIY	Open Workshops	2
DIY	Fablabs	2
DIY	Knitting Shops	1
MOG	E-sports Events	2
MOG[a]	Gaming house	2

Data collection was done by Urszula Wudarski, Karsten D. Wolf, Burcin Nar, Julien Eissing, Sabine Schaaf, Carina Lohfeld, Katharina Ellmers, Freya Kuhn, Lilith Wilkening, Svenja Gottschalk, Michael Berndt, Kerstin Kreis, and Hilka Neunaber

[a]only male participants

specific LDME (cases A, B, C, D), such as watching movies in a cinema. Empirically, we have so far been unable to find individual learners with a repertoire *smaller* than an ensemble (hypothetical case E). While an individual learner's *learning specific media repertoire* (LSMR)—the subset of an individual learner's media repertoire used in a learning domain—in most cases only covers a part of a LDME (e.g. a learner using only printed DIY journals and not much else), non-learning-centred media usage outside the LDME was always present, such as watching the news on TV or reading books as a pastime. Compared to the real size of individual's media repertoires and the encompassing media environment, the shown LDME is often much smaller in relation.

Empirically, we rarely found LSMR with more than ten media types, while learners' complete media repertoire were much larger. Case D shows a somewhat common situation, where a specific learner does use a specific media such as WhatsApp in other communicative contexts (therefore it is a part of his or her media repertoire), ***but not within*** the learning domain (marked as a white 'non-usage' spot in Fig. 6.1). Nevertheless, other learners use it commonly for learning, so that it becomes part of the LDME. Mainstream communication platforms in particular, such as Facebook, Twitter, WhatsApp or Instagram, are often used from nearly anybody in a certain age range, but not necessarily for informal learning ***within*** the learning domain.

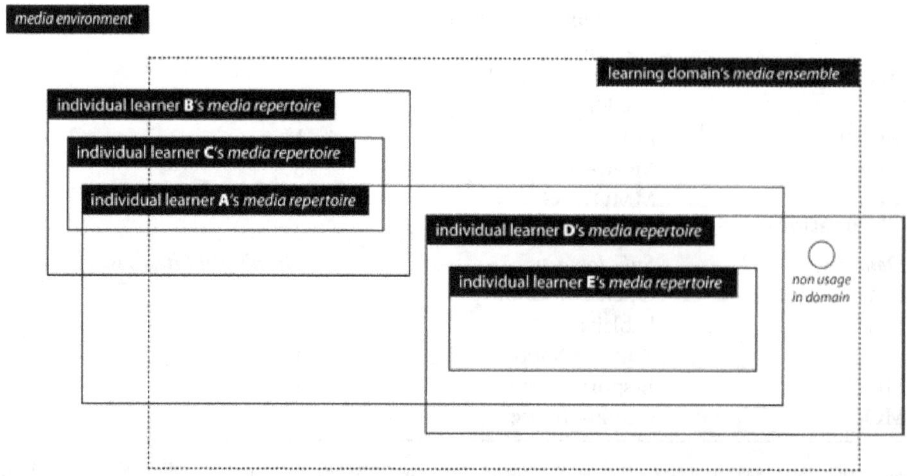

Fig. 6.1 Schematic view of media environment, learning domain's media ensemble and individual learners' media repertoires

Typical for empirical maps of LDME is the *clustering* of media repertoires. Within a media ensemble, there will be larger groups of individuals with similar media usage, and these clusters do not necessarily overlap (cluster B + C; cluster D + E). Some individuals connect these clusters (case A), either by *sourcing* both clusters for individual deeper knowledge or by *bridging* in the form of taking knowledge from one communicative learning cluster and sharing it in another cluster.

In our research of individuals' *media repertoires*, we were interested not only in *what* media they were using, but *how* they used media for *what* (communicative practices). One thus has to add a dimension of communicative activity type. As a first simple analytical step, one can differentiate between consumptive and productive usage of media, such as reading versus posting tweets on Twitter, or reading versus editing Wiki articles. Within media *ensembles* of learning, these types of activity can be much more differentiated. For example, writing a blog can be a straightforward posting of blog articles, or include rich interactions with other bloggers and readers. Even with the same set of media, different clusters can be identified because of different sets of communicative activity.

Obviously, both DIY_MAKER and MOG are huge domains and encompass divergent subcultures of learning. In a first step, both domains' communicative figurations of learning will be described and compared with each other *on a high aggregation level.* In a second step, we explore differences within sub-domains.

6.5.1 Media Ensembles and Communicative Practices of Learning

We can distinguish four basic types of communication (Krotz 2007; Hepp 2013): *direct communication*, which happens in a co-present context; *reciprocal media communication*, with separation of contexts in a synchronous or asynchronous way, of which both are oriented to specific others in a dialogic mode of communication; *produced media communication*, which is a monologic mode of communication oriented to an indefinite potential number of addressees; and finally, *virtualized media communication*, which is a form of interlogical communication, where human-made algorithms simulate communicative processes.

In the case of MOG, most learning happens in *reciprocal media com munication*. Players chat either synchronously via in-game text or audio chats, or use external chat systems such as TeamSpeak; or asynchronously use forums for discussing the 'meta game', which is a deep analysis of the game mechanics, often impacted by game patches. Player interaction within the game by acting out ways to do things is also an important element of reciprocal, *virtual embodied* communication. All levels of learners are intensive users of reciprocal communication channels, sometimes even outside the game. For instance, we observed clan members using mobile audio chat apps such as TeamSpeak on their smartphones to listen constantly to a clan's conversation outside the gaming context, for example when they went to a supermarket to buy supplies. Produced media communication such as frequently asked questions (FAQs), Walkthroughs, Let's-Play-Videos or Twitch.tv-Streaming are especially important for beginners to mid-level players. In contrast, *direct* communication is only important in competitive e-sports tournament settings, when teams train and play in co-presence, although even then audio chat programs (reciprocal media) are used.

Additionally, MOGs are a domain with rich virtualized media communication, mostly in the form of Non-Player Characters (NPCs; computer controlled players) and Bots (computer controlled enemies). NPCs often suggest tasks based on the players' current abilities. This helps to accelerate the learning curve of players. Bots are important training partners for deliberate practice. Again, this communication becomes less important with higher levels of expertise.

In comparison, DIY_MAKER learners are much more involved in direct communication within co-present contexts, such as in co-workspaces, workshops, fairs, shops or private homes. The physical (hardware) nature of objects with a need to feel and show fosters such direct communication. Produced communication is also very important in form of written, visual or audio-visual tutorials on blogs, Instagram, Facebook, tutorial websites or YouTube. There is also a depth of asynchronous reciprocal media communication in forums or comment systems. There is no virtualized media communication.

Figure 6.2 shows a high level comparison of media ensembles between MOG and DIY_MAKER. While mainstream media such as Facebook or YouTube are part of both ensembles, each learning domain has very specific media types not used in the other. One reason for this is the different needs and affordances of the domains' skill sets. In DIY_MAKER, it is common to search for creative inspiration for new products to make, so social (image) sharing becomes very popular; hence Instagram and Pinterest are very important parts of media ensembles. In MOG, watching performance and following live commentary is an

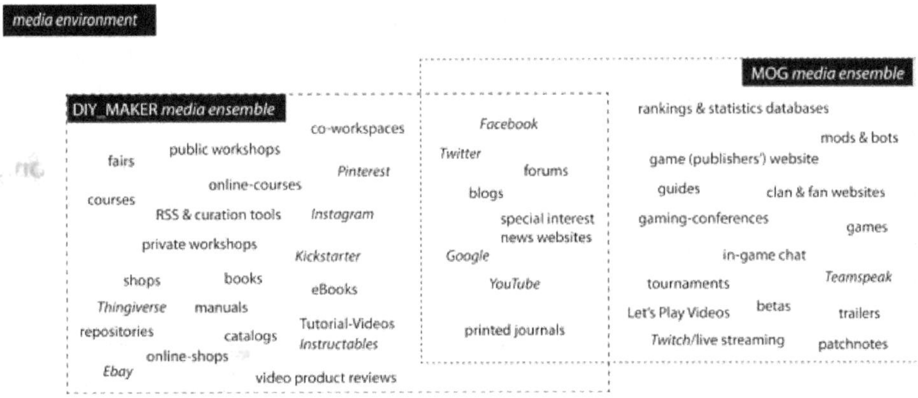

Fig. 6.2 Comparison between two learning domains' media ensembles (DIY_MAKER versus MOG)

important part of skill building, so live streams of gaming on Twitch or YouTube Live generate thousands of views. While there is a strong trend to visual media such as video or photographs, very specialized knowledge topics are still being discussed in written form on forums.

Within each of the sub-domains, there are further layers of details and differentiation. For example, within 'gearheads in trending bike activities', the relative age and maturity of a learning domain plays a role for its media ensemble. While BMX is a well established 'old school' activity with a rich body of mediatized knowledge bases, Dirtbike is more of an upcoming activity, which has yet to be systematized. Therefore, it is nearly impossible for semi-pro and amateur learners in BMX to create interesting tutorial videos. Everything has been done and the production value is extremely high ('better than I can do it'), therefore participation in sharing videos is lower than in Dirtbike.

6.5.2 *Constellation of Actors*

Actors are manifold in communicative figurations of informal learning: learners as individual actors, groups of problem-solving learners as collective actors, corporate actors such as publishers and commercial training providers.

In the MOG constellation of actors, most games are produced by commercial companies. MOG represents a huge market, but also require expensive resources such as servers. Even successful community 'mods' (modifications of a game) have been 'sucked' into commercial products, such as popular MOBA Defense of the Ancients (DoTA) or FPS Counter Strike. Because of their competitive nature, MOGs were especially fitting to be established as an e-sport with high prize money for tournaments. Together with both professional and amateur press, this formed a strong commercialization arena of MOG, further increased by lifestyle brands acting as sponsors.

A second arena is the meta-game discourse. Here, all game mechanics are discussed and contested. Game developers are at the centre of both commercialization and meta-game. Their task is to make games attractive both from a gamer's (enjoyment) and publisher's (profit) perspective. At the centre of the learning arena are both serious/competitive amateur gamers, who often share their knowledge with each other, and commercially oriented Twitch live streamers and Let's Players on YouTube. Casual and hobby gamers are mostly playing and not analyzing. With higher knowledge of the meta-game, actors become more influential on the meta-game discourse, eventually directing the development of patches and future games (Fig. 6.3).

While Massive Multiplayer Online Games (MMORPG) can be played within larger groups such as clans and raid groups against NPCs and other players, in most cases MOGs are played in smaller teams, such as in groups of five (MOBA) or even singly against other individuals (arcade FPS). The competitive nature and the game mechanisms induce

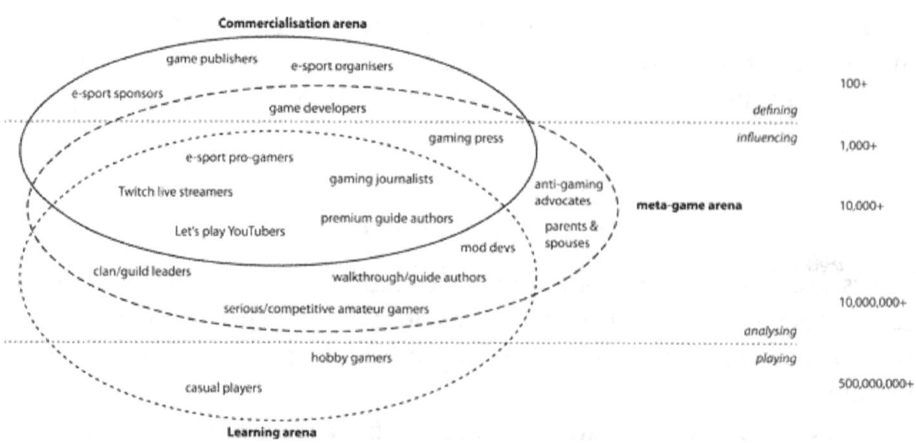

Fig. 6.3 Constellation of actors for learning domain Multiplayer Online Gaming

a necessary command structure and therefore a hierarchy within groups of players. Furthermore. the performance level becomes very visible and quantifiable via ladder systems, trophies and other ranking systems. Pro-gamers can become 'stars' with a fan following.

Because most of the learning happens within games, the learning constellation of actors is focused on smaller groups of people. People are dependent on one another to work as a team. If the competence levels of players are too diverse, they often don't stay connected. For beginners or newbies, it is obvious that other players are on a higher expertise level. Outside interpersonal communication in clans or other groups, only few experts provide their knowledge actively in produced media for others to follow, such as tutorials and Let'sPlay videos on YouTube or in live streams on Twitch. Much of the reciprocal communication on meta-game issues happens in blogs or forums, as well as collaboratively in FAQs and Walkthroughs.

In our interviews with semi-pro FPS gamers, it became clear that learners move easily between different sets of actor constellations: they played Real Time Strategy Games alone against other anonymous players for relaxation, mostly in a learning-by-doing style; with their spouses they played puzzle games or MMORPG in a co-present setting, helping each other in direct communication; with family members and friends they played 'accessible' FPS such as Halo on their video game console, sharing their deep knowledge with their co-players as an expert; but in their Battlefield Clan they practised in a commando structure, led by more experienced players.

In e-sports settings such as professional MOBA teams we observed an even higher specialization. Analysts were profiling other teams, creating video analyses of other players, and coaches were setting up training routines for the players based on these profiles.

In comparison, in DIY_MAKER we find a much more egalitarian constellation of actors, as there are no ranking systems or other competitive elements. For example, a vegan food blogging expert stated that she learned a lot from the comments and ideas of her readers, who often transformed her recipes and shared new knowledge. Again, we found a social arena of commercialization, although it is smaller in volume. While the computer game industry is huge (e.g. computer game publisher Electronic Arts made 4.52 billion dollars in revenue in 2015), important MAKER projects such as Arduino/Genuino are open source,

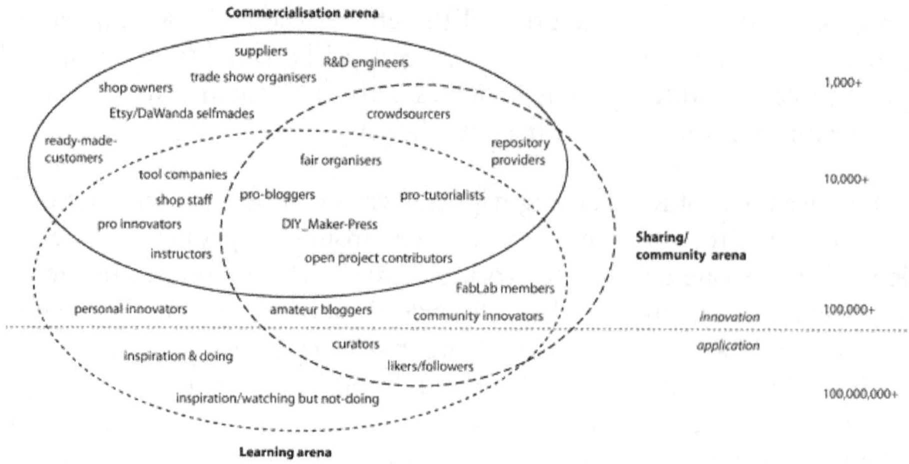

Fig. 6.4 Constellation of actors for learning domain DIY_MAKER

grassroots projects. As there are many different interests and projects in DIY_MAKER, companies tend to be smaller and less dominant.

A very important social arena in the learning constellation of DIY_MAKER actors is sharing and community, because most innovation and learning resources are created collaboratively, so even the commercial DIY_MAKER press is participating in these sharing activities (Fig. 6.4).

6.6 Conclusion

Taking a figurational perspective on learning domains, we could show that both maps of *media ensembles* and *constellation of actors* are helping us to describe the complexity of communicative practices and the role of media in two exemplary learning domains. Several things can be learned:

Media ensembles of learning are highly dependent on the learning domain, because a domain consists of specific knowledge and skills, which demand different forms of media. For example, in 3D printing, objects are often described in STL (STereoLithography) files, which can be shared in file repositories such as Thingiverse. These files open up information about the construction of the models and are a very important resource for further learning. For MOG players, on the other hand, information about new successful strategies cannot be shared in repositories but instead more easily on YouTube or Twitch.

In the analysis of the constellation of actors, we can identify different social arenas of discourse. Within both learning domains, there are direct intersections between commercialization and learning arenas: amateurs trying to earn some money by providing learning resources; learners turned into possible customers of companies; or companies trying to support the development of their customers' expertise so they become interested in more advanced commercial offerings.

In DIY_MAKER, there exists a strong sharing/community arena, which acts as a counterforce to the commercialization arena to support self-development instead of customer education. In MOG, we can find a stronger commercialization arena. Tensions between 'gaming industry', 'cultural values of games' and 'fun' are negotiated in the meta-game arena by developers, journalists, pro and amateur gamers. One could argue, furthermore, that the commercialization arena and the learning arena together form a competition arena, which is further moulding the learning aspiration of amateur learners.

Empirical reconstructions of learning domains' communicative figurations have proven to be very promising for the further analysis of informal learning in times of deep mediatization.

References

Attwell, Graham. 2007. Personal learning environments-the future of eLearning? *Elearning papers* 2 (1): 1–8.

Attwell, Graham. 2011. The future learning environments. In *IATEL: Interdisciplinary approaches to technology-enhanced learning*, ed. Max Mühlhäuser, Werner Sesink, Andreas Kaminski, and Jürgen Steimle, 75–94. Münster, New York, München, and Berlin: Waxmann.

Bernhardt, Thomas, and Karsten D. Wolf. 2012. Akzeptanz und Nutzungsintensität von Blogs als Lernmedium in Onlinekursen [Acceptance and usage of blogs in online courses]. In *Digitale Medien. Werkzeuge für exzellente Forschung und* Lehre [Digital media. Tools for excellent research and teaching], eds. Gottfried Csanyi, Franz Reichl, and Andreas Steiner, 141–152. Münster: Waxmann.

Boud, David, and John Garrick, J. 1999. *Understanding learning at work.* London and New York: Psychology Press.

Brookfield, Stephen D. 2005. *The power of critical theory for adult learning and teaching.* Maidenhead: Open University Press.

Bruns, A. 2008. *Blogs, Wikipedia, second life, and beyond: From production to produsage.* Frankfurt am Main: Peter Lang.

Bruns, Axel. 2011. Beyond difference. In *Digital difference. Perspective on online learning. Educational futures: Rethinking theory and practice*, eds. Ray Land and Siân Bayne, 133–144. Rotterdam: Sense Publishers.

Buckingham, David. 2013. *Media education: Literacy, learning and contemporary culture*. Chichester: Wiley.

Candy, Philip C. 1991. *Self-direction for lifelong learning: A comprehensive guide to theory and practice*. Chichester: Wiley.

Candy, Philip C. 2004. *Linking thinking: Self-directed learning in the digital age. PANDORA electronic collection*. Canberra: Dept. of Education, Science and Training.

Carr, Nicholas. G. 2010. *The shallows: What the internet is doing to our brains*. New York: W.W. Norton.

D'Angelo, William. 2016. "Call of Duty: Black Ops 3 Tops an Estimated 25M Units Sold Worldwide at Retail." VGChartz. http://www.vgchartz.com/article/266166/call-of-duty-black-ops-3-tops-an-estimated-25m-units-sold-worldwide-at-retail/. Accessed 23 Aug 2017.

Dochy, Filip, David Gijbels, Mien Segers, and Piet van den Bossche. 2012. *Theories of learning for the workplace: Building blocks for training and professional development programs*. Abingdon, NY: Routledge.

Downes, Stephen. 2006. Learning networks and connective knowledge. *Collective intelligence and elearning* 20: 1–26.

Drotner, Kirsten. 2008. Leisure is hard work: Digital practices and future competences. In *Youth, identity, and digital media*, ed. David Buckingham, 187–211. Cambridge MA: Heinemann (The MacArthur Foundation series on digital media and learning).

Drotner, Kirsten. 2009. Informal learning and digital media: Perceptions, practices and perspectives. In *Informal learning and digital media*, ed. Kirsten Drotner, Hans S. Jensen, and Kim C. Schrøder, 10–28. Cambridge: Cambridge Scholars Publishing.

Drotner, Kirsten, and Ola Erstad. 2014. Inclusive media literacies: Interlacing media studies and education studies. *International Journal of Learning and Media* 4 (2): 19–34.

Eraut, Michael. 2000. Non-formal learning and tacit knowledge in professional work. *British Journal of Educational Psychology* 70 (1): 113–136.

Ericsson, Karl A. 1996. The acquisition of expert performance: An introduction to some of the issues. In *The road to excellence: The acquisition of expert performance in the arts and sciences, sports, and games*, ed. Karl A. Ericsson, 1–50. Hillsdale, NJ: Lawrence Erlbaum Associates.

Ericsson, K.A. 2006. The influence of experience and deliberate practice on the development of superior expert performance. In *The Cambridge handbook of expertise and expert performance*, eds. Karl A. Ericsson, Neil Charness, Paul J. Feltovich, and Robert R. Hoffman, 683–703. Cambridge: Cambridge University Press.

Ericsson, Karl A. 2008. Deliberate practice and acquisition of expert performance: A general overview. *Academic Emergency Medicine* 15 (11): 988–994.

Ericsson, K.A. 2009. *Development of Professional Expertise: Toward Measurement of Expert Performance and Design of Optimal Learning Environments.* Cambridge: Cambridge University Press.

Feist, Gregory J. 2014. Psychometric studies of scientific talent and eminence. In *The Wiley handbook of genius*, ed. Dean K. Simonton, 62–86. Malden, Oxford, and Chichester: Wiley.

Fiedler, Sebastian H.D., and Terje Väljataga. 2013. Personal learning environments: A conceptual landscape revisited. *eLearning Papers* 35: 1–16.

Fischer, Gerhard, and Karsten D. Wolf. 2015. What can residential, research-based universities learn about their core competencies from MOOCs (Massive Open Online Courses)? In *Teaching is touching the future. Academic teaching within and across disciplines*, eds. Heidi Schelhowe, Melanie Schaumburg, and Judith Jasper, 65–75. Bielefeld: UniversitätsVerlagWebler.

Friesen, Norm, and Theo Hug. 2009. The mediatic turn: Exploring concepts for media pedagogy. In *Mediatization: Concept, changes, consequences*, ed. Knut Lundby, 63–83. Frankfurt am Main: Lang.

Friesen, Norm, and Shannon Lowe. 2012. The questionable promise of social media for education: Connective learning and the commercial imperative. *Journal of Computer Assisted learning* 28 (3): 183–194.

Fuchs, Christian. 2013. *Social media: A critical introduction.* Los Angeles: Sage.

Fuchs, Christian, and Marisol Sandoval. 2013. *Critique, social media and the information society.* New York: Routledge.

Gebel, Christa, Nadine Jünger, and Ulrike Wagner. 2014. Informations- und engagementbezogenes Medienhandeln von Jugendlichen [Adolescents' media activitiy regarding information and engagement]. In *Jugendliche und die Aneignung politischer Information in Online-Medien [Adolescents and appropriation of political information in online media]*, ed. Ulrike Wagner, and Christa Gebel, 53–136. Wiesbaden: Springer Fachmedien.

Gee, James P. 2008. *What video games have to teach us about learning and literacy.* New York: St. Martin's Press.

Gibbons, Michael. C. 2008. Digital disparities. In *eHealth solutions for healthcare disparities*, ed. Michael C. Gibbons, 66–71. New York: Springer.

Greer, Betsy. 2014. *Craftivism: The art of craft and activism.* Vancouver: Arsenal Pulp Press.

Gruber, Hans, Petra Jansen, Joerg Marienhagen, and Eckart Altenmueller. 2010. Adaptations during the acquisition of expertise. *Talent Development & Excellence* 2 (1): 3–15.

Hasebrink, Uwe, and Claudia Lampert. 2011. Kinder und Jugendliche im Web 2.0—Befunde, Chancen und Risiken [Children and adolescents in Web 2.0]. *Aus Politik und Zeitgeschichte* 3: 3–17.

Hartung, Anja. 2010. Medien als Orte informellen Lernens? [Media as informal learning spaces?]. In *Soziale Arbeit und Medien [Social work and media]*, ed. Georg Cleppien, and Ulrike Lerche, 71–83. Wiesbaden: VS Verlag für Sozialwissenschaften.

Hepp, Andreas. 2013. The communicative figurations of mediatized worlds: Mediatization research in times of the 'mediation of everything'. *European Journal of Communication* 28 (6): 615–629.

Hepp, Andreas, and Uwe Hasebrink. 2014. Human interaction and communicative figurations. The transformation of mediatized cultures and societies. In *Mediatization of communication*, ed. Knut Lundby, 249–271. Berlin: Walter de Gruyter.

Hills, Matt. 2002. *Fan cultures*. London and New York: Routledge.

Horst, Heather A., Becky Herr-Stephenson, and Laura Robinson. 2009. Media ecologies. In *Hanging out, messing around, and geeking out*, eds. Mizuko Ito, Sonja Baumer, Matteo Bittani, danah boyd, et al., 29–78. Cambridge, MA: MIT University Press Group.

Hugger, Kai-Uwe. 2009. *Junge Migranten online [Young immigrants online]*. Wiesbaden: Springer.

Hull, Glynda A., and Katherine Schultz. 2002. *School's out: Bridging out-of-school literacies with classroom practice*. New York: Teachers College Press.

Hungerland, Beatrice, and Bernd Overwien. 2004. *Kompetenzentwicklung im Wandel. Auf dem Weg zu einer informellen Lernkultur?* Wiesbaden: VS Verlag für Sozialwissenschaften.

Illich, Ivan. 1971. *Deschooling society*. New York: Harper & Row.

Ito, Mizuko, Sonja Baumer, Matteo Bittani, Danah Boyd, et al. 2009. *Hanging out, messing around, and geeking out: Kids living and learning with new media*. Cambridge, MA: MIT University Press Group.

Ito, Mizuko, Daisuke Okabe, and Izumi Tsuji. 2012. *Fandom unbound: Otaku culture in a connected world*. New Haven, CT: Yale University Press.

Ito, Mizuko, Kris Gutierrez, Sonia Livingstone, Bill Penuel, Jean Rhodes, Katie Salen, Juliet Schor, et al. 2013. *Connected learning: An agenda for research and design. Digital media and learning research hub*. Irvine, CA: BookBaby.

James, Nalita, and Hugh Busher. 2013. Researching hybrid learning communities in the digital age through educational ethnography. *Ethnography and Education* 8 (2): 194–209.

Jenkins, Henry. 2006. *Fans, bloggers, and gamers: Exploring participatory culture*. New York: New York University Press.

Jenkins, Henry, Ravi Purushotma, Margaret Weigel, Katie Clinton, and Alice J. Robison. 2009. *Confronting the challenges of participatory culture: Media education for the 21st century*. Cambridge, MA: MIT Press.

Jenkins, Henry, Mizuko Ito, and Danah Boyd. 2015. *Participatory culture in a networked era: A conversation on youth, learning, commerce, and politics*. Cambridge and Malden, MA: Wiley.

Jörissen, Benjamin. 2007. Informelle Lernkulturen in Online-Communities. Mediale Rahmungen und rituelle Gestaltungsweisen. In *Lernkulturen im Umbruch. Rituelle Praktiken in Schule, Medien, Familie und Jugend*, eds. Christoph Wulf, Birgit Althans, Gerald Blaschke, Nino Ferrin, et al., 184–219. Wiesbaden: VS Verlag für Sozialwissenschaften.

Kammerl, Rudolf. 2011. Schulische und außerschulische Sozialisation: Mediensozialisation in einer zunehmend mediatisierten Welt [School and extra-school socialisation. Media socialisation in an increasingly mediatized world]. In *Sozialpsychologie, Sozialisation und Schule* [Social psychology, socialisation, and school], ed. Erich H. Witte, Lutz-Michael Alisch, and Jörg Doll, 77–96. Lengerich: Pabst.

Keen, Andrew. 2007. *The cult of the amateur: How blogs, MySpace, YouTube, and the rest of today's user-generated media are destroying our economy, our culture, and our values.* New York: Doubleday.

Knowles, Malcolm S. 1975. *Self-directed learning. A guide for learners and teachers.* New York: Cambridge Books.

Koller, Hans-Christoph. 2011. The research of transformational education processes: Exemplary considerations on the relation of the philosophy of education and educational research. *European Educational Research Journal* 10 (3): 375–382.

Kop, Rita, Hélène Fournier, and Sui F.J. Mak. 2011. A pedagogy of abundance or a pedagogy to support human beings? Participant support on massive open online courses. *The International Review of Research in Open and Distance Learning* 12 (7): 74–93.

Krotz, Friedrich. 2007. *Mediatisierung: Fallstudien zum Wandel von Kommunikation.* Wiesbaden: VS Verlag für Sozialwissenschaften.

Lachmann, Richard. 1988. Graffiti as career and ideology. *American Journal of Sociology* 94 (2): 229–250.

Lane, Andy. 2009. The impact of openness on bridging educational digital divides. *The International Review of Research in Open and Distributed Learning* 10(5): 1–12. http://www.irrodl.org/index.php/irrodl/article/view/637. Accessed 30 Mar 2017.

Lanier, Jaron. 2013. *Who owns the future?*. New York: Simon & Schuster.

Lave, Jean. 1988. *Cognition in practice: Mind, mathematics and culture in everyday life.* Cambridge, New York: Cambridge University Press.

Lave, Jean. 2011. *Apprenticeship in critical ethnographic practice.* Chicago: University of Chicago Press.

Lave, Jean, and Etienne Wenger. 1991. *Situated learning: Legitimate peripheral participation.* Cambridge: Cambridge University Press.

Livingstone, David W. 1999. Exploring the icebergs of adult learning: Findings of the first Canadian survey of informal learning practices. *Canadian Journal for the Study of Adult Education* 13 (2): 49–72.

Livingstone, David W. 2001. Adults' informal learning: Definitions, findings, gaps, and future research. NALL Working Paper #21.

Luckin, R. 2010. *Re-designing learning contexts: Technology-rich*. Learner-centred Ecologies: Routledge.

Marsick, Victoria J., and Karen E. Watkins. 2001. Informal and incidental learning. *New Directions for Adult and Continuing Education* 89: 25–34.

Marsick, Victoria. J., Karen E. Watkins, and Barbara Lovin. 2011. Revisiting informal and incidental learning as a vehicle for professional learning and development. In *Elaborating professionalism. Studies in practice and theory*, ed. Clive Kanes, 59–76. Dordrecht: Springer.

McGaghie, W.C., S.B. Issenberg, E.R. Cohen, J.H. Barsuk, and D.B. Wayne. 2011. Does Simulation-based Medical Education with Deliberate Practice Yield Better Results than Traditional Clinical Education? A Meta-Analytic Comparative Review of the Evidence. *Academic Medicine: Journal of the Association of American Medical Colleges* 86 (6): 706–711. doi:10.1097/ACM.0b013e318217e119.

Mieg, Harald A. 2008. Expertisierung vs. Professionalisierung: relative und andere Experten aus Sicht der psychologischen Expertiseforschung. In *Die Natur der Gesellschaft (Verhandlungsband des 33. DGS-Kongresses)*, ed. Karl-Siegbert Rehberg, 3265–3275. Frankfurt am Main: Campus.

Moravec, John W. 2013. Knowmad society: The "new" work and education. *On the Horizon* 21 (2): 79–83.

Peña-López, Ismael. 2013. Heavy switchers in translearning: From formal teaching to ubiquitous learning. *On the Horizon* 21 (2): 127–137.

Ponti, Marisa. 2014. Self-directed learning and guidance in non-formal open courses. *Learning, Media and Technology* 39 (2): 154–168.

Ragnedda, Massimo, and Glenn W. Muschert. 2013. *The digital divide: The internet and social inequality in international perspective*. Abingdon, NY: Routledge.

Ranieri, Maria, and Norbert Pachler. 2014. Inventing and re-inventing identity: Exploring the potential of mobile learning in adult education. *Prospects* 44 (1): 61–79.

Rogoff, Barbara. 2008. Observing sociocultural activity on three planes: Participatory appropriation, guided participation, and apprenticeship. In *Pedagogy and practice: Culture and identities*, ed. Kathy Hall, Patricia Murphy, and Janet Soler, 58–74. London: Sage.

Rogoff, Barbara E., and Jean E. Lave. 1984. *Everyday cognition: Its development in social context*. Cambridge MA, London: Harvard University Press.

Sargant, Naomi. 1991. *Learning and „leisure": A study of adult participation in learning and its policy implications*. Leicester: National Institute of Adult Continuing Education.

Sargant, N. 1993. Learning for a purpose: Participation in education and training by adults from the ethnic minorities. National Institute of Adult Continuing Education.

Schnoor, Oliver, and Michaela Pfadenhauer. 2009. Kompetenzentwicklung in Jugendszenen. Das Karriere-Konzept als Zugang zur Rekonstruktion situierter Lernprozesse [Literacy development in youth scenes]. *Zeitschrift für Qualitative. Forschung* 10 (2): 293–320.

Schorb, Bernd, Thomas Rakebrand, and Nadine Jünger. 2013. *Die Aneignung konvergenter Medienwelten durch Jugendliche: Das Medienkonvergenz Monitoring [Adolescents' appropriation of convergent media worlds: The media convergence monitoring]*. Berlin: VISTAS.

Selwyn, Neil. 2013. *Distrusting educational technology: Critical questions for changing times*. Abingdon, NY: Routledge.

Siemens, George. 2005. Connectivism: Learning as network-creation. *ASTD Learning News* 10(1). http://www.itdl.org/journal/jan_05/article01.htm.

Simons, Robert-Jan. 2000. Various kinds of life long learning. In *Lebenslanges Lernen im Beruf—seine Grundlegung im Kindes- und Jugendalter*, ed. Frank Achtenhagen, and Wolfgang Lempert, 23–38. Wiesbaden: VS Verlag für Sozialwissenschaften.

Smith, Rochelle. 2010. Antislick to postslick: DIY books and youth culture then and now. *The Journal of American Culture* 33 (3): 207–216.

Spencer, Amy. 2008. *DIY: The rise of lo-fi culture*. London and New York: Marion Boyars Publishers.

Squire, Kurt. 2011. *Video games and learning: Teaching and participatory culture in the digital age. Technology, education–connections (the TEC series)*. New York: Teachers College Press.

Tanenbaum, Joshua. G., Amanda M. Williams, Audrey Desjardins, and Karen Tanenbaum. 2013. Democratizing technology: Pleasure, utility and expressiveness in DIY and maker practice. Proceedings of the SIGCHI Conference on Human Factors in Computing Systems. ACM, 2603–2612.

Thomas, Doug, and John S. Brown. 2011. *A new culture of learning: Cultivating the imagination for a world of constant change*. Lexington, KY: CreateSpace Independent Publishing Platform.

Tough, Allen M. 1971. *The adults' learning projects: A fresh approach to theory and practice in adult education*. Toronto: Ontario Institute for Studies. In Education.

Tully, Claus. J. 2008. Alltagslernen in technisierten Welten: Kompetenzerwerb durch Computer, Internet und Handy [Everyday learning in technologized worlds: Competence development with computers, internet, and cellphones]. In *Jugendliche in neuen Lernwelten* [Adolescents in new learning worlds], ed. Peter Wahler, Claus J. Tully, and Christine Preiß, 165–199. Wiesbaden: Springer.

van de Wiel, Margje W.J., Piet van den Bossche, Richard P. Koopmans, Filip Dochy, David Gijbels, and Mien Segers. 2011. Deliberate practice, the high road to expertise. In *Theories of learning for the workplace: Building blocks for training and professional development programs*, ed. Filip Dochy, David

Gijbels, Mien Segers, and Piet van den Bossche, 1–16. Abingdon, NY: Routledge.

Vygotsky, Lev S. 1980. *Mind in society: The development of higher psychological processes.* Cambridge, MA: Harvard University Press.

Wagner, Ulrike, Helga Theunert, Christa Gebel, and Bernd Schorb. 2012. Jugend und Information im Kontext gesellschaftlicher Mediatisierung. In *Mediatisierte Welten*, ed. Friedrich Krotz, and Andreas Hepp, 307–329. Wiesbaden: VS Verlag für Sozialwissenschaften.

Wenger, Etienne. 2001. Supporting communities of practice: A survey of community-oriented technologies. Report to the Council of CIOs of the US Federal Government. Available at https://guard.canberra.edu.au/opus/copyright_register/repository/53/153/01_03_CP_technology_survey_v3.pdf.

Wenger, Etienne, Nancy White, and John D. Smith. 2009. *Digital habitats: Stewarding technology for communities.* Portland, OR: Cpsquare.

Wheeler, Steve. 2009. Learning space mashups: Combining Web 2.0 tools to create collaborative and reflective learning spaces. *Future Internet* 1(1): 3–13.

Wolf, Karsten D. 2006. Software für Online-Communities auswählen. In *Handbuch E-Learning*, ed. Andreas Hohenstein, and Karl Wilbers, 1–28. Köln: Fachverlag Deutscher Wirtschaftsdienst.

Wolf, Karsten D. 2012. The instructional design and motivational mechanisms of world of warcraft. In *Computer games and new media cultures. A handbook of digital games studies*, eds. Johannes Fromme and Alexander J. Unger, 557–569. Dordrecht: Springer.

Wolf, Karsten D., and Andreas Breiter. 2014. Integration informeller und formaler Bildungsprozesse zur beruflichen Orientierung von Jugendlichen am Beispiel draufhaber.tv. In *Lernen im Web 2.0—Erfahrungen aus Berufsbildung und Studium*, eds. Nicole C. Krämer, Nicole Sträfling, Nils Malzahn, Tina Ganster, and Ulrich H. Hoppe, 85–101. Bielefeld: Bertelsmann.

Yee, Nick. 2017. "Beyond 50/50: Breaking Down The Percentage of Female Gamers By Genre." Quantic Foundry. http://quanticfoundry.com/2017/01/19/female-gamers-by-genre/. Accessed 23 Aug 2017.

Zawacki-Richter, Olaf. 2015. Zur Mediennutzung im Studium–unter besonderer Berücksichtigung heterogener Studierender [Media usage patterns in higher education]. *Zeitschrift für Erziehungswissenschaft* 18: 527–549.

Ziegler, Albert. 2012. Gifted education from a systemic perspective: The importance of educational capital and learning capital for the development of actiotopes. In *Development of excellence in East-Asia: Explorations in the actiotope model of giftedness*, ed. Shane N. Phillipson, Heidrun Stoeger, and Albert Ziegler, 18–39. London: Routledge.

7

Hamburg and Leipzig: Construction of Space-Related Identities

Yvonne Robel and Inge Marszolek

7.1 Introduction

'Leipzig—not the gate to the world as Hamburg is', claimed the authors of a broadcast celebrating Leipzig's millennium jubilee on *Deutschlandradio* in 2015.[1] Their statement captured the common feeling in Leipzig: that it was not as famous as Paris or Hamburg, although the citizens of Leipzig have

---

A first, preliminary version of this chapter was published as: I. Marszolek and Y. Robel, The communicative construction of space-related identities. Hamburg and Leipzig between the local and the global. Communicative Figurations Working Paper No. 13 (2016).

Y. Robel (✉)
Research Centre for Contemporary History in Hamburg,
Hamburg, Germany
e-mail: robel@zeitgeschichte-hamburg.de

I. Marszolek
ZeMKI, Centre for Media, Communication and Information
Research, University of Bremen, Bremen, Germany

always been proud of their metropolitan traditions. This is true for Hamburg too: Both cities have frequently presented themselves as cosmopolitan and open to the world (Rembold 2003; Amenda and Grünen 2008). Therefore, both have been able to look back on a long tradition of highlighting their respective importance by stressing their global connections and declaring their specific locality as world territory, with responsibilities and privileges on a global scale. No wonder that both cities were constantly classified as open-minded metropolises in media discourses of the 1950s. What we observe here is the communicative construction of space-related identities in mass communication. Focusing on the 1950s, our chapter will deal with the medial construction of space-related identities in Hamburg and Leipzig. Our main interest is to follow up the complex process of how the changing cities' media ensembles relate to transformations in urban collectivity building. In so doing, we ask from a historical point of view how collective space-related identities were imagined, constructed and changed in mediated communication processes. In particular, how were global reference points produced in mass media discourses? How were they connected to local characteristics?

After some notes on the state of research and our methodology, we will first examine the historical, political and media contexts that affect the construction of the cities' global self-images. Second, we will elaborate to what extent *the local* in Hamburg and Leipzig was constantly constructed by discourses on *the global*. In consequence, we argue that the constructions of global images are very stable umbrella notions, even though the changing media ensembles and the worsening Cold War during the 1950s had some impact on gradual new formations of space-related identities. In a third step, we will discuss different visual examples to show that media communication plays a decisive part in constructing multiple collective identities. Accordingly, we will show that markers of mobility and modernity, in particular, were important for the mediated construction of the cities' cosmopolitanism, which besides all similarities were framed by special discourses in the East and the West. Because of these similarities and differences in Hamburg and Leipzig, we finally discuss the idea of an *entangled perspective*, which could enrich the historical view on communicative figurations in a special way.

7.2 State of Research and Methodology

There is a wide range of studies from different disciplines concerned with the constructions of identities and space. In particular, research in social and cultural studies has underlined that collective identities aren't genuine, essential and homogeneous entities, which we are born with, but constructed and transformed permanently in relation to our socio-cultural environment (Hall 1992). Based on that assumption, historians have contributed in many ways to processes of collectivity building. Some have focused on how special social domains (milieus) have emerged and asked for common values and standards of groups (e.g. Schmiechen-Ackermann 1997; von Reeken 1999; Bösch 2002). Others have researched the relevance of 'inventing traditions' (Hobsbawm and Ranger 1992) or 'imagining communities' (Anderson 2006) for processes of nation building. Like the latter, many have concentrated on the spread of nationalism (see also Balakrishnan 2012; Glasze 2013), but have overlooked the interlinkage between different 'spaces'; for example, between the nation, the region, the local and the global.

Furthermore, it is astonishing that the role of communication and mediatization for the process of—especially urban—collective identity building has so far not been investigated in depth (Arnold et al. 2008; Daniel and Schildt 2010: 9–32; Schildt 2012). Currently, there is a widespread argument that space has to be thought of as 'relational', which means space isn't deep-rooted or static but a mutable outcome of an ongoing process of communication (cf. Geppert et al. 2005). This theoretical assumption also affects our view on identities, as Doreen Massey has pointed out: 'if we make space through interactions at all levels, from the (so-called) local to the (so-called) global then those spatial identities such as places, regions, nations, and the local and the global must be forged in this relational way too, as internally complex, (…) and inevitably historically changing' (2004: 5). Within this complex field, *media* not only mirror changeable ideas of space and connected ideas of collective identities but play a decisive role in their construction.

Referring to Stuart Hall (1992), we argue that urban dwellers in Hamburg and Leipzig were confronted with multiple identities: media communication in the 1950s comprehended different space-related identities—both in an interwoven and in a competitive way. Especially *the local* and *the global* closely interacted in the construction of particular urban space-related identities and were parts of changing communitization processes within the two cities.

Analyzing the cities' identity constructions by using the concept of communicative figurations enables us to ask for the dynamic interrelation between the medial, political and social contexts that shape these processes of communicative construction. As the concept stresses the significance of the different media ensembles, it helps us to research their significance for transformation and, at the same time, to overcome the focus on one single 'dominant medium' that until today is characteristic for most of historic media research (Marszolek and Robel 2016). Following the non-mediacentric understanding of communicative figurations, we argue that different aspects were crucial for changes in or the persistence of Hamburg's and Leipzig's identity constructions. Only one of them was the framing of different political systems. Deeply connected with this, the changing cities' media ensembles were another.

As Hepp and other scholars have pointed out, referring to times of deep mediatization, communicative figurations are shaped by media and by the differentiated use of media. Thus, the concept of figurations exhibits a strong bias to the investigation of communicative practices. However, not only individuals are involved in these communicative practices but also collectivities and organizations. Taking our historical perspective, it is mostly impossible to investigate the use of media by individuals; but we can ask for the role of media for collective processes of identity building.

In this respect, ideas of critical discourse theory are helpful. To work on the spatiality of collective identities and imagined communities we employ discourse analysis as a particular research perspective as well as a methodological approach to our sources (e.g. Landwehr 2008; Keller 2011; Dreesen et al. 2012). In this framework, we argue that media not only figure themselves as places of structures, but generate structures and negotiate—in our case—space related to exclusion and inclusion.

Our chapter is based on profound research into historical sources we mostly found in media themselves. We examined the local newspapers, radio and television programmes as well as the programme guides. Archive sources rounded up the research. We focused mainly on visual material, identifying the interrelations between the local and the global in the constructions of self-images.

A comparative perspective is inherent in all stages of our argument. As we concentrate on the 1950s, we are dealing (1) in Leipzig with the first decade of the development of a socialist society and its close links to the Soviet Union and (2) in Hamburg with the reconstruction of democracy and self-positioning in the Western world. Besides standard methods of comparison in historiography (Haupt 2001; Kaelble and Schriewer 2003; Häberlen et al. 2011), finally we pick up the latest concepts of entanglement probed in transnational historiography (Middell 2000; Werner and Zimmermann 2006).

7.3 Changing Cities' Media Ensembles and Their Impact on Identity Constructions

Traditionally, Hamburg and Leipzig were places of particularly dense communication and as prominent media locations allocated highly diversified media ensembles.

Accordingly, Hamburg, within the newly founded Federal Republic of Germany (FRG), could build on its traditions as a media location, especially with respect to audio media. After 1945, the radio station Nordwestdeutscher Rundfunk (NWDR), based in Hamburg and Cologne, broadcast within the British occupation zone (von Rüden and Wagner 2005). In 1956 it was separated into Norddeutscher Rundfunk (NDR) and Westdeutscher Rundfunk (WDR). The former has remained in Hamburg. The city had a pioneer role in the development of television as well, since the Nordwestdeutscher Fernsehdienst in Hamburg started its experimental broadcasts as early as 1950 (Wagner 2008). Even after the West German public television broadcasting service (ARD) was founded in the same year, Hamburg didn't lose its significance, as can be seen from the fact that the daily news has been produced in Hamburg since 1952. It later became the popular Tagesschau. Although Hamburg wasn't a major location for magazines during the Weimar Republic, in the 1950s in particular the magazine market expanded rapidly (Führer 2008: 246–269). The most successful magazine, not only in the north, was the TV programme guide *Hör zu!*, which has been published since 1946 (Seegers 2001). In addition, the *Hamburger Abendblatt*, which was first published in 1948, and has been the highest circulating and most-read daily newspaper in Hamburg since as early as 1950 (Führer 2008: 515). The trans-local daily newspaper *Die Welt*, the illustrated magazine *Stern*, the political magazine *Der Spiegel* and the weekly newspaper *Die Zeit*, as well as the tabloid *Bild*, all of which have been produced in Hamburg since the beginning of the 1950s, clearly made the city the 'centre of the west German press' (Führer 2008: 261).

Leipzig lost its international importance as a distinguished location for press and publishing houses after 1945 (this being especially the case before and at the beginning of the Weimar Republic), but the city still continued to be important for media in the German Democratic Republic (GDR). The *Leipziger Volkszeitung* has been published since July 1945 (Schlimper 1997) and later became one of the big regional organs of the Socialist Unity Party of Germany (SED). In 1946 the radio station Mitteldeutscher Rundfunk, Sender Leipzig started to broadcast regularly. From 1949 to 1952, the popular regional radio programme guide *Der Rundfunk. Mitteldeutscher Rundfunk Leipzig* was published. And it was Leipzig which—because of the trade fair in autumn 1953—opened the so-called *Fernsehstuben* (locations for public TV-viewing) as one of the first cities in the GDR (Meyen 1999: 120).

Both German media environments after 1945 were characterized by the reorganization of media institutions after the war, the initially strong influence of the occupying powers, the continuing and increasing importance of radio and finally by the (second) beginning of TV during the 1950s. The re-establishment of media and the media organization in Hamburg and Leipzig showed some similarities owing to the same starting point after the Nazi period and the lost war. However, the different political systems had various impacts on the (ideological) alignments of their media ensembles, the professionalization of journalists and so on. Even though there was no direct competition between the cities, the media ensembles were active players in the rivalry between the systems in the Cold War.

With the founding of the FRG in 1949 in the West, a federal political system was established that particularly affected media organization. Accordingly, during the 1950s a regional media structure developed. Owing to Hamburg's character as a city state, *the regional* and *the local* were difficult to keep apart. Already in 1950, the NWDR devised special programmes for the North and the South within the VHF transmission area. Since then, Hamburg has broadcast a special music programme for the North (titled '*Welle der Freude*'). The separation into NDR and WDR in 1956 led to the regional broadcasting structure of the Weimar republic being re-established for good (Führer 2008: 129–131).

Television, still a young medium, picked up the growing regional and local trend in the programmes offered (Schildt 2012: 259), and Hamburg was one of the first cities to start a regional television magazine in 1957. The so-called '*Nordschau*' included political and cultural reports from the four Northern federal states of Hamburg, Bremen, Schleswig-Holstein and Lower Saxony, special reports on rural areas, as well as series on the East German state.[2] The '*Aktuelle Schaubude*', an entertainment show produced in a glass box in the city centre, thus enabling urban dwellers to watch the live production every Saturday, became particularly popular. Walter Hilpert, general director of the

NDR, opened the first '*Nordschau*' with the following words: 'Our aim: The *Nordschau* should observe and listen to the diverse topics in North Germany; especially to the persons and characters who are working there. This programme will live *out* of the space which we are broadcasting to. At the same time, it is to be made *for* a northern Germany without any provincial narrowness.'[3] Beside the regional concept of the '*Nordschau*', it seemed important to claim Hamburg's and Northern Germany's trans-local open-mindedness.

In the GDR, at the latest from 1952 onwards, well-established older *regional* references for the construction of identities were officially undesirable. When enforcing the administrative reform of 1952, the party replaced the five states created after 1945 with 14 newly formed districts and 217 completely new counties. Accordingly, media were directly influenced by the reform of 1952 and the diffusion rates of regional pages in newspapers were adapted to the newly formed districts. Thus, until 1952 readers in Leipzig received the edition for north-west Saxony, and from 1952 the edition for the district of Leipzig. Presumably that changed the reports in their spatial range. Regional radio stations such as Mitteldeutscher Rundfunk were abolished. Although this didn't mean constructions of regional identities ceased to exist (cf. Palmowski 2009), this step did strengthen the interconnection between Leipzig's local characteristics and global references.

An important role for the permanent construction of local identity was played by Leipziger Stadtfunk. This was produced by a small studio located in the town hall and could be listened to through loudspeakers in the city centre, in different urban quarters and in some factories in town. The airtime could be from just one hour a day to the whole day (especially during trade fairs). In addition to official statements from the government or local leisure time recommendations, distributed radio reporters (Funkkorrespondenten)[4] provided reports from local factories or about leisure-time activities with their co-workers.[5] Stadtfunk can be seen as a special part of the urban soundscape of Leipzig's past—understood as an acoustic surrounding of people in a particular place at a particular time (Birdsall 2012). Leipzig Stadtfunk, in a way a child of the Cold War,[6] existed from 1950 until 1995. It couldn't be switched off and replaced by another broadcast as radio or television programmes could be, but belonged to daily (acoustic) life—for example, while people were waiting at the tram station. In this way Stadtfunk immediately impacted on the communicative construction of social reality in Leipzig.

Not only through Stadtfunk could people in the performative sense listen to their Saxon speaking 'neighbours'. Even after the abolition of Mitteldeutscher Rundfunk, the radio reported from urban quarters, from factories and from the streets of Leipzig.[7]

While Stadtfunk primarily strengthened the local space, locally labelled music shows such as the '*Leipziger Allerlei*' ('Leipzig Potpourri')[8] or the '*Hamburger Hafenkonzert*' ('Hamburg harbour concert') (Tiews 2014), permanently reinforced the global importance of the respective cities. The interlinkage between *the local* and *the global,* especially in Hamburg, became obvious in special broadcasting formats which connected the city to global travel. The best-known example was the weekly radio programme '*Zwischen Hamburg und Haiti*' ('Between Hamburg and Haiti'), which was broadcast from 1951.[9] Even today, every Sunday listeners can 'accompany' reporters on their travels around the world. In the 1950s, Hamburg acted as the port location of departure; the world 'outside' was shown as manifold and exotic (cf. Klamroth 1956). Certainly, 'the faraway' always referred to spaces of proximity and the home as well. For example, in the radio programme guide *Hör zu!* of 1955 one could read: 'It is so easy: The Sunday morning coffee behind you, waiting for lunch, you switch on the radio—and promptly you are a foreign people's guest.'[10] In a way, this statement illustrates the increasing retreat into the private sphere which was characteristic for the 1950s.

The examples of Hamburg and Leipzig both show that the historical context not only affected the cities' media ensembles, but also the programmes on offer and the content alignments. Within the local or regional programme selections linked to Hamburg or Leipzig, *the global* was a very often-used reference.

7.4 Hamburg and Leipzig as 'Global Players'?

When researching the 'regularities' and 'predominant statements' (Foucault 2003) in media discourses on the cities' images, we are inevitably confronted with global references. During the 1950s, slogans such as 'Hamburg, the gate to the world' and 'Leipzig, the showcase to the world' were omnipresent. They were produced and reproduced cross-medially, both as part of image strategies and unintended discourses. The main reason for both cities to enhance their claim to be part of the world in the 1950s was of course that after the defeat of National Socialism both parts of Germany had to reinvent their positions in a world divided by the Cold

War. In this sort of very dense cross-media communication, the differences in the media ensembles were much fewer than in other periods. In our figurational perspective we can illustrate the differentiation within the communicative figurations by such cross-media references.

Stressing the importance of the yearly trade fairs, Leipzig had a multiple image as a city that had a particular standing across the globe. This can be shown cross-medially by textual, visual and audio sources. For instance, the radio and TV programme guide *Unser Rundfunk* frequently announced reports on the trade fairs with titles such as 'Leipzig—a global meeting point', 'Leipzig—in the spotlight of the world' or 'Leipzig—the global showcase'.[11] On television, the daily news '*Aktuelle Kamera*' frequently confirmed Leipzig's significance as the place of 'the greatest trade fair in the world'.[12] In about 1955, a 'corporate video' about the city, titled 'Leipzig—the bridge to the world', was produced. The movie, commissioned by the district council, introduced Leipzig as the 'heart of the European continent' because of its importance as *the* global city of trade fairs.[13] Books (e.g. Hennig 1959), and songs,[14] repeated the slogans of 'the global showcase' or 'the gate(way) to the world' again and again. Accordingly to them, Leipzig was not only seen as a global meeting point, but as a showcase, bridge or gate to the world.

However, Leipzig's image as a global showcase was deeply embedded in the city's narrative, although in the Weimar Republic Leipzig had not been given the official title as a trade fair city because different urban actors highlighted the city's manifold traditions as the location of the book trade or fur trade and as a place of music, art and science. Only in 1937 was it recognized as a trade fair city of the German Reich,[15] and framed by the nationalist narrative and identity constructions of the Nazi period. After 1989, Leipzig re-enhanced its image as a meeting point between the transformed East and West and as a 'global player'.

For Hamburg, a similar dominance of global references is apparent, even though they aren't connected to a single event like the trade fair in Leipzig. It is striking how consistently Hamburg has been called the 'gateway to the world' even right up to the present day. Lars Amenda has stressed how this slogan has become increasingly important for the image policy of the city since the Weimar Republic, and that it was nationally framed and overemphasized during National Socialism and reinvented after the Second World War (Amenda and Grünen 2008). During the 1950s, the metaphor of the world's gateway was omnipresent, especially within media discourses. We can find it as a visual signal within the logo of the *Hamburger Abendblatt*, the most important local newspaper: Since 1948, the logo has shown a gate between two towers, surrounded by the text: 'With home in your heart, embrace the world.'[16] The slogan 'gateway to the world' was again used in 1951 as the title for a broadcast on schools radio (Schulfunk) of Norddeutscher Rundfunk.[17] In the same year, a documentary film titled '*Germany's Gateway to the World*' was produced in German and English language versions which showed the daily business of the Hamburg port (Landesmedienzentrum Hamburg 1999: 57f.). In 1953 and 1955 other movies were produced that used the slogan, too (1999: 61–64/78). Another example is the book *Hamburg—gateway to the world*, which was published in various editions during the 1950s (Amenda and Grünen 2008: 82). Like Leipzig, Hamburg was not only thought of as the gateway to the world, but also as a global meeting point and bridge between different worlds.[18]

These metaphors are accompanied by their own connotations and open up a range of diverse associations. Whereas especially the meeting point and showcase metaphors emphasize an integrative moment and the world in one's own home, the gateway to the world metaphor stresses ideas about travel and departure. But in the Hamburg and Leipzig cross-media sources it is evident that these connotations seem to be interchangeable. Both were important ways of claiming the cities' significance for the world and served as umbrella notions which were rather stable in their significance. However, what we can certainly show is that 'places are also the moments through which the global is constituted, invented, co-ordinated, produced' (Massey 2004: 11), and vice versa. *The local* and *the global* are closely interlinked and interact.

7.5 Visual Signs for the Cities' Cosmopolitism

During the 1950s, the *visual* dimension became more and more important for creating and communicating such space-related ideas of identity. In this period, the visual repertoire not only became larger but also more variegated, strengthening the visualization processes of the previous decades. Leipzig and Hamburg were very often presented via visual markers, thus reinforcing the interlinkage between *the local* and *the global*.

During the 1950s, the most striking visual marker for Leipzig was the globe. Functioning as a logo for the city's trade fair as well, it stands for the international importance of Leipzig. Together with pictures of Leipzig's town hall, of its rebuilt 'modern' central railway station or of lines of cars within the city centre,[19] the globe stressed the mobility, hence the modernity of Leipzig. Using signs like this, pictures showed a vivid city, open-minded, with its gates always open for visitors from all over the world.

For example, see Fig. 7.1: the cover of the radio programme guide in March 1955. As an announcement of the spring trade fair, the picture relates Leipzig to the world in a particular way. Reminiscent of Charlie Chaplin's dance with the globe, the woman seems to be playing cheerfully with the globes. We can see two globes—possibly symbolizing the two political worlds, which appear to meet easily in Leipzig. By placing the one world in front of the woman and the other in the middle of her hand, the picture confirms Leipzig's location in the middle (or rather the heart) of Europe and the globe.

As other pictures illustrate, Leipzig was very often seen as the centre or heart of the world. Without any doubt, one important spatial imagination during the 1950s deals with the difference between West and East. This was used as a reference point for that picture as well. The symbol of the globe was especially suitable to stress both Leipzig's and the GDR's openness to the world *and* the (dichotomic) territorial borders. The two globes symbolized this competitive situation with the West, while the reference to Charlie Chaplin strengthened the anti-fascist narration and the new invention of the GDR. As we know, photographs are not only influenced by culture and politics, but they also help to create and stabilize them (Christmann 2008). In this sense, they could formulate different and parallel existing space-related ideas of identity. On the one hand, the photograph of the woman dancing with the globes obviously goes hand in hand with gender constructions. On the other hand, it refers to older traditions of commercial photography, especially in a magazine such as this programme guide, which was a well-known medium itself, being an all-German tradition before 1945. The dynamic use and interpretation of a picture like this can only be understood if one knows about the cities' special (political and historical) framings, and about the changes within both German media environments and within Hamburg's and Leipzig's media ensembles. The concept of communicative figurations highlights these points and, in this way, helps to investigate the construction of identities as an intertwined process shaped by media and other political and social forces. With this in mind, we can ask

Fig. 7.1 Cover page *Unser Rundfunk*, 9/1955, © Burda News, TV Spielfilm Verlag GmbH, Redaktion F.F. dabei

for a media-related transformation of the communicative construction of 'social reality' during the 1950s and its impact on the transformations of communicative figurations and the social domains.

In Hamburg, visual signs of modernity and mobility played a similar key role in the construction of a cosmopolitan urban identity (cf. Stoetzer 2006) as in Leipzig during the 1950s. They were inseparable from the history of the city's media ensemble, as can be shown by 'Mecki'—a fictional hedgehog who was designed to create a feeling of identification with the programme guide *Hör zu!* in West Germany. Existing since 1949, Mecki's most conspicuous attribute was his role as a globetrotter,[20] who on the one hand permanently crossed boundaries, but on the other was deeply entrenched in his hometown, Hamburg. Hence, he was a well-known globetrotter with familial background. The world he was living in was a very cosy one, free from social or political conflicts. Mecki's 'personal life' (he became engaged to Micki in 1952) was shaped by traditional civic values and morals. To some extent, he stood symbolically for the cosmopolitan and bourgeois part of 'the Hanseatic' that was reinvented during the 1950s (Seegers 2015).

However, the most dominant sign for Hamburg's mobility and its global mindset was the port. Thus, the visual representation of the city during the 1950s was accompanied by pictures of industrial docks, cranes, tugboats or sailing boats, ships' ropes and, of course, the Elbe river with its renowned landing stages.[21] Sometimes it was reduced to a few maritime signs, such as the anchor or seagulls.[22] Sometimes male actors represented it; for example, the dockers or the more romantic figure of the sailor setting out as a young man from Hamburg into the world.[23] These pictures and the combination of visual markers give an impression of an industrious city set in relaxing surroundings that at the same time was a place of departure into the world.[24] In a way, the general social and economic departure of the 1950s was represented in those pictures. Moreover, the port in particular was very often seen as a mysterious and shady space that had its own special atmosphere. It is striking how often the Port of Hamburg was depicted in romantic light at night time.[25]

Whereas Hamburg stressed the metaphor of departure into the outside world, Leipzig (imaginarily) opened its doors to invite the world into the city. Beneath the superficial similarities, we have to deal with the underlying differences in ascribing the mediated constructions of Hamburg and Leipzig as cosmopolitan cities. Of course, these differing understandings of cosmopolitism depended on the historical context of the divided world. For instance, the strong references to mobility and modernity in Leipzig are embedded in the efforts to demonstrate the '*Weltniveau*' of the GDR and the orientation to a socialist future. Thus, media discourses on *the global* and imagined transnational spaces confirmed very real territorial political borders.

The prominent role of *visual* media for the imagination of those 'modern' and 'mobile' global spaces within national borders is remarkable. According to approaches of visual history (Paul 2006), images are not only representations of a reality which is formed 'somewhere else', but have to be seen as an important part of the construction of social sense and values. Harald Welzer et al. (2002) have clearly shown how visual and audio-visual media produce people's ideas of 'reality', and even form their 'own personal' memories and identities. During the 1950s in Hamburg and Leipzig, programme guides or movies, in particular, dealt with global references, much more so than daily newspapers. Moreover, it is striking that visual metaphors such as 'showcase into the world' or 'global viewpoint' were used progressively after 1953—while the experimental time of TV broadcasting in both German states fascinated large parts of society.[26] However, the growing differentiation within the cities' media ensembles strengthened the spread and popularization of the modern, mobile and open-minded images of Hamburg and Leipzig during this decade.

7.6 A Plea for an Entangled and Cross-Media Historical Approach

Media in East and West always reacted to each other and to the dynamics of the Cold War. Dominant discourses on the 'economic miracle' in the West and the 'building of socialism' in the East stressed the differences between the systems. Nevertheless, the link between *the local*, *the national* and *the global* was variable, as can be shown for Leipzig: In the early 1950s, the Leipzig trade fair was presented as a symbol of German unity and a perfect example of border crossing.[27] As an all-German event, it was considered to be part of the fight for the reunification of the German 'fatherland'.[28] Yet, from 1952 onwards it was to demonstrate the economic growth of the young GDR and the growth of socialism in a divided world.[29] As such, the trade fair's logo changed from one world in 1952 to two worlds placed next to each other in 1953. At the same time the trade fair's significance was seen from an increasingly international perspective.[30] The picture of the woman dancing with two globes represents this as well. By the second half of the 1950s at the latest, the Leipzig trade fair acted definitely as a symbol of strength of the GDR in the increasingly competitive situation with the West.[31]

Likewise in the West, even the 'unpolitical' character of Mecki, not without reason, again and again travelled to the United States of America.[32] But how can we highlight the historic political context for identity constructions and at the same time overcome the problem that comparisons between totalitarian and democratic systems often tend to grow too dichotomic and normative? To investigate communicative figurations means to enhance the comparative perspective. For historians, one of the main problems with comparison is to identify the different levels of transformations, since in the past this has often led to neglecting the similarities of the two political systems. As a result, for our comparative investigation on Hamburg and Leipzig, ideas of entanglement or '*histoire croisée*' (Middell 2000; Werner and Zimmermann 2006) come in useful because—with the shift to global or transnational history—they focus on mutual influences and entanglement beyond relatively plain comparisons. The interrelation of space plays an important role in these studies, as scholars enhance the entanglement between *the national*, *the regional* and *the local*, as well as in *transnational* relations (Middell 2000; Werner and Zimmermann 2006). These ideas of entanglement not only help to shed light on the interrelations between the East and the West in the context of the Cold War, but also take into account that in Germany, in particular, experiences and mentalities as well as (mediated) routines and expectations have been deeply shaped by a common past (Bösch 2015; Wierling 2015). This could explain why the global metaphors in Hamburg and Leipzig in a way functioned as open umbrella notions, interchangeable and overlapping. However, these entanglements were far away from being on the same level. In fact, they were asymmetric. The young GDR had to struggle far more to position itself in the divided world of that time. The state (and Leipzig) had to invent new traditions or interpret old metaphors by embedding them in a new narrative, whereas Hamburg enhanced more or less the continuities of the story of the port overlapping the 'dark years' of the Nazi regime.

Furthermore, space-related identity constructions in Hamburg and Leipzig have to be analyzed in an entangled perspective because people in the East often participated in Western media and vice versa. Having this in mind, media also reported on the cities beyond the border; for example, when the programme guide *Der Rundfunk* announced a radio broadcast entitled '*Beautiful German Heimat*', reporting on Hamburg as the 'gateway to the world'.[33] The other way around, the print press in Hamburg frequently reported on the Leipzig trade fair, amongst other things asking whether Leipzig should be seen as the 'gateway to the East'.[34] Thus, we can understand both cities as communicative figurations whose borders permanently blurred. Then again, the research on entangled communicative figurations highlights the cross-medial character of the identity constructions and, at the same time, observes the dynamics of changing media ensembles, as is apparent in the special role given to the visual within both cities' image building. Moreover, the cities communicative figurations seem to be variable and very stable at the same time—besides the differences between a dictatorship and a democracy and connected to different political, social and medial frame conditions.

Notes

1. http://www.deutschlandradiokultur.de/eine-lange-nacht-ueber-eine-tausendjaehrige-stadt-mein.1024.de.html?dram:article_id=336721. Accessed: 30 March 2017.
2. NDR Unternehmensarchiv, Nachlass Proske.
3. NDR Fernseharchiv, No 0001009705, Nordschau, 01.12.1957, 2.04–2.31 min (quote translated by the authors).
4. The *Funkkorrespondenten* as one active group within Leipzig's communicative figuration were a special mixture of semi-professional and non-professional journalists. Reaching back to older socialist traditions, in the GDR they were part of the ideology of 'democratic' mass media in general. Cf. Richter (1993).
5. Stadtarchiv Leipzig, StVuR Nr. 22020; Rohr (2011).
6. Especially after the construction of the Berlin Wall in 1961, loudspeakers played an important role for the (listenable) demarcation from each other. Cf. Stratenschulte (2013).
7. From the second half of the 1950s at the latest, local and regional programmes were being promoted again. The Sender Leipzig then regularly broadcast its own programmes once or twice a day, including the '*Stadtreporter*'. At first, these programmes of the district broadcasting stations (*Bezirksstudios*) were part of the schedules of Berliner Rundfunk; after 1956 they became part of Radio DDR.

8. 'Hörerstimmen zu Leipziger allerlei', *Der Rundfunk* 2/1951: 4; 'Nicht zerstreuen, sondern erfreuen!', *Unser Rundfunk* 18/1958: 7.
9. Staatsarchiv Hamburg, Best. 621–1/144, Nr. 1201 (transcriptions 1956–1960).
10. 'Zwischen Hamburg und Haiti', *Hör zu!* 46/1955: 3 (quote translated by the authors).
11. Cf. *Unser Rundfunk* 36/1953: 9–11, 37/1954: 16–17, 9/1955: 10–11, 10/1957: 12–13, 36/1954: 14.
12. Deutsches Rundfunkarchiv Potsdam, Deutscher Fernsehfunk, Aktuelle Kamera, 03.03.1959.
13. Staatsarchiv Leipzig, Best. 22043, Leipzig—Brücke zur Welt', around 1955, 17 min.
14. In 1960 the radio broadcast the song 'Leipzig—the gate(way) to the world'. Deutsches Rundfunkarchiv Potsdam, ZMV8349.
15. Stadtarchiv Leipzig, Kap. 66, Nr. 27.
16. Cf.: 'Anno Domini 1241', *Hamburger Abendblatt* 14.10.1948: 3.
17. Staatsarchiv Hamburg, Best. 621–1/144 Nr. 1759, 'Hamburg – Tor zur Welt'.
18. Cf. 'Treffpunkt am Tor zur Welt', *Hör zu!* 27/1953: 24–25. See also: 'Blaue Nacht am Hafen', *Hör zu!* 43/1952: 3.
19. 'Leipzig Treffpunkt der Welt', *Leipziger Volkszeitung* 25.02.1956: 1.
20. Symptomatically, *Hör zu!* several times reported on Meckis's voyages under the heading 'Look out into the world'. Cf. 10/1951: 5; 10/1952: 4.
21. Cf. 'Menschen im Hafen', *Hör zu!* 44/1957: 12–13.
22. Cf. *Hör zu!* 29/1950: Cover.
23. Cf. 'Kapitäne von morgen', *Hör zu!* 18/1954: 8; 'Vorzimmer der weiten Welt', *Hör zu!* 48/1956: 20.
24. Cf. 'Um die Ecke geht es nach Amerika', *Hör zu!* 01/1957: 3.
25. Cf. 'Tausende Kontorhauslichter am Tor zur Welt', *Hamburger Abendblatt* 23.02.1953: 3.
26. Moreover, the television itself was titled as the 'showcase into the world'. Cf. 'Fernsehstart', *Hör zu!* 52/1952: 6–7; Diercks (2000).
27. Cf. 'Messe der Erfolge. Leipziger Herbstmesse 1950', *Der Rundfunk* 35/1950: 3; 'Messegäste grüßen aus Leipzig', *Der Rundfunk* 10/1951: 16. Deutsches Rundfunkarchiv Potsdam, Hörfunk, Nr. 2025527, MDR, 'Zeitgeschehen vom Funk gesehen', broadcasting from 10.09.1951.
28. 'Die Messe hat eine wichtige Friedensmission zu erfüllen', *Leipziger Volkszeitung* 05.09.1952: 1.
29. 'Leipziger Messe 1952 – Erste Messe im Aufbau des Sozialismus', *Leipziger Volkszeitung* 07.09.1952: 1; 'Größte Gebrauchsgütermesse eröffnet', *Leipziger Volkszeitung* 07.09.1958: 1.
30. Appropriately, the '*Leipziger Stadtreporter*' of Berliner Rundfunk explained: 'Particularly from the licence plates and the cars

manufacturers' logos [within the city] one can see which role Leipzig has to fulfil as a city of trade fairs and as a connection between two global markets. Yes, because of this, there are the two globes and the traditional MM within the emblem of the trade fair.' Deutsches Rundfunkarchiv Potsdam, Schriftgut, F094-01-00/0054, p. 0072-0075, undated broadcasting, presumably March 1954 (quote translated by the authors).

31. 'Die Herbstmesse 1958 – ein Schlag in Erhards Wirtschaftswunder', *Leipziger Volkszeitung* 17.09.1958: 2; 'Treffpunkt Leipzig', *Unser Rundfunk* 37/1958: 2.
32. E.g. 'Mecki in Amerika', *Hör zu!* 33/1951: 32–33.
33. 'Schöne deutsche Heimat', *Der Rundfunk* 39/1952: 7.
34. 'Leipziger Messe – Tor zum Osten?', *Die Zeit* 37/1954: 9.

References

Amenda, Lars, and Sonja Grünen. 2008. "*Tor zur Welt*": *Hamburg-Bilder und Hamburg-Werbung im 20. Jahrhundert* [Hamburg in images and advertising in the 20th century]. Hamburg: Dölling und Galitz.

Anderson, Benedict. 2006. *Imagined communities. Reflections on the origin and spread of nationalism.* London: Verso.

Arnold, Klaus, Markus Behmer, and Bernd Semrad. 2008. *Kommunikationsgeschichte. Positionen und Werkzeuge. Ein diskursives Hand- und Lehrbuch.* LIT: Münster.

Balakrishnan, Gopal. 2012. *Mapping the nation.* London: Verso.

Birdsall, Carolyn. 2012. *Nazi soundscapes: Sound, technology and urban space in Germany, 1933–1945.* Amsterdam: Amsterdam University Press.

Bösch, Frank. 2002. *Das konservative Milieu. Vereinskultur und lokale Sammlungspolitik* [The conservative milieu]. Göttingen: Wallstein.

Bösch, Frank. 2015. Geteilte Geschichte: Plädoyer für eine deutsch-deutsche Perspektive auf die jüngere Zeitgeschichte [Plea for a German-German perspective in recent contemporary history]. *Zeithistorische Forschungen* 12 (1): 98–114.

Christmann, Gabriela B. 2008. The power of photographs of buildings in the Dresden urban discourse: Towards a visual discourse analysis. *Forum: Qualitative Social Research* 9 (3): Art. 11.

Daniel, Ute, and Axel Schildt. 2010. Einleitung. In *Massenmedien im Europa des 20. Jahrhunderts* [European mass media in the 20th century], ed. Ute Daniel and Axel Schildt, 9–32. Köln: Böhlau.

Diercks, Carsten. 2000. *Die Welt kommt in die Stube. Es begann 1952: Die Anfänge des Fernseh-Dokumentarfilms im NWDR/ARD* [The beginning of television documentaries on NWDR/ARD]. Hamburg: Druckerei Zollenspieker.

Dreesen, Philipp, Łukasz Kumięga, and Constanze Spieß. 2012. *Mediendiskursanalyse. Diskurse – Dispositive – Medien – Macht* [Discourse analysis of media]. Wiesbaden: VS Verlag für Sozialwissenschaften.

Foucault, Michel. 2003. *Die Ordnung des Diskurses* [The discourse of language]. Frankfurt am Main: Fischer.

Führer, Karl C. 2008. *Medienmetropole Hamburg: Mediale Öffentlichkeiten 1930–1960* [Media metropolis Hamburg]. Hamburg: Dölling und Galitz.

Geppert, Alexander C.T., Uffa Jensen, and Jörn Weinhold. 2005. *Ortsgespräche: Raum und Kommunikation im 19. und 20. Jahrhundert* [Space and communication in the 19th and 20th centuries]. Bielefeld: Transcript.

Glasze, Georg. 2013. *Politische Räume. Die diskursive Konstitution eines "geokulturellen Raums" – die* Frankophonie [The discoursive constitution of a geocultural space—the *francophonie*]. Bielefeld: Transcript.

Häberlen, Joachim C., Agnes Arndt, and Christiane Reinecke. 2011. Vergleichen, verflechten, verwirren? Europäische Geschichtsschreibung zwischen Theorie und Praxis [European historiography between theory and practice]. Göttingen: Vandenhoeck & Ruprecht.

Hall, Stuart. 1992. The question of cultural identity. In *Modernity and its futures*, ed. Stuart Hall, David Held, and Tony McGrew, 273–316. Oxford: The Open University.

Haupt, Heinz-Gerhardt. 2001. Comparative history. *International Encyclopedia of the Social and Behavioral Sciences* 4: 2397–2403.

Hennig, Reinhold. 1959. *Leipzig: Schaufenster der Welt. Messe-ABC* [Leipzig: the global showcase]. Berlin: Kongress-Verlag.

Hobsbawm, Eric, and Terence Ranger. 1992. *The invention of tradition.* Cambridge: Cambridge University Press.

Kaelble, Hartmut, and Jürgen Schriewer. 2003. *Vergleich und Transfer. Komparatistik in den Sozial-, Geschichts- und Kulturwissenschaften* [Comparatistics in social sciences, history and cultural studies]. Frankfurt am Main: Campus.

Keller, Reiner. 2011. *Wissenssoziologische Diskursanalyse. Grundlegung eines Forschungsprogramms* [The sociology of knowledge approach to discourse]. Wiesbaden: VS Verlag für Sozialwissenschaften.

Klamroth, Ursula. 1956. *Zwischen Hamburg und Haiti: Weltenbummler erzählen* [Between Hamburg and Haiti]. Braunschweig: Bertelsmann Lesering.

Landesmedienzentrum Hamburg, M.F. 1999. *Filmdokumente zur Entwicklung Hamburgs* [Television documents on the development of Hamburg]. Hamburg: Landesmedienzentrum.

Landwehr, Achim. 2008. *Historische Diskursanalyse* [Historical discourse analysis]. Frankfurt am Main: Campus.

Marszolek, Inge, and Yvonne Robel. 2016. The communicative construction of collectivities: An interdisciplinary approach to media history. *Historical Social Research* 41 (1): 328–357.

Massey, Doreen. 2004. Geographies of responsibility. *Human Geography* 86 (1): 5–18.

Meyen, Michael. 1999. Fernsehstuben in der DDR und anderswo [Television parlors/"Fernsehstuben" in the GDR and elsewhere]. Rundfunk und Geschichte 25: 118–126.

Middell, Matthias. 2000. *Kulturtransfer und Vergleich* [Culture transfer and comparison]. Leipzig: Leipziger Universitätsverlag.

Palmowski, Jan. 2009. *Inventing a socialist nation: Heimat and the politics of everyday life in the GDR 1945–1990.* Cambridge: Cambridge University Press.

Paul, Gerhard. 2006. *Visual history. Ein Studienbuch.* Göttingen: Vandenhoeck & Ruprecht.

Rembold, Elfie. 2003. Staatsinteresse, Messegeist und Stadtkultur: Das Beispiel Leipzig [State interest, trade fair spirit and urban culture]. In *Inszenierte Einigkeit: Herrschaftsrepräsentationen in DDR-Städten*, ed. Adelheid von Saldern, 275–353. Stuttgart: Steiner.

Richter, Sigrun. 1993. *Die Volkskorrespondenten-Bewegung der SED-Bezirkspresse: Theorie, Geschichte und Entwicklung einer Kommunikatorfigur* [The movement of folk correspondents of the SED district press]. Frankfurt am Main: Lang.

Rohr, Sylvia. 2011. *Stadtfunk Leipzig: Ein Feature von Sylvia Rohr. Dokumentation* ['Stadtfunk'/Broadcasting Leipzig]. Weimar: Unpublished Masters thesis.

Schildt, Axel. 2012. Großstadt und Massenmedien: Hamburg von den 1950er bis zu den 1980er Jahren' [City and mass media]. In *Stadt und Medien: Vom Mittelalter bis zur Gegenwart*, ed. Clemens Zimmermann, 249–263. Köln: Böhlau.

Schlimper, Jürgen. 1997. *"Natürlich - die Tauchaer Straße!": Beiträge zur Geschichte der "Leipziger Volkszeitung"* [Contributions to the history of the 'Leipziger Volkszeitung']. Leipzig: Rosa-Luxemburg-Stiftung Sachsen.

Schmiechen-Ackermann, Detlef. 1997. *Anpassung, Verweigerung, Widerstand. Soziale Milieus, politische Kultur und der Widerstand gegen den Nationalsozialismus in Deutschland im regionalen Vergleich* [Social milieus, political culture and resistance against the Nazi regime in Germany]. Berlin: Edition Hentrich.

Seegers, Lu. 2001. Hör zu! Eduard Rhein und die Rundfunkprogrammzeitschriften: 1931–1965 [Eduard Rhein and the broadcasting programme guide]. Potsdam: Verlag für Berlin-Brandenburg.

Seegers, Lu. 2015. Hanseaten und das Hanseatische in Diktatur und Demokratie: Politisch-ideologische Zuschreibungen und Praxen [The Hanseatic under dictatorship and democracy]. In *Zeitgeschichte in Hamburg 2014*, ed. Forschungsstelle für Zeitgeschichte in Hamburg, 71–83. Hamburg: Forschungsstelle für Zeitgeschichte.

Stoetzer, Sergej. 2006. Picturing urban identities. In *Negotiating urban conflicts: interaction, space and control*, ed. Helmuth Berking, Sybille Frank, Lars Frers, Martina Löw, Lars Meier, Silke Steets, and Sergej Stoetzer, 177–194. Bielefeld: Transcript.

Stratenschulte, Eckart. D. 2013. Lasst euch nicht verhetzen! Der Lautsprecherkrieg in Berlin [The war of loudspeakers in Berlin]. In *Sound des Jahrhunderts: Geräusche, Töne, Stimmen. 1989 bis heute*, ed. Gerhard Paul and Ralph Schock, 432–435. Bonn: Bundeszentrale für politische Bildung.

Tiews, Alina L. 2014. *Jeden Sonntag um sechs: Das Hamburger "Hafenkonzert" der Norag ist die traditionsreichste Rundfunksendung der Welt* [The 'Hamburger Hafenkonzert' of the Norag is the most rich in tradition broadcasting show in the world]. http://www.hans-bredow-institut.de/de/fgrn/jeden-sonntag-sechs-„hamburger-hafenkonzert"-norag-ist-traditionsreichste-rundfunksendung-welt. Accessed 30 Mar 2017.

von Reeken, Dietmar. 1999. *Kirchen im Umbruch der Moderne. Milieubildungsprozesse im nordwestdeutschen Protestantismus 1849–1914* [Protestant milieus in North-West Germany]. Gütersloh: Gütersloher Verlagshaus.

von Rüden, Peter, and Hans-Ulrich Wagner. 2005. *Die Geschichte des Nordwestdeutschen Rundfunks* [The history of the North-West German broadcasting station], vol. 1. Hamburg: Hoffmann und Campe.

Wagner, Hans-Ulrich. 2008. *Die Geschichte des Nordwestdeutschen Rundfunks* [The history of the North-West German broadcasting station], vol. 2. Hamburg: Hoffmann und Campe.

Welzer, Harald, Sabine Moller, and Karoline Tschuggnall. 2002. *"Opa war kein Nazi": Nationalsozialismus und Holocaust im Familiengedächtnis* [National Socialism and Holocaust in family memory]. Frankfurt am Main: Fischer.

Werner, Michael, and Benedicte Zimmermann. 2006. Beyond comparison: Histoire Croisée and the challenge of reflexivity. *History and Theory* 45: 30–50.

Wierling, Dorothee. 2015. Über Asymmetrien. Ein Kommentar zu Frank Bösch [About asymmetries. A comment on Frank Bösch]. *Zeithistorische Forschungen* 12 (1): 115–123.

8

Collectivities and their Communicative Construction through Media

Thomas N. Friemel and Matthias Bixler

8.1 Introduction

People use media to communicate and thereby create and maintain social relations in two ways. First, media provide technological means to bypass time and space and enable otherwise unconnected individuals to interact. Second, media provide topics for communication. Hence, media are able to fulfil two functions for relationships between individuals and for the collectivities they are part of at the same time: as a technology for and as

T.N. Friemel (✉) · M. Bixler
Institute of Mass Communication and Media Research, University of Zurich, Andreasstrasse 15, 8050 Zurich, Switzerland
e-mail: th.friemel@ipmz.uzh.ch

M. Bixler
e-mail: m.bixler@ipmz.uzh.ch

subject of communication. For decades, these two aspects were separated by two distinct types of media. For example, the telephone can be seen as a traditional medium that provides the technology for *mediated interpersonal communication* and to bypass geographical distance. In contrast to this, the content of newspapers, TV and other *mass media* are typically referred to as important subjects for everyday conversation. Theoretical concepts and empirical research on the social context and social relevance of media use have a long history (Friemel 2013). Based on the general trend towards an increasing relevance of media for our society (Esser and Strömbäck 2014; Lundby 2014), collectivities are affected by mediatization as well (Couldry and Hepp 2017).

The current mediatization might not only be a gradual shift by means of a quantitative increase of media use and media references: we assume that the fundamental change in media environment will lead to a qualitative change of how collectivities are constructed by and through media. For example, the online social networking platforms that have emerged in the past decade have made apparent how numerous and interwoven our personal networks are. They enable us to display activities, preferences and relationships to friends as well as to more distant persons or even strangers in a way which was not possible with any media before. Online media also facilitate an easy sharing of mass media content through computer-mediated interpersonal communication and thereby blur the above-mentioned line between the two kinds of media (i.e. technology and content). Hence, the emergence and pervasiveness of 'new' digital communication technologies will change the way people connect and communicate by various means. Owing to the expected fundamental change of how social collectivities are constructed, this trend can be referred to as *deep mediatization* (cf. Chap. 2).

With respect to our subject of collectivities, we regard the following trends in the changing media environment as the most important: (1) *Connectivity*. Digital communication technologies such as social network services (SNS) and instant messengers (IM) empower people to connect with a vast number of others and relax the boundedness of time and space for social interaction. A consequence of this trend is that social borders are blurring and personal networks may become more diverse (Erickson 2003; Gruzd et al. 2011). (2) *Omnipresence*. The development of Internet-enabled mobile devices to make these technologies available on the go. For many people, this means they have become accessible almost anywhere and at any time (van Eimeren 2013). At the same time, people permanently create digital traces that may be tracked by various actors and create new possibilities for intended but also unintended control. Managing this omnipresence is likely to become a major challenge for individuals as well as collectivities. (3) *Differentiation.* Omnipresent connectivity is not limited to a single medium but is diversified across several communication technologies (DIVSI 2014). At the same time, the number of subjects to communicate on vastly increases owing to the large number of digital media outlets (e.g. special interest media) and the abundance of user-generated content. It is likely that beside algorithmic content selection the selection by collectivities will become of increasing importance (Friemel 2013). (4) *Datafication.* The possibility to embed (mass) media content in computer-mediated interpersonal communication and the large amount of user-generated data leads to new forms of communication that let previously distinct media types converge (Jensen 2010), but also set the ground for entirely new ways in which media are used. All four trends are likely to alter the way people communicate, establish relationships, collectivities and social capital.

In order to track these trends and study the consequences of deep mediatization of collectivities, we develop the theoretical concept of networked media collectivities and an empirical research design based on social network analysis. The goal of this contribution is to introduce the theoretical concept and the respective research design and to provide an initial measure to enable future comparisons. The next two sections discuss the literature related to this endeavour and define the most important terms. Section 8.2 focuses on the concept of networked media collectivities and how these are constructed. This sets the ground for the discussion of how the changing media environment has an impact on social capital emerging from the collectivities (Sect. 8.3). Based on this literature review and theoretical reasoning, five research questions are derived in Sect. 8.4. Section 8.5 explains the research design of our study and introduces the chosen sample and methods. The results are presented and discussed in two subsequent sections. In Sect. 8.6 relevant descriptives for media use and communication about media content are discussed, and Sect. 8.7 provides insight into the network perspective of media-related communication. Section 8.8 summarizes our findings.

8.2 Mediatized Construction of Collectivities

Drawing on a definition proposed by Couldry and Hepp, we use the term *collectivity* to describe a 'figuration of individuals that share a certain meaningful belonging that provides a basis for action- and orientation-in-common' (Couldry and Hepp 2017: 168). They further distinguish between *media-based collectivities* and *mediatized collectivities*. The first are only made possible by the use of media technologies. The latter are able to exist without the use of media in principle, but are substantially shaped by media-related communication (Couldry and Hepp 2017: 170). Purely media-based and purely mediatized collectivities can be regarded as two theoretical poles of a continuum encompassing the phenomenon of collectivism as defined above. In reality, they are most likely to be encountered as hybrids or in transition from one type to the other.

The research presented in this chapter deals with collectivities in which both media and strong social relationships play a crucial role for their members. Therefore we put a special focus on the actor constellations that emerge from media-related communication on the one hand and friendship on the other. To be able to identify several actor constellations and how they are interrelated with media use as well as with each other, we apply a social network approach. According to Lin, we can define a collectivity as 'a social network with members as actors' (Lin 2008: 62), which includes the necessity that the actors are at least partially directly linked to each other. The loosest link hereby is the possibility to perceive others and their actions. More obvious links would be any form of direct interaction, such as conversations. The relevance of these direct links can be explained by the criteria Baym lists for online communities and networked collectivism. In addition to the shared practice by means of using a specific medium, this includes social norms (Baym 2015), since social norms require at least a minimal level of perception of others. Hence, direct links become a necessary prerequisite for what we call collectivities.

In a broad understanding, any audience could be seen as a *media-based collectivity* since it has an orientation towards the respective media content in common (Grunig and Stamm 1973: 567). However, to emphasize the aspect of direct orientation to each other and respective actions, we subsequently use the term of *networked media collectivities*. Thus, these are defined as networked sets of actors with shared communicative practices (e.g. a strong orientation towards specific *media contents* and/or specific *media technologies*). Examples are a group of people who discuss TV series, football fans who gather to watch a match or avid users of a micro-blogging service commenting on an ongoing political discussion. In all three instances, media play a constitutive role for the communicative construction of a collectivity, either as conversation topics, as means of communication or both. Networked media collectivities can be densely knit or even be congruent to families, groups of friends, groups of work colleagues or other kinds of collectivities. However, they can also transcend these or may even construct detached collectivities and thereby lead to blurring of traditional social borders. Networked media collectivities can differ in size from small social groups to whole societies that follow a large media event and interact with reference to it, and stability (short and long lasting) which influences their visibility/observability. In cases of frequent and direct interaction, members of networked media collectivities may develop a strong identification with group membership. However, especially in ephemeral and larger collectivities, their 'members' may feel to be part of a collectivity, but may not even be aware of its exact boundaries and composition. The networks formed by those collectivities rapidly exceed the point where any actor can have a complete overview over their structure or identify their boundaries. With our concept of collectivities and our network analytic approach we draw also on Elias's idea of *figurations* that conceptualizes school classes, families, occupational groups or any other social aggregate as networks of individuals that are 'linked with each other in the most diverse ways' (1978: 15).

With respect to *'new' media as communication technologies*, it is of great interest to find out how digital media affect current media and non-mediated communication. Several studies argue that there still is a strong relationship between face-to-face and online communication. Caughlin and Sharabi (2013) show that there is a positive correlation between the frequency of online and face-to-face communication. That is to say that online communication is most frequent with those persons we communicate with in person as well. The strong overlap of computer-mediated and face-to-face communication networks can at least partially be explained by the fact that new communication technologies are diffusing within the pre-existing social structures that are represented by face-to-face communication (Baym et al. 2004; Subrahmanyam et al.

2008; Neuberger 2011; Reich et al. 2012; van Zalk et al. 2014). Offline relationships may not only be relevant for the adoption of new communication technologies. Latent tie theory assumes that offline relationships are also crucial for the maintenance of online communication (Haythornthwaite 2002, 2005). Digital communication technologies make it very low cost to socialize (van Zalk et al. 2014), to maintain or to reactivate old relationships (Ramirez and Bryant 2014), and some media seem to be typical for different social groups (Kim et al. 2007). But normally they remain weak ties (Granovetter 1973; Baym and Ledbetter 2009) that dissolve when the communication technologies lapse (Haythornthwaite 2005).

The relevance of *media content as an object for everyday interpersonal communication* is documented in various empirical studies. In fact, a substantial proportion of everyday conversations is related to mass media content (Friemel 2013; Keppler 2014; Weber 2015). For Germany, Kepplinger and Martin (1986) found in their observational study that 77% of all conversations in public places, bars and restaurants, at universities and in homes referred to media content. Since then, it has been pointed out that conversation topics have become more heterogeneous (differentiated) and media themselves have become more important as a conversation topic (Gehrau and Goertz 2010). Moreover, conversations about media content are able to fulfil important social functions (Friemel 2013). Media provide a constant source of conversation topics. Mass media content especially has the potential to serve as a ground of common knowledge from which conversations can arise (DiMaggio 1987; Friemel 2009). This can be a means to define inner structures and boundaries of collectivities. To display a shared preference for specific media content, to give an example, is one of several possibilities to express a sense of belonging and distinction from others (Hepp 1998). It has been shown that conversations surrounding mass media content can be an instrument to constitute hierarchy in relationships (Lull 1980). On a more general level, media content can also provide a starting point for the negotiation of norms and values in groups (Hurrelmann 1989) and in this way serve as one foundation for the construction of collectivities (Hepp et al. 2014). Conversations surrounding media content can thus be seen both as a means to facilitate the construction of media-based collectivities as well as a factor that mediatizes collectivities.

8.3 The Impact of Changing Media Environment on Social Capital

Collectivities are important for their members as they provide access to various forms of resources and support. This is generally referred to as the concept of *social capital*, which is closely related to social network theory (Bourdieu 1983; Coleman 1988). Social capital can be defined as the resources that an actor is able to access or profit from because of his or her embeddedness in a social network (Lin 2001; Esser 2008). Well-known studies have shown the importance of social relationships for access to information when looking for a new job (Granovetter 1973; Marsden and Gorman 2001). However, the concept of social capital is not limited to the perspective of single actors. A whole collectivity can be researched as a social network to assess the resources brought to bear by its members as *internal social capital* (Lin 2008: 62f.). Other forms of a collectivity's social capital have been referred to as *system capital*. They are not directly accessed by actors through specific relationships, but can be seen as a feature of a specific collectivity itself. Examples range from the development of a climate of trust, to the adherence to and reinforcement of social norms, and the emergence of morality among a defined set of actors (Coleman 1988; Esser 2008).

In analogy to the general notion of mediatization and the idea of mediatized collectivities, we can assume that networked media collectivities are likely to become more prevalent in various types of social settings. In a nutshell, communication technologies make new means available to interconnect, and diversified media contents provide more topics for communication (the assumed consequences of optionality, social contingency and new chances for participation). Both play a crucial role in the establishment and maintenance of collectivities. The trends of a changing media environment mentioned in the introduction are assumed to affect the development and maintenance of various forms of collectivities and their social capital. At a first glance, the trend of *differentiation* of media as contents and technologies might lead to an erosion of traditional social structures. It has been argued that both weaken boundaries of families, groups or even whole societies. In a widely discussed work, Robert Putnam argued that the increase in consumption of mass media—particularly watching TV—led to a dramatic decline in various forms of civic engagement in US society (Putnam 2000). His empirical data show strong negative correlations between screen hours and attending public meetings, writing letters to Congress and being member or officer in a local organization. Similar effects are found for the relevance of TV for entertainment. Dependent on the relevance of TV as the primary form of entertainment, he found lower values for volunteering, writing letters to friends and relatives, attending club meetings, going to church and working on community projects. Putnam admits that the correlations reported cannot answer the question regarding the causal direction between TV use and the various forms of civic engagement. Nevertheless, based on other research such as the natural experiment on television reception in three Canadian communities in the 1970s (MacBeth 1986), he argues that the causal direction is likely to be directed from TV use towards civic and social life. Hence, according to Putnam, an increase of media use (e.g. TV), and especially the use of entertaining content (versus news and information) has a negative effect on various forms of collectivities.

The negative trend towards social isolation in the USA was supported by findings from the General Social Survey (GSS). McPherson and colleagues found that the core networks of US citizens decreased by about a third between 1985 and 2004, while the number of social isolates rose substantially (McPherson et al. 2006). This publication had a strong impact and is widely discussed in academia owing to its strong empirical foundation, since it is based on GSS data. However, subsequent methodological tests have revealed that the decrease is likely to be an effect of questionnaire design that made people name fewer persons (Marsden 2013) and an interviewer effect (Paik and Sanchagrin 2013). Furthermore, the finding of a decline is corroborated by almost no other evidence. Hence, no general decline in socializing since the 1970s can be found, apart from the downward trend in socializing with neighbours (Fischer 2011; Marsden and Srivastava 2012).

With a reference to technologies for interpersonal communication, Manuel Castells predicted fundamental changes for the organization of groups, social structures and societies as a whole (Castells 1996). Moreover, other authors assume that traditional groups and their structures are changing through the influence of the Internet. Boyd (2006) argues that on social networking sites every person is embedded in their very own egocentric network and the context of every person is different and only partially publicly visible. Wellman et al. describe a turn towards *networked individualism* which is driven by the Internet. It is described as a change from densely knit groups to sparsely knit networks (2003).

In contrast to the negative connotation of Putnam's 'bowling alone', Rainie and Wellman (2012) come to a rather positive interpretation. They argue that nowadays an individual's main resource for social capital is to be found in each individual's personal relationships, which provide access to a wider range of contacts and thus more diverse resources. They therefore propose the term *networked individualism* as 'the new social operating system'.

8.4 Research Questions

Summarizing the previous paragraphs, we are facing theoretical and empirical arguments which suggest either a decay, a transformation or a renaissance of social patterns and collectivism in a networked society (Castells 1996, 2013; van Dijk 2006). The divergent interpretations can partly be explained by the different foci of the respective studies. While some offline activities seem to vanish, focusing on these leads to pessimistic conclusions. On the other hand, the Internet makes new forms of social support and civic engagement possible that draw a more positive picture of the societal changes related to the changing media environment. Therefore, the only valid approach to studying collectivities in a changing media environment is to study multiple relations simultaneously. Methodologically speaking, we have to collect multiplex network data (Wasserman and Faust 1994) in which multiple relations are taken into account and can be analyzed in relation to each other. In our case, these multiple relations can be various types of media technologies and different media content that people interact with (through these different media technologies). However, pushed to its extreme, this would result in a research design with an immense number of dimensions (number of media content *x* number of communication technologies *x* number of communication partners *x* types of social support). We therefore decided to focus on the question of *how communication about different media content is linked with friendship ties.* Hence, differences in communication technologies are not considered and friendship is used as a proxy for social capital. For the empirical analysis of these hard-to-grasp collectivities, we investigate *networked media collectivities among adolescents* for two reasons: First, adolescents are known to have a more focused social network among their peers than is the case for other cohorts. For younger children, their parents are still a much more important point of reference. Adults are often simultaneously embedded in different social settings such as family, friends and workplace. Second, adolescents are usually among the early adopters when it comes to new communication technologies and services.

To investigate the figurations of networked media collectivities empiri cally, we have to address the communicative practices, the frames of relevance and the constellation of actors (Hepp and Hasebrink 2014). Hence, our first research question is *RQ1: What are the communicative practices of today's adolescents?* Hereby, the communicative practices are operationalized as the frequency of use and the frequency of interpersonal communication about different mass media contents which are important to adolescents. This includes the question whether there is still enough shared interest in specific content even though media content has diversified.

Based on the results of these two kinds of communicative practices, we proceed to analyze the relationship between the two. With a reference to the concept of figuration, the second research question gives an insight into the frames of relevance. It is about the importance of different media content, to be able to communicate about them and thereby construct a networked media collectivity. *RQ2: Are frequencies of mass media use and interpersonal communication about these contents correlated with each other?*

The remaining constitutive feature of a communicative figuration is its actor constellation. This includes both the actors as well as the ties between them. In contrast to most of the previous research, we are not only interested to find out the type of persons the adolescents talk to (e.g. peers versus parents versus siblings versus teachers). Since we focus on the figurations among adolescents we are able to zoom into the actor constellation and reveal the actual network structure among all persons participating in our study. From the literature review in Sect. 8.2, it can be concluded that communication about media content provides a basis for stronger forms of social relationships. In Sect. 8.3, it was pointed out that they are the prerequisite for access to social capital. With our multiplex approach, we are able to disentangle the structural patterns of several overlapping collectivities before we assess their individual relevance for friendship in a later step. Our third research question therefore is *RQ3: How frequently and within what actor constellation do people communicate about different media?*

In addition to the individual analysis of communication about different media, we are interested in the relationship between these different networks of media use and media-related communication. How similar are the patterns of different actor constellations? Phrased in methodological terms, *RQ4: What is the structural correlation of different communication networks?*

Finally, we turn to the link between media use and social capital. To carve out the relationship between media use, media-related communication and friendship ties we include the friendship network in the same analysis as above. Again in methodological terms, *RQ5: What is the structural correlation between communication networks and friendship networks?*

Answering these five research questions allows us to empirically describe networked media collectivities with respect to different features that are constitutive for communicative figurations. Furthermore, we are able to answer the question concerning the relationship between networked media collectivities and access to social capital. Finally, this provides a good starting point to reflect on the potential consequences of deep mediatization for collectivities and our society.

8.5 Sample and Methods

The first aim of the present study is to describe the social domain of networked media collectivities as communicative figurations. Hence, it is necessary to extend the scope beyond that of individual attributes and take the actor constellations, communicative practices and frames of relevance into account that constitute these figurations. In order to do so, we apply a social network approach. Social network analysis is especially suitable to detect actor constellations and allows us to quantify how media collectivities coexist and interfere with each other.

The data were collected in three middle schools in a major German city (Bremen). As social network structures are of particular interest here, we sampled four grades in which all students were invited to participate in our survey. This includes two 10th grades as well as one 11th and one 12th grade, respectively. The students and their parents were informed about the study in advance by letter and asked for written consent to participate. In total 335 students between 15 and 21 years of age participated in the survey (53.2% female, $M_{AGE} = 17.1$, $SE_{AGE} = 0.53$). Data collection took place during class hours in the computer labs of the respective schools on a class-by-class basis. The students answered an online questionnaire (CASI) while a member of the project team was present.

The questionnaire consisted of questions regarding ownership and use of several technological media devices, use of specific media content such as TV programmes, YouTube channels and video games, and how often students engage in interpersonal communication about these contents. To measure social network structures several sociometric questions, so-called name generator questions, were asked. Name generator questions ask for other persons with whom a respondent is in a certain type of relationship. In this study, we gathered data on friendship ties and on interpersonal communication about TV programmes, YouTube channels and video games. These media were selected because they are among the most important for this age group with respect to usage and interpersonal communication. To get a comprehensive overview of the pattern of networked media collectivities, we allowed for cross-class nominations. Thus, for the social network analyses we have four different structures at hand for each school grade, that is to say the friendship network and three communication networks, one for each type of media content.

To answer research question RQ1, we applied frequency analyzes for six media types which are of special relevance for adolescents and the communication about these media. For RQ2, bivariate correlations between frequency of media use and conversation on the level of the students were calculated. Sociograms as a specific kind of visualization of social networks were used to answer RQ3 regarding actor constellations. Finally, to answer RQ4 and RQ5 regarding the structural correlation of communication networks and the friendship network, we performed Quadratic Assignment Procedure (QAP), which provides correlation statistics for social networks (Krackhardt 1987). The QAP can be used as a stochastical method to test whether two networks are significantly correlated, that is to say, for example, whether two students who talk about what they have seen on YouTube also tend to be friends or whether two students who talk about TV programmes also talk about video games, and so on.

8.6 Media Use and Communication About Media Content

To be able to identify networked media collectivities as defined above, it is necessary to evaluate the relevance of several media in our sample. *RQ1 addresses the communicative practices by means of frequencies of*

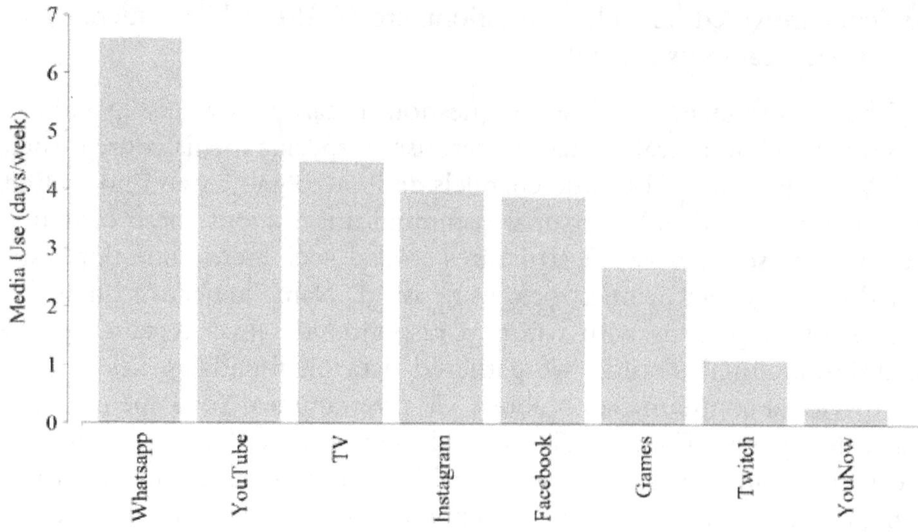

Fig. 8.1 Most frequently used media (days/week)

media use by adolescents. Figure 8.1 shows on how many days per week eight electronic media are used by the adolescents.

The media included were the most used screen-based media at the time of our survey. The set consists of one instant messenger service, several social media platforms and video sharing platforms as well as linear TV and video games. Results show that the instant messenger service Whatsapp was used most frequently of all media technologies. Most of our respondents reported using it every day or almost every day of a normal week ($M = 6.6$, SE = 0.08). When the survey was conducted, the installation of this application was not yet supported on desktop PCs, so a smartphone was necessary to use the service: 99.4% of our respondents indicated that they owned a mobile phone, 97.9% of whom owned a smartphone. Only two respondents out of four school grades reported that they did not own any kind of mobile phone. However, one of them explained in an open-ended question that his smartphone had been stolen only recently before the survey. These numbers are almost exactly in line with other representative studies in Germany (Feierabend et al. 2015).

In our sample, the video sharing platform YouTube was used slightly more often ($M = 4.7$, SE = 0.12) than linear TV ($M = 4.5$, SE = 0.14). Among social network sites, the picture and video sharing platform

Instagram ($M = 4.0$, SE = 0.17) was slightly more frequently used than Facebook ($M = 3.9$, SE = 0.16). Our respondents indicated to play video games on 2.7 days per week on average (SE = 0.15). Further, the video streaming platforms Twitch ($M = 1.1$, SE = 0.14) and YouNow ($M = 0.3$, SE = 0.08) were used least often.

According to our definition of networked media collectivities, to speak of a collectivity it is not sufficient that the students use the same media. Our understanding requires a direct link among the actors. Only in collectivities in which actors can act and react upon each other are meanings and opinions negotiated and diffusion of information take place. Hence, a necessary requirement for these processes is that media content is the subject of interpersonal communication. To assess the importance of media content in interpersonal communication, we asked our respondents to indicate how frequently they talk about their most-used media on a five point scale. We also included 'school exams' as a conversation topic to have a point of reference for other important everyday matters. Figure 8.2 shows the results. School exams were the topic that was most frequently discussed at the time of our survey ($M = 3.6$, SE = 0.05). Almost as frequent was communication about content sent via the instant messenger service Whatsapp ($M = 3.5$, SE = 0.07). Despite some differences in frequency of use, all other types of media content were about equally often the

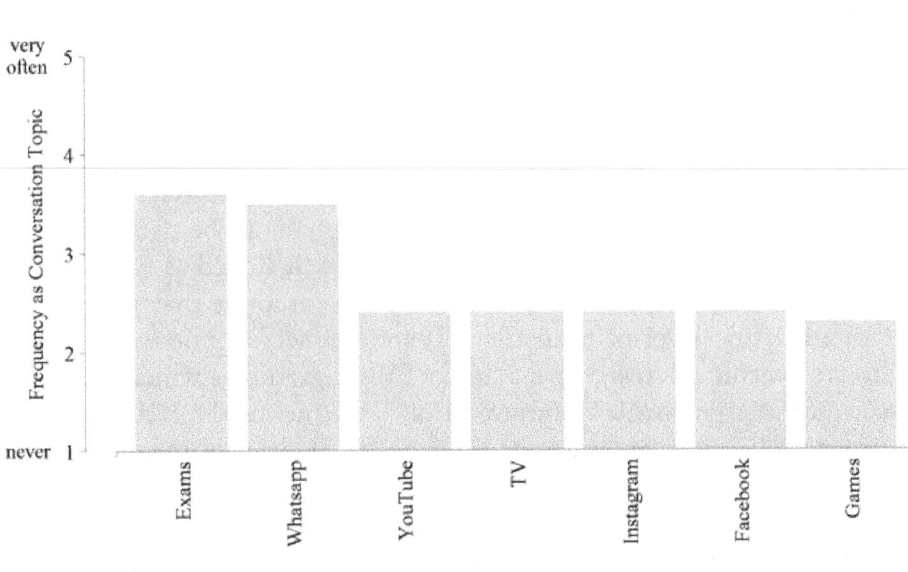

Fig. 8.2 Most frequent conversation topics

subject of interpersonal communication (YouTube: $M = 2.4$, SE = 0.06, TV: $M = 2.4$, SE = 0.06, Instagram: $M = 2.4$, SE = 0.08, Facebook: $M = 2.4$, SE = 0.07, Video games: $M = 2.3$, SE = 0.08). These data show that despite the general trend towards a diversified media content, people still have enough in common to be able to talk about a topic. Whether this is because they have used the same content or another function of interpersonal communication about mass media content (Friemel 2013) is of relevance cannot be answered by this data.

A comparison between the frequencies of media use and the frequencies of media-related interpersonal communication for each of the media shows that Whatsapp stands out as a communication technology as well as a source for conversation topics. All other media differ mainly in frequency of use, but not in their ability to provide conversation topics. Nevertheless, the communicative practices regarding all included media seem to meet our criteria to be constitutive for a communicative figuration of networked media collectivities. Hence, it will be of interest to further characterize these figurations. We will do so by answering the next three research questions (RQ2–RQ4).

RQ2 goes a step further by addressing the *correlation between media use and communication about media content.* As can be expected, bivariate correlation (Table 8.1) shows that the frequencies of use and the frequencies of media-related communication are positively correlated with substantial effect sizes for each media type (grey-coloured cells). The strongest correlation is found for games. The value of $r = 0.78$ means that the frequency of gaming and game-related communication is very strongly correlated. The more someone plays computer games the more this person also talks about it (and vice versa). At the same time, TV use and TV-related communication are only moderately correlated. Hence, while TV is among the most frequently used media to be used, interpersonal communication on the topic is not so closely linked as for the other media types. However, it has to be taken into account that this finding is limited to the level of frequency. Therefore, we cannot rule out that there are specific genres or even single TV programmes which are closer linked to interpersonal communication (Friemel 2012, 2015). With respect to RQ2, we can conclude that the frequencies of mass media use and interpersonal communication about these contents are indeed correlated with each other, and for most media this correlation is rather strong. Almost all of the other parameters in the top right quadrant of Table 8.1 are non-significant or negatively correlated. Hence, beside the

Table 8.1 Correlation matrix for media use and media-related communication

	Media use					*Media-related communication*					
	YT	*FB*	*WA*	*I*	*G*	*TV-C*	*YT-C*	*FB-C*	*WA-C*	*I-C*	*G-C*
TV	−0.251*	−0.103	0.124*	0.111	−0.096	0.302**	−0.315**	0.007	0.138	0.084	−0.162
YouTube	-	0.167	0.011	0.038	0.188	−0.101	0.532**	0.055	−0.116	−0.037	0.208
Facebook		-	0.260*	0.139	0.191	−0.019	0.063	0.587**	0.048	0.042	0.183
Whatsapp			-	0.328**	−0.184	0.172	−0.248*	0.153	0.536**	0.210	−0.233*
Instagram				-	−0.142	0.213	0.020	0.130	0.420**	0.661**	−0.125
Games					-	−0.002	0.243*	0.077	−0.254*	−0.152	0.777**
TV-C						-	0.036	0.264*	0.337**	0.480**	0.026
YT-C							-	0.241*	−0.021	0.146	0.468**
FB-C								-	0.380**	0.285*	0.216
WA-C									-	0.581**	−0.075
I-C										-	−0.070

*$p < .05$
**$p < .01$

correlation between the frequencies of Instagram use and Whatsapp-related communication, the communicative practices of the various media seem to be independent from one another.

The top left quadrant of the matrix reveals patterns of media use by means of indicating whether the frequency of use is correlated with the use of other media types. It is found that only instant messenger and social media services—which are mainly designed as means for interpersonal communication—can be regarded as a bundle of media that are used in combination and thereby form a common media repertoire (Hasebrink and Domeyer 2012). In addition, we find also negative relations between frequencies of media use. Results show that TV and YouTube tend to be negatively associated, which can be interpreted as an indicator for substitution of one by the other.

Likewise, we can also focus on how communication about various media is related (bottom right quadrant). There are several media which seem to be often talked about by the same people, but also some that seem to be mutually exclusive. Again, Facebook, Whatsapp and Instagram form a bundle of conversation topics. For YouTube-related communication, positive correlations are found for Facebook and game-related communication. Both are highly plausible, since a substantial share of the most popular YouTube channels are about gaming and Facebook is a common platform to share YouTube videos.

Besides answering RQ2 with a clear yes (correlations between media use and communication about these media), the data reveal a complex constellation of communicative practices. While the correlation values reported here provide an overall indicator for communicative practices, they neglect the actor constellation in which these practices take place. We now turn to social network analytic approaches to identify networked media collectivities.

8.7 Networks of Media-Related Communication

In this section we look at actor constellations emerging from communication about media content to identify networked media collectivities and thus answer RQ3 (How frequent and within what actor constellation do people communicate about different media?). In doing so, we compare structural patterns for different media types as well as with the underlying actor constellation of the friendship network. This allow us to answer in a next step RQ4 and RQ5 by testing to which extent networked media collectivities emerge across different media types and whether they are linked to social capital (RQ4 and RQ5).

Table 8.2 Network descriptives by school grade

	School grade A (10th)			*School grade B (10th)*			*School grade C (11th)*			*School grade D (12th)*		
	D (%)	*M*	*SE*	*D (%)*	*M*	*SE*	*D (%)*	*M*	*SE*	*D (%)*	*M*	*SE*
Friendship	5.1	4.10	0.33	6.7	5.89	0.34	4.2	4.74	0.28	4.2	5.54	0.30
TV communication	1.7	1.39	0.17	1.9	1.67	0.15	1.4	1.65	0.14	1.4	1.89	0.17
YouTube communication	1.6	1.26	0.16	1.7	1.53	0.18	0.3	1.40	0.13	1.2	0.41	0.08
Video game communication	1.2	1.00	0.16	1.8	1.56	0.23	0.7	1.08	0.17	0.9	0.97	0.14

Since networked media collectivities require direct ties among the actors, we analyze the four grades' levels as separate actor constellations. In each grade level, three communication networks and a friendship network were collected (see Sect. 8.5). Table 8.2 gives the network density and the mean number of ties for each network from each school grade. The school grades are in ascending order and labelled A, B, C and D. Network density (*D*) is defined as the proportion of existing ties in a network in relation to the maximum number of possible ties. The friendship network of school grade B, for example, has a density of 6.7%, which means that almost 7% of all possible friendship ties were present at the time of the survey. Given the size of the networks (89–132 students per grade level), this is a reasonable value. In addition, the average number of ties per actor for each of the networks is given (*M*) as well as corresponding standard errors (SE).

Results show that in all four grade levels the density of the friendship networks is substantially higher than for the communication networks. In fact, it is at least three times the density of each of the communication networks in the same school grade. Comparing the three communication networks over all grade levels, it can be seen that the communication networks on TV content have the highest density. This might surprise since the frequency in which students talk about the three media (Fig. 8.2) is almost equal. Hence, our network analytic measures provide a more granular insight that is not possible based on a frequency scale. An alternative explanation could be that communication about YouTube and video games is less bound to the school context than communication about TV.

Sociograms enable us to *assess how frequently and within what actor con stellation people communicate about different media* (RQ3). Figures 8.3, 8.4, 8.5, 8.6 show the sociograms of all four networks from school grade

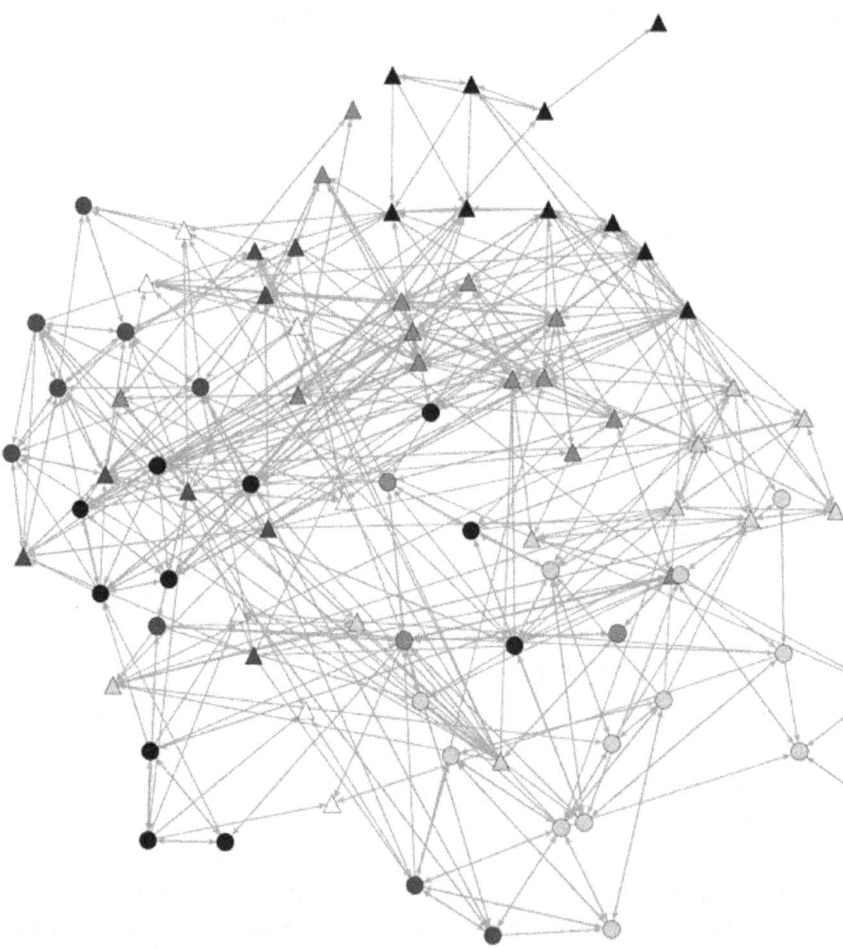

Fig. 8.3 School grade B friendship. *Triangles* male; *circle* female; *greyscale* class membership; *tie* friendship nomination

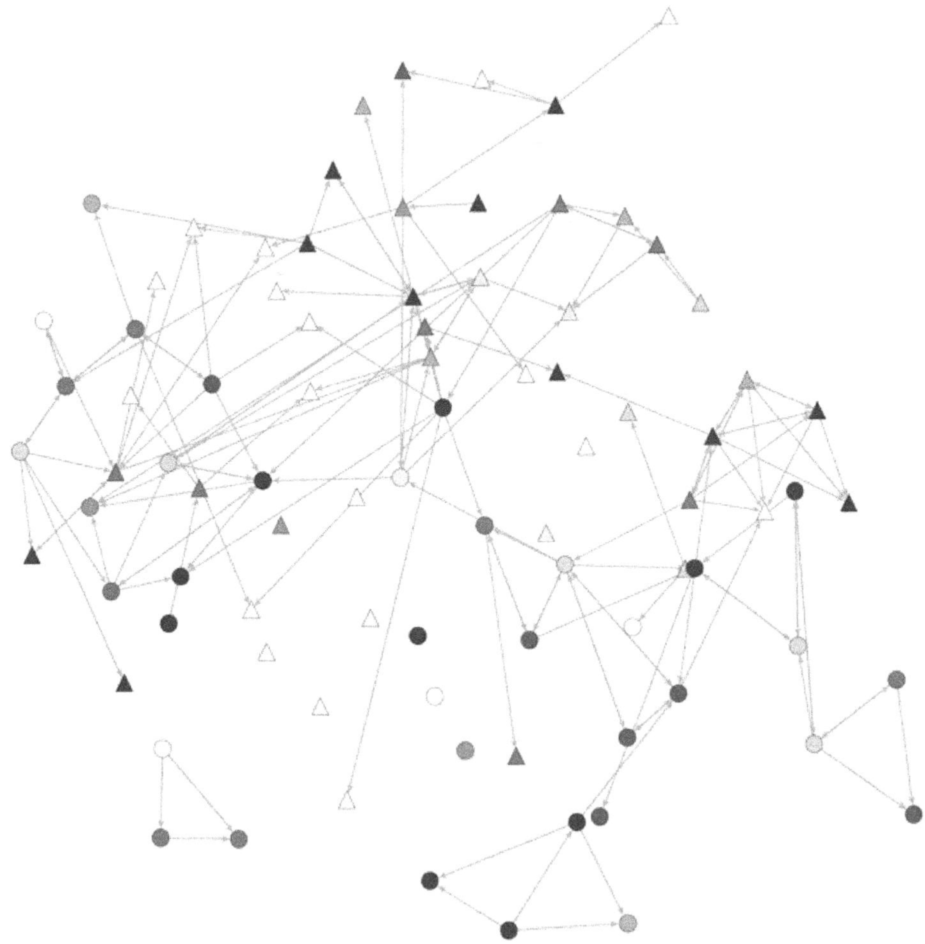

Fig. 8.4 School grade B TV communication. *Triangles* male; *circle* female; *greyscale* intensity frequency of TV use; *tie* interpersonal communication about TV

B. Each node represents one student, whereas triangles stand for male students and circles for female students. An edge indicates a tie between two students (i.e. friendship or conversation tie). The positioning of the nodes is fixed over all visualizations to facilitate comparison. Figure 8.3 shows the friendship network for school grade B. Classroom membership is indicated by different shades of grey. The way they are distributed over the graph suggests that a substantial proportion of friendship ties occur within classrooms, but there is also a considerable amount of cross-class nominations. Hence, this supports the chosen research design that was not bound to

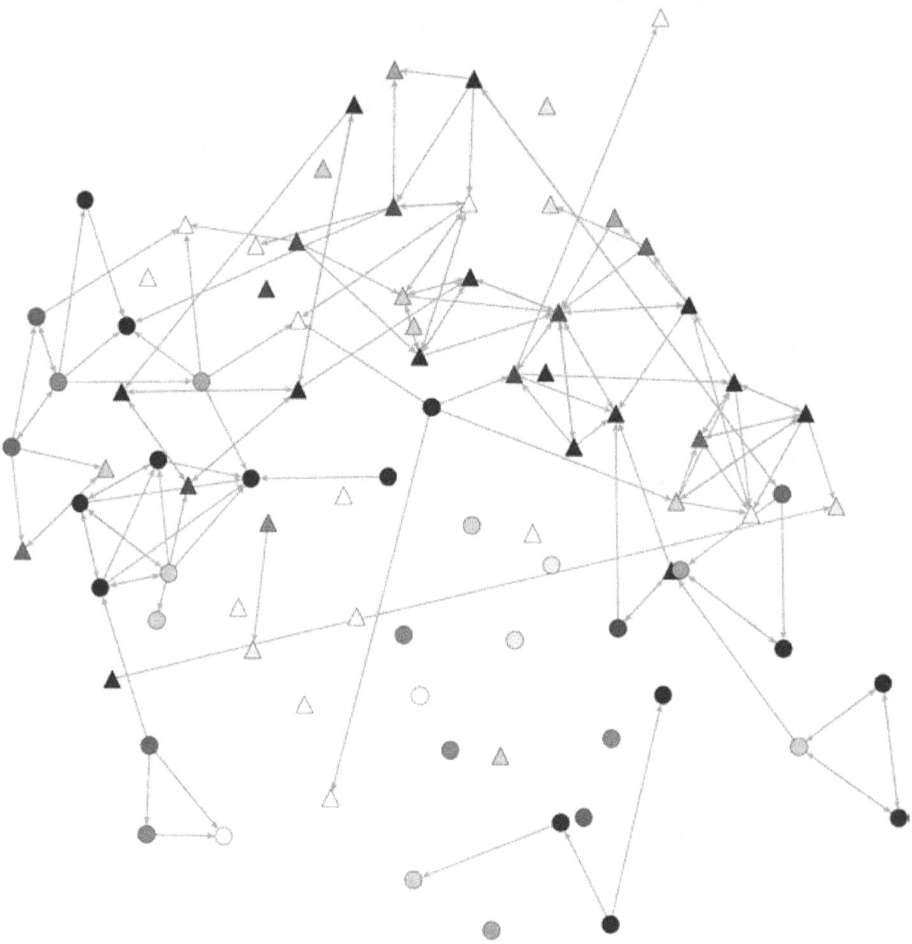

Fig. 8.5 School grade B YouTube communication. *Triangles* male; *circle* female; *greyscale* intensity frequency of YouTube use; *tie* interpersonal communication about YouTube

classrooms but included entire grade levels (Friemel and Knecht 2009). Denser parts of the network suggest the existence of cliques of friends. Figures 8.4, 8.5, 8.6 show the respective networks for communication about TV, YouTube and video games. In these networks, the intensity of the greyscale indicates the frequency of use of the medium in question; for example, the darker a node in Fig. 8.4 the more frequently that person watches TV. A visual exploration of each of these communication networks supports the results from correlation analysis above (cf. Table 8.2). In all three networks, darker coloured nodes tend to be linked by more

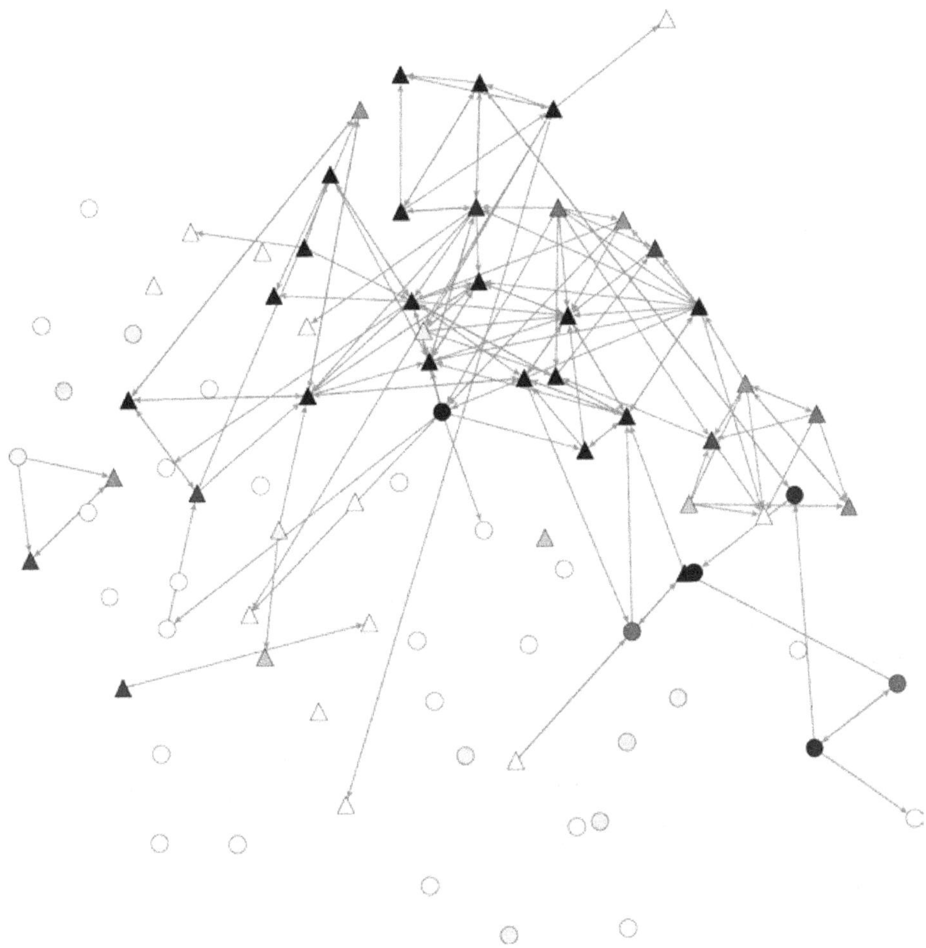

Fig. 8.6 School grade B gaming communication. *Triangles* male; *circle* female; *greyscale* intensity frequency of video game use; *tie* interpersonal communication about video games

ties to other nodes. Light-coloured nodes tend to be weakly connected or even isolated from the rest of the network. This is most striking in Figs. 8.5 (YouTube communication) and 8.6 (video game communication). Furthermore, the clustering of ties in certain parts of the communication networks and their absence in others indicates that communication about media content often takes place among groups of friends. Finally, some regions of the graphs show similar actor constellations for two or more media types, resulting in multiplex relationships in collectivities.

Table 8.3 QAP correlations by school grade

School grade A	*TV-C*	*YT-C*	*G-C*	*Multiplex communication*
Friendship	0.373***	0.456***	0.459***	0.576***
TV communication	-	0.369***	0.606***	
YouTube communication		-	0.464***	
Games communication			-	
School grade B	*TV*	*YT*	*G*	*Multiplex communication*
Friendship	0.354***	0.396***	0.429***	0.508***
TV communication	-	0.371***	0.515***	
YouTube communication		-	0.464***	
Games communication			-	
School grade C	*TV*	*YT*	*G*	*Multiplex communication*
Friendship	0.327***	0.513***	0.469***	0.580***
TV communication	-	0.267***	0.411***	
YouTube communication		-	0.505***	
Games communication			-	
School grade D	*TV*	*YT*	*G*	*Multiplex communication*
Friendship	0.320***	0.491***	0.240***	0.541***
TV communication	-	0.294***	0.212***	
YouTube communication		-	0.253***	
Games communication			-	

***$p < 0.001$

Similar patterns can be found for grade levels A, C and D that are not visualized here. With respect to RQ3, we can conclude that networked media collectivities show the same general pattern as are found for other media-related social networks (Friemel 2012, 2015; Shoham et al. 2012; Steglich et al. 2006). First, media use serves as a resource to create and maintain social ties. Second, this leads to a pattern of network auto-correlation in which actors of similar media use tend to be stronger linked than other actors.

RQ4 *regarding the structural correlation of different communication networks* can be answered by computing correlation coefficients and estimated significance values with QAP. Table 8.3 shows the results for these correlations between all networks within each school grade. They can be interpreted in the same ways as the bivariate correlations in Table 8.1. For all school grades, we find positive and significant correlations between all networks and RQ4 can be answered with a clear yes (there is substantial structural correlation). However, effect sizes are varying. Except for school grade D, they seem to follow a certain pattern, in which the correlation between the TV and YouTube network is the lowest of all communication networks. For example the networks regarding

TV and video games are more similar than the TV and YouTube networks. Even though this finding might be surprising at first, this is consistent with the findings reported in Table 8.1 (negative correlation between YouTube and TV use and positive correlation between YouTube and game-related communication). Only in school grade D are correlations in general rather weak. All differences between the correlation coefficients are significant at the 1% level. In sum, we can conclude that networked media collectivities are transcending different media types by ascertaining that actor constellations are somewhat similar across TV, YouTube and game-related interpersonal communication.

Finally, we turn to RQ5 to answer *whether there is a structural correlation between communication and friendship networks*. This is of relevance since friendship ties are an important source for various kinds of support and thus are a proxy for the social capital of and within collectivities. The analytic approach of calculating QAP correlations is the same as for RQ4. Again, we find positive and highly significant correlations between each of the media-related communication networks and the friendship network. All school grades but school grade D follow a similar pattern, in that communication about TV content shows the lowest overlap with the friendship network. In addition, we calculated the overlap of the friendship network with the multiplex network of all three media-related communication. Here, even higher correlations are found than for the individual communication networks, indicating that the friendship network is most similar with a multiplex operationalization of networked media collectivities. This supports our theoretical and empirical approach that builds on the idea of a figuration as a combination of multiple networks of interpersonal communication, friendship and media use.

8.8 Current Findings and Future Research on Networked Media Collectivities

We started our contribution with a two-sided perspective of how media are related to the communicative construction of collectivities. First, they serve as technologies to bypass time and space. Second, media provide content for various forms of interpersonal communication. Based on this distinction and the literature on media use in social contexts, we subsequently developed the concept of networked media collectivities. These are defined as networked sets of actors with shared communicative practices. We furthermore emphasized the necessity of direct links between the individuals, since the concept otherwise would be a synonym for the audience of media content or all users of a media technology. The idea of networked media collectivities is linked to the literature on social capital. We therefore summarized the theoretically assumed and empirically identified impact of a changing media environment on social capital. In sum, this includes both arguments for an increase of social capital, as well as a decline. However, the unidirectional perspective of how a changing media environment influences social structures is short sighted in that it is rather a mutual dependency. It is likely that the social context also has an influence on media use and media-related communication.

Based on these lines of reasoning, we developed five research questions to investigate the figurations of networked media collectivities and tested them based on networks of four German school grades encompassing 335 students. The research questions address the three defining features of a communicative figuration: the communicative practices, the frames of relevance and the constellation of actors.

RQ1 concerned the communicative practices of today's adolescents. Our results show that the instant messaging service Whatsapp is used nearly every day by most of the participants. Whatsapp and related issues were also the topic adolescents talked most about in person. YouTube, TV, Instagram, Facebook and video games were both less used and talked about. Based on these data, it was also tested whether frequencies of mass media use and interpersonal communication about these contents are correlated with each other and therefore define a frame of relevance for adolescents (RQ2). The respective results show that media use and media-related communication are strongly correlated on the level of the various media types. Hence, this supports the general idea that media use provides sources for interpersonal communication. Finally, we addressed the actor constellation of the communicative figuration by analyzing the friendship networks and the networks of interpersonal communication about TV, YouTube and gaming (RQ3), the structural correlation among the communication networks (RQ4) and their correlation with the friendship network (RQ5). The friendship network hereby serves as a proxy for social capital. The respective results show that media in fact seem to serve as a resource to create and maintain social ties, since people with a similar intensity of media use are more likely to communicate about the respective media compared to dissimilar others. This is also supported by the findings regarding the positive structural correlation between the different networks (RQ4). This finding supports our assumption that the figuration of networked media collectivities should be understood as a combination of multiple (partially overlapping) networks. The findings regarding RQ5 finally show that these media-related communication networks are strongly related to the friendship network.

These findings suggest multiple conclusions. First, networked media collectivities should not be limited to a single medium. The structures transcend various types, but every network also has its own characteristics that help to reach a holistic representation of the figurations. Second, networked media collectivities are likely to be a resource of social capital. Media-related conversations are found to be of substantial relevance for everyday interaction and can be assumed to help create and maintain social ties. In fact, we are able to show strong overlap between media-related communication networks and friendship structures. Third, if figurations of friendship networks among adolescents are regarded as a benchmark for what structural properties a figuration should have, we are able to validate our theoretical and empirical approach of networked media collectivities.

The proposed concept of networked media collectivities seems to provide an appropriate theoretical and methodological approach to describe today's media use of adolescents and its interdependence with social structures. However, only a longitudinal extension of this research design will be able to test how the changing media environment alters processes and characteristics of networked media collectivities. Hence, the consequences of the four trends described in the introduction (connectivity, omnipresence, differentiation, datafication) need to be analyzed in future studies.

References

Baym, Nancy. 2015. *Personal connections in the digital age*. Cambridge: Polity Press.

Baym, Nancy, and Andrew Ledbetter. 2009. Tunes that bind? *Information, Communication & Society* 12 (3): 408–427.

Baym, Nancy, Yan B. Zhang, and Mei-Chen Lin. 2004. Social interactions across media: Interpersonal communication on the Internet, telephone and face-to-face. *New Media & Society* 6 (3): 299–318.

Bourdieu, Pierre. 1983. Ökonomisches Kapital, kulturelles Kapital, soziales Kapital. In *Soziale Ungleichheiten*, ed. Reinhard Kreckel, 183–198. Göttingen: Schwartz.

Boyd, Danah. 2006. Friends, friendsters, and MySpace Top 8. Writing community into being on social network sites. *First Monday* 11 (12). http://firstmonday.org/ojs/index.php/fm/article/view/1418/1336. Accessed 30 Mar 2017.

Castells, Manuel. 1996. *The information age. The rise of the network society*. Oxford: Blackwell.

Castells, Manuel. 2013. *Communication power*. Oxford: Oxford University Press.

Caughlin, John P., and Liesel L. Sharabi. 2013. A communicative interdependence perspective of close relationships: The connections between mediated and unmediated interactions matter. *Journal of Communication* 63 (5): 873–893.

Coleman, James S. 1988. Social capital in the creation of human capital. *The American Journal of Sociology* 94: 95–120.

Couldry, Nick, and Andreas Hepp. 2017. *The mediated construction of reality*. Cambridge: Polity Press.

DiMaggio, Paul. 1987. Classification in art. *American Sociological Review* 52 (4): 440–455.

DIVSI. 2014. DIVSI U25-Studie. Kinder, Jugendliche und junge Erwachsene in der digitalen Welt [Survey Children, teenagers and young adults in the digital world]. https://www.divsi.de/wp-content/uploads/2014/02/DIVSI-U25-Studie.pdf. Accessed 30 Mar 2017.

Elias, Norbert. 1978. *What is sociology?* New York: Columbia University Press.

Erickson, Bonnie. 2003. Social networks. The value of variety. *Contexts* 2 (1): 25–31.

Esser, Hartmut. 2008. The two meanings of social capital. In *The handbook of social capital*, ed. Dario Castiglione, Jan W. van Deth, and Guglielmo Wolleb, 22–49. Oxford: Oxford University Press.

Esser, Frank, and Jesper Strömbäck. 2014. *Mediatization of politics*. Houndmills: Palgrave.

Feierabend, Sabine, Theresa Plankenhorn, and Thomas Rathgeb. 2015. *JIM 2012. Jugend, information. (Multi-) media. Basisstudie zum Medienumgang 12- bis 19-Jähriger in Deutschland*. Stuttgart: mpfs.

Fischer, Claude S. 2011. *Still connected: Family and friends in America since 1970*. New York: Russell Sage Foundation.

Friemel, Thomas N. 2009. Mediensport als Gesprächsthema. Sozialpsychologische Betrachtung der interpersonalen Kommunikation über Sportberichterstattung in Massenmedien [Media sport as conversation topic. A social-psychological perspective on interpersonal communication about sport coverage in mass media]. In *Die Sozialpsychologie des Sports in den Medien*, eds. Holger Schramm and Mirko Marr, 199–222. Köln: Halem.

Friemel, Thomas N. 2012. Network dynamics of television use in school classes. *Social Networks* 34 (2): 346–358.

Friemel, Thomas. N. 2013. *Sozialpsychologie der Mediennutzung*. Konstanz: UVK.

Friemel, Thomas N. 2015. Influence vs. selection: A network perspective on opinion leadership. *International Journal of Communication* 1002–1022. http://ijoc.org/index.php/ijoc/article/view/2806. Accessed 30 Mar 2017.

Friemel, Thomas N., and Andrea Knecht. 2009. Praktische Grenzen vs. effektive Netzwerke. In *Netzwerkgrenzen*, eds. Christian Stegbauer and Roger Häußling, 15–32. Wiesbaden: VS.

Gehrau, Volker, and Lutz Goertz. 2010. Gespräche über Medien unter veränderten medialen Bedingungen. *Publizistik* 55 (2): 153–172.

Granovetter, Mark S. 1973. The strength of weak ties. *The American Journal of Sociology* 78 (6): 1360–1380.

Grunig, James E., and Keith R. Stamm. 1973. Communication and coorientation of collectives. *American Behavioral Scientist* 16 (4): 567–591.

Gruzd, Anatoliy, Barry Wellman, and Yuri Takhteyev. 2011. Imagining Twitter as an imagined community. *American Behavioral Scientist* 55 (10): 1294–1318.

Hasebrink, Uwe, and Hanna Domeyer. 2012. Media repertoires as patterns of behaviour and as meaningful practices: A multimethod approach to media use in converging media environments. *Participations* 9 (2): 757–783.

Haythornthwaite, Caroline. 2002. Strong, weak, and latent ties and the impact of new media. *The Information Society* 18 (5): 385–401.

Haythornthwaite, Caroline. 2005. Social networks and Internet connectivity effects. *Information, Communication & Society* 8 (2): 125–147.

Hepp, Andreas. 1998. *Fernsehaneignung und Alltagsgespräche. Fernsehnutzung aus der Perspektive der Cultural Studies.* Opladen: Westdeutscher Verlag.

Hepp, Andreas, Matthias Berg, and Cindy Roitsch. 2014. *Mediatisierte Welten der Vergemeinschaftung. Kommunikative Vernetzung und das Gemeinschaftsleben junger Menschen.* Wiesbaden: Springer VS.

Hepp, Andreas, and Uwe Hasebrink. 2014. Human interaction and communicative figurations: The transformation of mediatized cultures and societies. In *Mediatization of communication*, ed. Knut Lundby, 249–272. Berlin and New York: de Gruyter.

Hurrelmann, Bettina. 1989. *Fernsehen in der Familie.* Weinheim and München: Juventa.

Jensen, Klaus B. 2010. *Media convergence.* London and New York: Routledge.

Keppler, Angela. 2014. Reichweiten alltäglicher Gespräche. In *Unser Alltag ist voll von Gesellschaft*, ed. Alfred Bellebaum and Robert Hettlage, 85–104. Wiesbaden: VS.

Kepplinger, Hans-Martin, and Verena Martin. 1986. Die Funktionen der Massenmedien in der Alltagskommunikation. *Publizistik* 31 (1–2): 118–128.

Kim, Hyo, Gwang J. Kim, Han W. Park, and Ronald E. Rice. 2007. Configurations of relationships in different media: FtF, email, instant messenger, mobile phone, and SMS. *Journal of Computer-Mediated Communication* 12 (4): 1183–1207.

Krackhardt, David. 1987. QAP partialling as a test of spuriousness. *Social Networks* 9 (2): 171–186.

Lin, Nan. 2001. *Social capital. A theory of social structure and action.* New York: Cambridge University Press.

Lin, Nan. 2008. A network theory of social capital. In *The handbook of social capital*, ed. Dario Castiglione, Jan W. van Deth, and Guglielmo Wolleb, 50–69. Oxford: Oxford University Press.

Lull, James. 1980. The social uses of television. *Human Communication Research* 6 (3): 197–209.

Lundby, Knut. 2014. *Mediatization of communication*. Berlin and New York: de Gruyter.

MacBeth, Tannis M. 1986. *The impact of television: A natural experiment in three communities*. Orlando, FL: Academic Press.

Marsden, Peter V. 2013. An experiment about questionnaire context effects on name generator data. Invited presentation at *ARS '13 fourth international workshop, "Networks in Space and Time: Models, Data Collection and Applications"*, Rome, Italy, June, 2013.

Marsden, Peter V., and Elizabeth H. Gorman. 2001. Social networks, job changes, and recruitment. In *Sourcebook on labor markets. Evolving structures and processes*, eds. Ivar Berg and Arne L. Kalleberg, 476–502. New York: Kluwer Academic/Plenum.

Marsden, Peter V., and Sameer B. Srivastava. 2012. Trends in informal social participation, 1974–2008. In *Social trends in American life: Findings from the general social survey since 1972*, ed. Peter V. Marsden, 240–263. Princeton, NJ: Princeton University Press.

McPherson, Miller, Lynn Smith-Lovin, and Matthew E. Brashears. 2006. Social isolation in America: Changes in core discussion networks over two decades. *American Sociological Review* 71: 353–375.

Neuberger, Christoph. 2011. Soziale Netzwerke im Internet. Kommunikationswissenschaftliche Einordnung und Forschungsüberblick. In *StudiVZ. Diffusion, Nutzung und Wirkung eines sozialen Netzwerks im Internet*, eds. Volker Gehrau and Christoph Neuberger, 33–96. Wiesbaden: Springer VS.

Paik, Anthony, and Kenneth Sanchagrin. 2013. Social isolation in America: An artifact. *American Sociological Review* 78: 339–360.

Putnam, Robert D. 2000. *Bowling alone. The collapse and revival of American community*. New York: Simon & Schuster.

Rainie, Lee, and Barry Wellman. 2012. *Networked. The new social operating system*. Cambridge, MA: MIT Press.

Ramirez, Artemio, and Erin M. Bryant. 2014. Relational reconnection on social network sites: An examination of relationship persistence and modality switching. *Communication Reports* 27 (1): 1–12.

Reich, Stephanie M., Kaveri Subrahmanyam, and Guadalupe Espinoza. 2012. Friending, IMing, and hanging out face-to-face: Overlap in adolescents' online and offline social networks. *Developmental Psychology* 48 (2): 356–368.

Shoham, David A., Liping Tong, Peter J. Lamberson, Amy H. Auchincloss, Jun Zhang, Lara Dugas, and Kathleen A. O'Connor. 2012. An actorbased model of social network influence on adolescent body size, screen time, and playing sports. *PLoS ONE 7* (6): e39795. doi:10.1371/journal.pone.0039795.

Steglich, Christian, Tom A.B. Snijders, and Patrick West. 2006. Applying SIENA. An illustrative analysis of the coevolution of adolescents' friendship networks, taste in music, and alcohol consumption. *Methodology* 2 (1): 48–56.

Subrahmanyam, Kaveri, Stephanie M. Reich, Natalia Waechter, and Guadalupe Espinoza. 2008. Online and offline social networks: Use of social networking sites by emerging adults. *Journal of Applied Developmental Psychology* 29 (6): 420–433.

van Dijk, Jan. 2006. *The network society. Social aspects of new media*. Thousand Oaks, CA: Sage.

van Eimeren, Birgit. 2013. 'Always on'. Smartphone, Tablet & Co. als neue Taktgeber im Netz. *Media Perspektiven* 7–8: 386–390.

van Zalk, Maarten H.W., Nejra van Zalk, Margaret Kerr, and Hakan Stattin. 2014. Influences between online-exclusive, conjoint and offline-exclusive friendship networks: The moderating role of shyness. *European Journal of Personality* 28 (2): 134–146.

Wasserman, Stanley, and Katherine Faust. 1994. *Social network analysis. Methods and applications*. Cambridge: Cambridge University Press.

Weber, Mathias. 2015. *Der soziale Rezipient*. Wiesbaden: Springer.

Wellman, B., A., Quan-Haase, J., Boase, W., Chen, K., Hampton, I., Díaz, and K., Miyata. 2003. The Social Affordances of the Internet for Networked Individualism. *Journal of Computer-Mediated Communication*, 8: 0. doi:10.1111/j.1083-6101.2003.tb00216.x.

PART III

Exploring Organizations and Institutions

9

Journalism and its Transformation: An Empirical Study

Leif Kramp and Wiebke Loosen

9.1 Introduction

Journalism is profoundly affected by a changing media environment that has contributed to an ever-increasing pace of innovation and a differentiation of media channels and platforms that simultaneously follows and fosters individualized media use. The digitalization of news media has enabled changes in news production as well as in news consumption, both on the level of individual practices and of organizational and social structures (cf. Klinenberg 2005; Paulussen 2012; Venkatesch and Dunkle 2013; Hermida 2014; Meijer and Kormelink 2015).

L. Kramp (✉)
ZeMKI, Centre for Media, Communication and Information Research, University of Bremen, Bremen, Germany
e-mail: kramp@uni-bremen.de

W. Loosen
Hans Bredow Institute for Media Research, University of Hamburg, Rothenbaumchaussee 36, 20148 Hamburg, Germany
e-mail: w.loosen@hans-bredow-institut.de

In particular, social media have enlarged and multiplied the possibilities for public participation in journalism: Terms such as "participatory journalism" (Singer et al. 2011), "collaborative journalism" (Bruns 2005) or "network journalism" (Heinrich 2011) have been used to characterize how these trends affect the journalism-audience relationship and our understandings of and demands on journalism. Since the 1990s the major challenges confronting journalism – and research into it – has been seen in the developments around the internet and the new communicative conditions that came with it (for an overview see Mitchelstein and Boczkowski 2009). This illustrates that journalism as a genuine media phenomenon is intrinsically intertwined with the changing media environment which affects how journalism is produced, distributed and used by audiences (for a historical perspective see Birkner 2012).

Today, journalistic content is produced, used and distributed via multiple platforms, and social media increasingly complement traditional mass media while expanding the communicative options between journalists and their audiences. One consequence is an increased connectivity between journalists and audiences as well as an omnipresence of audience feedback: News organizations must now manage an increasing amount of audience-led comments, for example, in forums, comment sections and through user interaction on their social media channels which fundamentally changes how today's journalists and their audiences perceive, use and manage these kinds of interactions (Bergström and Wadbring 2015; Loosen and Schmidt 2016). The steady growth of user comments is probably one of the most notable examples in this context – and it illustrates that the idea of audience participation in journalism has changed relatively quickly over the past few years. What we are presently observing is a shift in the understanding of the comment section from being "a space for a new 'deliberative democratic potential' to emerge" (Collins and Nerlich 2015) to a necessary evil or even a threat to deliberation.[1] As a consequence, and also owing to limited resources – and also because of a mixture of a certain professional distance towards their audiences, scepticism or even resistance against audience participation – there are already various examples of newsrooms that have completely shut down the comments sections of their websites.[2]

These developments should be seen in the context of a news industry struggling with disrupted business models and declining audiences (Phillips 2015), where one decisive challenge is to (re-)discover and (re-)engage audiences – also through new (social) media channels. Some of the newer journalistic media organizations in the field, for instance, start-ups such as the German *Krautreporter* or the Dutch *De Correspondent*, even explicitly build their foundations upon a new understanding of the journalism-audience relationship, for instance as a financer of crowdfunded projects (Carvajal et al. 2012), as collaborators in enterprises relying on crowdsourcing or as co-decision-makers.

Even if these developments neither follow a linear process nor take place simultaneously within all newsrooms or for all individual journalists, there is no doubt that "the audience" plays a much more central and explicit role in everyday newsroom routines than has been the case under the communicative conditions of mass media where journalism mainly observed its audiences via audience research and punctual feedback, for example, via letters to the editors. Generally speaking, this illustrates how the journalism-audience relationship is a mediated one and is subsequently changing with an expansion and differentiation of the media ensemble it is based on (for a historical perspective see Reader 2015). From the perspective of journalism (as a social field or system), media organizations (as enterprises), newsrooms (as journalistic organizations) and individual journalists (who may work in different contexts and under different conditions), these transformation processes inevitably lead to a tension between a (certain indispensable) professional distance towards their audiences and an increasing proximity that comes together with social media channels and their particular modes of communication. These spaces have become "meeting point[s]" (Bergström and Wadbring 2015: 140) for journalists and their audiences – meeting points where both groups meet on still 'uncommon ground'.

With this chapter, we want to discuss empirical evidence of this transformative stage for journalism in terms of its communicative orientation towards its audience(s). For this, we analyze empirical data from three of our recent surveys with the help of the approach of communicative figurations. It then becomes possible to identify patterns of a transforming communicative relationship between journalism and audiences.

9.2 The Communicative Figuration of the Journalism-Audience Relationship

One of the most often used notions to describe consequences of a changing media environment is "the notion of the blurring boundaries" (Loosen 2015) between communicator and recipient, the distinctions between whom are becoming increasingly porous. These fundamental changes in the media environment appear in journalism as if seen under a magnifying glass:

- Journalism's communication conditions are no longer solely characterized by mass media, but increasingly complemented by social media (e.g. Deuze et al. 2007; Singer et al. 2011).
- Consequently, journalism has become a form of "multichannel communication", that is, content is produced, distributed and used via various kinds of media and platforms; and these platforms are also used for various purposes: research, audience engagement, marketing, audience monitoring and so on (cf. Neuberger et al. 2014).

One main consequence of these developments is the expansion and the amplification of the communicative options between journalism and audiences, leading to a diversification and dynamization of roles and relations between them (Loosen and Schmidt 2012). There seems to be little doubt that the journalism-audience relationship is transforming in the context of continuous mediatization; that is, an interwoven change of media, culture and society. However, such a catch-all-diagnosis also conceals the fact that this transition follows neither a linear nor a simultaneous process for all segments of journalism, for all journalists or audience members. Thus, the vital question becomes how we can better assess and analyze this transformation theoretically and empirically.

Here, the concept of communicative figurations (Hepp and Hasebrink 2014) is helpful as it acknowledges three features of communicative interdependencies between individuals, collectivities and organizations that are of particular importance for the transformation of the journalism-audience relationship (cf. Hasebrink and Hepp 2016):

- A communicative figuration has a certain *constellation of actors* that makes up its structural basis.
- It has a dominating *frame of relevance*, a certain sense orientation that serves to guide its constitutive practices, and
- it is built upon specific *communicative practices* that draw upon and are entangled with a particular *media ensemble*.

We want to use this heuristic to describe the previously mentioned changes in the journalism-audience relationship systematically from a social constructivist perspective. Studying the transformation of the communicative figuration of the journalism-audience relationship requires a clear understanding of its social factors: the actors involved, their forms of communication (social interaction) and their shared frames of relevance which make up the basis upon which a communicative relationship is moulded and oriented (see Table 9.1).

Against the background of the above highlighted body of research and following Hasebrink and Hepp (2016: 4f.), we can identify five general trends in a changing media environment that are of particular relevance for journalism:

- The *differentiation* of media and communicative practices that also provides audiences with new chances to participate.
- Increasing *connectivity* between journalists and their audiences through these media and various technical intermediaries.
- The *omnipresence* of audience feedback and other contributions.
- An ever-increasing *pace of innovation* of media technologies and their use by journalists and audiences alike.
- The *datafication* and monitoring of audience behaviour based on increasingly diverse digital traces such as click rates and social media analytics that reveal information about news preferences, evaluation and engagement.

Obviously, these trends (can) have various consequences for journalism in general and for the journalism-audience relationship in particular (Loosen 2016). Here, the concept of communicative figurations helps us to reflect on how the journalism-audience relationship transforms with the changing conditions of media and communications – with respect to the communicative practices that are used by journalists and the audience, and the actor constellations in terms of who participates in the production and dissemination of news with respect to the dominating frames of relevance that characterize this relationship.

Therefore, if we very broadly define a point in time as the "pre-internet age" (t1) and compare that with "the internet and social media age" (t2), we can trace how the communicative figuration of the journalism-audience relationship has changed over time in terms of the dimensions described – and how it continues to change. With respect to the briefly outlined state of research, we come to the following orienting hypotheses:

Table 9.1 The transformation of the communicative figuration of the journalism-audience relationship

Trends of a changing media environment	*Features of figuration*	*t1* → *"pre-internet age"*	*t2* *"internet/social media age"*	*Consequences/transformation of figuration*
Differentiation Connectivity Omnipresence Pace of innovation Datafication	communicative practices	monologic, predominantly mass media oriented	dialogic, also social media oriented	increasing variety of practices, acceleration of communication processes
	actor constellation	producer/recipient	e.g. "social media editor", "active user", "measured audience/user", multiple audiences	role shifts, role diversification, dynamization of relationships
	dominating frames of relevance	supply/demand	dialogue, participation, reciprocity	increase of contingency, increasing demands on transparency, …

1. The communicative practices between journalism and (its) audiences are no longer only/predominantly mass media-oriented and monologic, but are increasingly social media-oriented and dialogic as well. Consequently, this transformation process leads to increasingly accelerated and varied communicative practices.

2. With respect to the actor constellation we can observe shifts and diversifications in the roles journalists and audiences play as well as the dynamization of their relationships: To differentiate between producer and recipient has become much too static. Instead we notice users operating at different degrees of participation, "measured audiences" coming together at different levels of aggregation and a multiplication of audiences media brands reach through a variety of platforms (e.g. via its printed edition or its Facebook page), which leads to a balancing act between "multiple audiences".

3. Overall, the defining characteristic of mass media – the asymmetry between journalism and audience in terms of supply and demand – is about to give way to a more reciprocal, participatory and dialogue-oriented framing. One effect of this is an increase of contingency because follow-up communication is, in a new quality and quantity, as visible as journalistic communication. Propositions are instantly discussed and criticized as well as stimulated by user contributions. Another consequence is an increasing demand for transparency – that is, for instance, that newsrooms and journalists increasingly discuss topic selections, ways of covering or not covering certain topics with their audiences.

Even if the three research projects we draw from in the following sections weren't already conceptualized and operationalized with respect to the concept of communicative figurations, it offers a fruitful framework to interconnect the different empirical evidence to trace and illustrate the changing nature of the communicative relationship between newsroom staff and audiences in a digital age. That is, we use communicative figurations as a theoretical lens through which we can reinterpret our empirical findings. Section 9.3 refers (1) to a survey among editors of German newspapers and (2) to in-depth-interviews with ten editors-in-chief of so-called "millennial news media" for young audiences in Germany (2.1). In Sect. 9.4 we switch and simultaneously widen the perspective by drawing on some empirical examples through a newsroom case-study that looks "at both sides of the story" (Schmidt and Loosen 2015) by looking at the (in-)congruence of mutual expectations between journalists and audience members.

9.3 Tentative Openness and Structural Drawbacks in German Newspaper Newsrooms

The following reflections on the communicative reorientation in German newspapers draw on two surveys that focus on the ongoing transformation of journalism practices in German newspaper newsrooms against the background of a changing (digital) media environment. The first study is a comprehensive survey of all newspapers in Germany with a complete editorial team ("*publizistische Einheiten*"). This survey was conducted in 2012 with a quantitative design and had a response rate of 56% (cf. Kramp and Weichert 2015; Weichert et al. 2015).[3] Its main question was: How and to what extent do newsrooms facilitate a reorganization of dominating frames of relevance in journalism with respect to its communicative orientation? The second survey was conducted in 2016 with a qualitative design, collecting the experiences and expectations of twelve editors-in-chiefs of millennial news media outlets in Germany, including *Bento*, *BUNTEnow*, *BusinessInsider*, *Buzzfeed Germany*, *BYou*, *Headline24*, *HuffingtonPost Germany*, *jetzt*, *orange by Handelsblatt*, *Refinery29*, *Vice Germany* and *Ze.tt* (cf. Kramp and Weichert 2016).[4] In recent years, a considerable number of German publishing houses have launched specific news outlets that are geared towards attracting teenagers and young adults (summarized under the generational term "millennials"), encouraging them to engage with the news. They compete with other new market entries by international media corporations that have launched German subsidiaries and also canvas for a young target market that is characterized by an intensely digital lifestyle, but who are difficult to reach through the conventional news offerings of established newspaper websites (cf. Kramp 2016: 21f.).

Considering the two survey periods, the results of the studies can be understood as building upon each other in a transformative process in which publishers and newsrooms have tried to adapt to and even shape their changing (digital) media environment by changing their newsroom cultures and their communicative orientation towards audiences. In 2012, when the first survey was conducted, newspaper publishing in

Germany had already been through a period of massive cutbacks and a continuous decline in circulation and advertizing revenue. By then, the industry had already been working on options to secure its core newspaper business and expand its digital outreach (cf. Esser and Brüggemann 2010; Kramp 2015). The subsequent development of alternative platforms, and new ways of attracting new (young) audiences by engaging them with interactive and participatory modes of mediating the news, not only corresponds with economical determinants but to journalists' professional perceptions of audiences' changing needs, demands and attitudes towards making news and its mediation as well. This combination of perceptions that change and the attitudes and demands that change with them constitute the wider transformation of the very communicative figuration that is the journalism-audience relationship.

9.3.1 Changing Newsroom Cultures Through New Professional Roles

Role conceptions in journalism are the result of a complex interdependence between self-perceptions and imposed expectations to fulfil normative and empirical functions (cf. Mellado et al. 2017). With the dawn of social media and its widespread dissemination, newsrooms became increasingly confronted with a continued differentiation, vast connectivity and the growing omnipresence of media affordances provided by digital information and communication technology (ICT). Journalistic roles were confronted with differentiated tasks and practices. Undertaking several efforts to adapt to this transforming media environment, the journalistic profession has experienced a rapid diversification with the implementation of various new professional roles that add to the existing range of tasks in integrated newsrooms (Bakker 2014): According to the 2012 survey, traditional roles still tend to dominate the self-perception of editorial staff in (German newspaper) newsrooms, and innovative job profiles seem to evolve in reaction to a communicatively interwoven public sphere encompassing new constellations of actors that include both journalists and audiences. These profiles can already be understood as the outcome of a professional reconsideration of journalism's efficiency in disseminating information and generating public interest for critical issues of broader societal relevance: An omnipresence of audience articulations (including feedback) and user-generated content has triggered an awareness that new tasks such as moderating the public discourse, editorial community management or curating social media content have emerged and that they should be taken seriously in the context of the newsroom. What these tasks have in common is that they are not so much focused on the production of original news content as they are on the mediation, classification and discussion of it by various (new) communicative practices through social media, with a strong emphasis on user dialogue.

The integration of additional professional fields with a variety of communicative requirements and orientations, which solidify into a range of job profiles and role perceptions, might not only change editorial procedures but also the social reality and self-perception of newsrooms. This is because it affects an adjustment of the dominating *frames of relevance*. This transformation process naturally depends on a variety of factors, including the particular nature and extent of the reorganization of professional roles. If a journalist's main task is to literally *moderate* a public discussion among members of the audience (and/or other journalists and public stakeholders), this means that a profound change in the communicative orientation of a newsroom that has previously been characterized by mass-media news production and distribution focus – or by a relevance frame of 'supply and demand' – occurs (see Table 9.1). If journalists act as *managers* of a community of users who share their opinions amongst themselves, who contribute their observations to their personal public spheres, who engage with the news dynamically, then we can see a significant change in newsroom culture: Against this background, the ability to master various emerging *communicative practices* in an ever-changing (social) media environment becomes increasingly relevant for journalists. And, if a journalist lives up to a self-perception that places a special emphasis on the content of others circulating through social media by curating it for the sake of providing an overview of a complex discourse or issue, it also shifts editorial priorities.

Nearly half of the respondents (48%, n = 127) in the 2012 newsroom survey identified the "community manager" as an increasingly relevant job profile in journalism. The approval rate was even higher for a prospectively increasing demand for journalists as "moderators" (66.1%), "curators" (55.9%) and "bloggers/commentators" (56.7%). The formation of new role perceptions in the newsroom that place emphasis on follow-up communication with the audience and building and managing a community of users is a novelty in newspaper journalism, as reader service has formerly been a task undertaken exclusively by the marketing and public relations (PR) division of publishing houses (cf. Schoenbach et al. 1999). In 2016, editors-in-chiefs of millennial news media do not only confirm the high(er) relevance of journalistic roles that focus on audience engagement. Social media are at the centre of newsroom activities for both the subsidiaries of established newspaper companies and for newly established digital news organizations that exclusively address adolescents and/or young adults. Here, facing young, volatile, media users, the dominant *frame of relevance* has shifted towards a systematically dialogic communicative orientation towards audiences. Here, according to the surveyed editors, each and every journalist is expected to also act as a moderator, curator, community manager and blogger/commentator. In addition, the editorial staff of millennial news media are generally quite young, belonging almost exclusively to the very same generation that is targeted by the new editorial strategies (e.g. the age array at the newsroom of *orange by Handelsblatt* is 16–22 years, according to its editor Hans-Jürgen Jakobs). As stated by the surveyed editors of the millennial news media, the recruitment of young journalists is often focused on digital literacy in terms of an inherent understanding of and affinity towards emerging *communicative forms* in the digital ecosphere. Although classic journalistic competencies stay relevant, experiences in social media content production, networking expertise and the willingness to experiment with emerging media technologies are considered to be equally important.

9.3.2 Differentiating the Media Ensemble

Only 43% of the respondents in the newspaper newsroom survey stated that they would agree to focus on news that was interesting for a broad audience; one of the most supported role perceptions traditionally attributed to journalists (among themselves) related to the key idea of objective reporting (Weischenberg et al. 2012: 213–215). Here, it had by far the lowest approval rate for all surveyed items.

We consider this an indicator of the shifting priorities of communicative orientation for journalists: from a traditional mass media news dissemination perspective to a differentiated media ensemble with an audience that is fragmented and/or, indeed, “multiple audiences” (Hasebrink 2008, own translation) – it appears that journalists are increasingly acknowledging that they serve different audiences via different media channels and platforms during their daily work routines (Loosen and Schmidt 2016b). This is corroborated by the relevance that is ascribed to social networks in the newsroom compared to other internet services: More than 70% of the respondents deem social networks "very important" or "important" for their everyday work with an average approval rate of 2.2 (1 = very important, 5 = unimportant); all other surveyed items had lower approval rates (blogs 3.6, podcasts 3.9, video 2.8, Twitter 3.0, data-driven journalism 2.6). A high level of importance placed on social networks is mentioned particularly by those respondents who think that community management will become more important for journalists in the future. This also points to the increased relevance of interactive and dialogic formats and practices in journalism. The results in detail:

- For *younger journalists* (39 and younger) social network services such as Facebook, Xing and Google+ are by far the most important online platforms for their editorial work. They also use short messaging services such as Twitter and appreciate video as a new form of mediation within integrated newspaper newsrooms as well as methods for data visualization.
- For *middle-aged journalists* (40–49) social web and data-driven journalism is the first choice when it comes to online activities. They also consider short messaging services and video important for their reporting. Blogs and podcasts, however, are deemed mostly unimportant.
- For *older journalists* (50 and over) Facebook and other social networks, data visualization and video are the most important online activities in the context of the newsroom, but Twitter is also considered relevant. Blogs and podcasts are regarded as rather conventional and less innovative forms of journalism practice compared with social networking and more challenging multimedia formats.

The relevance of online communicative interaction with the audience relates to both research tasks in everyday news production and content distribution. Journalists increasingly participate in the versatile distribution of (their) content by posting and sharing on social media.

This *differentiation of media ensembles* in the distribution of editorial content has been encouraged in a concerted effort to reach younger audiences with news content. Millennials are regarded as crucial for the future development of the news environment (cf. Poindexter 2012). Attracting young media users is in many respects challenging for traditional news organizations: With a declining readership for mass-distributed news products, young consumers do not necessarily develop an affinity to legacy media as former generations have done in the past (cf. Duggan 2015a, b; Newman et al. 2016). Instead, they tend to turn towards digital media affordances that are not necessarily provided by established news organizations, but might lack a journalistic background (e.g. user-generated content by 'YouTube stars'; marketing, public relations or propaganda content disseminated virally through social networks; direct messaging/group communication). Furthermore, a considerably large body of research suggests that the respective millennial audience, born between the early 1980s and the late 1990s, is not at all a group of coherent interests and habits, but that its members are on the contrary as heterogeneous in their life plans as they are volatile in their preferences towards and motivations for using (mainly) digital media (cf. Albert et al. 2015; American Press Institute et al. 2015; Deloitte 2016).

This has stimulated editorial strategies that resulted in the emergence of millennial news media such as *Ze.tt* (an online venture of the German weekly *Die Zeit*), orange (the young subsidiary of the financial daily *Handelsblatt*) and *Headline24* (a news portal for young audiences by the local media group Dr. Haas). As the 2016 survey shows, these media still operate a website as a steady destination for loyal users, but also as a hub that is connected to a multitude of social media platforms, channels and accounts operated by newsroom staff and actively engages with other users by distributing content in various ways and formats. According to all the editors of millennial news media that we surveyed, most users consume, share and comment on the news through Facebook, diverting it to a wide array of other communication services and social networks. For the responsible editors, this is a main driving force to not only adopt a "viral seeding" strategy (Sebastian Horn, *Ze.tt*) from marketing to expand their outreach to younger audiences, but even more so to develop distinctive news concepts for every single popular social media service, such as Facebook, Instagram, WhatsApp and Snapchat. This is pursued in the knowledge that this might lead to a procession of dependence on social media providers that are incrementally behaving like publishers themselves. However, assessing advantages and disadvantages, the surveyed millennial news media continue to walk a "thin line" (Juliane Leopold, *Buzzfeed Germany*) between not surrendering themselves to these uncontrollable social media partners and to gain as much valuable target group coverage as possible.

9.3.3 Adapting to the Communicative Habits of the Audience

The ways millennial news media address adolescents and young adults are striking. Editorial strategies among the surveyed newsrooms mainly focus on two aims: first, to contribute to the conversations among users on social networks and messaging services such as WhatsApp, Facebook Messenger and Snapchat, and, second, to build an audience for their news brand. Therefore, the integration of social media concepts into newsroom practices does not necessarily have a supplementary character, but rather is more in line with the core of editorial self-perception. This communicative orientation is comparably radical: In order to attract young audiences with news, millennial news media strive to *engage* them with it. In doing so, they adopt various prevalent and emerging forms of communication that are used by adolescents and young adults and adapt their reporting to these communicative forms: from, for instance, interpersonal messaging to posting personal pictures and videos to circulating internet memes through peer networks.

Theoretically, against this background, users could also become a more active part of the news-making process – not only as a source, but also as a collaborator or as a corrective to false information mediated by journalists: This might be the case if a newsroom manages to successfully engage users to systematically contribute observations or even private research endeavours on public issues and versatile constructive feedback on editorial content.[5] However, the communicative figuration between newsrooms and audiences is clearly more complicated than that. Even for millennial news media, the interviewed editors-in-chief note in surprising unity that user feedback would be an important factor in the editorial strategy. However, besides sharing feedback, the audience would not – yet – be as interested in contributing original content to news production as it could be, for example, on their personal living environment (in terms of hyperlocal citizen journalism). Therefore, a constructive inclusion of the audience into editorial processes of news-gathering remains a long-term perspective for some of the newsrooms.

With respect to the 2012 survey on transformations in newspaper newsrooms, a fundamental hesitation towards user participation in traditional areas of expertise in newsroom work prevails (Robinson 2010). According to the results of the survey, readers were hardly integrated into news production at all. To some extent, journalists welcomed the participation of readers while doing research (e.g. "crowdsourcing"): 11% of the journalists surveyed stated that reader participation is high when it comes to research; 33% said that it was at a normal level. Rather unpopular in news making contexts is user participation as a corrective: Only 22% of the respondents answered that users would participate like this in their editorial work. Other forms of participation such as contributing to the editing process or joining newsroom conferences (or the respective decision-making procedures) virtually or in person are widely ruled out, with 96% and 88% of respondents stating that this is not offered by their newsroom.

Participation in journalistic research can be understood in various ways and should be relativized. Journalists might not only think of it as helpful input for their research but also ascribe a certain relevance towards user-generated material such as photographs or notifications about opinions or complaints that are sent in. Therefore, we asked a further, more specific, question about whether the respondents would be willing to collaborate with readers if working on more complex and difficult issues. Here, the results demonstrate a hesitant reaction: 40% of the respondents had a neutral attitude towards the participation of users in this context. A third would let users participate, but more than a quarter were strictly against collaborations of this kind. We checked how strong the participation options correlate with other activities. The 2012 data show that there were significant correlations for all surveyed participation options. Therefore, if the reader is provided with an opportunity to participate in editorial research, it is also likely that he or she participates in other editorial contexts. However, in the case of sophisticated or sensitive stories that are deemed important by the journalist we found a negative correlation (Fig. 9.1).

Nonetheless, the surveyed journalists did not feel extraordinarily distant from their readers: more than half of the respondents were undecided. They stated that their readership was neither "far away" nor "very close" in terms of the assumed professional distance to the newsroom. Approximately one third of respondents attested to their newsroom as having a relatively close proximity to its readers. The overall professional distance between newsrooms and audiences was rated significantly lower (2.64 at 1 = very high, 5 = very low) than the attitude towards user participation might suggest. An explanation for this difference might be the

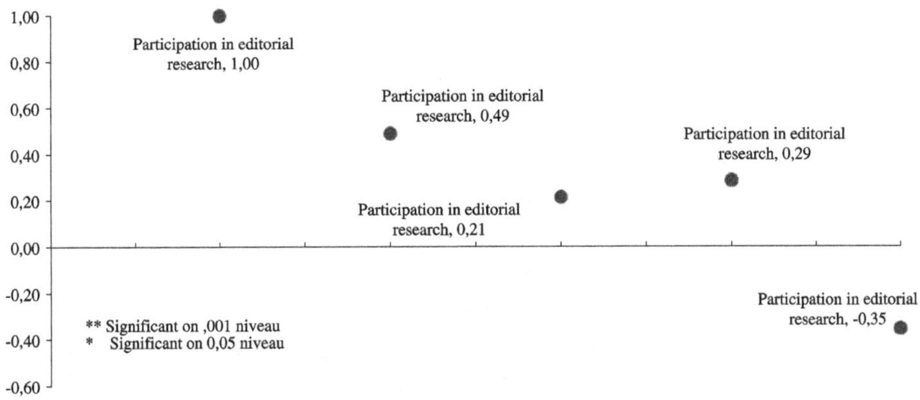

Fig. 9.1 2012 survey on transformation in newspaper newsrooms: willingness to let the reader participate in editorial research correlated with further options to participate. Pearson corr., sign. both sides; N = 127

multi-factorial nature of professional distance that does not only comprise readers' participation in editorial activities, but also the editorial performance in relation to the reader. It is therefore conceivable that the editors think they take up and reflect the needs and desires of their audience in their articles to the correct degree.

Furthermore, the perceived distance to the reader is significantly lower for respondents who have a higher approval rate for the increasing relevance of the "community manager" role. Journalists who see a demand for their profession to adopt a stronger moderation and dialogic job profile tend rather more to involve their readers in their research and publication of a story. However, the results suggest that newspaper newsrooms in Germany (still) do not show a systematic involvement of audiences in their editorial workflows. Instead, editorial cultures in newspaper companies are evidently still dominated by a decades-old mass media approach characterized by very few participation options for users. Strong inertial forces seem to be at play, at least in newsrooms that address a wider audience of all ages.

The results show a divergence between general news media and those that target younger audiences. As nearly all interviewed editors-in-chief of millennial news media emphasized that their editorial strategy explicitly excludes a regular editorial exchange of knowledge and developed formats between their respective venture and their parent company, this gap might grow even further.

9.4 Mutual Observation: Participatory Expectations and Attitudes of Journalists and Audience Members

In this section, we switch the perspective by drawing on empirical examples of a newsroom case study while simultaneously widening it by "including the audience in journalism (research)" (Loosen and Schmidt 2016a). That is, we take both journalists and audiences into theoretical and methodological account by considering both groups in the actor constellation of the journalism-audience relationship. Since journalism research mainly focuses on the journalist as the central actor or role in the field, the journalist is considered the basic unit of empirical investigation and as such the primary social address or access point for data collection. However, if we deem the transformation of the journalism-audience relationship from a communicative orientation towards "supply and demand" to one of "dialog and participation" as a remarkable process (see Table 9.1), we consequently take a step further which means that we need to widen our focus by including not only journalists but audiences as an empirical subject into journalism research as well (Costera Meijer 2016).

To achieve this we will draw on a research project on audience participation that investigated how increasing opportunities for audience participation and expanding communicative options between journalists and their audiences, in light of a changing media environment, reshape the relationship between journalism and its audiences in four case studies of German journalistic outlets.[6] The special character of this research lies in the fact that the theoretical frame and empirical design were chosen to assess and compare participatory practices and related expectations for journalists and audience members within one integrated framework. The project followed a multi-method design that combined in-depth interviews and online surveys with standardized content analyses (of journalistic output, user comments and participatory features on news sites) (Loosen and Schmidt 2016).

The data we present here were collected in July 2013 (a survey of journalists) and October 2013 (an audience survey), via online surveys among journalists and audiences. For this chapter, we focus on one of the four case studies, that of the German national newspaper *Süddeutsche Zeitung* and on two selected findings (Heise et al. 2014). These are related to a theoretical construct we term "inclusion distance" – understood as the extent of congruence and/or mismatch of inclusion expectations journalists and audience members hold (Loosen and Schmidt 2012; Schmidt and Loosen 2015). Among journalists, these inclusion expectations consist of journalistic role conceptions, images of the audience, its place and its function within journalistic practices and their assumed motivations for participation, as well as some general and strategic considerations of media organizations when it comes to audience participation. Among the audience, inclusion expectations consist of motivations for participation, the importance placed on participatory features and their general expectations of journalism and its functions.

We consider journalistic role conceptions and the (assumed) importance of participatory features the two richest aspects in the context of this chapter as they represent, in particular, "the tension between professional control and participatory openness" (Lewis 2012) – influencing a shift in, or at least an expansion of, the dominating frames of relevance in the journalism-audience relationship from "supply and demand" to "dialogue and participation" (see Table 9.1). Moreover, the concept of journalistic role conceptions is one of the classic tropes in journalism research (Weaver and Wilhoit 1986; Cassidy 2005; Mellado 2011; van Dalen et al. 2012; Mellado and van Dalen 2013) that helps us understand whether journalists consider themselves as mainly independent from audience influence (i.e. as a "gatekeeper" who provides a mass audience with objective information), as partners in a conversation with audiences, or if they aim to "stand up for the disadvantaged population" (Weischenberg et al. 2012: 214). For our purposes, we complemented the established scales to measure journalistic role conceptions with new participation- and dialogue-oriented tasks.[7]

To assess the mutual expectations of journalists and audience members the respective item batteries were worded in parallel in both the journalist and the audience surveys, and the same answer scales (five-point Likert scales, e.g. "agree completely" to "disagree completely" and "very important" to "very unimportant") were given, while the question text was directed to either one's own expectations or the assumed expectations of the other side.

In each case study, the differences between journalists' and users' mean item assessments are used to measure inclusion distance. Mathematically, we subtract for each item of the users' mean from the journalists' mean. Thus, the sign of the difference shows whether journalists rate the item higher (positive sign) or lower (negative sign) than their audience. The value of the differences in means conveys information about the extent of congruence. Table 9.2 shows that the difference in mean is already becoming highly significant with the absolute value of 0.36; below that, differences can be significant as well but need to interpreted with caution.

The mean scores and the differences in the assessments of journalists and audiences become clearer if we present the data not only in tables, but also in a particular visualization which enables the identification of patterns in the data (Schmidt and Loosen 2015): see Fig. 9.2. In this way, each item becomes a data point that is placed on a two-dimensional plane according to its mean value among journalists (x-axis; scale from 1 to 5) and audience members (y-axis; scale from 1 to 5). A diagonal line from bottom left to top right indicates those points where the mean values for journalists and audience members are identical. Thus, the closer an item is to the diagonal line, the more similar are the means and the shorter is the distance. Items in the top-right corner are mainly agreed on by both journalists and users, while items in the bottom-left corner are mainly not agreed on.

All in all, we find a high congruency between journalists and audience members regarding journalistic role conceptions at *Süddeutsche Zeitung*; only four of these show a difference of means larger than 0.5 (see Table 9.2). Both audience members and journalists agree on specific functions that news journalism by *Süddeutsche Zeitung* should fulfil. Accordingly, the tasks to explain and convey complex issues ($\Delta = 0.17$) as well as to criticize problems and grievances ($\Delta = -0.15$) and report as objectively and precisely as possible ($\Delta = -0.20$) have a high priority among both journalists and audience members (see also Fig. 9.1). This shows that both groups more or less agree on the traditional tasks of journalists as explainers of complex topics, as critics and as disseminators of objective information (see Hanitzsch 2011; Weischenberg et al. 2012). Moreover, there is also notable agreement on what is not seen as a journalistic task: audience members and journalists alike reject the idea that journalism should "provide the audience with the opportunity to maintain ties among themselves" (item 2).

This is not to say that journalists and users agree on everything and there are some notable differences in opinion: journalists agree more strongly than users that it is their task to concentrate on news and information that is interesting for the widest possible audience ($\Delta = 0.65$; significant with $p < 0.001$). Users, on the other hand, expect journalists to also act as watchdogs ("control politics, business and society") to a

Table 9.2 Case study *Süddeutsche Zeitung*: congruence of journalistic role conceptions among journalists and audience members

"What are your personal goals in your profession?"/"Süddeutsche Zeitung journalists should…"	*Journalists (n = 128–136)*	*Users (n = 476–510)*	Δ	*t*
1. Encourage and moderate discussion among the audience	2.77	2.81	−0.03	0.30
2. Provide the audience with the opportunity to maintain relationships among themselves	1.80	1.83	−0.04	0.36
3. Build and maintain a relationship to the audience	2.87	2.83	0.04	0.36
4. Share positive ideals	3.08	3.15	−0.07	0.53
5. Inform the audience as fast as possible	3.98	4.06	−0.08	0.82
6. Show new trends and highlight new ideas	3.90	3.78	0.13	−1.27
7. Point out interesting topics to the audience and show them where to get further information on them	4.02	4.15	−0.13	1.37
8. Criticize problems and grievances*	4.40	4.56	−0.15	2.16
9. Give the audience the opportunity to express opinion on topics of public interest	2.82	3.00	−0.17	1.53
10. Explain and convey complex issues**	4.78	4.61	0.17	−3.17
11. Inform the audience as objectively and precisely as possible*	4.33	4.53	−0.20	2.43
12. Get into conversation with the audience about current events and topics*	2.81	3.09	−0.28	2.53
13. Present my/their own opinion(s) to the audience/ to the public***	3.19	3.55	−0.36	3.34
14. Provide useful information for the audience and act as advisor/guidance***	3.02	2.56	0.46	−4.02

(continued)

Table 9.2 (continued)

"What are your personal goals in your profession?"/"Süddeutsche Zeitung journalists should…"	*Journalists (n = 128–136)*	*Users (n = 476–510)*	Δ	*t*
15. Provide people with opportunity to publish their own content***	1.79	2.29	−0.50	5.01
16. Give the audience topics to talk about***	3.98	3.47	0.52	−4.91
17. Monitor politics, the economy and society***	2.90	3.49	−0.58	4.19
18. Offer the audience entertainment and relaxation***	3.50	2.88	0.62	−5.84
19. Concentrate on news that is interesting to an audience as wide as possible***	3.35	2.70	0.65	−5.99

Items are sorted by size of difference in means (Δ). Scales were 5-point Likert scale ranging from 1 ("strongly disagree") to 5 ("strongly agree"). Answers "Don't know./Can't say." were excluded for calculation of means. Tagged differences in means are statistically significant on levels: *$p < 0.05$; **$p < 0.01$; ***$p < 0.001$

greater extent than journalists themselves feel professionally obliged to ($\Delta = -0.58$, $p < 0.001$).

Another dimension of our understanding of "inclusion distance" between journalists and their audiences is the congruence of the (assumed) importance of participatory features. Here we asked journalists what they consider important to their audiences and we also asked audiences members themselves. What is striking at first is that all differences in means are highly significant (see Table 9.3). Additionally, Fig. 9.3 indicates that in almost all cases journalists overestimate the importance the queried participation- and transparency-oriented features actually have for their audiences (=almost all items are situated right from the diagonal line) – or at least what they claim they have for them.

Table 9.3 Case study *Süddeutsche Zeitung*: congruence of (assumed) importance of participatory features

"How important are the following aspects to your audience/to you?"	*Journalists (n = 119–129)*	*Users (n = 480–515)*	Δ	*t*
1. To be able to get further information on editorial routines and practices***	2.95	2.51	0.44	−4.22
2. To have editorial staff introduced to them/me***	3.26	2.78	0.48	−4.55
3. To be able to quickly forward and recommend news items to friends and family***	3.77	3.25	0.52	−4.93
4. To have a platform for discussing the practices and quality of news reporting***	3.57	3.03	0.54	−4.93
5. To be able to provide own material (pictures, videos, interview questions) for news reporting***	2.55	1.87	0.68	−6.65
6. To be able to make suggestions to the editorial staff (e.g. on topics for reporting, interview partners)***	3.29	2.56	0.73	−7.38
7. To get additional information on the sources the reporting is based on***	3.15	3.89	−0.75	7.06
8. To be able to see which stories are viewed, shared and commented on by many other people***	3.24	2.46	0.78	−7.51
9. To be able to interact and/or make contact with other readers/users and exchange opinions***	3.01	1.93	1.08	−10.23
10. To be able to rate and comment on journalistic content***	3.95	2.81	1.13	−11.49
11. To be able to make contact and enter into a dialogue with editorial staff directly***	3.70	2.55	1.14	−12.14

(continued)

Table 9.3 (continued)

"How important are the following aspects to your audience/to you?"	*Journalists (n = 119–129)*	*Users (n = 480–515)*	Δ	*t*
12. To have the editorial staff be present and responsive (on social media)***	3.48	2.08	1.39	−11.67
13. To be taken seriously by journalists***	4.63	3.24	1.40	−16.03
14. To be able to publicly show their/my attachment to the *Süddeutsche Zeitung****	3.39	1.99	1.40	−12.15
15. To be able to discuss the topics of news reporting with other readers/users***	3.83	2.34	1.48	−15.92

Items are sorted by size of difference in means (Δ). Scales were 5-point Likert scale ranging from 1 ("very unimportant") to 5 ("very important"). Answers "Don't know./Can't say." were excluded for calculation of means. Tagged differences in means are statistically significant on levels: *$p < 0.05$; **$p < 0.01$; ***$p < 0.001$

The only exception is item number 7. For audience members, the most important thing is "to get additional information on the sources the reporting is based on", while, to some extent, journalists underestimate this desire for source transparency ($\Delta = -0.75$, $p < 0.001$). In contrast, they think that the most important thing for audiences is to be taken seriously – a desire that journalists overestimate as the user survey reveals ($\Delta = 1.40$, $p < 0.001$). We also found a similar pattern in a case study on the German TV newscast "*Tagesschau*" (Heise et al. 2014). In sum, we only found four out of 15 items in this item battery that users rate important rather than unimportant (=mean > 3.0): the already mentioned item no. 7; 3 ("to be able to quickly forward and recommend news items to friends and family"); 13 ("to be taken seriously by journalists") and 4 ("to have a platform for discussing the practices and quality of news reporting").

The item with the most significant difference of means is the possibility of discussing the topics of news reporting with other users ($\Delta = 1.48$). While journalists expect this aspect to be more important for audience members, users care less about it and deem it rather unimportant.

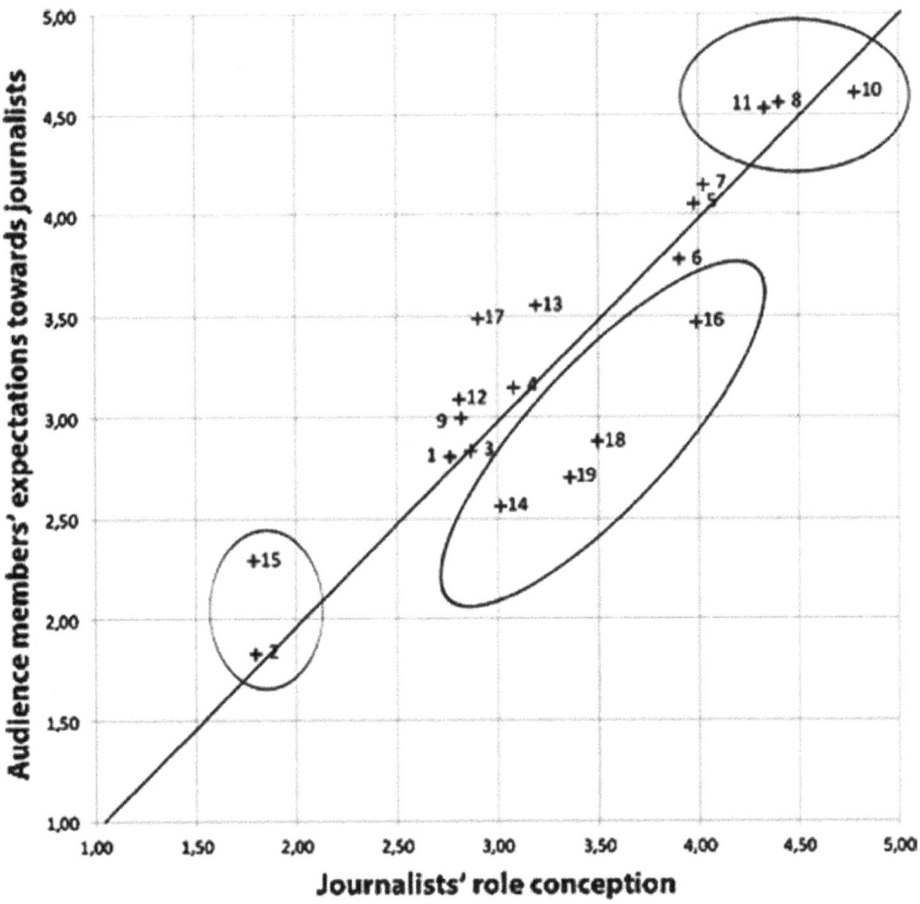

Fig. 9.2 Case study *Süddeutsche Zeitung*: journalistic role conception among journalists and audience members (numbers refer to items in Table 9.2)

In sum, both findings leave a mixed impression. The inclusion distance, in other words the difference between inclusion expectations as far as journalists and audiences are concerned, is rather low with respect to journalistic role conceptions. Journalists at the *Süddeutsche Zeitung* tend to wholeheartedly lend their support to role perceptions that are related to the concept of *objective reporting* (e.g. "inform the audience as objectively and precisely as possible") and partly to *advocacy journalism* ("criticize problems and grievances") (Weischenberg et al. 2012: 213) – and this, in the view of their audience, is exactly what they should be doing. The comparison of the (assumed) importance of particular aspects of audience participation, however, shows a rather obvious inclusion distance. With respect to almost all aspects, journalists assume a greater interest in participation- and transparency-oriented practices than users specify for themselves. The only exception here is an aspect that relates source to transparency: audience members have significantly higher expectations of acquiring additional information and references to the sources of a news story than journalists anticipate.

9.5 Conclusions

We have discussed here empirical evidence of a transformation that is taking place in the journalism-audience relationship through the examples of three different studies that focused, first, on the anticipated expectations of journalists in newspaper newsrooms concerning their audience and, second, on the comparison of expectations of journalists in a newsroom with those of their audience. The survey results indicate that the transformation of the journalism-audience relationship is a complex, non-linear and quite ambivalent process that is moulded by a plethora of factors that have primarily social determinants. They are deeply rooted and interrelated with what journalists want to achieve professionally and what they should according to audiences. With the help of the communicative figurations approach, we can describe the implications of these interdependencies as follows:

1. The *constellation of actors* in an increasingly fragmented and diverse public sphere contribute to journalists' construction of their image of and their relationship to audiences, including, among others, audience members themselves who contact journalists, write online comments, collaborate in investigating issues and so on, as well as social media editors and other colleagues who provide information about the audience. Analyses of the surveys showed that journalists assess the feedback they receive by members of the audience as valuable and guiding. However, this has rather limited implications for the willingness of journalists to allow users to participate in their editorial work beyond appreciating their feedback. Nevertheless, journalists learn a lot about their fragmented audience that has already developed into multiple audiences against the background of the proliferation of channels and platforms in the digital media environment where journalism is distributed, consumed, shared and discussed. Newsrooms no longer serve a

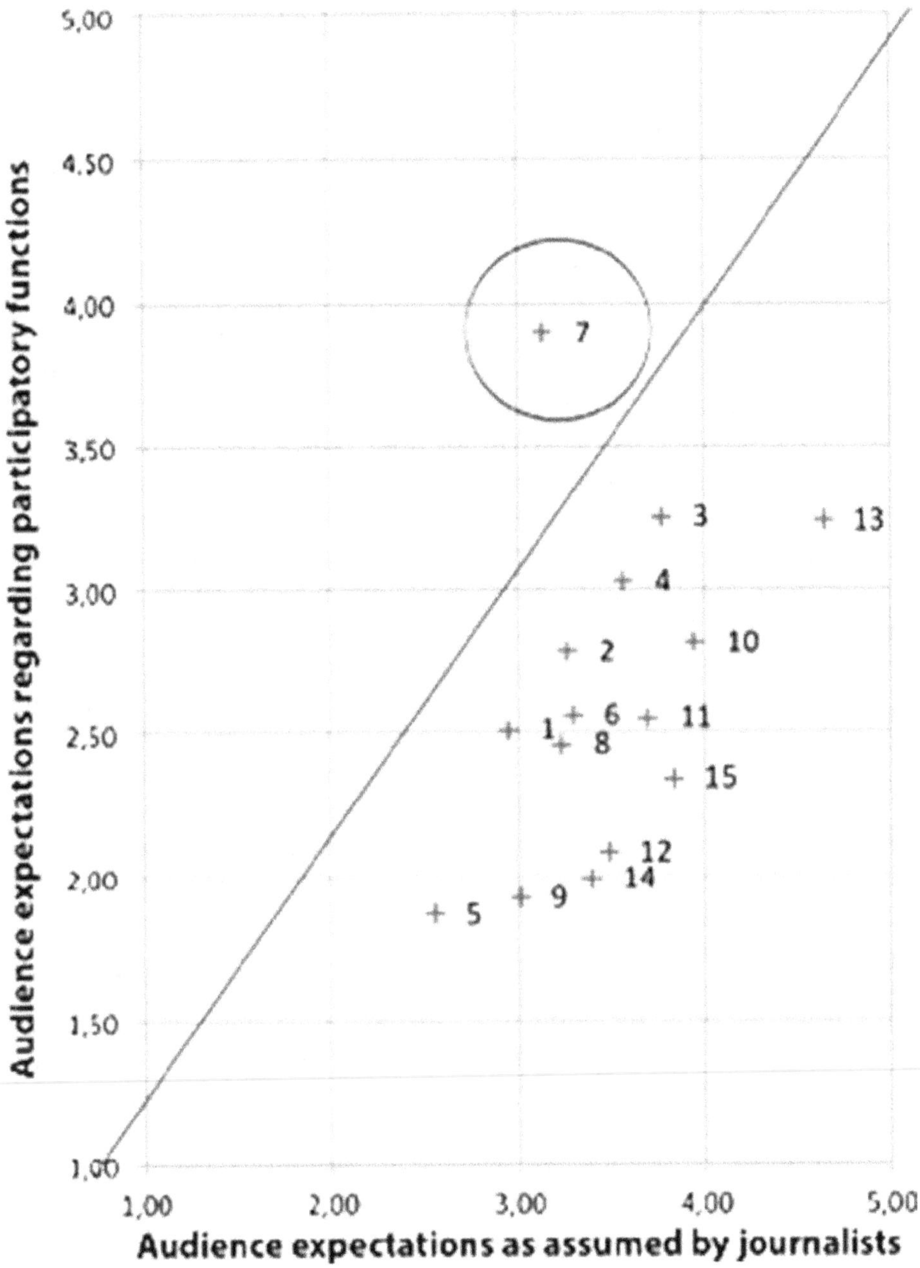

Fig. 9.3 Case study *Süddeutsche Zeitung*: congruence of (assumed) importance of participatory features (numbers refer to items in Table 9.3)

coherent audience, but have to approach their (different) target groups at various levels through different routes in order to reach them, catch their attention and increase audience loyalty and retention. Therefore, as the survey results underline, journalism has already become more dialogue oriented and more open towards the (online) social interaction of its audiences.

2. Newsrooms have eagerly adapted to new *communicative practices*, that is, modes of communication, to reach their audiences on diverse media channels and platforms (the respective media ensemble). This is mainly the product of a learning process that has been stimulated by changing habits of media use: as social media have become more relevant in both private and public communications, so has the information seeking and entertainment needs among all age groups – especially for adolescents and young adults – journalists try to adapt to and explore new ways of distributing their content and engaging (with) their audiences on social media platforms. Social networks – along with their versatile communication, information and entertainment tools – have entered the newsroom and are used by journalists in various ways in their editorial work. Even more importantly, newsrooms are beginning to systematically develop their own journalistic distribution and audience engagement strategies for communicative forms that are popular among audiences, such as interpersonal direct messaging and chatting (text/video).

3. Consequentially, journalism undergoes a profound transformation with respect to the dominant *frames of relevance* that guide these practices, including the (shared) understandings of (1) the journalist's role in his/her organizational environment(s), (2) the position of the respective organization(s) in the wider journalistic field and (3) the function of journalism for society as a whole. As the survey results indicate, newsrooms become an increasingly contested field of interrelated individual and organizational levels of journalistic role conceptions that are, on the one hand, oriented towards 'information supply and demand' (with a hesitation to let the reader participate in editorial work), or on the other, towards 'dialogue and participation' (with a stronger emphasis on the moderating role and a more conversational mediation of information). At a glance, journalism experiences a vast expansion of professional self-perceptions and role expectations among audiences

> oriented towards dialogue and participation. However, these new roles do not displace traditional expectations towards journalism, but instead contribute to a differentiation of expectations towards journalists even though the majority of the audience might not be overly interested in participating editorially.

Considering these profound aspects of the transformation of the journalism-audience relationship as demonstrated by the results of the three separate surveys, our three hypotheses turned out to be fairly accurate.

Our first hypothesis assumed that the communicative orientation between journalism and its audiences would be characterized by a combination of a rather monological approach and an increasingly dialogic relation to audiences. The empirical data not only demonstrate this blending of communicative orientations to be accurate, but also highlight that there are different sets of priorities regarding the insistence of promoting social media-oriented strategies in newsroom work that depend on the perceived needs and demands of different target groups.

The second hypothesis was concerned with shifts and diversifications in perceptions within the newsroom that might lead to a dynamization of the communicative journalism-audience relationship. By analyzing the survey data, we found that there is indeed an emergence of new roles in newsrooms that is being accepted by journalists as a reaction to the shifting media environment characterized by popular social media that require additional editorial tasks to be able to reach and inform audiences properly. However, the empirical data also show that this one-sided dynamization of self-perceptions is not (yet) reflected by a more reflexive understanding between journalists and audiences – especially when it comes to audience participation: journalists and audiences do not necessarily know what the other wants, what they deem important and what they expect from each other. Rather, journalists seem to pursue a fairly one-sided approach of adding more dynamism to their relationship with their audiences and trying to meet their assumed expectations. This suggests that the journalism-audience relationship is not (yet) characterized by a communicative exchange that leads to a deeper understanding of each other's needs and demands.

Our third hypothesis focused on the asymmetry between journalism and audiences in terms of supply and demand which could be complemented by a more dialogue and participation-oriented framing and reciprocity. The analyzed data show that journalists are not completely ready to share the details of their editorial work. Most journalists see the necessity of explaining the background and context of their reporting with their audiences to a certain degree, but not to engage readers in sovereign newsroom activities such as taking part in editorial conferences, discussing and selecting issues to report on or in fact checking articles. This shows that there is still a considerable communicative distance between newsrooms and audiences with respect to tasks that are deemed exceptionally relevant to the professional self-understanding of journalists in their traditional privileged role as (mass media) gatekeepers and agenda setters.

Overall, we can conclude that journalism is going through a transition phase that challenges the established roles, tasks and even functions traditionally ascribed to journalists and to journalism as a social system or field. In this chapter, we have discussed empirical evidence indicating that as journalists grow accustomed to and more intensely consider new dialogic tasks as important in prospective newsroom work and the more that they integrate social media communication in their editorial work, the more likely it is that legacy news media change profoundly in their communicative orientation and refresh their journalism-audience relationship in light of new media use.

Notes

1. See, as an example, a study on the British *Guardian*'s comment section published under the title: "The dark side of Guardian comments". Here, the gender of authors and the topical area of an article were found to be predictors of attraction to hateful comments. https://www.theguardian.com/technology/2016/apr/12/the-dark-side-of-guardian-comments. Accessed: 30 Mar 2017.
2. For examples see the list on news organizations that shot down onsite comments collected by the "Coral Project": https://community.coralproject.net/t/shutting-down-onsite-comments-a-comprehensive-list-of-all-news-organisations/347.
3. The study *"Die Zeitungsmacher"* [*'The Newspaper Makers'*] was conducted in 2012 among newsrooms with complete editorial team ("*publizistische Einheiten*") of all German daily newspapers (130). The sample has been generated randomly by a multistage selection process with different size classes on newsroom level (one, two or three journalists each). The response was 56.2 per cent with a total of 127 journalists in the sample. Study was funded by the Foundation Press House NRZ, the Otto-Brenner-Foundation and the FAZIT Foundation.

4. The study on millennial news media was conducted in 2016 (Kramp 2017; Kramp/Weichert 2017; Weichert/Kramp 2017a; 2017b). The empirical multi-method design included expert interviews with editors-in-chief of millennial news media in Germany, focus groups with participants of four different birth cohorts (1981–1985, 1986–1991, 1992–1996, 1997–2000) and in-depth interviews with participants of the focus groups, combined with network maps and media diaries. The study was commission by the Federation of German Newspaper Publishers (BDZV). For this chapter, we analyzed the interviews with the following editors-in-chief (in the order of interview date): Sebastian Horn (*Ze.tt*), Juliane Leopold (*Buzzfeed Germany*), Christian Helten (*jetzt*), Christian Grospitz (*BUNTEnow*), Hans-Jürgen Jakobs (*orange by Handelsblatt*), Manfred Hart (*BYou*), Sebastian Matthes (*HuffingtonPostGermany*), Tom Littlewood (*Vice Germany*), Volker Pfau (*Headline24*) and Nora Beckerhaus (*Refinery29*).

5. This kind of systematic inclusion of the audience in editorial research is being tested by the foundation-funded newsroom Correct!v on its online platform crowdnewsroom.org. An exemplary research collaboration between the journalists in the newsroom and members of the audience has led to the publication of an investigative dossier on the situation of German saving banks ("*Sparkassen*").

6. The project was based on theoretical assumptions and analytical heuristics derived from sociological inclusion theory (Loosen and Schmidt 2012). In a nutshell, audience inclusion into journalism is realized through both inclusion practices (e.g. certain patterns of media use) and inclusion expectations (e.g. assumptions about the professional role of journalists), which can be assessed for either journalists or audience members. The central methodological innovation of the project was to systematically relate and connect methods focusing on either side in order to address the relationship between them.

7. Items were partly drawn from established scales, partly created by the research team. A documentation of the survey instruments can be found in our project blog at http://jpub20.hans-bredow-institut.de/?p=768.

References

Albert, Mathias, Klaus Hurrelmann, Gudrun Quenzel, and TNS Infratest Social Research. 2015. *Jugend 2015. 17. Shell Jugendstudie* [Youth 2015. 17th Shell youth study]. Frankfurt am Main: Fischer TB.

American Press Institute, Associated Press, and NORC Center for Public Affairs Research. 2015. How millennials get news: Inside the habits of America's first digital generation. Media insight project, March 2015. http://www.

mediainsight.org/PDFs/Millennials/Millennials%20Report%20FINAL.pdf. Accessed 30 Mar 2017.

Bakker, Piet. 2014. Mr. Gates returns: Curation, community management and other new roles for journalists. *Journalism Studies* 15 (5): 596–606.

Bergström, Annika, and Ingela Wadbring. 2015. Beneficial yet crappy: Journalists and audiences on obstacles and opportunities in reader comments. *European Journal of Communication* 30 (2): 137–151.

Birkner, Thomas. 2012. *Das Selbstgespräch der Zeit. Die Geschichte des Journalismus in Deutschland 1605–1914* [The self-talk of time. The history of journalism in Germany 1605–1914]. Köln: von Halem.

Bruns, Axel. 2005. *Gatewatching. Collaborative online news production.* New York: Peter Lang.

Carvajal, Miguel, José A. García-Avilés, and José L. González. 2012. Crowdfunding and non-profit media. The emergence of new models for public interest journalism. *Journalism Practice* 6 (5–6): 638–647.

Cassidy, William P. 2005. Variations on a theme: The professional role conceptions of print and online newspaper journalists. *Journalism & Mass Communication Quarterly* 82 (2): 264–280.

Collins, Luke, and Brigitte Nerlich. 2015. Examining user comments for deliberative democracy: A corpus-driven analysis of the climate change debate online. *Environmental Communication* 9 (2): 189–207.

Deloitte. 2016. The 2016 Deloitte Millennial Survey. https://www2.deloitte.com/content/dam/Deloitte/global/Documents/About-Deloitte/gx-millenial-survey-2016-exec-summary.pdf. Accessed 30 Mar 2017.

Deuze, Mark, Axel Bruns, and Christoph Neuberger. 2007. Preparing for an age of participatory news. *Journalism Practice* 1 (3): 322–338.

Duggan, Maeve. 2015a. Mobile messaging and social media 2015. *Pew Research Center*, 19.08.2015. http://www.pewinternet.org/2015/08/19/mobile-messaging-and-social-media-2015/. Accessed: 30 Mar 2017.

Duggan, Maeve. 2015b. The demographics of social media users. *Pew Research Center.* 19.08.2015. http://www.pewinternet.org/2015/08/19/the-demographics-of-social-media-users/. Accessed: 30 Mar 2017.

Esser, Frank, and Michael Brüggemann. 2010. The changing business of journalism and its implications for democracy: The case of Germany. In *The changing business of journalism and its impact on democracy*, ed. David A.L. Levy and Rasmus K. Nielsen, 39–54. Oxford: Reuters Institute for the Study of Journalism.

Hanitzsch, Thomas. 2011. Populist disseminators, detached watchdogs, critical change agents and opportunist facilitators: Professional milieus, the journalistic field and autonomy in 18 countries. *International Communication Gazette* 73 (6): 477–494.

Hasebrink, Uwe. 2008. Das multiple Publikum. Paradoxien im Verhältnis von Journalismus und Mediennutzung. In *Paradoxien des Journalismus. Theorie – Empirie – Praxis*, ed. Bernhard Pörksen, Wiebke Loosen, and Armin Scholl, 513–530. Wiesbaden: VS.

Hasebrink, Uwe, and Andreas Hepp. 2016. How to research cross-media practices? Investigating media repertoires and media ensembles. Communicative Figurations Working Paper Series 15. http://www.kommunikative-figurationen.de/fileadmin/redak_kofi/Arbeitspapiere/CoFi_EWP_No-15_Hasebrink_Hepp.pdf. Accessed 30 Mar 2017.

Heinrich, Ansgar. 2011. *Network journalism. Journalistic practice in interactive spheres*. New York, Oxford: Routledge.

Heise, Nele, Wiebke Loosen, Julius Reimer, and Jan-Hinrik Schmidt. 2014. Including the audience. Comparing attitudes and expectations of journalists and users towards participation in German TV news journalism. *Journalism Studies* 15 (4): 411–430.

Hepp, Andreas, and Uwe Hasebrink. 2014. Human interaction and communicative figurations: The transformation of mediatized cultures and societies. In *Mediatization of communication*, ed. Knut Lundby, 249–272. Berlin, New York: de Gruyter.

Hermida, Alfred. 2014. *Open journalism: Dynamics of change and continuity in news work in the 21st century*. Doctoral thesis. City University London.

Klinenberg, Eric. 2005. Convergence: News production in a digital age. *Convergence* 597 (1): 48–64.

Kramp, Leif. 2015. The rumbling years. The communicative figurations approach as a heuristic concept to study – and shape – the transformation of journalism. In *Journalism, representation and the public sphere*, ed. Leif Kramp, Nico Carpentier, Andreas Hepp, Ilija Tomanić Trivundža, Hannu Nieminen, Risto Kunelius, Tobias Olsson, Ebba Sundin, and Richard Kilborn, 23–55. Bremen: edition lumière.

Kramp, Leif. 2016. Conceptualizing metropolitan journalism: New approaches, new communicative practices, new perspectives? Communicative Figurations Working Paper Series 10. March 2016. http://www.kommunikative-figurationen.de/fileadmin/redak_kofi/Arbeitspapiere/CoFi_EWP_No-10_Kramp.pdf. Accessed 30 Mar 2017.

Kramp, Leif, and Stephan Weichert. 2015. From crisis to departure? Newsroom culture under the impact of digital structural change in Germany. Paper presented at the 2015 Negotiating Culture Conference: News Production Culture, Reuters Institute for the Study of Journalism at the University of Oxford. 30.10.2015. Oxford.

Kramp, Leif, and Stephan Weichert. 2016. Understanding the millennial way: Implications of young users' volatile media practices for journalism practice. Paper presented at the 2016 European Communication Research and Education Association's Biannual Conference, 11.11.2016, Prague, CZ.

Kramp, Leif. 2017. "We need to keep moving": Strategies of news media to attract young audiences in Germany. In *Present scenarios of media production and engagement*, ed. Simone Tosoni, Nico Carpentier, Maria Francesca Murru, Richard Kilborn, Leif Kramp, Risto Kunelius, Tobias Olsson, Pille Pruulmann-Vengerfeldt, 107–122. Bremen: edition lumière.

Kramp, Leif, and Stephan Weichert. 2017. *Der Millennial Code. Junge Mediennutzer verstehen – und handeln* [The millennial code. Understanding young media users – and act]. Leipzig: Vistas.

Lewis, Seth C. 2012. The tension between professional control and open participation. Journalism and its boundaries. *Information, Communication & Society* 15 (6): 836–866.

Loosen, Wiebke 2016. Publikumsbeteiligung im Journalismus [Audience participation in journalism]. In *Journalismusforschung. Stand und Perspektiven* [Journalism research], ed. Klaus Meier and Christoph Neuberger, 287–316. Baden-Baden: Nomos.

Loosen, Wiebke. 2015. The notion of the 'blurring boundaries': Journalism as a (de-)differentiated phenomenon. *Digital Journalism* 3 (1): 68–84.

Loosen, Wiebke, and Jan-Hinrik Schmidt. 2012. (Re-)discovering the audience. The relationship between journalism and audience in networked digital media. *Information, Communication & Society* 15 (6): 867–887.

Loosen, Wiebke, and Jan-Hinrik Schmidt. 2016a. Multi-method approaches. In *The Sage handbook of digital journalism*, ed. Tamara Witschge, Chris W. Anderson, David Domingo, and Alfred Hermida, 562–575. London et al.: Sage.

Loosen, Wiebke, and Jan-Hinrik Schmidt. 2016b, forthcoming. Between proximity and distance: Including the audience in journalism (research). In *The Routledge companion to digital journalism studies*, ed. Bob Franklin and Scott Eldridge II. New York, London: Routledge.

Meijer, Irene Costera, and Tim Groot Kormelink. 2015. Checking, sharing, clicking and linking. Changing patterns of news use between 2004 and 2014. *Digital Journalism* 3 (5): 664–679.

Meijer, Irene Costera. 2016. Practicing audience-centred journalism research. In *The SAGE Handbook of Digital Journalism*, eds Tamara Witschge, C.W. Anderson, David Domingo, and Alfred Hermida, 546–561. London: SAGE Publications.

Mellado, Claudia. 2011. Modeling individual and organizational effects on Chilean journalism: A multilevel analysis of professional role conceptions. *Comunicación y Sociedad* 24 (2): 269–304.

Mellado, Claudia, and Arjen van Dalen. 2013. Between rhetoric and practice: Explaining the gap between role conception and performance in journalism. *Journalism Studies* 15 (6): 859–878.

Mellado, Claudia, Lea Hellmueller, and Wolfgang Donsbach. 2017. *Journalistic role performance. Concepts, contexts, and methods.* New York, Oxon: Routledge.

Mitchelstein, Eugenia, and Pablo J. Boczkowski. 2009. Between tradition and change. A review of recent research on online news production. *Journalism* 10 (5): 562–586.

Neuberger, Christoph, Susanne Langenohl, and Christian Nuernbergk. 2014. *Social Media und Journalismus* [Social media and journalism]. Düsseldorf: LfM.

Newman, Nic, Richard Fletcher, David A. L. Levy, and Rasmus K. Nielsen. 2016. *Reuters institute digital news report 2016.* Oxford: Reuters Institute for the Study of Journalism. http://reutersinstitute.politics.ox.ac.uk/sites/default/files/Digital-News-Report-2016.pdf. Accessed 30 Mar 2017.

Paulussen, Steve. 2012. Technology and the transformation of news work: Are labor conditions in (online) journalism changing? In *The handbook of global online journalism*, ed. Eugenia Siapera, and Andreas Veglis, 192–208. Malden, MA: Wiley.

Phillips, Angela. 2015. *Journalism in context. Practice and theory for the digital age.* Abingdon, New York: Routledge.

Poindexter, Paula M. 2012. *Millennials, news, and social media. Is news engagement a thing of the past?* New York: Peter Lang.

Reader, Bill. 2015. *Audience feedback in the media.* London, New York: Routledge.

Robinson, Sue. 2010. Traditionalists vs. convergers. Textual privilege, boundary work, and the journalist-audience relationship in the commenting policies of online news sites. *Convergence: The International Journal of Research into New Media Technologies* 16 (1): 125–143.

Schmidt, Jan-Hinrik, and Wiebke Loosen. 2015. Both sides of the story. Assessing audience participation in journalism through the concept of inclusion distance. *Digital Journalism* 3 (2): 259–278.

Schoenbach, Klaus, Edmund Lauf, Dieter Stürzebecher, and Silvia Knobloch. 1999. Evaluating 350 newspapers – Factors contributing to their success: A summary of a large-scale empirical study. *Document Design* 1 (2): 75–84.

Singer, Jane B., Alfred Hermida, David Domingo, Ari Heinonen, Steve Paulussen, Thorsten Quandt, Zvi Reich, and Marina Vujnovic. 2011. *Participatory journalism. Guarding open gates at online newspapers.* Chichester: Wiley.

van Dalen, Arjen, Claes H. de Vreese, and Erik Albæk. 2012. Different roles, different content? A four-country comparison of the role conceptions and reporting style of political journalists. *Journalism* 13 (7): 903–922.

Venkatesch, Alladi, and Debora Dunkle. 2013. Digitizing physical objects in the home. In *The Routledge companion to digital consumption*, ed. Russell W. Belk, and Rosa Llamas, 14–27. Oxon, New York: Routledge.

Weaver, David H., and G. Cleveland Wilhoit. 1986. *The American journalist: A portrait of U.S. news people and their work.* Bloomington: Indiana University Press.

Weichert, Stephan, Leif Kramp, and Martin Welker. 2015. *Die Zeitungsmacher. Aufbruch in die digitale Moderne* [The newspaper makers]. Wiesbaden: Springer VS.

Weichert, Stephan, and Leif Kramp. 2017a. *Millennials. Mediennutzungsverhalten und Optionen für Zeitungsverlage* [Millennials. Media use behaviour and options for newspaper publishers]. Berlin: BDZV.

Weichert, Stephan, and Leif Kramp. 2017b. *Trendreport 2020. Medien für Millennials* [Trend report 2020. Media for millennials]. Berlin: BDZV.

Weischenberg, Siegfried, Maja Malik, and Armin Scholl. 2012. Journalism in Germany in the 21st century. In *The global journalist in the 21st century*, ed. David H. Weaver, and Lars Willnat, 205–219. Mahwah: L. Erlbaum Associates.

10

Moral Debates and Financial Blogging

Rebecca Venema and Stefanie Averbeck-Lietz

10.1 Introduction

Banking crisis, financial crisis, euro crisis—these keywords decisively shaped the public debate in the recent years. Questions of causes, responsibilities, regulations and possible solutions were intensively discussed in everyday communication, political decision-making processes and media reporting, accompanied by normative controversies about (im)proper ways of acting and communicating. These crisis-related normative controversies are the starting point of this chapter. To which

R. Venema (✉)
Institute for Communication Technologies, USI – Università della Svizzera italiana, Via Giuseppe Buffi 13, 6904 Lugano, Switzerland
e-mail: rebecca.venema@usi.ch

S. Averbeck-Lietz
ZeMKI, Centre for Media, Communication and Information Research, University of Bremen, Bremen, Germany
e-mail: averbeck.lietz@uni-bremen.de

norms and values do the actors refer to and in what way? How are the actors who are communicatively engaged in the public debates analyzed? Is it all about moralization? What role does deliberating play? The aim of this chapter is to provide a detailed discussion of communicative practices and of how norms, values and ethics were communicatively constructed in the crisis situation in 2008 after the bankruptcy of the investment bank Lehman Brothers. The figurational perspective allows us to show the dynamics of these constructions by analyzing a selected *constellation of actors*, realizations of moralizing and deliberating as specific *communicative practices* that draw on and are entangled with a specific *media ensemble*, as well as the references to norms and values within the debates about the crisis that are understood as the figuration's *frame of relevance*.

Focusing on the engagement in financial blog communication, including readers' comments, we examine specific 'voices' (Silverstone 2007; Couldry 2010) in transforming public spheres and 'networked publics' (boyd 2010). Hence, we investigate the practices, negotiations and constructions of meaning in a specific, heterogeneous media-related constellation of actors at the junction of journalism,[1] non-professional content production, and (expert) advocacy of bloggers (cf. Debatin 2011; Schenk et al. [in press]). This is a part of wider actor constellations of publics in which the role of 'non-professionals', complementing or probably stimulating traditional media, shifts. The communicative figuration analyzed is based on a particular way of participation[2]: Individuals opt to contribute to a debate in 'voluntary associations' (Perlmutter 2008) by their acts of blogging or commenting in a chosen media ensemble.

Against this backdrop, we develop a four-step argument. First, we give brief insights into the state of research concerning crisis-related (re) constructions of norms and values and shifting constellations of actors in public debates. After this, we explain our empirical approach. We then discuss central empirical findings of our study, while initially characterizing the specific actor constellation analyzed. As regards communicative constructions of norms and values and communicative practices, we then underline two aspects: First, the actors' engagement with the crisis is not limited to the financial crisis itself but also deals with (general) procedural norms of public communication in situations of crisis. Second, communicative practices of moralizing relate to different types and kinds of 'social evaluation' (Bergmann and Luckmann 1999: 23) and are often intermingled with aspects of deliberation. Concluding, we discuss our findings, arguing for the necessity to integrate approaches of deliberation and moralization research in order to understand controversial public debates and their dynamics of interaction more profoundly.

10.2 Crisis-Related (Re)Constructions of Norms and Values and Shifting Constellations of Actors in Public Debates

The current state of research indicates that the public engagement with the crisis can be described as a process of (re)discussing, (re)negotiating and communicative (re)constructing norms, values and ethics.[3] Studies of mass media coverage as well as citizen discussions in online forums reveal that the debates on, causes of and solutions to the financial crisis and its regulation are themselves often *related with explicit and implicit references to norms and values* such as responsibility, justice, solidarity or claims for the same (cf. for example Schranz and Eisenegger 2012; Kuhn 2014). However, the concrete way in which norms and values are communicatively constructed is mostly neglected, as Schmidt (2015) states for media content research of public debates in general. Schranz and Eisenegger (2012) or Cetin (2012) give certain hints to modes of communication, stating strongly moralizing reporting of the financial crisis with personalized as well as system-related blame attributions. This proffers a starting point for a more detailed analysis of communicative practices and constructions of values and related norms, as we present in this chapter. Relating to a social constructivist conception of norms and values, we emphasize their dynamics and conflictual contestations, but also their endurance. Values are understood as the normative, evaluative base frames of what is desirable, 'right or wrong' that are specified in terms of norms, as explicit codes of conduct, or 'rules of behaviour' in certain situational settings. They are conceived as collective 'structures of relevance' that are maintained and transmitted in and through long-term social and communicative interaction (Schütz and Luckmann 1973; Tomin and Averbeck-Lietz 2015: 229). The particular moral (dis)order of each social world relies on an intersubjective and communicative construction or—in the terms of Goffman—an 'interaction order' (Luckmann 1997: 8, referring to Goffman). Often taken for granted, guiding principles become visible in situations of crisis with their moral instability, insecurity of expectations and mistrust in public institutions (Imhof 2014). Crisis communication, then, is structured by public complaints of 'immoral' or 'inadequate' (communicative) performance on the part of actors involved within the crisis and their loss of reputation.

Constellations of actors, process dynamics and 'arenas' of these crisis-related negotiations—for example, public debates in general—may change under conditions of deep mediatization and with changing media environments. With the emergence of digital media and hyperlinked connections, we are dealing with a certain change in the preconditions of public communication. Those 'formerly known as the audience' (Rosen 2006) are able to immediately comment on media coverage, to blog or tweet, and gain public visibility and resonance with their own inputs and positions, thus strengthening the diversity of viewpoints available that complement traditional media (cf. Baden and Springer 2014). The implications of the changes alongside shifting actor constellations with communicators beyond organized media institutions as 'professional producers' are controversially discussed in academic discourse. Such discourses emphasize the potentials to foster interaction and dialogue (cf. Debatin 2011), to improve deliberative qualities of debates (cf. Papacharissi 2004) or, contrarily, the radicalization of public debates via moralization, elements of scandalization (Imhof 2014) or even incivility, flaming and hate speech (cf. Sobieraj and Berry 2011; Friemel and Dötsch 2015; Stroud et al. 2015; Suhay et al. 2015). The latter tendency is generally discussed for virtual online communication, often attributed to the possibilities and dysfunctions of anonymous communication (Averbeck-Lietz 2014). However, there are few empirical findings that shed light on specific communicative practices and interaction patterns under conditions of deep mediatization (Neuberger 2014) or in blog communication, including blog readers' comments (Baumer et al. 2008). So, how to characterize communicative practices and communicative constructions of norms and values in the actor constellation of debates in financial blogs? Ways of communicating about moral problems and processes of (re)negotiating norms and values are reflected by two at first sight rather different approaches and research traditions: by Jürgen Habermas's concept of 'practical discourse' relating to his model of deliberation and Thomas Luckmann's and Jörg Bergmann's social constructivist concept of 'moralization'. More or less contrary to Habermas's dictum that 'practical discourses' deal with *moral problems* (Arens 1997; Habermas 1990) and despite reflections on 'competitive' or 'plebiscitory' discourses with potentially low levels of respect and justification (Bächtiger et al. 2010: 11), up to now research on moral communication (Schmidt 2015)—or related phenomena such as scandalization (Kepplinger 2009)—and deliberation research mostly remained parallel and seperate concerns in different areas or disciplines of social research with different methodological approaches.

By contrast, we argue for the necessity to integrate approaches of deliberation and moralization research for a comprehensive analysis of the dynamics of (moral) public debates, communicative practices and constructions of values and their related norms. We therefore propose a framework for analysis of communicative practices that links (a) deliberation theory in the tradition of Habermas and (b) concepts for empirical deliberation research 'post Habermas' with (c) social and communicative constructivist approaches to moral communication in the tradition of Bergmann and Luckmann (in detail cf. Averbeck-Lietz et al. 2015; Averbeck-Lietz and Sanko 2015).

10.3 Methods and Empirical Approach

Moralizing and deliberating are thereby conceptualized as two superordinate, ideal-typical and distinguishable but in fact (as real-type) interrelated modes of communication, each characterized by specific communicative practices. We use Bergmann's and Luckmann's conceptual definition (Bergmann and Luckmann 1999: 23) of moralizing as socially evaluating statements concerning persons and/or their actions that convey esteem or contempt which are able to affect or increase the reputation or image of the given person(s) and which are linked with a broader reference to conceptions of what is 'right' or wrong' or—even stronger—'good' or 'bad' (Luckmann 1997: 9f.; Bergmann and Luckmann 1999: 19–23).

Deliberating is generally defined by reasoning, mutual respect and the absence of external pressure. For an analytical conceptualization and operationalization of deliberating, we relate to Mansbridge (2015: 1–3), who describes respect and argumentation as main traits of deliberative communication (in the same sense Wessler 2008). Deliberating is then understood as a mutual, respectful justification of ideas and claims. Hence, we examine specific ways of articulating justifications and evaluations—which both relate to the notion of and expressions of respect and/or disrespect in a certain sense. Respect can be understood as a procedural norm for social action and communication and a precondition of a consensus in the normative ideal-typical Habermasian discourse ethics as well as a concrete way to treat and evaluate others—also in forms of negative social evaluation or 'overtly communicative disrespect' (cf. Bergmann 1998: 286). The integrative consideration of both approaches, coming from discourse ethics on the one hand and from social constructivism on the other hand, allows us to describe in what ways the actors meet or abandon ideal-typical norms of communication and to discern their expressions of (dis)regard.

Assuming that blog posts and comments cannot be characterized by one single mode of communication and in order to identify single deliberative or moralizing elements, we operationalize a sequential approach (for sequential analysis in quantitative and qualitative deliberation research see Bächtiger et al. 2010; for sequential analysis in conversation analysis see Ayaß and Meyer 2012 and Luckmann 2012: 22, 25). Consequently, the unit of coding was not a given post or comment in its entirety, but a *sequence*—understood as a semantic unit of meaning in which a specific issue is taken up and covered with a specific communicative practice. Our empirical study is based on the analysis of four purposively selected German financial blogs: *Blick Log*,[4] *Die Wunderbare Welt der Wirtschaft [The Wonderful World of Economics]*,[5] *ZEIT Herdentrieb [ZEIT Herd Instinct]*,[6] and *Neue Wirtschaftswunder [New Economic Miracles]*.[7] Thus, we draw on a sample which integrates different types of bloggers or blogs: (1) award-winning,[8] renowned independent media amateur blogs,[9] providing specific specialist perspectives thanks to the authors' professional background, (2) a blog with a journalist's column and experts' guest commentaries affiliated to a media institution, and (3) a blog that is incorporated in a media institution's online presence, in other words a media integrated blog. So we investigate journalists (in the case of *Herdentrieb* the leading editors, 'talking heads') from well-known brands and established in economic journalism as well as actors who are not professional communicators but professionals in the field of economics—and their commenting readers.

Our analysis focuses on the period between 1 September 2008 and 30 November 2008, covering the time immediately before the bankruptcy of Lehman Brothers until two weeks after the G20 summit in Washington with an agreement on the main features of a reform and intensified control of the global financial system. We analyzed such posts that include at least one statement regarding the financial crisis, its causes, solutions and (future) regulations or the practices and statements of actors involved in the crisis. With these criteria, the sample for the study presented here includes 74 blog posts and their related 643 readers' comments.[10]

We conducted a qualitative content analysis (cf. Nawratil and Schönhagen 2009; Kuckartz 2014; Schreier 2014) in order to systematically grasp communicative practices as well as references to norms and values and their constructions. The basic deductive categorical scheme comprised references to norms and values, elements of moralizing and deliberating (developed in previous research, cf. Averbeck-Lietz et al. 2015) to be refined inductively and, in order to describe the specific constellation of actors, the bloggers' backgrounds and mission statements.

10.4 Findings

10.4.1 Characterizing the Actor Constellation

In order to characterize the actor constellation and the specific media ensemble, Table 10.1 provides an overview of the blogs' particular contexts and self-conceptions at the time of crisis, 2008.

We are dealing with a heterogeneous but in fact interrelated constellation of actors that can be designated as a specific and dynamic collectivity of debate emerging in cross-media debates on the crisis. The journalists and bloggers involved share a specific idea of 'advocating communication' (Debatin 2011; Schenk et al. [in press]) inasmuch as they explicitly characterize themselves and their contributions to public communication as guided by their personal opinions and interests. To illustrate the actors' interactions and interrelations: the bloggers comment on each other (e.g. Robert von Heusinger (*Herdentrieb*) or Dirk Elsner (*Blick Log*) on *Die Wunderbare Welt der Wirtschaft*, Ulrich Voß, in turn, on *Blick Log*) and have common regularly commenting readers, partly professional journalists (e.g. Frank Lübberding, a blogging journalist) or an actor named 'Caspar Hauser', both commenting on *Herdentrieb* as well as *Die wunderbare Welt der Wirtschaft*. This also shows that in this specific figuration journalists in fact do notice discussions on independent blogs as well as the bloggers' engagement with the journalistic coverage of the crisis. Moreover, the comment section on the media blog *Herdentrieb* functions as the venue where the different types of actors or 'communicators' (independent media amateurs, blogging journalists and commenting readers) get together and discuss directly with each other.

Table 10.1 Contexts and self-conceptions of blogs analyzed

	Blick Log	*Die Wunderbare Welt der Wirtschaft*	*Neue Wirtschaftswunder*	*ZEIT Herdentrieb*
authors	Dirk Elsner	Ulrich Voß (pseudonyms: egghat, Dieter Meyeer)	Thomas Fricke	Multi-author group, in 2008: Robert von Heusinger, Uwe Richter, Dieter Wermuth, Fabian Lindner, Lucas Zeise
established	2008	2006	2007[a]	2005
type	media amateur/expert in finance and markets, independent	media amateur/expert in finance and markets, independent	media professional/affiliated to a mass media institution (*Financial Times Deutschland*)	media professionals/ incorporated part of a mass media institution's online presence *(ZEIT)*
authors' background	consultant (financial sector, medium-sized enterprises)	business IT specialist, CEO of a company for app development	specialized journalist	specialized Journalists
mission statement	blog as a complement to mass media coverage offering different, critical perspective—'But, I'm not interested in bank-bashing'	selecting and commenting: 'Reading (…), linking the interesting things and have my say to it'	'The other perspective on boom and crises'. Aim to contribute a perspective 'beyond the old mainstream', ambition to provide contextual knowledge and orientation	Contribute a different perspective to core trends in the capital market, interfere in the current macro-economic or economic policy debates, provide contextual knowledge

[a] In 2013, the blog became independent from the publisher Gruner + Jahr. Thomas Fricke was chief economist and columnist of the *Financial Times Deutschland*, then he worked as a columnist for *Süddeutsche Zeitung*; now he is a columnist for *Spiegel Online*

Thereby the bloggers, who are often directly addressed in the comments, themselves act as commentators and engage with their readers as they respond to various comments, reply to questions or counterargue (e.g. Dieter Wermuth, Fabian Linder, Robert von Heusinger, Ulrich Voß as egghat) and hence enter into a conversation and exchange views as ideal-typically described for blog communication (Debatin 2011: 826).

These interactions and debates are primarily situated in a specific media ensemble: the aforementioned blogs. However, the actors' debates are related to the figurations of other publics, to (moral) debates within a broader constellation of actors and media ensembles, including for example expert journals or newspaper and television coverage about the crisis. As regards explicit links and connections to these broader figurations, we can show specific structural differences between the blogs analyzed. With regard to cross-media references and linkage patterns, *Blick Log* in particular has to be characterized as highly contextualized and referential, as this blog connects to other blogs as well as national and international mass and specialist media. For the media blog *Herdentrieb*, in contrast, it may be noted that the posts mainly refer to research institutes or to well-known experts' contributions. Hence, the references and link structures within the posts are directed to specialized segments, not to a wider blogosphere.[11]

10.4.2 Moralizing, Deliberating and Constructions of Norms and Values in Blog Communication

To give insights to constructions of norms and values, Table 10.2 initially provides an overview of norms and values that the bloggers and commenting readers refer to in their posts and comments.

Table 10.2 Norms and values the actors refer to

general values	*specific norms and values of communication*
solidarity	veracity
moderate risk tolerance/moderate Action	respectfulness
common good	celf-reflexion
justice	transparency
diligence	participation
(assumption of) responsibility	objectivity/appropriateness
trust in an actor	trust in an Actor's Communication

We can identify references to general values as maxims and guiding principles for social action such as responsibility (also as a claim for assumption of responsibility for the consequences of the crisis), justice or trust as well as to procedural norms of communication such as transparency. These norms and values of communication explicitly refer to ideas of desirable, appropriate, 'good' public communication in a Habermasian sense, such as veracity or respectfulness (for such types of validity claims in the sense of Habermas cf. Brosda 2008: 314–319; Averbeck-Lietz 2014). In the readers' comments analyzed, we partially find explicit references to general values such as justice and their requirement as priority maxims of political and economic action, as for example in the following quote:

> 'A functioning economy that is not exclusively profit-oriented but which also includes aspects of justice is particularly important in this regard.' (paradoxus 2008)

Mostly, however, values particularly serve as implicit reference point for interpretations, critique of concrete actions, problematizations or claims (cf. Averbeck-Lietz et al. 2015) as 'glasses'—in the sense of filters—to evaluate social actions and/or persons (Bergmann and Luckmann 1999: 14) and as implicit justifications. Consequently, in a first step we can note that in our data norms, their 'rightness' and thus the legitimacy of practices are introduced and negotiated via specific *claims* (to better a situation), which are implicitly linked to ideas of preferable guiding principles or general maxims for action. This can be shown exemplarily when Dirk Elsner refers back to the idea of the so-called user-pays principle and the principles of (assumption of) responsibility when pleading for the involvement of financial institutes in financing the external effects and costs caused by them as a requirement of fairness and justice:

> 'First and foremost, one has to reflect upon how the costs caused by the banks can be borne by the causal agent [...] the financial institutes participating in financing the external effects caused by them – this can possibly be an approach.' (Elsner 2008a)

As regards the question how norms and values are communicatively constructed we can state that our data norms and values are first and foremost constructed via *critique and stated deficiencies.* Claims for transparency as a relevant norm of communication, for instance, are established by reproaches of a lack of transparency and insincerity while accusing politicians of wilful deceit, of deliberately misleading and the attempt to disguise their own faults in handling the financial crisis.

In the following section, we elaborate further on this specific communicative practice while showing and illustrating selected realizations of moralizing and deliberating.

10.4.3 Moralization: Social Evaluations

The analysis reveals two general core aspects with regard to moralization in the specific figuration analyzed: realizations of moralization relate to different types of social evaluation and are frequently intermingled with aspects of deliberation.

A further point here is that moralization exclusively appears as *negative evaluations*, as a display of contempt, a condemnation of behaviour and actions—presumably owing to financial crisis as a negative frame per se. There seem to be neither heroes or heroines nor moments requiring positive social evaluation for the actors we focus on in the financial crisis in 2008. In the posts as well as in the comments, moralization is first and foremost established by the *reproach of a lack of transparency and insincerity*. *Politicians* (as individuals as well as a vague collective) and *bankers* (as a vague collective) are especially blamed for 'lying and cheating' (otti 2008), as illustrated in the exemplary sequences (Table 10.3).[12]

Our analysis indicates differences between the tone of reader comments and bloggers' contributions. For the comments, we notice more pronounced moralizations with communicative practices such as the *reproach of culpable (personal) failure* (to central banks, bankers and several political actors) and the *denunciation of motives such as greed* of bankers or financial institutions as a vague collective. But even in reader commentaries, this practice of reproaching culpable failure is intermingled with at least 'traces of deliberation' (Bächtiger et al. 2010: 212). The actors in the figuration of financial blog communication maintain principles of deliberation, as they do not completely abandon mechanisms of argumentation and reasoning. The selected sequences in Table 10.4 illustrate these reproaches of culpable failures intermingled with sequences of arguing:

Another particular interrelation of specific practices of moralizing and deliberating is in evidence in sequences relating to denunciations of greed in blog posts as well as in reader comments (for the deconstruction

Table 10.3 Reproaches of a lack of transparency and insincerity in blog posts and comments

reproach of a lack of transparency and insincerity	*selected exemplary sequences*
to individual politicians	'It is not about a fair evaluation (as stated publically) but to give more money to the banks than the stuff is worth.' (Voß 2008a)
to politicians as vague collective	'The official figures show that the turbulences in the past weeks caused the current downturn just to a limited extent as the federal government and the European Central Bank willingly lead to believe in order to divert attention from their own faults.' (Fricke 2008) 'Politicians naturally want to divert attention from their own faults.' (Voß 2008b)
to bankers as a vague collective	'De facto, it was a systematic, nearly criminal disguising of risks by the banks and rating agencies.' (Wermuth 2008) 'For years banks made billions in profits for years, aimed at returns on equity of 25 per cent and thus took the other market participants' money. And now? Now they are nursed with the money of those they have fooled and betrayed to start over again their perfidious game next year.' (Bartels 2008)

of the greed-metaphor related to the financial crisis[13] cf. Neckel 2011). We find a rather striking example in a comment on *Blick Log* referring back to the idea of the so-called user-pays principle and the principles of (assumption of) responsibility: 'These greedy bankers ought to be held liable for their actions with their personal assets—then those crises would never arise!' (Marc 2008). But at the same time *Blick Log*'s blogger Dirk Elsner himself reasons about the public function of the reproach of greed and de-constructs it as an interest-guided communication strategy (see realizations of deliberating discussed further below). It is highly interesting to think about the process factor of time here. As Wunden (1994: 168) points out, indignation and outrage are not always the end but sometimes the beginning of ethics, as these communicative practices are able to initiate a critical reflection on an issue.

A central finding regarding realizations of moralization is that they relate to different types or forms of social evaluation: the actors' social

Table 10.4 Reproaches of culpable (personal) failure in comments

reproach of culpable (personal) failure	*selected exemplary sequences*
to institutions (central banks)	'Moreover, the central banks had already bowed out of the control of financial markets. They have left the banks free to act—and helped in case of fire. This was called Greenspan-Put.' (Lübberding 2008a) 'What is less understandable for me is that the European Central Bank gets off relatively lightly. The experts who pursue financial policies *sine ira et studio* and without political ulterior motifs should actually be found here. Instead they have raised interest rates when it long was predictable that Europe will be affected by an economic crisis.' (Zeise 2008)
to bankers/managers	'So it remained that all experts were aware of the imbalance for years, BUT that the top managers wanted to push the limits of this predictably catastrophic game and to pocket the immoral profits until the ultimate end.' (Frank 2008)
to politics/(union of) states	'Basically, this helplessness is comprehensible, but one has to reproach politics for the failure to prepare for this situation. One had 12 months. They could have followed the discussions here.' (Lübberding 2008b)

evaluations and expressions of disregard are not always associated with distinct conceptions of good and bad. Instead of reproaches of personal guilt and default in simplifying good–bad dichotomies as Bergmann's and Luckmann's (1999: 19–23) approach outlines, in our data, social evaluation and (dis)respect are frequently expressed by more general reproaches of professional misconduct in politics, financial markets and the banking sector. Such—even possibly argumentative—reproaches deny a person's or institutions' competence and ability. Consequently, bloggers and reader commentators judge or evaluate (professional) actors as being naïve or overburdened—as in a certain sense helpless against structural constraints of financial markets. In both posts as well as in comments, the questioning of competencies and skills as a specific form of social evaluation is first and foremost formulated with regard to politicians (as individuals as well as a generalized, collective actor) and their management of the crisis.

> 'We have first-class losers at the head of government.' (Stadler 2008)

> 'This not solely requires a solid knowledge about the world of finance but also knowledge of human nature in order to understand in advance how clever bankers will sneak past the regulation. And as most politicians don't even comply with one of these abilities...' (horst_m 2008)

In the blog *Neues Wirtschaftswunder* and in several comments on the blog *Herdentrieb*, these denials of a person's competence are also directed at economic experts, partly described as 'disorientated' or 'shamans'.

> 'NOTHING could be more irresponsible. They stare at their graphs and scream as if they are on a rollercoaster. No analyses, no reflections on causes, consequences, risks, sustainable systemic changes, nothing. Just propagandistic roaring, the old, cheap, wrong prescriptions. Depressing.' (edicius 2008)

Apparently blog communication is not exclusively a narrow critical engagement with developments in the financial sector. In fact, particularly for the bloggers of *Herdentrieb*, the financial crisis is a moment and a reason to critically assess political actors and negotiate 'appropriate' political action.

10.4.4 Deliberating: Meta-Communicative Elements

Among practices of moralizing, we do find deliberative elements in blog communication, in posts and in comments, particularly in terms of *multi-dimensional reasoning and background information* or *argumentation based on explanations of fiscal phenomena and contexts* as provisions of evidence—and in terms of meta-communicative elements such as communication about communication (cf. Burkart 2002: 105f.). In the following, we expand on the latter as they show that the bloggers' and commenters' critical engagement with the crisis goes far beyond a theme-centred discussion on a factual level. Instead, the actors critically deal with processes, contents and desirable norms of appropriate public (crisis) communication including values of 'good' communication in a Habermasian sense. Thus, blog communication in this particular figuration can also be described as a meta-communicative sphere. Of particular relevance are: (1) the *reference to the characteristics of (public) debates*, (2) the *claim of a differentiated consideration* and (3) *meta-communicative deconstructions*, for example of motifs in public debates like greed. Claims of a differentiated consideration—mixed with critical comments on objectivity, neutrality and their abilities to explicate complex relationships—are often established in readers' comments, such as these:

> 'You question state activity fundamentally. This is something different—you need to explain this.' (Tischer 2008)

> 'However, I cannot help thinking that you cultivate old oppositions or antagonisms and that each of you focuses on individual sub-aspects that actually should be merged to an overall picture. Basically, the question is whether the financial crisis was caused by institutional or macro-economic factors. Presumably that is not your intention, but the neutral reader gets the impression that each of you prefer mono-causal explanations denying the other factor´s impact.' (Peter JK 2008)

Contrary to these findings, analyses in research on readers' comments often underline their *emotional* tone, that it is rather about 'venting one's anger' (cf. Friemel and Dötsch 2015: 262) than sharing and exchanging ideas. For the analysis presented here, we also want to stress the deliberative elements in readers' comments notwithstanding the practices of moralizing illustrated above.

Motifs of public debates such as greed—in other research described as a specific frame (cf. Bach et al. 2012)—and their strategic uses in public communication are themselves repeatedly discussed. The deconstruction of metaphors as a clearly meta-communicative act (in detail Averbeck-Lietz et al. 2015) seems to be a typical argumentative pattern in deliberative sequences in the expert's blog posts analyzed in this study. Contrasting moralizations, the bloggers request a more differentiated view instead of limiting the analysis of causes on a personalized and personality-related level to personal defaults such as the 'greed' of some bankers, to outrage or populism while neglecting to discuss measures and regulatory approaches to overcome the crisis:

> 'I think that the public discussion falls short of the aspect of regulation. But it does not cost anyone headline hitting billions, and you cannot complain but you have to have a clue, at least to some extent.' (Voß 2008c)

> 'However, we should be careful not to limit the debate of causes of the financial crisis to a debate on greed. This does not meet and satisfy the requirements of an analysis of causes but is useful during election campaigns.' (Elsner 2008b)

10.5 Conclusion

With the analysis presented here we exemplarily shed light on a specific part of multi-faceted moral debates during the financial crisis in 2008 and the communicative practices and communicative constructions of norms and values in a media-related constellation of actors constituting a specific collectivity of debate. The figurational approach thereby offered the chance for an integrative, cross-media analysis of crisis-related normative controversies while reflecting on the specific interplay of actors, practices and structures characterizing and moulding these processes. Hence, it is a fruitful way to reflect on and to provide insight into *how* norms, values and ethics are constructed within debates and negotiations in situations of crises.

As we have illustrated, the communicative engagement with the crisis in the constellation of actors and media ensemble of financial blogs is not simply a matter of 'blaming and shaming' (Habermas 2007: 420), of indignation and contempt in a stereotyping sense (for semantic mechanisms of blaming cf. Bergmann 1998: 286f.). Rather, we have shown the interplay of practices of moralizing and deliberating—including critical reflections on an issue as well as on processes of public communication—by arguing, giving and searching background information, claiming for differentiated considerations of complex problems, and deconstructing populist metaphors. Public welfare and its hindrances, measures of regulation of financial markets, 'appropriate' (political) action but also desirable norms of 'appropriate' public (crisis) communication in terms of transparency, respect and veracity are negotiated in blogs and reader comments. Two mechanisms are central to characterize communicative construction of norms and values in the figuration analyzed: they are constructed (1) via claims implicitly linked to specific ideas of preferable guiding principles for action and (2) via critique and stated deficiencies.

The references to norms and values in the data presented here validate norms reflected in settings of 'deliberation experiments' (Grönlund et al. 2010: 96), being leading principles for professional deliberative discourses such as parliamentary debates (Bächtiger et al. 2010).

Nevertheless, we find some differences between blogs with their more or less implicitly accepted rules of a netiquette (cf. Schenk et al. [in press]) and their readers' comments: namely stronger moralizations related to latent *emotionalization and dramatization*, which is typical for communication of unreflected indignation (cf. Münch 1995: 214–240) in a part of the readers' comments. This underlines the necessity to examine further specific constellations of actors, their communicative practices and the entangled media ensembles in order to shed light on heterogeneities as well as overarching common characteristics in crisis-related debates and processes of communicative constructions of norms and values under conditions of deep mediatization and within different specific media settings and their specific affordances.

Against the backdrop of communicative practices of moralizing relating to different types and forms of social evaluation, their commingling with aspects of deliberation and the visible reflection and argumentation of norms and values—not at least the verbal deconstruction of populist metaphors by some bloggers—we propose a concept of deliberating beyond the pure ideal-type of just and interest-free speech without power plays and strategic communication. This matches the current status quo of deliberation research which refers to practices of bargaining, promising, story-telling, even of threatening (cf. Schaal and Ritzi: 2009; Bächtiger and Wyss 2013). Similarly, Mansbridge (2015: 14) highlights citizens' moralizations as 'compatible' with public deliberation. Complementary to such findings concerning mixtures of communicative practices in deliberation research, in our own research we mostly identify intermingled processes between real type-deliberations and real type-moralizations. Correspondingly, we conclude that social research on public debates cannot neglect neither moralization nor deliberation as crucial concepts to rethink social communication and to describe dynamics and negotiations in public debates profoundly.

In this context, further reflection is required on the theoretical and empirical conceptualization of moralization and deliberation *as a kind of continuum* of two intermingled but also differentiated modes of communication and complementary sets of communicative practices.

Notes

1. In Germany, blogs do not have the same rights and protective mechanisms as traditional journalism, as for example the protection of sources and informants (Arnold 2014: 146–160; Averbeck-Lietz 2014: 95–97).
2. If we speak of 'participation' we are aware that we refer to a mostly privileged segment of bloggers and their (partly journalist) readers. Blogging, active commenting on posts and even reading blogs are relatively rare practices among German onliners older than the age of 14 (van Eimeren and Frees 2014: 388). Citizens who actively engage and participate in

public mostly have a certain motivation related to their positioning and further engagement in the respective social field (Couldry et al. 2007).

3. As generally in social sciences and philosophy, ethics are understood as the critical reflection of morals (Rath 2014: 37f.) or a kind of meta-morality (Greene 2014: 15). Bergmann and Luckmann (1999: 18, 22) mention that people are potentially able to reflexively observe their own (moral) actions.
4. http://www.blicklog.com.
5. http://www.diewunderbareweltderwirtschaft.de/.
6. http://blog.zeit.de/herdentrieb/.
7. http://neuewirtschaftswunder.de.
8. *Blick Log* and *Wunderbare Welt der Wirtschaft* were both winners of the comdirect finanzblog award in 2012, the most prestigious award for financial blogging in Germany. The award aims to honour outstanding independent, competent, easily comprehensible blogs which give their readers an understanding of the complexities of the financial world (comdirect finanzblog award n.d.).
9. We use the term 'media amateur' to describe the relation of these actors to professional media and therefore to institutionalized roles in an organized media environment. Yet this characteristic and the classification of communicator roles are rather a snapshot. The example of Dirk Elsner illustrates this strikingly: In July 2012, four years after having established his *Blick Log*, he became semi-professionalized within the media sector as a frequent commentator for the highly specialized branch of digital finance in the German edition of *Wallstreet Journal* and the magazine *Capital* (Elsner n.d).
10. 22 blogposts of *Blick Log*, 16 of *Die wunderbare Welt der Wirtschaft*, 23 of *Neue Wirtschaftswunder* and 13 blogposts of *ZEIT Herdentrieb*. In all, in the period covered the bloggers published 427 (*Blick Log*), 344 (*Die wunderbare Welt der Wirtschaft*), 131 (*Neue Wirtschaftswunder*) or 22 (*ZEIT Herdentrieb*) posts. Hence, we can state a broad range regarding the frequency of posting. The qualitative content analysis using MaxQDA was done by Rebecca Venema with the help of Levke Kehl as a student researcher.
11. One reason may be that *Herdentrieb* as a media blog is forced to 'objectivity' norms and validation including safe sources.
12. Occasionally injustice and the lack of transparency of political rescue measures are symbolized with drastic metaphors, such as 'Guantanamo' (Voß 2008a).
13. We also find other metaphors and verbal images in the readers' comments: Moralizations also co-occur in conjunction with metaphors of game and gambling, designating bankers and managers as 'gamblers' or 'finance-jugglers' (for game as a frame in international mass media coverage cf. Joris et al. 2014).

References

Arens, Edmund. 1997. Discourse ethics and its relevance for communication and media ethics. In *Communication ethics and universal values*, eds. Clifford Christians, and Michael Traber, 46–68. Thousand Oaks, CA, London and New Delhi: Sage.

Arnold, Dirk. 2014. *Medienregulierung in Europa. Vergleich der Medienregulierungsinstrumente und -formen der EU-Mitgliedsstaaten vor dem Hintergrund technischer Konvergenz und Europäisierung*. Baden-Baden: Nomos.

Averbeck-Lietz, Stefanie. 2014. Transparenz, Verantwortung und Diskursivität als Herausforderungen einer Ethik der Online-Kommunikation. In *Kommunikation über Grenzen. Studien deutschsprachiger Kommunikationswissenschaftler zu Ehren von Joan Hemels*, eds. Arnulf Kutsch, Stefanie Averbeck-Lietz, and Heinz Eickmans, 79–107. Münster: LIT.

Averbeck-Lietz, Stefanie, and Christina Sanko. 2015. Kommunikationsethik im Feld der Wirtschaft: Praktischer Diskurs oder Moralisierung? Konzeption eines Forschungsprojektes und Fallstudie. In *Neuvermessung der Medienethik. Bilanz, Themen und Herausforderungen seit 2000*, eds. Marlies Prinzing, Matthias Rath, Christian Schicha, and Ingrid Stapf, 162–176. Weinheim: Beltz/Juventa.

Averbeck-Lietz, Stefanie, Andreas Hepp, and Rebecca Venema. 2015. Communicative figurations of financial blogging: Deliberative and moralising modes of crisis communication during the Eurocrisis. In *The dynamics of mediatized conflicts*, eds. Mikkel F. Eskjær, Stig Hjarvard, and Mette Mortensen, 71–89. New York: Peter Lang.

Ayaß, Ruth, and Christian Meyer. 2012. *Sozialität in slow motion: Theoretische und empirische Perspektiven. Festschrift für Jörg Bergmann*. Wiesbaden: Springer VS.

Bach, Thomas, Mathias Weber, and Oliver Quiring. 2012. Das Framing der Finanzkrise. Deutungsmuster und Inter-Media Frame Transfer im Krisenherbst 2008. *SCM* 1 (2): 193–224.

Bächtiger, André, and Dominik Wyss. 2013. Deliberationsforschung – eine systematische Übersicht. *Zeitschrift für Vergleichende Politikwissenschaft* 7 (2): 155–181.

Bächtiger, André, Seraina Pedrini, and Mirjam Ryser. 2010. Prozessanalyse politischer Entscheidungen: Deliberative Standards, Diskurstypen und Sequenzialisierung. In *Jahrbuch für Handlungs- und Entscheidungstheorie*, eds. Joachim Behnke, Thomas Bräuninger, and Susumu Shikano, 194–226. Wiesbaden: Springer VS.

Baden, Christian, and Nina Springer. 2014. Com(ple)menting the news on the financial crisis: The contribution of news users' commentary to the diversity of viewpoints in the public debate. *European Journal of Communication* 29 (5): 529–548.

Bartels, Hans. 2008, Oktober 14. [Comment to blogpost 'Dünne und enttäuschende Erklärung vom Bankenverband zu Fehlern der Branche'] *Blick Log.* http://www.blicklog.com/2008/10/14/dunne-und-enttauschende-erklarung-vom-bankenverband-zu-fehlern-der-branche/. Accessed 30 Mar 2017.

Baumer, Eric, Mark Sueyoshi, and Bill Tomlinson. 2008. Exploring the role of the reader in the activity of blogging. In *CHI 2008. The 26th Annual CHI Conference on Human Factors in Computing Systems*, ed. Margaret Burnett, 1111–1120. Florence: Association for Computing Machinery.

Bergmann, Jörg. 1998. Introduction: Morality in discourse. *Discourse, Research on Language and Interaction* 31 (3–4): 279–294.

Bergmann, Jörg R., and Thomas Luckmann. 1999. Moral und Kommunikation. In *Kommunikative Konstruktion von Moral. Struktur und Dynamik der Formen moralischer Kommunikation*, eds. Jörg R. Bergmann and Thomas Luckmann, 13–38. Wiesbaden: Westdeutscher Verlag.

boyd, danah. 2010. Social network sites as networked publics: Affordances, dynamics, and implications. In *Networked self: Identity, community, and culture on social network sites*, ed. Zizi Papacharissi, 39–58. London: Routledge.

Brosda, Carsten. 2008. *Diskursiver Journalismus: Journalistisches Handeln zwischen kommunikativer Vernunft und mediensystemischem Zwang*. Wiesbaden: Springer VS.

Burkart, Roland. 2002. *Kommunikationswissenschaft: Grundlagen und Problemfelder. Umrisse einer interdisziplinären Sozialwissenschaft.* Wien: Böhlau.

Cetin, Emel. 2012. 'Denn sie wissen nicht was sie tun.' Eine Diskursanalyse über die Finanzkrise 2008 in deutschen Tageszeitungen. In *Krise, Cash und Kommunikation – Die Finanzkrise in den Medien*, eds. Anja Peltzer, Kathrin Lämmle, and Andreas Wagenknecht, 95–110. Konstanz: UVK.

comdirect finanzblog award. n.d. Der comdirect finanzblog award. http://finanzblog-award.de/award/. Accessed 30 Mar 2017.

Couldry, Nick. 2010. *Why voice matters: Culture and politics after neoliberalism.* London: Sage.

Couldry, Nick, Sonia M. Livingstone, and Tim Markham. 2007. *Media consumption and public engagement. Beyond the presumption of attention.* Houndmills: Palgrave.

Debatin, Bernhard. 2011. Ethical implications of blogging. In *The handbook of global communication and media ethics*, ed. Robert S. Fortner, 823–843. London: Blackwell.

edicius. 2008. [Comment #22 to blogpost 'Eiszeit in Deutschland'] *ZEIT Herdentrieb.* http://blog.zeit.de/herdentrieb/2008/11/27/eiszeit-in-deutschland_446. Accessed 30 Mar 2017.

Elsner, Dirk. 2008a, September 10. Wir brauchen eine Debatte über eine neue Finanzmarktordnung! [blogpost]. http://www.blicklog.com/2008/09/10/wir-brauchen-eine-debatte-uber-eine-neue-finanzmarktordnung/.

Elsner, Dirk. 2008b, October 20. Die von Ackermann beschleunigte Gier-Debatte führt von den Krisenursachen weg [blogpost]. http://www.blicklog.com/2008/10/20/die-von-ackermann-beschleunigte-gierdebatte-fuhrt-von-krisenursachen-weg/. Accessed 30 Mar 2017.

Elsner, Dirk. n.d.. Digital Finance: Kolumne Bankenwandel für das Wall Street Journal [blogpost]. http://www.blicklog.com/finanzmarkte/trends-im-banking-20/digital-finance-kolumne-bankenwandel-fr-das-wall-street-journal/. Accessed 30 Mar 2017.

Frank. 2008. [Comment # 9 to blogpost 'Von Financial Engineers und Betrügern'] *ZEIT Herdentrieb*. http://blog.zeit.de/herdentrieb/2008/09/25/von-financial-engineers-und-betrugern_365. Accessed 30 Mar 2017.

Fricke, Thomas. 2008, November 13. Das ist Ihre Rezession, Frau Merkel [blogpost]. https://neuewirtschaftswunder.de/2008/11/13/das-ist-ihre-rezession-frau-merkel/#more-16747. Accessed 30 Mar 2017.

Friemel, Thomas N., and Mareike Dötsch. 2015. Online reader comments as indicators for perceived public opinion. In *Kommunikationspolitik für die digitale Gesellschaft*, eds. Martin Emmer and Christian Strippel, 151–172. Berlin. doi: 10.17174/dcr.v1.0.

Greene, Joshua. 2014. *Moral tribes. Emotion, reason and the gap between us and them*. New York: Penguin.

Grönlund, Kimmo, Maija Setälä, and Kaisa Herne. 2010. Deliberation and civic virtue: Lessons from a citizen deliberation experiment. *European Political Science Review* 1 (1): 95–117.

Habermas, Jürgen. 1990. Discourse ethics. Notes on a program of philosophical justification. In *The communicative ethics controversy*, eds. Seyla Benhabib and Fred R. Dallmayr. 60–110. Cambridge, MA: MIT Press.

Habermas, Jürgen. 2007. Kommunikative Rationalität und grenzüberschreitende Politik: eine Replik. In *Anarchie der kommunikativen Freiheit*, eds. Peter Niesen, and Benjamin Herborth, 406–459. Frankfurt am Main: Suhrkamp.

horst_m. 2008, September 17. [Comment to blogpost 'Der Marshallplan war auch ein Bailout!'] *Die wunderbare Welt der Wirtschaft*. http://www.diewunderbareweltderwirtschaft.de/2008/09/der-marshallplan-war-auch-ein-bailout.html. Accessed 30 Mar 2017.

Imhof, Kurt. 2014. Medien und Öffentlichkeit: Krisenanalytik. In *Kommunikationswissenschaft als Integrationsdisziplin*, ed. Matthias Karmasin, Matthias Rath, and Barbara Thomaß, 341–366. Wiesbaden: Springer VS.

Joris, Willem, Leen d'Haenens, and Baldwin van Gorp. 2014. The euro crisis in metaphors and frames: Focus on the press in the low countries. *European Journal of Communication* 29 (5): 608–617.

Kepplinger, Hans M. 2009. *Publizistische Konflikte und Skandale*. Wiesbaden: Springer VS.

Kuckartz, Udo. 2014. *Qualitative Inhaltsanalyse. Methoden, Praxis, Computerunterstützung*. Weinheim: Beltz Juventa.

Kuhn, Oliver E. 2014. *Alltagswissen in der Krise: Über die Zurechnung der Verantwortung für die Finanzkrise*. Wiesbaden: Springer VS.

Lübberding, Frank. 2008a. [Comment #46 to blogpost 'Ehrfurcht vor der Hochfinanz'] *ZEIT Herdentrieb*. http://blog.zeit.de/herdentrieb/2008/10/23/ehrfurcht-vor-der-hochfinanz_378. Accessed 30 Mar 2017.

Lübberding, Frank. 2008b. [Comment #38 to blogpost 'Strategie in Rettungsaktionen'] *ZEIT Herdentrieb*. http://blog.zeit.de/herdentrieb/2008/10/02/strategie-in-rettungsaktionen_366. Accessed 30 Mar 2017.

Luckmann, Thomas. 1997. The moral order of modern societies, moral communication and indirect moralising. *Budapest Collegium: Public Lectures No. 17*. http://www.infoamerica.org/documentos_pdf/luckmann01.pdf. Accessed 30 Mar 2017.

Luckmann, Thomas. 2012. Alles Soziale besteht aus verschiedenen Niveaus der Objektivierung. Ein Gespräch mit Thomas Luckmann. In *Sozialität in Slow Motion. Theoretische und Empirische Perspektiven. Festschrift für Jörg Bergmann*, eds. Ruth Ayaß and Christian Meyer, 21–39. Wiesbaden: Springer VS.

Mansbridge, Jane. 2015. Deliberative und nicht-deliberative Verhandlungen. In *Jahrbuch für Handlungs- und Entscheidungstheorie*, eds. André Bächtiger, Susumu Shikano, and Eric Linhart, 1–39. Wiesbaden: Springer VS.

Marc. 2008, September 30. [Comment to blogpost 'Notpaket übersieht Krebsgeschwür der Finanzmarktkrise'] *Blick Log*. http://www.blicklog.com/2008/09/19/notpaket-ubersieht-krebsgeschwur-der-finanzmarkt-krise/. Accessed 30 Mar 2017.

Münch, Richard. 1995. *Dynamik der Kommunikationsgesellschaft*. Frankfurt am Main: Suhrkamp.

Nawratil, Ute, and Philomen Schönhagen. 2009. Die qualitative Inhaltsanalyse: Rekonstruktion der Kommunikationswirklichkeit. In *Qualitative Methoden in der Kommunikationswissenschaft*, ed. Hans Wagner, 333–346. Baden-Baden: Nomos.

Neckel, Sighard. 2011. Der Gefühlskapitalismus der Banken: Vom Ende der Gier als 'ruhiger Leidenschaft'. *Leviathan* 39: 39–53.

Neuberger, Christoph. 2014. Konflikt, Konkurrenz und Kooperation. Interaktionsmodi in einer Theorie der dynamischen Netzwerköffentlichkeit. *Medien- und Kommunikationswissenschaft* 62(4): 567–587.

otti. 2008. [Comment # 27 to blogpost 'Strategie in Rettungsaktionen'] *ZEIT Herdentrieb*. http://blog.zeit.de/herdentrieb/2008/10/02/strategie-in-rettungsaktionen_366. Accessed 30 Mar 2017.

Papacharissi, Zizi. 2004. Democracy online: Cavity, politeness, and the democratic potential of online political discussion groups. *New Media and Society* 6 (4): 259–283.

paradoxus. 2008. [Comment # 35 to blogpost 'Von Financial Engineers und Betrügern']. *ZEIT Herdentrieb.* http://blog.zeit.de/herdentrieb/2008/09/25/von-financial-engineers-und-betrugern_365. Accessed 30 Mar 2017.

Perlmutter, David D. 2008. *Blog wars.* New York: Oxford University Press.

Peter JK. 2008. [Comment # 28 to blogpost 'Ehrfurcht vor der Hochfinanz'] *ZEIT Herdentrieb.* http://blog.zeit.de/herdentrieb/2008/10/23/ehrfurcht-vor-der-hochfinanz_378. Accessed 30 Mar 2017.

Rath, Matthias. 2014. *Ethik der mediatisierten Welt: Grundlagen und Perspektiven.* Wiesbaden: Springer VS.

Rosen, Jay. 2006, June 27. The people formerly known as the audience. Press Think. http://archive.pressthink.org/2006/06/27/ppl_frmr_p.html. Accessed 30 Mar 2017.

Schaal, Gary S., and Claudia Ritzi. 2009. Empirische Deliberationsforschung. *Max Planck Institute for the Study of Societies, Cologne MPIfG Working Paper 09/9.* http://www.mpifg.de/pu/workpap/wp09-9.pdf. Accessed 30 Mar 2017.

Schenk, Michael, Julia Niemann, and Andrea Briehl. in press. Das Selbstverständnis von Themenbloggern und ihr Beitrag zur Meinungsbildung. In *Medienwandel – Wandel der Demokratie? Das demokratische Potenzial der Social Media*, eds. Tobias Eberwein, Gabriele Melischek, Josef Seethaler, and Corinna Wenzel. Wien: Verlag der Österreichischen Akademie der Wissenschaften.

Schmidt, Andreas. 2015. Moralvorstellungen in der öffentlichen Debatte: Konzeptionelle und methodische Überlegungen zu Relevanz und empirischer Untersuchung. *Studies in Communication | Media* 4 (2): 69–134.

Schranz, Mario, and Mark Eisenegger. 2012. The media construction of the financial crisis in a comparative perspective—An analysis of newspapers in the UK, USA and Switzerland between 2007 and 2009. *Swiss Journal of Sociology* 37 (2): 241–258.

Schreier, Margrit. 2014. Qualitative content analysis. In *The SAGE handbook of qualitative data analysis*, ed. Uwe Flick, 170–183. London: Sage.

Schütz, Alfred, and Thomas Luckmann. 1973. *The structures of the life-world*, vol. 1. Evanston, IL: Northwestern University Press.

Silverstone, Roger. 2007. *Media and morality: On the rise of mediapolis.* London: Polity Press.

Sobieraj, Sarah, and Jeffrey M. Berry. 2011. From incivility to outrage: Political discourse in blogs, talk radio, and cable news. *Political Communication* 28 (1): 19–41.

Stadler, Detlef. 2008. [Comment #22 to blogpost 'Die EZB muss – und wird – die Zinsen senken'] *ZEIT Herdentrieb.* http://blog.zeit.de/herdentrieb/2008/10/07/die-ezb-muss-und-wird-die-zinsen-senken_367. Accessed 30 Mar 2017.

Stroud, Natalie J., Joshua M. Sacco, Ashley Muddiman, and Alexander L. Curry. 2015. Changing deliberative norms on news organizations' Facebook sites. *Journal of Computer-Mediated Communication* 20 (2): 1–16.

Suhay, Elisabeth, Allyson Blackwell, Cameron Roche, and Lucien Bruggeman. 2015. Forging bonds and burning bridges: Polarization and incivility in blog discussions about occupy wall street. *American Politics Research* 43 (4): 643–679.

Tischer, Dietmar. 2008. [Comment #26 to blogpost 'Kein Land kann sich von der Krise abkoppeln'] *ZEIT Herdentrieb.* http://blog.zeit.de/herdentrieb/2008/11/04/kein-land-kann-sich-von-der-krise-abkoppeln_386. Accessed 30 Mar 2017.

Tomin, Marijana, and Stefanie Averbeck-Lietz. 2015. Thomas Luckmann – Sozialkonstruktivismus und Kommunikation. In *Soziologie der Kommunikation. Die Mediatisierung der Gesellschaft und die Theoriebildung der Klassiker,* Stefanie Averbeck-Lietz, 195–230. Berlin and Boston: De Gruyter-Oldenbourg.

van Eimeren, Birgit, and Beate Frees. 2014. 79 Prozent der Deutschen online – Zuwachs bei mobiler Internetnutzung und Bewegtbild. *Media Perspektiven* 7–8: 378–396.

Voß, Ulrich. 2008a. September 22. Meine Meinung zum Rettungspaket: Gut, gut, richtig schlecht, totaler Mist [blogpost]. http://www.diewunderbareweltderwirtschaft.de/2008/09/meine-meinung-zum-rettungspaket-gut-gut.html. Accessed 30 Mar 2017.

Voß, Ulrich. 2008b. October 9. Heli-Heusi fordert Banken in Staatsbesitz! [blogpost]. http://www.diewunderbareweltderwirtschaft.de/2008/10/heli-heusi-fordert-banken-in.html. Accessed 30 Mar 2017.

Voß, Ulrich. 2008c. November 5. EZB unterstützt Börse für CDS. Ich will mehr [blogpost]. http://www.diewunderbareweltderwirtschaft.de/2008/11/ezb-untersttzt-brse-fr-cds-ich-will.html. Accessed 30 Mar 2017.

Wermuth, Dieter. 2008, September 25. Von Financial Engineers und Betrügern [blogpost]. http://blog.zeit.de/herdentrieb/2008/09/25/von-financial-engineers-und-betrugern_365. Accessed 30 Mar 2017.

Wessler, Hartmut. 2008. Investigating deliberativeness comparatively. *Political Communication* 25 (1): 1–22.

Wunden, Wolfgang. 1994. Grenzen öffentlichen Zeigens. Privatheit als Element einer Kultur der Öffentlichkeit. In *Öffentlichkeit und Kommunikationskultur. Beiträge zur Medienethik*, ed. Wolfgang Wunden, 165–179. Hamburg, Stuttgart: Steinkopf Verlag.

Zeise, Lucas. 2008. [Comment # 5 to blogpost 'Wunschdenken reicht nicht'] *ZEIT Herdentrieb.* http://blog.zeit.de/herdentrieb/2008/11/07/wunschdenken-reicht-nicht_394. Accessed 30 Mar 2017.

11

Mediatization of the Roman Catholic Church

Kerstin Radde-Antweiler, Hannah Grünenthal and Sina Gogolok

11.1 Introduction

In June 2016, a wedding of German celebrities was broadcast on television with great media attention. For the preparation of this TV wedding, the bridal couple used a new online portal 'MeineTrauKirche',[1] a service run by the archdiocese of Cologne. The wedding itself was conducted by a Roman Catholic priest who gave interviews on the occasion.

K. Radde-Antweiler (✉) · H. Grünenthal · S. Gogolok
Zentrum für Medien-, Kommunikations- und Informationsforschung (ZeMKI), University of Bremen, Linzer Str. 4, 28359 Bremen, Germany
e-mail: radde@uni-bremen.de

H. Grünenthal
e-mail: gruenenthal@uni-bremen.de

Questioned on the necessity of such a broadcasting of belief which was often perceived as inappropriate, he stressed that '(i)t is important to bring things together, things that have nothing to do with each other at first sight, because God wants to be everywhere. And if the world does not go to church, then the Church has to go to the world.'[2] This priest is a youth priest with an active Facebook profile. He preaches and gives film reviews on local radio, publishes his own songs and preaches sermons on his YouTube channel. There are other examples which suggest that social media are an integral part of the Roman Catholic Church in Germany; for example, the organization for clerical professions and ecclesiastical services of the German bishop conference [Zentrum für Berufungspastoral der Deutschen Bischofskonferenz] started the project 'ValerieundderPriester' in 2016,[3] in which a young non-religious female journalist accompanies a priest and publishes her observations on different media formats such as blogs, Facebook, and YouTube. And even some of the German bishops themselves have begun to tweet.

At first glance, social media seem to have arrived in the world of religious organizations: namely the Church. Nevertheless, religious organizations—and the Catholic Church in particular—are said to be more reluctant to accept change than many other organizations. And furthermore, people seem to have different expectations of how the Catholic Church has to deal and interact with media: one example is the response to the aforementioned wedding, where reactions—in magazines, television, newspapers as well as in social media—ranged widely, from statements such as 'Finally a Catholic priest who speaks casually and touches my heart!' to responses such as 'Not a Church for pagans but a Church of pagans!' And within the religious organization itself, we can observe quite critical remarks regarding digital media: for example, the leader of the German bishop conference, Cardinal Marx, who stressed during a press conference in 2015 that 'blogging sometimes leads to dementia, doesn't it?'.[4]

So, the crucial question remains: how exactly does the Roman Catholic Church act and react towards media? Depending on their perspective, academic studies emphasize either a high mediatization or a low mediatization of religious organizations with resistance to media change. What is the reason for such contradicting evaluations concerning religious organizations and how can they be explained? In this article, we analyze an exemplary religious organization, namely the Roman Catholic Church, and ask for specific resistance to media change. As religious organizations are not monolithic entities but have their own inner dynamics, we call for a necessary distinction between different actors and especially religious authority figures involved within the religious organization. By taking a figurational point of view, it is possible to make those inner dynamics visible and thus explain the aforementioned contradictions.

11.2 Current State of Research

There are divergent research positions concerning the transformation of religious organizations in times of deep mediatization. Dawson and Cowan (2004), for example, stressed that the change of media equalizes different actors and positions and that such richness of communication tools was believed to open and disseminate many stocks of knowledge, as well as to prevent a control of their interpretation through traditional authorities. Furthermore, Possamai and Turner state that 'global information technologies undermine traditional forms of religious authority because they expand conventional modes of communication, open up new opportunities for debate and dispute, and create alternative visions of what religion is, how it should operate, and how it should answer to the larger society' (Possamai and Turner 2012: 199). The invention of modern mass media, and then of the internet, was from the very beginning seen as a threat to established authorities. The thesis that mass media are a danger to traditional organizations is based on the assumption that a low-threshold access to information and a massive distribution of knowledge implies a loss of control for the established authorities. Eickelman and Anderson (1999), for example, believe that new media technologies challenge established authorities within organizations such as the Catholic Church, and in some cases even replace them. They state that through the development and the widespread accessibility of new communicational technologies, individuals are able to interpret their religious texts autonomously from established organizations. The consequences of such an actor-specific ascription would be a loss of interpretational sovereignty for the established Churches as well as new constructions of religious authority (Hjarvard 2008, 2013; Lövheim 2011; Lundby 2013).

In the established Christian Churches, ecclesiastical structures such as office and theological knowledge were perceived as particularly vulnerable owing to privatization and secularization (Norris and Inglehart 2004; Turner 2007; Knoblauch 2008, 2009). Therefore, most studies in the field of church sociology emphasize the influence of new media technologies as a weakening of religious authorities. For example, Gabriel (1999) notes a crisis of Western European Churches which is caused by individualization and, as a result of that, an explosion of diversity within the Church. The church members' attitude towards the Church changed from their commitment to a value community organization to a simple binding to the Church as an organization (Gabriel 1999: 33). But the public accessibility of religious knowledge is not seen as the only way in which new media question religious authorities. Hepp, for example, deduces from his research of Catholicism as a non-territorial community, among other things that mediatization makes visible the plurality of individual beliefs within the Catholic discourse (Hepp 2009, cf. also Knoblauch 2014). As an example, he evaluated the coverage of the World Youth Day in 2005, where a heterogeneous image of Catholicism is depicted that is quite opposite to the homogeneous value horizon often postulated by the Catholic Church. The mediatized coverage produced a public sphere in which different actors—not only officials—were visible and therefore had the possibility to negotiate their respective values of faith (cf. also Gebhardt et al. 2007 and Dorsch-Jungsberger 2014). According to Hepp, another consequence of mediatization is the establishment of translocal media communication, which can hardly be controlled by the Church and consequently leads to a changing social construction of reality. Thus, the different religious organizations have to position themselves and their concepts of meaning and compete within the media. As a consequence, Hepp diagnosed a branding of religion for Catholicism. Religious authority figures such as the pope have to follow the rules of the recent media-society to be perceived in the public sphere. Such a staging of the pope as a 'celebrity' and 'brand' of Catholicism results in a changing papal office in general (cf. Gabriel 2008).

In contrast to that, other studies, supported among others by Campbell (2010, 2013), are based on the assumption that the changing media environment, and particularly the possibilities of the new media technologies, strengthens and confirms the structures of established organizations at the same time. Not only individual actors, but in particular representatives of the Churches, use the new social space as a platform to communicate and position themselves (e.g. Arasa et al. 2010). These changing media environments offer manifold possibilities to spread legitimate recommendations and prohibitions concerning the religious value system. For instance, a pope who is tweeting is able to address a completely new audience, irrespective of place and time. Hence, the intensified online activities of the established authorities have the effect of consolidating and confirming existing hierarchies and religious organizations. Barzilai-Nahon and Barzilai show how established authorities raise and enforce their claims. They describe ultra-orthodox Jewish elites in Israel, who monitor and censor online information with the aim of stabilizing the hierarchical order within their community, the so-called forming or cultural shaping of the internet (Barzilai-Nahon and Barzilai 2005). Campbell also refers to a similar interdependence and demonstrates with regard to the Vatican's website and its YouTube channel how the Catholic Church is trying to keep control of the new media by reducing interactive tools such as the ranking or comment features.

Regarding the results of those studies, both aspects—the stabilization and confirmation of authority in religious organizations as well as its destabilization and challenge—can be observed in line with a changing media environment. So it is not surprising that besides studies which follow one of the two outlined perspectives there is an increasing number of studies that point out that modern mass media have the potential both to threaten and to support established religious organizations. This means that the two perspectives need not exclude each other but can be combined. One prominent example is the analysis by Pauline Cheong. Based on an analysis of the influence on new media on the authority of Protestant pastors in Singapore, she develops a theory of 'dialectics and paradox' (Cheong et al. 2011: 82–84): Representatives of the established religious organizations try to preserve the existing structure of power by communicating via new media, attain public visibility in this new social space and offensively make a stand for their claim of authority. While participating in this public discourse they are simultaneously becoming more vulnerable. Therefore, according to Cheong, they run the risk of being understood as ordinary and approachable. She states that epistemic authority is threatened because communication structures are changing and traditional norms are no longer sufficient. It is also threatened because 'the nature of epistemic function and thereby authority relationships' (Cheong et al. 2011: 944) are questioned. Because people have access to different theological sources and religious knowledge, pastors have to justify their point of view to their followers. Cheong observes among her interviewees the perception that 'the pastoral profession has become proletarianised and de-professionalised' (Cheong et al. 2011: 949). She concludes that on the one hand the established authorities have to participate in the public negotiating processes, if they don't want to completely lose their influence. On the other hand, their status is up for public discussion at the same time. Thus, the new variety of religious voices in public discourse indicates shifts in the conventional criteria of religious authority. Furthermore, criteria such as charisma, which can be represented most plausibly within the new media, become more important (Horsfield 2012).

But does this media-related changing religious authority have consequences for the religious organization as such? Chang (2003) as well as Tracey (2012) stressed the fact that despite the increasing relevance of religious organizations especially in Europe, research on the intersection between religion and organizations plays a minor role; furthermore, the relation to media is nearly neglected. However, the question remains as to whether the transformation of religious organizations in times of deep mediatization can be critically analyzed sufficiently without considering the role of a changing media environment. Regarding the current state of research, our hypothesis is that even if the changing media environment in times of deep mediatization does not dissolve religious authority within religious organizations, one can observe multi-level transformation in them. But to answer this question, we first have to clarify the term 'organization' in the sense of a communicative figurations model.

11.3 The Catholic Church as an Organization

The definition of religious communities as organizations is not without problems (Tyrell 2008; Tracey 2012). Even though Luhmann (1972) pointed early on to the relevance of the three levels of interaction, organizations and society, the sociology of religion was primarily dominated by the discussions on church–sect typology (Kehrer 1988: 8; Tyrell 2005: 32f.). Nevertheless, Beyer stresses that '(m)ore than any of the other forms, it is organizations that give religions the concrete presence that is at issue here' (Beyer 2003: 54). In line with Gabriel (1992), we can speak of different social forms of aggregations which we can assume for Christianity in recent society: ecclesiastical–institutional forms, non-ecclesiastical–social forms and personal, individual forms. Today, research on religious organizations is mostly done by practical theology or church sociology (e.g. Beyer 2006; Daiber 2008) that define Church as a hybrid between institution, organization and movement

(Hauschildt and Pohl-Patalong 2013: 218), which stands in contrast to the community of faith (Hermelink 2011: 110f.). As opposed to religious sociology's focus on individualization, privatization, and migration, research into changes in religious organizations is mostly done by organization sociologists (e.g. Etzioni 1975), although in times of deep mediatization change is pending. With regard to Etzioni (1961), religious organizations differ from other organizations in the means of compliance; that is, the power to influence the behaviour of members (coercive, remunerative or normative) and the latter's involvement (alienative, calculative and moral). A religious organization can be identified as a mainly normative organization, which relies on normative power and controls through the distribution of intrinsic rewards, such as symbolic capital or the additional benefit for society. The interesting question, however, is whether a changing media environment leads to a change of these two variables, which are no longer congruent.

Schimank states that organizations, although acting as one formal organization, consist of different actors who realize the organizations' plans individually. He therefore speaks of organizations as 'supra-individual actors' (Schimank 2010: 327), which are constructed in an everlasting process of 'organizing and organized sense-making' (Weick et al. 2005: 410) via communicative practices. Williams also emphasizes that '(w)hile organizational names, logos, and chains-of-command are meant to provide both the reality and image of unity, that unity should not be assumed' (Williams 2003: 328). In the case of the Catholic Church, it seems particularly natural to assume this unity, as the narrative of the unity is already in the name itself (Greek καθολικός (katholikós): universal). Still, as an organization communicatively constructed by those who are in it, and also by the society in which it exists, it is not enough to analyze the official statements of the Church's representatives. In general, we have to distinguish between the outside (e.g. the representation of the specific organization in the public discourse) and the inside (e.g. the ascription of meaning by the involved actors to the organization as such) of organizations. Both elements are part of the transformation processes of the organization. Therefore, it is important to analyze how different actors are involved in this twofold communicative construction of the organization and whether there are differences which hint to internal dynamics.

11.3.1 *The Communicative Figuration of the Roman Catholic Church*

Taking a figurational approach, we are able to describe the aforementioned communicative construction of organization in a differentiated way. We conducted qualitative empirical research from 2013 to 2015 in the Archbishopric of Cologne, Germany. It was our aim to explore the religious organizations' communicative figurations in times of deep mediatization related to religious authority. Hence, in a first step we analyzed the specific *actor constellations*, *communicative practices* and the character of the *frames of relevance*.

As we argue throughout this volume, each figuration has three features: frames of relevance, constellation of actors and communicative practices. In the case of the Roman Catholic Church as a communicative figuration, the frames of relevance comprise shared beliefs and a shared recognition of hierarchical structures which constitute the organization's practices. The actor's constellation of the Catholic Church is in a wider sense everybody who is baptized. Still, there are people who are more involved in the organization, those who are an active part of it and thus actively shape the organization as such. But next to holders of structurally implemented offices or consecrated priests, there are laypeople and volunteers who fulfil different tasks and duties in the parishes as well.

As the examples at the beginning of this chapter as well as the aforementioned academic studies suggest, the Catholic Church is highly mediatized at the scope of the translocal public discourse: the pope's media presence is professional. There are international events, such as the world youth day, at which a branding of religion becomes obvious. But is that true for the organization as a whole? In this chapter, we will focus on the priests as religious authorities, who serve as representatives and local key persons in the organization of the Roman Catholic Church in Germany. To gain a better understanding of the communicative figuration of the Catholic Church, we will look at a certain actors' constellation, which is the 'local scope' of parishes and their authority construction: namely the priests. In contrast to religious authority figures with a 'translocal scope'—who dominate the public discourse (e.g. the pope or cardinals)—the priests are engaged in the people's religious practices in everyday life. While the public discourse and therefore the translocal representatives of religious authority are by no means irrelevant for the religious actors, we looked for the local communicative practices entangled with media. By gathering the local priests' communicative practices and contextualizing them in the broader picture of the organization's media ensemble, we will differentiate between the various kinds of media practices in the Catholic Church.

11.4 METHODS

The sample selected for this chapter presents only a small part of the study and is focused on priests as local religious authorities. As part of the Creative Unit, we conducted an exploratory pilot study for communicative figurations of religious authorities in Germany, focusing on the archdiocese of Cologne. The media appropriation was explored at the levels of the religious institution, different religious groups within and beyond the religious institution (for example, 'We Are Church e.V.' Cologne, Benedictine Cologne) and three selected municipalities of the Cologne diocese. For this, we conducted 58 interviews with 26 different actors: parish priests and special priests, laypeople of different age and gender, parishes in areas with a majority and a minority of Catholics in relation to Protestants, monks and nuns, members of Catholic groups and secular institutes, and laypeople with an office in the Catholic Church.

The selected sample, however, focuses on the religious authority figures at a local level, namely six priests in the archdiocese of Cologne: three congregation priests, of whom two served in areas with a majority of Catholics and the other one in an area of a Catholic minority; one priest in a monastery, one priest in a leading position in the diocese, and one priest who works in the diocese without a specific parish. As they are all ordained as a priest they themselves are authorities in the organization of the Catholic Church and in the Catholic field. On the other hand, they are still involved in the structures of the Church.

We interviewed each person twice, at an interval of around one year. The first interview was an episodic interview (Flick 2011: 238ff.), in which we focused on semantic and narrative knowledge on authority—in general as well as in special cases, for example regarding the pope, the Bible or personal (religious) role models. We then conducted media questionnaires in order to collect information on their media repertoire (Hasebrink and Popp 2006). The second interview included a photo elicitation (Moser 2005) to trigger narratives and spontaneous reactions (Harper 2002) to visual discourse fragments that emerged in the first interview as well as media-related topics. It also included a networking card (Hepp et al. 2016) with which the participants portrayed their media use in a specific self-chosen scenario. At the end, open questions were discussed.

While the first step of analysis took place in between the first and the second interview, the main analysis was made including the full data. We first triangulated the data from the qualitative interviews that referred to media use, with the answers in the media questionnaire to reconstruct the priests' media appropriation (Ayaß and Gerhardt 2012). In general, we gathered data on the interviewees' media appropriation on three levels. We asked them about their attitude towards media and their media use in episodical interviews, they filled out a media questionnaire on their media use, and we made networking cards in which the priests' media use in one specific situation was collected. As we analyzed the material, we found inconsistencies between these levels. As Juliane Klein, Michael Walter and Uwe Schimank point out in Chap. 15 in this volume, there is a difficulty in investigating latent media usage by qualitative interviews. They suggest that people do not reflect on every practice, but master a lot of their daily life without even reflecting on it—as long as there is no problem, they do not even notice that they are using media to perform certain tasks. We observed the same in our context. When we first contacted people and asked them for an interview, they often gave responses like 'Media? Oh, I barely ever use media. I think you have to look for someone else.' Later, it became obvious that these people do in fact use media. This self-understanding as a minor or non-media user was not limited to priests: we observed the same processes within the Catholic laypeople sample. It seems that the Catholic Church encourages a media-critical attitude and that people who are—and work—in this context, think of themselves as non-media users.

In a second step, we analyzed the qualitative interviews with in vivo coding with focus on the priests' constructions of authority. We generated in vivo codes from the first six interviews until no further categories were found. After that, the in vivo categories were systematized and structured for the purpose of axial coding. Thereafter, we applied the core categories to the whole material. The textual elements related to the core categories were analyzed by means of discourse analysis, for example for speaker position, power relations or self-positioning. In a last step, we combined and compared the findings of those steps. We concentrated on the Catholic priests' attitude towards media, their media appropriation and their self-positioning as authorities in the light of a changing media environment.

11.5 Religious Organizations and Their Media Ensemble

The results of the research on media appropriation within the religious organizations were quite striking. In contrast to the—in the press discourse well-presented—social media activities and prominent media tools such as the YouTube channel 'ask the cardinal', the majority of the priests interviewed by us show quite different communicative practices entangled with media ensembles. What do we mean by that?

Regarding the media ensemble, the members of the Catholic Church's organizational elite use a very broad range of media. In official recommendations, workshops, statements and so on, members of the organization are often encouraged to make use of the broad media ensemble that is available for them. Still, as we will show, the local representatives' media repertoires are usually not as broad as the media environment their organization offers and advises them to make use of. One priest, for example, stated that his 'media landscape is relatively spartan' (KßD246150346_1). This gap between the media ensemble that is offered by the organization and the media repertoire that is actually used by its local representatives is also obvious in the local representatives' communicative practices. Regarding the priests' media repertoire, it becomes obvious that face-to-face communication, books (and, lower-ranked, emails) are defined as the most important media and the main communicative practices by the interviewed priests, as the networking cards and the media questionnaires showed. All interviewees state to prefer direct personal communication face to face, and assessed contact via email as an alternative in cases when personal contact is not possible: 'Well, we talk face to face, I am not a person who is much involved—well, I write emails, of course, but I am not very involved in social media' (BHW262150146_2). That books are seen as most important in order to gather information may be explained by the fact that priests as theologians are used to written texts. Another important medium for communication—which was stressed in nearly all interviews—is interestingly the priests' own sermons in church. These are seen as a platform to take up themes which matters to the parish and to position themselves on these issues: 'the sermon, of course, by which I bring amongst people (…) the topics I care about' (CRS263140126_2). During the sermon the interviewees have the feeling that they can control their words and message and felt therefore explicitly to be religious authority: 'you talk, you preach, and try to be true to life, towards the people—and well, that is something. You preach and you are an authority, telling the word of God as a priest, as a man of the Church' (NKG275140136_1); or 'I might also be an authority at another point, well, Sunday after Sunday at 12 o clock and at holidays I am preaching the sermon in the church' (GRK252140146_1).

In contrast to that, social media seem to be the most problematic medium for them. Only one priest uses social media daily, in this case for private as well as professional communication. For him, media play a very important role in being a priest, but he also mentions that he is an exception: 'Well, I do notice, I am one of very few (...) priests who for example dare to post their personal opinion publicly on Facebook (...) to put something to discussion' (NKG275140136_2). But the other priests who either have a Facebook account and do not use it or do not possess an account at all mention social media a lot, although they do so usually to distance themselves from it. Digital media are less integrated in the interviewees' daily routine than non-digital media. However, the smartphone plays a relevant role for using religious and non-religious apps regularly. Interestingly, this communicative practice doesn't seem to be obvious to most of the priests, who repeatedly emphasized that they don't use media at all or at least very little.

This matches with the priests' understanding of communication in relation to 'media'. Most of the interviewees referred primarily to reciprocal or direct communication (Krotz 2007). Mutual communication via media of personal communication (such as telephone, email, Skype, etc.) as well as standardized media communication referring to mass media played a minor role; virtualized media communication was never used. In addition, the priests often distinguish between media as a tool of communication in contrast to 'the media' as journalistic media with somehow 'standardized' contents. Their media critiques often referred to the latter, for example when one priest pointed out: 'In what derogatory ways some media have written about the time and work of our Cardinal, how he was apostrophized, that does not only hurt me, but it is just a distortion of reality' (GRK252140146_1). The interviewees' main concern was a presumed danger for the organization to be overruled by the press media in choosing specific topics, discussions and positions (and others not), and, moreover, lose its own profile. One priest, who explicitly told us that from time to time he gives interviews for local television or radio, also told us: 'When there is a call, a television

or radio interview, I usually do answer; but usually I don't pick up the topic, because I think you always have to be careful not to have the media set the agenda and dictate the topics' (BHW262150146_2). They fear a kind of powerful influence or patronizing by journalists, so that the media will gain the power to define Church topics, discussions and positions. One priest said: I think we do not have to hide. Just, there is this knockout argument: You postulate moral standards, so you have to live up to them, so you must not do this, and must not do that either ... that is difficult. Because I think that there will always be people who make mistakes (...) but still, as Church, we can talk about certain things (...) that are not mainstream. (...) And this is where I sometimes would like to ask the media to keep a sense of proportion. (CRS263140126_1)
With such a process—so is the priests' presumption—the Church has to adapt to specific media rules and lose its own profile and genuine mode of operation. In addition, they fear that they may lose control over content. The interviewees often stressed that from their perspective journalistic coverage about the Catholic Church is often incorrect. Thus, they are concerned that information is simplified or incorrect, or both, and therefore the public image of the Church is endangered by media rules and habits. In addition, media as the press discourse is often criticized because—often implicitly referred to—media is seen as something that makes things visible—even if they should have stayed invisible: 'Well, that's how media work: they reveal things—in the Church, but also elsewhere—that would otherwise be concealed. That is a service they offer, but the way they do it—I mean, that one bishop [i.e. Cardinal Tebartz-van Elst] dominates the headlines for a whole week, that's something I didn't understand' (JGK2571601246_1). In times of deep mediatization, communicative processes of constructing religious authority extend beyond the borders and classic hierarchies of religious organizations. With deep mediatization, such processes of construction extend beyond the locations and spaces dominated and controlled by religious organizations (churches, parish halls, religious media, etc.) into the public media. Thus, it is not surprising that we can observe reduced communicative practices owing to a limited application of the organization's media environment and, in addition, a very controlled relation to media, whether in the use of non-interactive media or in the refusal to be part of the press discourse.

Interestingly, at the same time we can observe quite different perspectives on media on the part of the priests when it comes to public figures of religious authority. While the majority of the interviewees refuse to be an active part of the media discourse (e.g. active in social media or giving interviews to journalists), all interviews emphasized the importance of social media. Social media is judged as a chance for the Catholic Church to reach people they would not reach otherwise: 'but if you want to reach people you have not reached before, then you have to walk new paths (…) find new paths which you haven't tried yet. And that can be done by using media' (NKG275140136_2). However, the majority referred to the level that we can call translocal scope. For example, the interviewees often approve the Catholic participation in public debates by referring to figures such as the chairman of the German Bishops' Conference or Pope Francis. Media is seen as a possibility for those representatives in translocal positions to communicate via a strong Catholic voice in the public. When one priest was asked about his opinion on Cardinal Marx, he said: 'All the others are very reserved. However, it needs people who have the courage to go there [in talkshows, *the authors*] and to do it and I think Marx can do that. He is very communicative' (KßD246150346_1). We can observe similar arguments when it comes to media coverage on Pope Francis. For example, one priest stressed the outstanding media-related characteristics of the pope: 'He was so good. Protestant colleagues envy us a little … because suddenly you are the subject of debate for a few days' (KßD246150346_1). Being active in media seems to be a necessary criterion for being part of the public discourse—and therefore abilities and character traits that are seen as compatible to the media are well appreciated in persons of a translocal authority position.

At this point, we can observe a distinction between the different religious figures and roles within the organization and their relation to media. Whereas certain media skills are seen as a necessary characteristic for a translocal figure of authority, the same is not characteristic for local authorities. As one priest put it: 'Well, I think it is important to say: we have to be active [in Facebook], as a parish. But that does not mean that I, as the priest, also have to do that, right?' Even if they stress the necessity for the Catholic Church to reach people outside the classical parishes, social media are not seen as the right tool for that within a local scope. Most of the priests see their area of influence as limited to their parish and try to hold up a local profile: 'I cannot reach the public from Flensburg to Munich, but let's say it like that: sometimes I'm glad that we are different here in situ' (KßD246150346_2).

11.6 Conclusion

What do our research results mean for a better understanding of the transformation of religious organizations in times of deep mediatization? There are several points we want to highlight. It became clear, that—in contrast to other organizations (cf. Chaps. 9 and 13 in this volume)—media change and media appropriation is seen in very different ways within the organization of the Catholic Church. We can observe that the priests use only a specific part of the organization's media environment. As a consequence, the organization's media environment isn't used by local authorities in its entirety. Therefore, the communicative practices with a local scope are less entangled with media than the activities with a translocal one. In contrast to public figures such as the pope or some of the bishops, the priests as local authorities show quite different communicative practices related to media. Even if the usage of new media technology is advertized in the public discourse, in the everyday life practices of the local religious authorities in the religious organization these technologies are not part of the priests' media repertoires with respect to the Church's media ensembles and therefore have no further relevance for the communicative practices of the Church's organizational elite. Sometimes new media practices, but also 'traditional' journalistic media, are judged critically. In contrast to social media activities on the part of the globalized, translocal elite in the religious organization, on a local level representatives of the Church are far more conservative and hold on to more traditional and less digital communicative practices. We even observed a broad tendency to try to ignore communicative practices related to social media.

Hepp diagnosed the invention of translocal media communication as a consequence of mediatization and—as a consequence of that—observed the necessity of religious organizations to position themselves within the media (Hepp 2009). However, it seems that such a 'branding of religion' refers only to religious authority figures—religious celebrities, for example the pope—with a translocal scope. From a figurational point of view, we are able to distinguish between different levels of actors' constellation and can critically analyze their specific communicative practices as well as their relation to the organization's media ensemble. Based on the distinction between the outside and the inside of organizations, it seems that deep mediatization affects both levels in quite different ways. Referring to the research discourse, the different results and hypothesis concerning religious organizations can be better understood by the different foci. Even if—and the examples at the beginning show this quite well—social media are an integral part of the organization's media ensemble within a translocal, globalized scope (a very 'deep' degree of mediatization), within the much more local scope of the parishes, the organizations can show resistance to media change at the same time (a much 'less deep' degree of mediatization). And furthermore, it seems that for both scopes there are different requirements for integrating digital media on the part of the religious authorities.

New possibilities for media use are not always chosen. Therefore, while the term mediatization grasps manifold interrelations between the change of media and communication on the one hand, and the changes in culture and society on the other, we also should take contrary movements into consideration when analyzing this process (cf. Hepp and Röser 2014: 165). By distinguishing a translocal and local scope, on the one hand and different forms of authority constructions on the other, we are able to critically analyze that the organization of the Catholic Church transforms in a more differentiated way when it comes to media: as other research shows, there are, for example, tendencies of 'branding' and 'professionalization' on a translocal level. Locally, however, we can observe quite different processes: a reluctant appropriation of the organization's media ensemble by the local authorities even though media-related communication is considered as necessary for translocal authority figures such as the pope or bishops. Regarding the religious organization, we can observe a tension between a 'deep' degree of mediatization in regard to a translocal scope in contrast to a 'less deep' degree of mediatization within a local scope. An interesting follow-up question and part of our own future research is how such different degrees of mediatization produce different tempi of transformations: a slower transformation process on a local level in contrast to a faster transformation process on a translocal level, the tensions that emerge and the negotiations that have to be made—not only between translocal and local, but between different localities worldwide.

Notes

1. http://www.meinetraukirche.de. Accessed: 30 March 2017.
2. http://www.meinetraukirche.de/pfarrer-fink.html. Accessed: 30 March 2017.

3. https://valerieundderpriester.de. Accessed: 30 March 2017.
4. http://www.katholisches.info/2015/09/25/verbloggung-fuehrt-zur-verbloedung-kardinal-marx-ueber-katholische-kritik-am-kurs-der-deutschen-kirche/. Accessed: 30 March 2017.

References

Arasa, Daniel, Lorenzo Cantoni, and Lucio A. Ruiz. 2010. *Religious internet communication. Facts, trends and experiences in the Catholic Church.* Rome: EDUSC.

Ayaß, Ruth, and Cornelia Gerhardt. 2012. *The appropriation of media in everyday life.* Amsterdam: John Benjamins Publishing.

Barzilai-Nahon, Karine, and Gad Barzilai. 2005. Cultured technology: Internet and religious fundamentalism. *The Information Society* 21 (1): 25–40.

Beyer, Peter. 2003. Social Forms of religion and religions in contemporary global society. In *Handbook of the sociology of religion*, ed. Michele Dillon, 45–60. Cambridge: Cambridge University Press.

Beyer, Peter. 2006. *Religions in global society.* London and New York: Routledge.

Campbell, Heidi. 2010. *When religion meets new media. Media, religion and culture.* London: Routledge.

Campbell, Heidi. 2013. *Digital religion. Understanding religious practices in new media worlds.* New York: Routledge.

Chang, Patricia, M.Y. 2003. Escaping the procrustean bed. A critical study of religious organizations, 1930–2001. In *Handbook of the study of the sociology of religion*, ed. Michele Dillon, 123–136. Cambridge: Cambridge University Press.

Cheong, Pauline H., Shirlena Huang, and Jessie P.H. Poon. 2011. Religious communication and epistemic authority of leaders in wired faith organizations. *Journal of Communication* 61 (5): 938–958.

Daiber, Karl-Fritz. 2008. Christliche Religion und ihre organisatorischen Ausprägungen. Überlegungen im Anschluss an Niklas Luhmann. In *Paradoxien kirchlicher Organisation. Niklas Luhmanns frühe Kirchensoziologie und die aktuelle Reform der evangelischen Kirche*, ed. Jan Hermelink and Gerhard Wegner, 25–69. Würzburg: Ergon.

Dawson, Lorne, and Douglas Cowan. 2004. *Religion online: Finding faith on the internet.* New York: Routledge.

Dorsch-Jungsberger, Petra E. 2014. *Papstkirche und Volkskirche im Konflikt: Die Kommunikationsstrategien von Johannes Paul II., Benedikt XVI. und Franziskus.* Berlin: Lit.

Eickelman, Dale, and Jon Anderson. 1999. *New media in the Muslim world. The emerging public sphere.* Bloomington: Indiana University Press.

Etzioni, Amitai. 1961. *A comparative analysis of complex organizations.* New York: Free Press.

Etzioni, Amitai. 1975. *A comparative analysis of complex organizations.* New York: Free Press.

Flick, Uwe. 2011. *Qualitative Sozialforschung. Eine Einführung.* Reinbek bei Hamburg: Rowohlt-Taschenbuch-Verlag.

Gabriel, Karl. 1992. *Christentum zwischen Tradition und Postmoderne.* Freiburg im Breisgau: Herder.

Gabriel, Karl. 1999. Modernisierung als die Organisierung von Religion. In *Institution—Organisation—Bewegung. Sozialformen der Religion im Wandel,* ed. Karl Gabriel, Martin Krüggeler, and Winfried Gebhardt, 19–37. Opladen: Leske + Budrich.

Gabriel, Karl. 2008. Die Versuche des Papstes, in der Welt der Gegenwart Autorität zu gewinnen [The Pope's attempts of achieving authority in today's world]. *Concilium* 44 (3): 361–367.

Gebhardt, Winfried, Ronald Hitzler, and Franz Liebl. 2007. *Megaparty Glaubensfest. Weltjugendtag: Erlebnis—Medien—Organisation.* Wiesbaden: Springer VS.

Harper, D. 2002. Talking about pictures: A case for photo elicitation. *Visual Studies* 17 (1): 13–26.

Hasebrink, Uwe, and Jutta Popp. 2006. Media repertoires as a result of selective media use. A conceptual approach to the analysis of patterns of exposure. *Communications* 31 (2): 369–387.

Hauschildt, Eberhard, and Uta Pohl-Patalong. 2013. *Kirche. Lehrbuch Praktische Theologie 4* [Church]. Gütersloh: Gütersloher Verlagshaus.

Hepp, Andreas. 2009. Der Katholizismus als deterritoriale Vergemeinschaftung. In *Medien—Event—Religion. Die Mediatisierung des Religiösen,* ed. Andreas Hepp and Veronika Krönert, 171–203. Wiesbaden: Springer VS.

Hepp, Andreas, and Jutta Röser. 2014. Beharrung in Mediatisierungsprozessen: Das mediatisierte Zuhause und die mediatisierte Vergemeinschaftung. *Die Mediatisierung sozialer Welten,* ed. Friedrich Krotz, Cathrin Despotovic, and Merle-Marie Kruse, 165–187. Wiesbaden: VS Verlag für Sozialwissenschaften.

Hepp, Andreas, Cindy Roitsch, and Matthias Berg. 2016. Investigating communication networks contextually. Qualitative network analysis as cross-media research. *MedieKultur* 32 (60): 87–106.

Hermelink, Jan. 2011. *Kirchliche Organisation und das Jenseits des Glaubens. Eine praktisch-theologische Theorie der evangelischen Kirche* [Ecclesiastic organisation and the afterlife of belief]. Gütersloh: Gütersloher Verlagshaus.

Hjarvard, Stig. 2008. *The mediatization of religion. Northern lights 2008.* Bristol: Intellect Press.

Hjarvard, Stig. 2013. The mediatization of religion: From the faith of the Church to the enchantment of the media. In *The mediatization of culture and society,* ed. Stig Hjarvard, 78–102. London: Routledge.

Horsfield, Peter. 2012. 'A moderate diversity of books?' The challenge of new media to the practice of Christian theology. In *Digital religion, social media and culture: Perspectives, practices and futures*, ed. Pauline H. Cheong, Peter Fischer-Nielsen, Stefan Gelfgren, and Charles Ess, 243–258. New York: Peter Lang.

Kehrer, Günter. 1988. *Einführung in die Religionssoziologie* [Introduction to the sociology of religion]. Darmstadt: Wiss. Buchgesellschaft.

Knoblauch, Hubert. 2008. Spiritualität und die Subjektivierung der Religion. In *Individualisierung, Spiritualität, Religion. Transformationsprozesse auf dem religiösen Feld in interdisziplinärer Perspektive*, ed. Wilhelm Gräb and Lars Charbonnier, 45–48. Münster: Lit.

Knoblauch, Hubert. 2009. *Populäre Religion. Auf dem Weg in eine spirituelle Gesellschaft*. Frankfurt am Main: Campus.

Knoblauch, Hubert. 2014. Benedict in Berlin. The mediatization of religion. In *Mediatized worlds. Culture and society in a media age*, ed. Andreas Hepp and Friedrich Krotz, 143–158. Basingstoke: Palgrave.

Krotz, Friedrich. 2007. *Mediatisierung. Fallstudien zum Wandel von Kommunikation*. Wiesbaden: VS Verlag für Sozialwissenschaften.

Lövheim, Mia. 2011. Mediatization of religion: A critical appraisal. *Culture and Religion* 12 (2): 153–166.

Luhmann, Niklas. 1972. Die Organisierbarkeit von Religionen und Kirchen. In *Religion im Umbruch: Soziologische Beiträge zur Situation von Religion und Kirche in der gegenwärtigen Gesellschaft*, ed. Jakobus Wössner, 245–285. Stuttgart: Enke.

Lundby, Knut. 2013. Media and transformations of religion. In *Religion across media. From early antiquity to late modernity*, ed. Knut Lundby, 185–202. New York: Peter Lang.

Moser, Heinz. 2005. Visuelle Forschung—Plädoyer für das Medium 'Fotografie'. *MedienPädagogik* 9: 1–27.

Norris, Pippa, and Ronald Inglehart. 2004. *Sacred and secular: Religion and politics worldwide*. Cambridge: Cambridge University Press.

Possamai, Adam, and Bryan Turner. 2012. Authority and liquid religion in cyber-space: The new territories of religious communication. *International Social Science Journal* 63 (208–210): 197–206.

Schimank, Uwe. 2010. *Handeln und Strukturen. Einführung in die akteurtheoretische Soziologie*. Weinheim and München: Juventa-Verlag.

Tracey, Paul. 2012. Religion and organization: A critical review of current trends and future directions. *The Academy of Management Annals* 6 (1): 87–134.

Turner, Bryan. 2007. Religious authority and the new media. *Theory, Culture & Society* 24 (2): 117–134.

Tyrell, Hartmann. 2005. Religion. Organisationen und Institutionen [Religion. Organizations and institutions]. In *Kultur und Religion, Institutionen und*

Charisma im Zivilisationsprozess, ed. Bernhard Schäfers and Justin Stagl, 25–56. Konstanz: Hartung-Gorre.

Tyrell, Hartmann. 2008. Religion und Organisation: Sechs kirchensoziologische Anmerkungen. In *Paradoxien kirchlicher Organisation. Niklas Luhmanns frühe Kirchensoziologie und die aktuelle Reform der evangelischen Kirche*, ed. Jan Hermelink and Gerhard Wegner, 25–69. Würzburg: Ergon.

Weick, Karl E., Kathleen Sutcliffe, and David Obstfeld. 2005. Organising and the process of sensemaking. *Organization Science* 16 (4): 409–421.

Williams, Rhys H. 2003. Religious social movements in the public sphere. In *Handbook of the sociology of religion*, ed. Michele Dillon, 315–330. Cambridge: Cambridge University Press.

12

Political Decision-Making, Face to Face Interactions and Communicative Practices

Tanja Pritzlaff-Scheele and Frank Nullmeier

12.1 Introduction

In the field of politics, mediatization processes have led to a lot of changes in the ways actors communicate with each other. Following the increased introduction of electronically mediated forms of communication, a vast range of communicative practices that constitute the day-to-day routines of politicians have shifted to the online sphere. But while daily routines—for example exchange of information material—are deeply affected by mediatization processes, practices of decision-making still rely on face-to-face interactions within communicative figurations such as working group meetings, briefings, cabinet meetings or committee meetings. Apparently, within actor constellations that produce

T. Pritzlaff-Scheele (✉) · F. Nullmeier
SOCIUM, University of Bremen, Mary-Somerville-Str. 7,
28359 Bremen, Germany
e-mail: tanja.pritzlaff@uni-bremen.de

F. Nullmeier
e-mail: frank.nullmeier@uni-bremen.de

political decisions, face-to-face communication is still looked upon as the most reliable and effective medium when compared with technically mediated forms of interaction. Therefore, figurations of political decision-making can be identified as an area of strong resistance against changes in the media environment. But why exactly are face-to-face interactions so important in decision-making contexts?

Based on a micro-analysis of face-to-face group experiments and a series of computer-mediated chat experiments, this chapter presents examples of typical sequences of face-to-face interaction that are significant within processes of joint decision-making. The aim of the chapter is to show that these typical sequences or patterns of interaction produce and reproduce specific forms of relatedness within figurations of political decision-making.

The underlying assumption of the analysis can be summed up as follows: the importance of face-to-face interaction leads to the prevalence of specific forms of communicative figurations within the field of politics. This finding can be observed when studying figurations such as working group meetings, briefings, cabinet meetings or committee meetings. While vast areas of day-to-day practices are entangled with electronically mediated forms of communication, face-to-face interaction manifests itself as the core medium when it comes to practices of decision-making. Within the field of politics, therefore, the transformation to deep mediatization takes place in a way that is not homogeneous. Eventually, in times of deep mediatization, changes in the media environment may even lead to an *increased importance* of face-to-face interaction within the field of politics.

Different from other social domains, politics still relies on 'direct communication', that is, on 'direct conversation with other people' (Hepp 2013: 64) in face-to-face meetings when actual decisions are made. While a vast range of practices and routines within the field of politics have changed owing to the mass distribution of electronic communication devices, the core practice of politics, collective decision-making (Easton 1957, 1965; Scharpf 1997), still relies on face-to-face encounters.

At first glance, this finding can be interpreted in line with observations from other social domains as well as with observations from other areas of research in political science: First of all, there are findings in research into other social domains on how issues of confidentiality and trust constitute a challenge to actors involved in technically mediated forms of communication (Riegelsberger et al. 2007). Second, the importance of face-to-face interactions is also supported by observations from other areas of decision-making, for example from the private business sector: Especially when it comes to complex decisions that require a significant amount of trust and/or involve decisions on resource allocation and distribution, actors rely on face-to-face meetings.[1] Finally, various shortcomings of technically mediated forms of decision-making interactions have been identified, for example in the context of studies on online deliberation or protest movements.[2]

But although these studies support the idea that face-to-face interactions are of particular importance to political decision-making, they do not present answers to the core question: Why exactly do face-to-face interactions structure figurations of political decision-making in this way? And, furthermore, why might a changing media environment lead to a point at which they become more important?

Following the concept of *communicative figurations*,[3] a promising approach of empirical research that tries to find an adequate answer to these questions is a focus on the construction of *relations* within actor constellations. If one analyzes the micro-level of political interactions, and especially the micro-level of decision-making interactions, it is possible to identify typical sequences of interaction that constitute important *relational structures* within figurations of political decision-making.

Furthermore, the micro-analysis of these typical sequences has implications for the meso-analysis of the political domain as a whole. This link becomes apparent if one takes a closer look at the way Norbert Elias introduces the concept of 'figuration':

> The network of interdependencies among human beings is what binds them together. Such interdependencies are the nexus of what is here called the figuration, a structure of mutually oriented and dependent people. Since people are more or less dependent on each other first by nature and then through social learning, through education, socialization, and socially generated reciprocal needs, they exist, one might venture to say, only as pluralities, only in figurations. (Elias 2012: 525)

For Elias, the concept of figuration is 'a theoretical conceptualization of interdependent human beings' (Kaspersen and Gabriel 2013: 59). Following this line of thought, human beings are social beings that are 'always embedded in figurations, interdependent webs and networks that are always moving, changing, and developing' (Kaspersen and Gabriel 2013: 59). Therefore, Elias focuses on 'relations, processes, and changes in figurations rather than on static structures and states' (Kaspersen and Gabriel 2013: 59).

According to Kaspersen and Gabriel, Elias presents a 'relational perspective' that is 'based on the concept of figuration, which explains that all social life is embedded in interdependent and interweaving social relations' (Kaspersen and Gabriel 2013: 67).

Within this relational perspective, special attention is paid to the embodied, bodily aspects of relational processes. Elias emphasizes the unique emotional and non-verbal capacities of human beings to relate to each other in interaction (Atkinson 2012: 54). He develops a complex, multi-disciplinary theory of embodiment (Atkinson 2012: 55). According to Elias, gestures and facial expressions are 'signals by means of which people communicate involuntarily or with intent the condition of the self-regulation of their emotions to other human beings. The term expression obscures the social, the communicative function of facial and other movements' (Elias 1987: 360).

Therefore, in order to analyze the fundamental differences between face-to-face and technically mediated forms of communicative practices from a relational perspective, it seems promising to take a closer look at communicative practices as speech–body acts (Nullmeier and Pritzlaff 2009: 365) that can be observed in political processes.

In the following, audio-visual data from face-to-face group experiments as well as data from chat-based computer experiments are studied. The analysis of the audio-visual material is based on a micro-ethnographic approach (Streeck and Mehus 2005; LeBaron 2008). Micro-ethnography moves beyond the study of language use in interaction and leads to a holistic study of language use, non-verbal aspects of communication as well as the meaning of bodies and artefacts within the space of interaction. With the help of a micro-ethnographic approach, typical sequences or patterns of face-to-face interactions can be identified in political decision-making contexts.[4]

These sequences of decision-making processes relate the participants of the decision-making interaction to one another. In the following, they are referred to as 'practices of relatedness'. The data from computer-mediated decision-making interactions in a chat environment shows that participants of computer-based decision interactions are more or less unable to perform the same or similar forms of practices or to 'electronically substitute' in a successful way the practices of relatedness observed in face-to-face interactions.

12.2 Face-to-Face Interactions in the Field of Politics

To a large extent, political decision-making takes place in face-to-face interactions within small groups (Sartori 1987: 228). Typical figurations within the field of politics can be identified if one analyzes decision-making contexts such as committee meetings, briefings, closed sessions or summits.

But meetings are not only forms of interaction in which resolutions are prepared and adopted and binding agreements are jointly produced. They are also instances of 'We'-creation within certain actor constellations in which the participants of a meeting have to relate to one another in order to produce a joint decision.

Following Peter L. Berger and Thomas Luckmann, it can be assumed that the 'most important experience of others takes place in the face-to-face situation, which is the prototypical case of social interaction. All other cases are derivatives of it' (Berger and Luckmann 1967: 28). If I interact with someone in a face-to-face meeting, a 'continuous reciprocity of expressive acts is simultaneously available to both of us. This means that, in the face-to-face situation, the other's subjectivity is available to me through a maximum of symptoms. [...] Only here is the other's subjectivity emphatically "close". All other forms of relating to the other are, in varying degrees, "remote"' (Berger and Luckmann 1967: 29).

If two or more actors interact with one another in order to arrive at an agreement or joint decision, the functioning of the process seems to improve in cases where multi-layered 'symptoms', as Berger and Luckmann call them, are mutually available. The focus on different 'forms of relating to the other', as outlined by Berger and Luckmann, suggests that there are sequences or patterns of interaction that constitute these different forms of relatedness.

As previous comparisons between face-to-face and technically mediated forms of communication have shown, actors can only to a lesser extent rely on normative resources such as trust in technically mediated episodes of communication (Anderson 2006; Zhou and Zhang 2006). Especially in computer-mediated contexts that rely only on text messages, the 'essential importance of embodied co-presence for the sake of developing and sustaining trust' (Ess 2011: 9) becomes apparent.[5]

Furthermore, online deliberation and decision processes are often characterized 'by the noise generated by online asynchronous text based discussion' (Spada et al. 2014: 13). Additionally, findings from studies of decision-making practices in protest movements also suggest that online forms of decision-making produce a lot of disruptive behaviour (Maeckelbergh 2009).

In an ethnographic study on *Direct Action* (Graeber 2009), David Graeber even comes to the conclusion that 'decision making is the one thing that is almost impossible to do on the Internet' (Graeber 2009: 237). Therefore, protest movements, at least for the most part, still rely on face-to-face interactions when it comes to joint decision-making.

In face-to-face interactions, actors can mutually rely on multi-layered expressive acts through which they evaluate the decision options at hand. Not only practical reasoning in the rational sense, but also emotional and bodily forms of evaluation and judgment are reciprocally available to the actors involved. Or, as Charles Ess points out, in 'the context of embodied co-presence', we are 'forced to confront "the gaze of the morally significant other"' (Ess 2011: 10). Physical, embodied co-presence involves 'the moral gaze of the other' (Ess 2011: 10). It allows us to 'learn to overcome our *distrust* of one another by "reading" [...] the Other as an embodied being, so to speak, in front of us' (Ess 2011: 24). Therefore, face-to-face communicative practices in general—and practices within figurations of political decision-making in particular—cannot simply be reduced to verbal communication in the sense of mere speech acts, and they cannot be studied in the way one studies written texts. They have to be understood as *speech–body acts* (Nullmeier and Pritzlaff 2009: 365), as material and embodied expressions that relate actors to one another and manifest themselves not only in time, but also in physical, embodied space. They have to be understood as manifestations and articulations within a dynamic relationship of artefacts, practices and social arrangements (Lievrouw 2014: 45–47).

12.3 Practices of Relatedness

Following Joseph Rouse, practices can be defined as 'complex relations of mutual interaction', as patterns of interaction that 'constitute something at issue and at stake in their outcome' (Rouse 2007: 50). Practices are 'complex patterns of mutual responsiveness' (Rouse 2007: 52) that relate individuals within constellations of actors to one another.[6]

In the above-cited quote, Berger and Luckmann discuss different 'forms of relating to the other' (Berger and Luckmann 1967: 29). Communicative practices that relate not only participants of an interaction in general, but also their individual positions or individually articulated contributory acts, can be characterized as—to use a term from family sociology—'practices of relatedness' (Jallinoja and Widmer 2011). Within figurations of political decision-making, these communicative practices produce elements of stability, mutuality and responsiveness. Mutual acts of securing and reassuring are necessary in order to add to the creation of a 'We'-perspective in the ongoing decision-making process and, therefore, are necessary in order to create a situation in which the group as a whole is willing and able to produce a joint decision.

In the context of a micro-analysis of real committee meetings, we identified various patterns or sequences of interaction that can be characterized as practices of relatedness in this sense. The following four examples are micro-elements of interaction that can be observed on a regular basis within figurations of political decision-making, examples being working group meetings, briefings and committee meetings:

- Practices of *translation*. Practices of translation can be identified as sequences in which participants in political face-to-face interactions try to integrate their different background assumptions and webs of meaning into a unified and harmonized use of concepts. These practices may not ensure that all participants talk about 'the exact same thing' when they talk about something, but since participants start using the same words in order to characterize what they are talking *about*, these practices promote the successful progression of the decision process.
- Practices of *repair*. Practices of repair can be identified as micro-interventions during sequences of conflict, misunderstanding or disagreement. These practices have the function of putting the respective interaction back on the right track. Practices of repair are usually performed by a third participant who intervenes in cases where the progress of a two-person conversation/dialogue is impeded by a misunderstanding or disagreement.[7] These practices are often based on non-verbal communication such as gestures and eye contact.
- Practices of *renarration*. Practices of renarration are sequences in which the participants of a meeting renarrate a proposal that has

already been made from their own perspective. By telling a slightly different version of the story from their own perspective, actors seem to be able to integrate the proposed decision into their own, differing, background assumptions. In addition, the multiple—although revised—repetitions of the suggested solution seem to add substance to the idea of a joint solution that the actors as a group can adopt as *their* decision. Through their non-verbal behaviour, participants signalize the growing coherence of the group, their increasing approval of the story that is told again and again in slight variations.

- Practices of *self-authorization*. Practices of self-authorization are sequences in which participants reassure each other of their authority as decision-makers. They define and reinforce their position to legitimately make the actual decision at hand. These practices serve to establish, or re-establish, the self-image of the participants as possessing authority and responsibility in the respective case/issue.

These are only four examples of practices of relatedness that we identified in an analysis of actual committee meetings (Nullmeier and Pritzlaff 2009; Pritzlaff and Nullmeier 2011). All of these practices, however, have one thing in common: they rest on a complex, triadic structure of interaction (Lindemann 2006a, 2006b, 2010, 2012) that includes verbal and non-verbal forms of communication and requires—to adapt Ess's above-cited term—a context in which participants can 'read' each other. In order to do this, referring back to Berger and Luckmann, the availability of a 'maximum of symptoms' is of crucial importance to the participants.

Triadic interaction sequences are characterized by relational dynamics that differ from dyadic types of interaction. And although these sequences in which a speaker 'is defining his or her relationship with two other people simultaneously' (Heatherington and Friedlander 2015: 109) have been analyzed mainly in the area of family therapy, it is important to point out that it is 'equally beneficial to capture these types of relational dynamics in other interactional settings involving three or more participants' (Escudero and Rogers 2015: 33). If one wants to analyze these kinds of relational dynamics within figurations of political decision-making, it is extremely important to move beyond the analysis of language use and to include non-verbal, bodily elements of interaction.

12.4 Empirical Findings

The empirical findings are based on data from two different research projects and a classroom experiment.[8] In a series of 50 face-to-face group experiments conducted in the first research project, participants were asked to deliberate and decide on three related issues/questions concerning possible regulations in the context of the world financial crisis.[9] The decision had to be unanimous. Participants were provided with individual role descriptions that led to differing preferences within the group. There was no chairperson assigned to the respective group. Within the given period of time (eight minutes), they were asked to debate and decide on the three issues simultaneously/combined. A decision form with the three questions on it and one ballpoint pen were placed in the middle of the table in order to document the results being reached by the group.

In the context of the second research project, face-to-face as well as chat-based group experiments were conducted. A group consisting of five participants (group A) was asked to decide on a distribution procedure for an extra amount of money that had to be divided between five members of another group consisting of members with different initial financial funding (group B). The group had to choose between three different distribution procedures by creating a rank order among the suggested procedures. The group decision had to be unanimous. In the second phase of the experiment, group B had to decide whether or not to accept the suggested distribution procedure. Again, the decision had to be unanimous. In case they didn't accept the suggested procedure, the participants had to come up with a numerical suggestion on how to distribute the amount. Some of the group A experiments were conducted in a face-to-face environment; the rest of the group A experiments as well as all of the group B experiments were conducted via chat, using the chat function of z-tree (Fischbacher 2007).

The experimental design of the data used shares similarities with political science experiments that are conducted in order to study deliberation processes (Karpowitz and Mendelberg 2011; Setälä and Herne 2014). The idea behind the comparison between the two extreme cases of face-to-face interaction (FTF) and mere text-based, in other words chat-based, computer-mediated communication (CMC), is similar to the research design presented in previous experiments in experimental political science (see for example Frohlich and Oppenheimer 1998). However, one thing is to be pointed out when labelling the text-only version an 'extreme case': When comparing FTF interactions to text-based forms of CMC, it seems to be an almost logical consequence to assume that the addition of other modes of communication, such as the combination of video data and text messages in the context of video conferencing systems, has a positive effect in the sense that it enables participants to have a richer form of conversation within a given constellation of actors. One may also assume that the addition of other modes of communication automatically leads to a higher level of cooperation and trust among the participants (Riegelsberger et al. 2007: 64). If this were the case, the conclusion would be that the presented shortcomings of text-based CMC are reduced when visual cues are available, for example through the use of video conferencing systems. It has to be pointed out, however, that there is also evidence to the contrary (see for example Walther 2011: 23).

12.4.1 Empirical Findings from Face-to-Face Experiments

In the course of the 50 sessions of face-to-face group experiments, the participants performed practices that were very similar to the practices of relatedness identified as important elements within real committee meetings. Owing to the differing preferences and role descriptions within the group that were provided to the participants of the experiments, the participants' attempts to reach a joint decision were rather 'confrontational'. While some of the interactions were dominated by classical practices such as 'coalition building' (Caplow 1968), other sequences of interaction were to a higher degree structured by attempts to address the group as a whole, appealing to the need for unanimity.

In this series of experiments, not only 'repair practices', but also a slightly different practice that furthered the progression of the establishment of common ground and, finally, the production of trust and a joint decision, was performed by various participants. When there was a confrontation between two different opinions/options, individual actors spontaneously took over the function of a chairperson or moderator, summed up the existing different positions within the group in a few sentences and offered a solution. In order to do this, they took a look around, made eye contact with the other group members and used verbal and non-verbal micro-interventions in order to move the decision interaction to the next stage. These 'moderator'-contributory acts served the function of moving the decision interaction to the next stage, by hinting at possible *relations* among the participants. They not only summed up and secured preliminary results, but also contributed to a 'stable' progression of the decision process.

In addition, another practice was performed quite frequently. It turned out to be very important during the analysis of the experiments to take a closer look at the act of writing down the results. In most cases, one of the participants took over the function of filling out the decision form. Although this finding might at first suggest that one participant took over a simple duty, a different reading seems to be more plausible: the respective participant who, at a certain point within the meeting, took the decision form and the pen usually also repeated and summed up the results (renarration) and stressed the importance of an agreement being reached by the group as a whole. This 'decision closing'-practice—with a focus on actually reaching a result—can be described as based on one participant's 'reading' of the group as a whole. The contributory acts performed by the participant who took over the function of the chairperson are similar to contributory acts that are usually performed by the chairperson in real committee meetings. In order to 'read' the group as a whole, the respective participant heavily relied on non-verbal cues. By performing this type of practice, the participants helped to establish a stable relational structure which served as the basis for the joint decision.

Similar findings were identified during the analysis of the audio-visual recordings of face-to-face group experiments conducted in the context of the FOR 2104 research project on needs-based distribution procedures.

12.4.2 Empirical Findings from Chat Experiments

In the context of the above-mentioned classroom experiment, computer-mediated chat experiments were conducted in an experimental economics laboratory,[10] to test the differences between face-to-face and computer-mediated decision interactions (hereafter referred to as classroom experiment). Similar to the face-to-face group experiments, participants were asked to decide on three related issues/questions. During the experiment, participants were able to deliberate with the members of their group using CMC, that is, an integrated chat function.[11]

In the course of the chat communication, participants tried to perform certain contributory acts in order to electronically substitute relational practices of translation and repair. But these attempts to relate to one another didn't work—not because of the time delay in written communication, but also because participants weren't able to create triadic communication constellations. In face-to-face interactions, this is done using non-verbal forms of communication, such as eye contact and non-verbal utterances. To substitute the lack of mutual availability of multi-layered 'symptoms', in other words the lack of those elements that create an emphatically 'close' subjectivity in the sense of Berger and Luckmann, the participants of the classroom experiment used 'emoticons' during chats (☹, ☺) or abbreviations and acronyms such as LOL (for 'laughing out loud').

Computer-mediated communication took longer, since all acts of signalizing acceptance had to be verbalized and put into written form. And communication didn't go too smoothly—in part because it was perceived as rather anonymous by the participants, but also because 'micro-interventions', in the sense of practices of relatedness, weren't possible in this setting. And although the participants of the classroom experiment knew each other, Table 12.1 shows that trust was still an issue in this CMC environment.

Obviously, although the remark concerning participant three being a spy is ironic, the participants find it difficult to build trust in this environment,[13] and joint decision-making doesn't proceed very smoothly.

In the context of the above-mentioned FOR 2104 research project on needs-based distribution procedures, another series of experiments was conducted using the chat function of z-tree. The section presented in Table 12.2 is an excerpt from these experiments. In this particular chat-based experiment, participants had to agree on a ranking between three different distribution procedures (Majority Decision by the concerned persons themselves [MAJ], Weaker First [WF] and Effort [EFF]). As the example shows, they struggle with the task to verify that each of them actually agrees with a suggested ranking (MAJ, EFF, WF). They repeat the proposal again and again, and try to figure out if all of the five members of the group actually understood the suggestion and are willing to join the group in a unanimous decision.

In the context of the FOR 2104 chat experiments, 36 groups with five participants each were assigned to the group B research design where a group had to discuss whether or not to accept a distribution procedure imposed on them by group A.[15] In case they did not accept the suggested distribution procedure, they had the opportunity to agree on

Table 12.1 Chat protocol from classroom experiment

P[12]	*Original text*	*Translation*
6	Frage 2: hat jemand Einwand gegen "sinnvoll"?	Question 2: does anyone object to "useful"?
5	ok	OK
3	also aufklärung weiter verstärken oder wie?	Thus, keeping people informed more or what?
1	ja	Yes
4	Ja	Yes
2	ja	Yes
3	nö! hab ich nichts gegen	Nope! I don't have anything against that
1	gut also angenommen	Fine, accepted then
6	was ja? Einwand?	What's the yes for? Objection?
1	nummer zwei: sinnvoll	Number 2: useful
6	oder einverstanden?	Or accepted?
2	ja	Yes
3	wie jetzt?	Meaning what?
2	keiner sagt was dagegen oder?	Nobody says anything against this, right?
4	einverstnden sinnvoll, was ist mit Frage 3	Accepted useful, what about question 3
3	was denn nu?	What now?
2	ja sinnvoll verdammt	Yes useful damn it
6	okay, also frage 3	Okay, so question 3
3	bin ich gegen!	I am against that!
1	du wurdest aber überstimmt	But you were overruled
2	keine maßnahmen	No measures
6	keine massnahmen finde ich auch	I agree, no measures
3	hä wo jetzt?	Huh? Where exactly?
6	bei 3	At 3
1	keine maßnahmen	No measures
3	genau keine maßnahmen!	Exactly, no measures!
3	**sag ich doch!**	**That's what I was saying!**
5	warum??	Why??
1	ich glaub, dass nummer drei ein spion ist, der alle verunsichern will;-)	I believe that number three is a spy who wants to unsettle us all;-)

an alternative distribution of 20 experimental tokens (which equals 10 euros). In the course of the 36 sessions, three groups came up with the idea to hand over all of the 20 tokens to one participant and to split the profit after the experiment had ended. In all of the three cases, this option was discussed in the chat environment, but in all of the three cases the participants weren't able to agree on the way to proceed. They all agreed that by 'cheating' on the experimental task in this way

Table 12.2 Chat protocol from FOR 2104 pre-test.[14] (Hamburg ID 2/group 2) structure: group chat; decision rule: unanimity

Player no.	*Chat*	*Translation*
4	jetzt schreibt jeder player seine vorschlagnummer, dann sehen wir mehr in der Mehrheit ist	Now, each player writes down his proposed numbers, then we'll see who has the majority
5	ZUSAMMENFASSUNG BITTE	SUMMARY PLEASE
3	aber hier ist es ja was anderes	But here it's something different
3	geringste ausstattu8ng	Least endowment
3	wenn wir	If we
3	sagen das side am meisten kriegen	Say that they receive the most
1	SG / MEHR / LEI	WF/MAJ/EFF
3	ist es unfair den anderen die sich anst-trengen eggenßüber	It is unfair with regard to those who try hard
3	ausserdem würde doch ehrlioch jeder am liebsten nix tuhen	Furthermore, to be honest, everyone would prefer to do nothing
3	und kohle kassieren	And just collect the cash
5	player 2, dein Vorschlag bitte	Player 2, your proposal please
4	player 1, kannst du dich nicht einfach bitte der Mehrheit anschliessen?	Player 1, could you please just join the majority?
1	die versuchen wir ja grad rauszufinden	We just try to figure out what that is
2	Jeder einmal seinen bevorzugten Vorschlag, dann haben wir Übersicht.	Everyone: your preferred proposal, so we can get an overview
3	haben wir doch schon	We already have it
3	das ist demokratie ;)	That's democracy ;)
1	jeder bitte nochmal genaue Rangfolge aufschreiben	Everyone please: write down your exact order of preference
5	player 1 war schon dran, nun player 2 bitte	Player 1 already had his turn, now player 2 please
3	haben nur noch 170 sek	We only have 170 sec
2	Mehr/SG/Lei	Maj/WF/Eff
3	...	...
5	player 3	Player 3
3	warum solen die die leistunge rbrignen schlechter egstellt werden als die die eh nix tunß	Why should those who perform well be worse off than those who do nothing
3	vorswchlag:	Suggestion:
4	Mehr/SG/Lei	Maj/WF/EFF
3	MEHR/LEI/SG	MAJ/EFF/WF
4	fuck sorry stimme 3 zu!	Fuck sorry I agree with 3!
3	hahahaah dachet schon :D	Hahahaah I thought so :D
4	MEHR LEI SG	MAJ EFF WF
3	jo	Yeah
5	mher lei sg	maj eff wf

(continued)

Table 12.2 (continued)

Player no.	*Chat*	*Translation*
1	also alle für MEHR / SG / LEI ????	Now, everyone for MAJ/ WF/ EFF???
4	JAAAAAA	YEAHHH
4		
1	außer mir ... menno	Except me ... gosh
3	what?	What?
5	mehr sg lei	maj wf eff
3	dachet mehrheit lesitungs chlechtgestellt	I thought majority effort weaker first
3		
4	3 sind für MEHR LEI SG	3 are in favour of MAJ EFF WF
3	jo	Yep
3	oki	OK
5	mehr lei sg, ok	maj eff wf, okay
1	okay MEHR / LEI / SG....	OK, MAJ/ EFF/ WF
4	PLAYER 5 und 1 schliesst ihr euch an?	PLAYER 5 and 1 do you join us?
5	ja	Yes
4	juhuu	Yay
3	player 2 meinst du ;)	You mean player 2 ;)
1	immer doch ... ;)	Still ... ;)
2	OK	OK
3	leute noch 25 sek :S	Folks only 25 sec :S
5	mehr lei sg	maj eff wf
1	MEHR LEI SG	MAJ EFF WF
4	geiloooo	Awesome

they would earn more money. But they were not sure whether or not they could trust the one person who would leave the lab with the total amount of money. Since the participants of the FOR 2104 experiments did not know each other, the creation of trust was even more difficult. In Table 12.3, player 5 identifies herself as 'the girl with the blue shirt'. But even after that, the other participants are not able to reach a decision that would end up by handing over all the money to player 5 and splitting the profit after the experiment ('We could meet on the staircase on first floor').

Table 12.3 Chat protocol from FOR 2104 experiments (Hamburg group no. 16)

P	*Original Text*	*Translation*
1	also wenn wir player 5 alles geben haben wir einen gewinn von 51,5, also 25,5 Euro, sind ca 6 euro für jeden	Now, if we hand over everything to player 5, we'll have a profit of 51,5, that is 25,5 Euros, and this is approx. 6 Euros per person
1	wenn wir das machen wir ihr meint haben wir einen gewinn von 42,5 token	If we do it the way you suggested we'll have a profit of 42,5 token
5	Ja super, Player 1 und 2, ich hoffe ihr seit damit einverstanden?	Yes, awesome, player 1 and 2, I hope you agree with that?
1	also 21 euro und die unfair verteilt	So, 21 Euros distributed unfairly
1	aber zur not bin ich damit einverstanden :D	But if necessary I agree with that :D
3	ok, wer stimmt für 11/6/3?	OK, who votes for 11/6/3?
1	11,6,3,0,0?	11,6,3,0,0?
5	moment	Just a moment
3	genau	exactly
5	6 euro für jeden	6 Euros each
1	sehe ich nicht als sinnvoll an aber na gut = D	I don't think this is reasonable but well, all right = D
5	pro diese runde?	Per round?
1	das risiko ist halt dass player 5 nicht solidarisch wäre und abhaut	There is a risk involved that player 5 doesn't show solidarity and disappears
5	Ich bin solidarisch!!!!!!	I show solidarity!!!!!!
4	sont wie option eins und wir vertrauen auf player 5;)	Otherwise like option one and we trust player 5;)
5		
1	:D	:D
5	jaaaa	Yeeeaaas
1	mir egal müsst ihr wissen	I don't care, I leave it to you
5	also ich bin player 5 und bin ein mädel mit blauem Shirt!!!	Now, I am player 5 and I am a girl in a blue shirt!!!
1	player 5 gibt uns einfach 6 euro nachm spiel	Player 5 will simply hand over 6 Euros to us after the game
4	:D na dann	:D OK…
1	können uns ja im ersten stock im treppenhaus treffen	We could meet on the staircase on first floor
4	ok	OK
3	ich wähle 11/6/3/0/0	I choose 11/6/3/0/0
5	moment	Just a moment
1	da sind nicht so viele leute	Since there are not that many people around
4	ja besser	Yes, that's better
5	oh	Oh

(continued)

Table 12.3 (continued)

P	*Original Text*	*Translation*
5	ich check das gerade nicht	I don't understand
5	6 euro pro runde oder was?	6 Euros per round or what?
2	leute was nun? draußen treffen und verteilen oder 11 6 3?	Folks, what now? Meet outside or distribute 11 6 3?
3	11 6 3	11 6 3
5	ja dann lass also bei der verteilung 11 6 3	Yes, let's stick to the distribution 11 6 3
1	ja soweit ich das verstanden habe 6 pro runde	Yes, as far as I understood it's 6 Euros per round
5	bleiben....	After all ...
1	ja ok = D	Yes OK = D
3	ich stimme jetzt ab	I'll vote now
5	also 6 runden ... moment	Well, 6 rounds ... just a moment
1	ich weiß nicht wie oft die verteilung statt findet	I don't know how often the distribution will take place
5	ja...	Yes...
1	ok also 11,6,3? müssen uns entscheiden	OK, 11,6,3 then? We have to reach a decision
5	ja	Yes

The examples seem to suggest that participants of text-based computer-mediated decision interactions are not able to create practices of relatedness—practices that rest on triadic constellations of interactions, non-verbal aspects of communication and micro-scale acts of reciprocal reassurance. And although they are able to reach a joint decision, the dominance of—rather unstable—dyadic constellations even leads to a point where two participants engaged in a dialogue are not sure whether the other participants are still present.

Obviously, the above-described practices of relatedness—practices that exhibit a complex, triadic, synchronous structure—cannot be performed or substituted in a chat environment. And although there are more sophisticated platforms for online deliberation available, difficulties remain (see for example Klein 2011; Spada et al. 2014).[16] Furthermore, empirical evidence from various areas of research in political science suggests that David Graeber might be right when he concludes that 'decision making is the one thing that is almost impossible to do on the Internet' (Graeber 2009: 237)—or while using other forms of technically mediated communication.

The presented findings suggest that practices of relatedness play a central role at the micro-level of decision-making interactions. And these findings are not only important for the study of specific figurations of political decision-making, but also for the meso-level of the political domain and the macro-level of society as a whole. It might also be assumed that the more complex—and the more important—joint decisions are, the more important it seems to be for the actors involved to meet each other face to face. Questions of resource distribution or redistribution, for example, require a level of relatedness within figurations of political decision-making that is difficult to create in a CMC environment.

12.5 Conclusion

The aim of this chapter has been to introduce a possible answer to the question why decision interactions within figurations of political decision-making still rely on face-to-face interactions. Certain features inherent in face-to-face, embodied communicative practices, performed under conditions of physical co-presence, seem to promote the production of trust and reciprocity within actor constellations. Among other things, sequences referred to as practices of relatedness ensure that the decision process runs smoothly. In cases of disagreements or misunderstandings, practices of repair can put the process back on the right track. But these are practices that have a very complex, synchronous structure. And they rely on verbal as well as non-verbal elements of communicative practices. Therefore, it seems almost impossible to perform similar practices in computer-mediated communication. Practices of relatedness contribute to the success of problem-solving interactions, for example in cases in which political decisions are made concerning resource distributions. Practices of relatedness have a triadic, synchronous structure, while chat environments seem to be restricted to dyadic—and often a-synchronous—forms of interaction. Therefore, the empirical results suggest that these micro-scale acts of correction, translation and repair are found exclusively in face-to-face interactions, where, to cite Berger and Luckmann again, 'the other's subjectivity is available to me through a maximum of symptoms' (Berger and Luckmann 1967: 29). These micro-level practices structure actor constellations within the field of politics in a way that has important implications for the study of communicative figurations and transforming communications in politics in general. While vast areas of day-to-day political practices and routines are backed up or substituted by electronically mediated forms of communication, face-to-face interaction manifests itself as the core medium of political decision-making. In a time of 'deep mediatization', figurations of political decision-making are a striking example for the fact that we are not dealing with a linear and homogeneous process. These figurations hint at the possibility of communicative practices and actor constellations that resist mediatization.

With regard to future studies of communicative figurations in the field of politics, other important aspects can be analyzed on the basis of the presented findings: In politics, at least for the most part, face-to-face meetings can be characterized as exclusive venues that usually involve limited access and restrictions of participation. If face-to-face meetings persist, and even gain importance within the political process, this increased importance raises issues of power relations, inequalities and exclusion. Even today, questions of who gets access to which face-to-face meeting and who has the power to decide about access within actor constellations already structure figurations of political decision-making in a crucial way. Therefore, the increasing significance and focal position of face-to-face interactions within the field of politics present an ongoing challenge to future studies of mediatization processes in politics and of typical figurations of political decision-making.

Notes

1. Although one would assume, as Judy Wajcman outlines, that the 'spatial-temporal practices' of highly mobile professionals have changed dramatically through the widespread use of technically mediated communication, it turned out that 'their time became dominated by a concern to connect in time and space because they considered face-to-face meetings to be the paramount means of communicating in organizations' (Wajcman 2015: 20; see also Brown and O'Hara 2003).
2. See, for example, Graeber 2009; Maeckelbergh 2009; Hartz-Karp and Sullivan 2014.
3. According to Hepp and Hasebrink, communicative figurations are 'patterns of processes of communicative interweaving that exist across various media and have a thematic framing that orients communicative action' (Hepp and Hasebrink 2014: 258).
4. Like other forms of qualitative data analysis, micro-ethnography has to carefully design and document 'procedures for coding to make

replication possible' (Neuman 1997: 274). Researchers have to 'take various steps to ensure this replicability' (Rose 2012: 96), including tests of coder reliability. The data coding and data organization process, including written transcripts of audio-visual material (Pink 2007: 136), have to be documented by the research team.

5. As Ess further outlines, this may change in cases where modalities other than text messages are available: 'In light of the way in which disembodiment online is a primary obstacle to our establishing and fostering trust with one another in online venues and environments, the return of the body—e.g., as more directly represented via video and audio in the various venues and modalities made possible by Web 2.0—thereby reduces online disembodiment and at least increases the possibilities of our re-presenting our bodies (including facial gestures and other components of nonverbal communication) in ways that may help establish and foster trust' (Ess 2011: 24). For a discussion on changes when it comes to 'issues around co-presence and embodiment' (Cumiskey and Hjorth 2013: 2) with regard to smartphone use and other mobile forms of mediated communication, see Cumiskey and Hjorth 2013.

6. For a detailed theoretical discussion on the concept of practice, see Pritzlaff-Scheele 2015.
7. Practices of repair are also discussed in Conversation Analysis (Schegloff et al. 1977; Goodwin 2003, 2006; Arminen 2005; Nielsen 2009). Schegloff refers to practices of repair as 'main guarantors of intersubjectivity and common ground in interaction' (Schegloff 2006: 79).
8. In the context of a research project funded by the NOWETAS foundation, 50 face-to-face group experiments with a total of 210 participants were conducted, as well as a series of chat experiments. The second project is part of the DFG Research Unit 'Needs-Based Distribution and Distribution Procedures' (FOR 2104).
9. The 'storyline' of the experimental design was that the participants were members of an advisory board that had to decide on the German position concerning the regulation of financial markets.
10. An experimental economics laboratory usually consists of a network of 20 to 30 connected subject stations (computers) and a monitor station for the researcher. The participants/experimental subjects are located in individual cabins separated by walls or shields in order to ensure anonymity. An experimental economics laboratory provides a controlled environment to observe individual and collective decision-making processes.
11. The experiments were conducted at the Carl-von-Ossietzky-Universität Oldenburg on 24 April 2008. The experiments were based on the software z-tree (Fischbacher 2007).
12. Number of the respective participant.

13. Again, it has to be pointed out that different from the experimental setting of the FOR 2104 chat experiments presented below, the participants of the classroom experiment knew each other—the experiment took place in the middle of a graduate class on experimental political science. Although they didn't know during the experiment who had what number—and so didn't know who number three was—they knew that number three had to be one of their fellow graduate students.
14. The pre-tests were conducted in the WISO Research Lab at the University of Hamburg on 17 September 2015.
15. The experiments were conducted in the WISO Research Lab at the University of Hamburg on 11 and 12 July 2016.
16. Hartz-Karp and Sullivan suggest using an integrated system based on 'synchronous video, voice and chat'—but according to them, in order to create a functioning 'public square' for deliberation, this integrated system has to be complemented by face-to-face deliberation (Hartz-Karp and Sullivan 2014: 4).

References

Anderson, Anne H. 2006. Achieving understanding in face-to-face and video-mediated multiparty interactions. *Discourse Processes* 41 (3): 251–287.

Arminen, Ilkka. 2005. *Institutional interaction: Studies of talk at work*. Aldershot and Burlington, VT: Ashgate.

Atkinson, Michael. 2012. Norbert Elias and the body. In *Routledge handbook of body studies*, ed. Bryan S. Turner, 49–61. Abingdon, Oxford: Routledge.

Berger, Peter L., and Thomas Luckmann. 1967. *The social construction of reality. A treatise in the sociology of knowledge*. New York: Anchor Books.

Brown, Barry, and Kenton O'Hara. 2003. Place as a practical concern of mobile workers. *Environment and Planning A* 35 (9): 1565–1587.

Caplow, Theodore. 1968. *Two against one. Coalitions in triads*. Englewood Cliffs, NJ: Prentice-Hall.

Cumiskey, Kathleen M., and Larissa Hjorth. 2013. Between the seams. Mobile media practice, presence and politics. In *Mobile media practices, presence and politics. The challenge of being seamlessly mobile*, ed. Kathleen M. Cumiskey and Larissa Hjorth, 1–11. New York and Abingdon, Oxford: Routledge.

Easton, David. 1957. An approach to the analysis of political systems. *World Politics* 9 (3): 383–400.

Easton, David. 1965. *A systems analysis of political life*. New York: Wiley.

Elias, Norbert. 1987. On human beings and their emotions: A process-sociological essay. *Theory, Culture & Society* 4 (2): 339–361.

Elias, Norbert. 2012. *On the process of civilisation. Collected works*, vol. 3. Dublin: UCD Press.

Escudero, Valentín, and L. Edna Rogers. 2015 [2004]. Observing relational communication. In *Relational communication. An interactional perspective to the study of process and form*, ed. Valentín Escudero and L. Edna Rogers, 23–49. New York and London: Psychology Press.

Ess, Charles. 2011. Self, community, and ethics in digital mediatized worlds. In *Trust and virtual worlds. Contemporary perspectives*, ed. Charles Ess and May Thorseth, 3–30. New York and Washington DC: Peter Lang.

Fischbacher, Urs. 2007. z-Tree: Zurich toolbox for readymade economic experiments. *Experimental Economics* 10 (2): 171–178.

Frohlich, Norman, and Joe Oppenheimer. 1998. Some consequences of e-mail vs. face-to-face communication in experiment. *Journal of Economic Behavior & Organization* 35 (3): 389–403.

Goodwin, Charles. 2003. Conversational frameworks for the accomplishment of meaning in aphasia. In *Conversation and brain damage*, ed. Charles Goodwin, 90–116. Oxford: Oxford University Press.

Goodwin, Charles. 2006. Human sociality as mutual orientation in a rich interactive environment: Multimodal utterances and pointing in aphasia. In *Roots of human sociality*, ed. Nicholas J. Enfield, and Stephen C. Levinson, 96–125. Oxford and New York: Berg Press.

Graeber, David. 2009. *Direct action. An ethnography*. Oakland, CA and Edinburgh: AK Press.

Hartz-Karp, Janette, and Brian Sullivan. 2014. The unfulfilled promise of online deliberation. *Journal of Public Deliberation* 10 (1): 1–5.

Heatherington, Laurie, and Myrna L. Friedlander. 2015 [2004]. From dyads to triads, and beyond: Relational control in individual and family therapy. In *Relational communication. An interactional perspective to the study of process and form*, ed. Valentín Escudero and L. Edna Rogers, 103–129. New York and London: Psychology Press.

Hepp, Andreas. 2013. *Cultures of mediatization*. Cambridge and Malden, MA: Polity Press.

Hepp, Andreas, and Uwe Hasebrink. 2014. Human interaction and communicative figurations. The transformation of mediatized cultures and societies. In *Mediatization of communication*, ed. Knut Lundby, 249–272. Berlin and New York: de Gruyter.

Jallinoja, Riitta, and Eric Widmer. 2011. Introduction. In *Families and kinship in contemporary Europe: Rules and practices of relatedness*, ed. Riitta Jallinoja, and Eric Widmer, 3–12. Basingstoke: Palgrave.

Karpowitz, Christopher, and Tali Mendelberg. 2011. An experimental approach to citizen deliberation. In *Cambridge handbook of experimental political science*, ed. James N. Druckman, Donald P. Green, James H. Kuklinski, and Arthur Lupia, 258–272. Cambridge, MA and New York: Cambridge University Press.

Kaspersen, Lars B., and Norman Gabriel. 2013. Survival units as the point of departure for a relational sociology. In *Applying relational sociology: Relations, networks, and society*, ed. François Dépelteau, and Christopher Powell, 51–82. New York: Palgrave.

Klein, Mark. 2011. *How to harvest collective wisdom on complex problems: An introduction to the MIT Deliberatorium*. MIT Center for Collective Intelligence Working Paper.

LeBaron, Curtis D. 2008. Microethnography. In *The international encyclopedia of communication, Vol. 7: Media corporations, forms of—objectivity in reporting*, ed. Wolfgang Donsbach, 3120–3124. Oxford and Malden, MA: Wiley-Blackwell.

Lievrouw, Leah A. 2014. Materiality and media in communication and technology studies: An unfinished project. In *Media technologies. Essays on communication, materiality, and society*, ed. Tarleton Gillespie, Pablo J. Boczkowski, and Kirsten A. Foot, 21–51. Cambridge and London: The MIT Press.

Lindemann, Gesa. 2006a. Die dritte Person—das konstitutive Minimum der Sozialtheorie. In *Philosophische Anthropologie im 21. Jahrhundert*, ed. Hans-Peter Krüger and Gesa Lindemann, 125–145. Berlin: Akademie Verlag.

Lindemann, Gesa. 2006b. Die Emergenzfunktion und die konstitutive Funktion des Dritten. Perspektiven einer kritisch-systematischen Theorieentwicklung. *Zeitschrift für Soziologie* 35 (2): 82–101.

Lindemann, Gesa. 2010. The lived body from the perspective of the shared world (Mitwelt). *Journal of Speculative Philosophy* 24 (3): 275–291.

Lindemann, Gesa. 2012. Die Kontingenz der Grenzen des Sozialen und die Notwendigkeit eines triadischen Kommunikationsbegriffs. *Berliner Journal für Soziologie* 22 (3): 317–340.

Maeckelbergh, Marianne. 2009. *The will of the many. How the Alter-globalization Movement is changing the face of democracy*. London and New York: Pluto Press.

Neuman, W.Lawrence. 1997. *Social research methods: Qualitative and quantitative approaches*. Boston, MA: Allyn & Bacon.

Nielsen, Mie F. 2009. Interpretative management in business meetings. Understanding managers' interactional strategies through conversation analysis. *Journal of Business Communication* 46 (1): 23–56.

Nullmeier, Frank, and Tanja Pritzlaff. 2009. The implicit normativity of political practices. Analyzing the dynamics and power relations of committee decision-making. *Critical Policy Studies* 3 (3–4): 357–374.

Pink, Sarah. 2007. *Doing visual ethnography*, 2nd ed. Los Angeles and London: Sage.

Pritzlaff-Scheele, Tanja. 2015. *Prefigurative politics. The normativity of political practice*. Unpublished Habilitation Manuscript, University of Bremen.

Pritzlaff, Tanja, and Frank Nullmeier. 2011. Capturing practice. *Evidence & Policy* 7 (2): 137–154.

Riegelsberger, Jens, M. Angela Sasse, and John D. McCarthy. 2007. Trust in mediated interactions. In *The Oxford handbook of internet psychology*, ed. Adam N. Joinson, Katelyn Y.A. McKenna, Tom Postmes, and Ulf-Dietrich Reips, 53–69. Oxford and New York: Oxford University Press.

Rose, Gillian. 2012. *Visual methodologies. An introduction to researching with visual materials*, 3rd ed. Los Angeles, CA and London: Sage.

Rouse, Joseph. 2007. Social practices and normativity. *Philosophy of the Social Sciences* 37 (1): 46–56.

Sartori, Giovanni. 1987. *The theory of democracy revisited. Part I: The contemporary debate.* Chatham, NJ: Chatham House.

Scharpf, Fritz W. 1997. *Games real actors play: Actor-centered institutionalism in policy research.* Boulder, CO: Westview Press.

Schegloff, Emanuel A. 2006. Interaction: The infrastructure for social institutions, the natural ecological niche for language, and the arena in which culture is enacted. In *Roots of human sociality*, ed. Nicholas J. Enfield, and Stephen C. Levinson, 70–96. Oxford and New York: Berg Press.

Schegloff, Emanuel A., Gail Jefferson, and Harvey Sacks. 1977. The preference for self-correction in the organization of repair in conversation. *Language* 53 (2): 361–382.

Setälä, Maija, and Kaisa Herne. 2014. Normative theory and experimental research in the study of deliberative mini-publics. In *Deliberative mini-publics. Involving citizens in the democratic process*, ed. Kimmo Grönlund, André Bächtiger, and Maija Setälä, 59–75. Colchester: ECPR Press.

Spada, Paolo, Mark Klein, Raffaele Calabretta, Luca Iandoli, and Ivana Quinto. 2014. *A first step towards scaling-up deliberation: Optimizing large group e-deliberation using argument maps.* Paper presented at the American Political Science Association (APSA). 110th Annual Meeting, *Politics after the Digital Revolution.* Washington DC, 28–31. 08. 2014.

Streeck, Jürgen, and Siri Mehus. 2005. Microethnography. The study of practices. In *Handbook of language and social interaction*, ed. Kristine L. Fitch and Robert E. Sanders, 381–404. Mahwah, NJ and London: Lawrence Erlbaum.

Wajcman, Judy. 2015. *Pressed for time. The acceleration of life in digital capitalism.* Chicago and London: University of Chicago Press.

Walther, Joseph B. 2011. Visual cues in computer-mediated communication: Sometimes less is more. In *Face-to-face communication over the internet. Emotions in a web of culture, language and technology*, ed. Arvid Kappas and Nicole C. Krämer, 17–38. Cambridge and New York: Cambridge University Press.

Zhou, Lina, and Donsong Zhang. 2006. A comparison of deception behavior in dyad and triadic group decision making in synchronous computer-mediated communication. *Small Group Research* 37 (2): 140–164.

13

Schools and their Mediatization

Andreas Breiter and Arne Hendrik Ruhe

13.1 Introduction

Teaching and learning are the core processes of schools, constituting their frame of relevance, in other words 'good education'. But, with changing educational governance as well as a changing media environment, administrative and strategic processes increasingly gain importance. This is because of the introduction of neo-liberal concepts such as new public management and other systems for accountability that are emerging on a global scale. The international competitiveness of the

A. Breiter (✉) · A.H. Ruhe
ZeMKI, Centre for Media, Communication and Information Research, University of Bremen, Bremen, Germany
e-mail: abreiter@uni-bremen.de

A.H. Ruhe
e-mail: ahruhe@ifib.de

education system has become an important playground for education politics (Grek 2009; Martens et al. 2010; Selwyn 2011, 2013). With the availability of large-scale databases, school data on pupils, staff, budget or infrastructure receive more attention. Schools can be compared with 'key performance indicators' locally, nationally and internationally. In this combination, these databases build 'infrastructures of accountability' (Anagnostopoulos et al. 2013) on different levels of educational governance. While pedagogical research on information and communication technology (ICT) integration in the core processes of schools is manifold, documented in handbooks and shows significant differences between and within countries, there is a lack of empirical results on communicative practices in school organization and the related managerial processes. What is more, the media ensemble related to these practices is only partially known—in contrast to the well-researched practices in classrooms. In particular, the widespread implementation of school management information systems in England and the lack thereof in Germany opens up the question as to whether and, if so, how governance structures shape the way schools are constituted as organizations and constructed as communicative figurations. The school's media ensemble is a moulding force for changes in communicative practices within the actor constellation of schools, among staff, students and administrators as well as in contact with parents. It is accompanied and reinforced by new public management procedures to reorganize school governance and control, which in turn require management information systems for decision-making as new parts of the media ensemble. This chapter will describe theoretically the frame of relevance in relation to educational governance and compare empirically media ensemble and communicative practices of secondary schools in England and Germany.

13.2 Schools as Communicative Figurations

The general concept of communicative figurations as introduced in this book allows us to draw attention to under-researched areas of educational institutions. In particular, the media-related communicative practices for organizing the school have shown a significant change during the last decade. This relates to communication between students, teachers, school management, parents and the administration. Mediatization in the life of children and young people (Livingstone 2009) as well as the impact on teaching and learning (e.g. Voogt and Knezek 2008;

Spector et al. 2014) have been widely researched. International comparative studies on ICT integration in both elementary and secondary schools show significant changes of teaching and learning practices (e.g. SITES: Kozma 2003a; Plomp et al. 2003) and student skills (e.g. ICILS: Fraillon et al. 2014). Additionally, they highlight country-specific differences in access and use of ICT, and learning outcomes. The role of ICT in this change process and its integration in institutionalized learning environments such as schools is under constant political discussion, ranging from high expectation attached to the next technological wave (Mayer-Schönberger and Cukier 2013) to profound scepticism (e.g. Cuban 2001; Ball 2007; Selwyn 2011). Compared with this, there are only a few studies from an organizational perspective.

Just recently, Livingstone and Sefton-Green (2016) finished their empirical research on a school class in an English suburban secondary school. Besides the detailed reconstruction of the 'digital life' of students (grade 8), they refer to organization-specific changes which affect the media ensemble of the school and the communicative practices between core actors:

> In the case of the VFS [the school, the authors], the information management system used was called SIMS, and talk of 'SIMS' figured routinely in students' and teachers' accounts of the school day. [...] Teachers entered and extracted information about any student's progress or behaviour throughout the school day via a range of computers available to them across the school. We observed that each student might attract between two and ten entries on any one day, resulting in a detailed database. (Livingstone and Sefton-Green 2016: 140)

If we regard an information management system as part of a school's media ensemble, this already indicates why a process perspective is necessary to understand transformations. In particular the relation between different actors within and outside the school and their individual media repertoire is relevant for the communicative construction of the school as a whole institution:

> In the class, connections between people and places were most sought among peers (locally or online) and most avoided between home and school. [...] Parents' efforts to bridge the home-school divide by organizing learning at home were unrecognized by or even problematic for the school, while teachers' efforts to bridge that same divide using digital technologies were fragile and short-lived. (Livingstone and Sefton-Green 2016: 247)

While integrated information management systems are less common in German schools, there is a growing number of learning management systems (LMS) which are used to exchange classroom material between students and teachers, to plan lessons or to distribute and collect homework (Avgeriou et al. 2003). Research in German schools (Karbautzki and Breiter 2011) showed that teachers used the system mainly to inform students. Instructional use was less prominent. This coincides with findings from Belgium (De Smet et al. 2012) and Switzerland (Petko and Moser 2009).

Schools are organizations that can be defined by their orientation to a shared purpose and practices (teaching, learning and administering), by a coordinated division of work or responsibility (staff, school management) and by certain rules of membership (Breiter 2001). In organizational studies, schools are often characterized as 'loosely coupled systems' (Weick 1976, 1982) with highly autonomous actors who work independently. March and Olsen (1986) used the 'garbage can model' to describe the cellular structure and the ambiguity of decision-making in educational institutions, as there are no exact measurable goals and an unclear hierarchy. Weick has described organizations as the 'process of organizing', referring to streams of practices, materials, actors, interests, solutions, problems and decisions (Weick 1969: 90). Organizations are neither static nor stable entities, and change according to negotiations and enactment. They are described by the practices of actors rather than by goals or objectives: 'When action is the central focus, interpretation, not choice, is the core phenomenon' (Weick et al. 2005: 409).

If we bring these concepts together, we can identify three interdependent aspects: actor constellation (students, teachers, parents, administrators, management, school board), media ensemble (SIMS, LMS, software products, internet resources) and communicative practices (from face-to-face to online communication). With respect to schools as organizations they centre around a specific frame of relevance, that is, providing 'good education' to future generations. This process-oriented view on social dynamics was described by Elias as figuration, that is, 'networks of individuals' (Elias 1978: 15). We built on this to introduce the concept of schools as communicatively constructed organizations, following the approach by Putnam and Nicotera (2009), and Taylor and van Every (2011). Schools as organizations are constructed through the communicative practices of the actors involved in their media ensemble and can, hence, be regarded as a communicative figuration.

Borrowing from sociological research on governance (Arnott and Raab 2000; Wong 2013), we follow the framework model of educational governance (Sergiovanni et al. 1987) introduced to the German context (Altrichter 2010) and contextualize it to the role of ICT in schooling (Kozma 2003b). Assuming that the structure of the school system as well as processes of governance influence or at least frame the organizing of schools, we will focus on the core difference and communalities on the first two levels of educational governance: macro and meso. The micro level of classroom management will be excluded from analysis. Although this theoretical concept is rather static and does not fully reflect the dynamic processes of the school as a communicative figuration particular to 'deep mediatization' (see Chap. 1) across the levels, we want to take educational governance as an external framework condition in order to focus on our empirical study on the school level.

In most countries, public pressure on changing education policy enforced by international non-governmental organizations can be observed since the publication of Programme for International Student Assessment (PISA) results in the 1990s. Martens and others explained different reactions of nation states to these pressures (Martens et al. 2007; Martens et al. 2010)—from adoption of achievement tests in the national education policy, to ignoring them. This is part of a larger movement of standardization in education, output measurement and accountability (Burch 2006; Jacobsen and Young 2013). This also affects the administrative level of schools by introducing methods of 'new public management' (Pollitt and Bouckaert 2000) for budget control, benchmarks and goals to measure effectiveness. While national standards and respective testing regimes are well established in the UK, Germany has only just started. Recently, education policy in Germany changed from input orientation to output orientation with forms of educational measurement (Huber and Gördel 2006). With PISA in 2001, a gap between student achievements within Germany was reported, and this started an extensive discussion about school quality and the best 'school structure'. As a consequence, most Länder introduced central student achievement tests, which were developed by universities and special state institutions, borrowing from experiences from the UK, the USA and the Netherlands. In Germany, national standards for the core subjects were not introduced until 2005 (KMK 2005). In order to understand the frame of relevance of education governance, we will highlight some specificities of the school systems in England and Germany. The German federal government has no legal or financial obligations in K-12 education. The Länder are responsible for all aspects of schooling. Furthermore, all Education Acts of the Länder define a division of responsibilities between the Länder, the district and the school. This combination of centralized power at the Länder level with limited management control at the school level and the responsibility for infrastructure at the district level is unique among OECD countries (OECD 2001). The Länder department of education is responsible for general education provision, curriculum, teacher training and teacher employment, and the school district or municipality is responsible for school buildings, facility management and administration. This shared responsibility and the limited autonomy of the school and its management lead to constant budget struggles concerning ICT infrastructure. This structure leads to a systematic 'digital divide' between richer and poorer districts as well as richer and poorer schools.

The meso level of school organization has often been underestimated (Pelgrum 2001). With regard to ICT and its innovative power, the organizational perspective becomes more crucial. First of all, dealing with change is a core process in school development. This is often related to schools as learning organizations (Leithwood and Seashore 1998; Fullan 2001; Fauske and Raybold 2005). Secondly, technological innovations have to be embedded in the organizational culture to secure sustainability (Volkoff et al. 2007). Particularly in schools, this is related to funding, training and management decisions (Hodas 1996). Within the organizational setting of the school, the principal plays the central role for change processes (e.g. Blumberg and Greenfield 1986; DuFour 2002; Wissinger 2002; Green 2010). While school leadership in England is often described with attributes from management science, the role of a German principal, even in larger secondary schools, is different. English head teachers are controlled by inspections, report data to other administrators and lead their schools on a competitive market which is made partly transparent by rankings. German principals have fewer responsibilities and just receive some teaching reduction. Teachers are hired by the Länder and distributed among the schools based on certain criteria. The influence of principals on staffing depends on their region. They are responsible only for a small budget, as many decisions are made at the Länder level or on a district level. Hence, they are in a fourfold sandwich position: between staff (without directives), Länder (as control entity), parents and district (as infrastructure provider).

This leads to our main research question. How can we describe the dynamics of the organization school as a communicative figuration and what are the interrelated aspects of educational governance? Although schools have a shared frame of relevance and a similar actor constellation, the process of organizing is rather different. We assume that communicative practices as well as differences in the media ensemble play an important role. This can only be answered on an empirical basis by comparing distinct school systems.

13.3 METHODOLOGY

In order to understand the internal organization of schools, we visited schools in England and Germany to gain insight into everyday practices. We base our empirical research on case studies carried out in a two-year project in two German secondary schools.[1] This is used as a fixed case to subsequently collect accordant data from English schools. Secondly, we follow the sampling method of most-different design (Lijphart 1971): England as a decentralized system with high autonomy of the school but central authority through inspections and national standards; Germany as a decentralized system on the national level with Länder in charge. Within the Länder, we find a highly centralized system with no school autonomy but limited control through standards and inspections. As our special focus is on ICT for school management as part of a school's media ensemble, we conducted qualitative interviews with key stakeholders (teachers, administrators) at school management level.

The sampling and selection of schools in England was based on the assumption that we search for ICT-savvy schools. Hence, we followed two different strategies, of which the first failed. The first attempt was to use the Department for Education's School and college performance tables.[2] The website offers school data for all English schools and includes all grades. 'The performance tables give information on the achievements of pupils in primary, secondary and 16–18 provision in schools and colleges, and how they compare with other schools and colleges in the local authority (LA) area and in England as a whole.'[3] Besides the school test scores (mainly key stage 2 and key stage 4), the tables also offer data about the financial situation of each school. One category is the ICT budget per pupil. We assumed a correlation between ICT investments, a superior ICT infrastructure within a school and a priority on ICT. Therefore, we tried to sample schools with the highest expenditures. This strategy was not successful. The main reason is the growing number of Academy schools in England. In 2010, the government passed the Academies Act,[4] which allowed both the conversion of existing schools into Academies and the creation of new Academies (Academies Act 2010). Academies are directly funded by the government instead of the Local Education Authority (LEA). They are no longer controlled by the LEA and report less information than Community Schools (and no data on ICT budget). Colleges and Independent Schools do not have to report detailed budget statistics, either. This means that of all 5905 active Secondary Schools in 2013, 3434 did not report any information on their ICT budget. The second attempt was to search for schools which received ICT awards. One notable award is the NAACE ICT Mark. This is given to schools '(...) with good use of technology to support teaching, learning and school administration. Deservedly popular with schools wanting to demonstrate both effective and mature use of technology. Schools use this award to drive change and many are, or go on to be, outstanding.'[5] NAACE is a charity ICT association that supports ICT in education.[6] The database included 121 Secondary Schools, which served as our sample. All schools were invited by an email to participate in our study. Six schools responded and showed interest, from which three schools were sampled (Table 13.1).

We visited all English schools for one day with two researchers. All site visits included an interview with a (vice-)principal and a head teacher. We conducted group discussions with teachers and other school staff in every school. All interviews and group discussions were recorded and transcribed. Guided tours of all schools offered the possibility to gain a deeper insight into media-related communicative practices and daily

Table 13.1 General information for English schools

School name (anonymized)	*No. pupils*	*Location*	*School form*	*NSI*[7]
Whitefall Secondary School	1200	Urban	Community school (mixed gender)	B
Jaynestown Academy	2000	Suburban	Converted academy (mixed gender)	C
Beaumonde Academy	1300	Suburban	Converted academy (mixed gender)	B

Table 13.2 General information for German schools

School name (anonymized)	*No. pupils*	*Location*	*School form*
Waldschule	1300	Urban	Gesamtschule (all tiers in secondary education)
Bergschule	1100	Urban	Gesamtschule (all tiers in secondary education)

routines. We took several pictures and notes during these tours which supplemented the interviews and transcripts.

The two German schools were visited over a period of two weeks by two researchers. As part of a larger research project, we focused on how communicative practices of teachers change owing to changing media (Welling et al. 2014). During the visits, participant observations were conducted. Wherever possible, spontaneous interviews with selected teachers took place. Additionally, group discussions with teachers and members of staff were conducted. Additionally, logfile analyses of the learning management system (Schulz and Breiter 2013) were done (Table 13.2).

In both cases, all observations, interviews and group discussions were analyzed by a qualitative research design. The recorded interviews and group discussions were transcribed. Together with notes from the observations, all data was analyzed using an inductive content analysis (Berg 2009; Flick 2014). The data is scanned for multiple iterations to ensure new categories are adapted to formerly scanned material. These categories are the basis for answering the research question.

13.4 Empirical Findings

During the visits to the three English and the two German schools, we gained insights into the media ensemble and the communicative practices of teachers and school administrators in everyday situations. With the help of interviews, group discussions, participant observations and school tours, it was possible to describe the school as a communicative figuration along the aspects of media ensemble and communicative practices of different actors. We start with media ensembles as they are a necessary condition to understand media-related communicative practices.

13.4.1 Media Ensemble

All three English schools have an ICT infrastructure that builds the technical backbone of their media ensemble in relation to organizational practices. At Jaynestown Academy, the school provides notebooks and tablets for all teachers. A state-of-the-art network including complete wireless coverage and a state-of-the-art server architecture ensure a smooth integration into the teachers' daily routine. The Beaumonde Academy also provides laptops for teachers. A full-coverage wireless network is available and can be used by teachers, pupils and guests. Customized Google spreadsheets are used by the teachers to monitor pupils' behaviour and performance. The Whitefall Secondary School does not provide mobile devices for teachers. Instead, every classroom is equipped with a desktop computer. In England, pupils change rooms between classes, in contrast to Germany where the teachers change classrooms after each lesson. A school-wide wireless network is available and accessible by teachers and pupils. All schools provide an open-minded network policy. Teachers and pupils can bring their own devices to school and log into the school's network.

The Waldschule has a comparably good ICT infrastructure. There are several computers in every staffroom, including faculty staffrooms. Most classrooms have at least one computer. A wireless network is not available. All teachers and pupils have school-wide and own network shares. Limiting is the aspect that the school's network is older and does not offer up-to-date transfer rates. The Bergschule is also focused on ICT. Every classroom is equipped with an interactive whiteboard, which is comparable to English schools. Unfortunately, there is no full network coverage within the school, which hinders the full usage of these whiteboards (e.g. internet videos, sharing of content). There are some computers in the main staffroom. A wireless network is not available.

There are differences in the media ensemble between Germany and England as well as between the schools within each country. The cross-national differences are more important and bigger. English schools have more intense usage of ICT. This has consequences for communication practices as well as for the actor constellation.

13.4.2 Media-Related Communicative Practices

As a common ground, and besides all differences of mediatized communication, the English as well as the German schools show strong and stable face-to-face communicative practices. We identified strong 'forces of persistence' against changing established practices just because of the advent of 'new' communication technologies. Teachers in English schools as well as their German counterparts emphasized the importance of direct face-to-face contact:

> (.) I am very often in my side room because my two [subject, note] colleagues are there and we exchange a lot face-to-face. That's why I'm rarely in the staff room which is not good, I force myself to go there at least every second day because it's good to see each other face to face. (teacher's group discussion 'Platane' at Waldschule)

Important communication media are the 'pigeon holes' for each teacher in the staffroom. This applies both to German and English schools. They are used for information exchange as well as for storing class material and work by pupils. Additionally, all staffrooms have pin boards with attached flyers and other information concerning everyday school life. Nevertheless, communication via pen and paper seems to be more important in German schools. One teacher mentions:

> The school is governed by slips of paper (notes during participant observation at Waldschule).

Differences between Germany and England are mainly in the role of mediatized communication. The main element of the media ensemble in all three English schools is email. Email is seen as a fast and reliable form of communication which transports important information within the schools. All teachers have an email account via the school server:

> A lot of (.)key information is communicated through the email system so (.) it's in people's interest to keep up to date what's going on and check (...) (interview vice-principal at Whitefall Secondary School)

Teachers and staff members check their emails regularly:

> '(...) I think people check their email' – 'Every morning' – 'Some, yeah, every morning (.) or through the day, depending on the nature of the work they do (...)' (interview vice-principal at Whitefall Secondary School)

The high frequency of checking for new emails is made possible by the reliable ICT infrastructure. Nevertheless, direct face-to-face contact is still seen as one of the most important communicative practice, especially between teachers and pupils. Teachers mention the importance of a physical appearance during classes and that not all communication could be mediatized. In daily routine, they need to make use of the whole range of communication media to make sure the spread information reaches the receiver:

> (…) the chances are that you're gonna need to use a range of methods, if you wanna make sure that you hit absolutely everybody (.) and that's the sort of the balance I think we have (…) (interview vice-principal at Whitefall Secondary School)

The importance of using digital and non-digital media and combining them dynamically is seen as a key competence for all members of staff:

> (…) personalizing the communication, erm, so that you make sure people are getting information in a way that (.) they're gonna be able to process it and deal with it(.) (interview vice-principal at Whitefall Secondary School)

The group discussions uncovered an extensive media ensemble in English schools. The Beaumonde Academy uses social networks (Twitter, Facebook, Vine) for communication between teachers, pupils and parents. Twitter is used for direct communication between teachers and pupils (e.g. homework reminders) and for informing pupils and parents. Communication with parents is also done by recording Vine videos from school trips aboard. This communication is mostly one way, whereas Twitter and Facebook are used in a bidirectional way. The other two schools do not use social networks as intensively. They use functionalities of their SIMS and LMS to communicate with pupils and parents.

The teachers also mention the use of mobile phones. All schools have group call systems to inform parents about news or reporting absence. Attendance plays an important role in English schools as it is a key performance indicator during school inspections. While some schools ban pupils' mobile phones, all teachers are allowed to use their personal devices. Voice calls are also an important communication media between parents and teachers, especially in a case of emergency:

> [We, editor's note] will use the phone, if it's (.) if it's something urgent like pretty much, certainly everybody on leadership has each other's

mobile phone numbers (.) erm so we can contact each other if there's that kind of situation, so if it's something immediate (.) we wouldn't use email, we'd use either the phone system or the (.) or a hand-delivered note(.) (interview vice-principal at Whitefall Secondary School)

(…) we also have kind of the in-school routes and the traditional routes of a mobile phone number that parents can contact in an emergency (…) (teacher group discussion at Beaumonde Academy)

A vice-principal mentioned the difficulties of mediated communication. Surprisingly, it was not seen as a step backwards when compared with face-to-face communication. The identified challenge was about the 'correct' use of the technology. Email is not seen as the right solution for every situation. This applies especially to urgent situations:

(.) if you're teaching five classes back-to-back (.) you may not be able to check your email from nine o'clock until half past three, so if you need somebody to do something at lunchtime (.) email wouldn't be the appropriate method to get that out, because staff may not be able to check it, and staff here are pretty good about working out when email is appropriate and, well you know, and when it's not (.) (teacher group discussion at Whitefall Secondary School)

Another drawback of email is that users get 'flooded'. They are likely to overlook important information. Therefore, important information is stored and spread via the SIMS. SIMS are mainly used to manage pupils, facility management and budgeting. All relevant pupil data such as grades, classes, attendances and characteristics are stored within the systems. The system provides a link to the Office for Standards in Education, Children's Services and Skills (OFSTED) database, which sends grades and attendance statistics automatically. The Beaumonde Academy uses Google spreadsheets to exchange data with the SIMS. Two benefits of SIMS are mentioned multiple times. First, the system allows the teachers a fast and complete overview about the current status of each pupil:

(…) it (SIMS, editor's note) collects the data on the children's performance essentially (.) although we've got attendance (…) but what we're really using it for (.) is tracking how the children are coming into the school (.) and how they're progressing through their time in the school (…) (teacher group discussion at Beaumonde Academy)

> (…) then with the key assessments, they go in there, and then they feed into a current sort of predicted level for the children, their effort and behaviour would go into SIMS (.) this is sort of where we're at in our thinking (…) (interview vice-principal at Whitefall Secondary School)

The second-mentioned advantage is the possibility to share pupils' information with parents. They can log into the SIMS from home and see current grades, absences and other notes concerning their child. SIMS are used intensively for the communication between teachers and parents. They also offer some kind of connection between different communication media. Some notes to parents are generated by the SIMS, printed and sent via postal mail. Additionally, they can be accessed online. SIMS are also connected to the group call system in the schools to send reminders to parents.

The media-related communicative practices are different in German schools. Teachers do not have an official school email address; they have to use their private accounts. Hence, communication via email exists, but is used significantly less frequently than in England:

> (…) newsletters do exist, but reach just 60 per cent of all colleagues (.) (principal interview at Waldschule)

Some teachers even refuse to use email:

> (…) [the usage of email] has been a major point for controversial discussions as many teachers do not want to communicate via email (.) (teacher interview at Waldschule)

The use of private email addresses conflicts with German privacy laws and acceptable use policies. German laws prohibit the storage of individual-related information in unsecure information technology (IT) environments, which applies to almost all commercial email providers. Besides the legal problems, this individual communicative practice is not embedded in the school's organizing practices. In both schools, the local education authority provides an LMS that helps the teachers to communicate among each other and pupils. As it is not compulsory and not embedded into the communicative practices, the usage is not very high (Schulz and Breiter 2013). This may also be owing to the limited ICT infrastructure within both schools. Combined with the lack of wireless networks, this hinders more intense usage from within the school.

> (…) there is the disadvantage that I cannot access OrgaTec [the LMS, note] directly (…) wireless coverage with an iPad would be perfect (.) (teacher group discussion 'Platane' at Bergschule)

In both cases of email and LMS, German principals cannot make the usage compulsory. This lowers their relevance within the media ensemble:

> (…) email is not the main component of our official communication (…) mainly, because we do not have the guarantee that colleagues on the one hand get in touch with us just in time and on the other we cannot be sure that they read their emails as there are no official policies (…) (group discussion head teachers at Bergschule)

These may be the reasons that German schools still rely on paper in pigeon holes. In both schools, we were able to see the routine that every teacher, when walking into the staffroom, first looked into the pigeon holes.

To summarize the findings, we can state that German schools are governed with slips of paper while English schools are governed with SIMS.

13.4.3 *School Stakeholders and the Media Ensemble*

In the next step, we investigated the school's media ensemble and mapped it into a matrix with all relevant actors (Fig. 13.1). The left column (teacher, pupils, parents, officials) is the sender, whereas the other four columns (teacher, pupils, parents, officials) are the receivers. Owing to the visits and group discussions, we were able to restore most of the communication practices between teachers, but we still do not know about the communicative behaviour between teachers, pupils and parents and between parents and school management (Table 13.3).

As mentioned above, the main communication media are email, SIMS, LMS and file sharing. Email is the most important and used through all combinations of sender and receiver, which includes parents and officials not only as receivers, but also as senders addressing teachers. SIMS, LMS and file sharing are used more selectively. File sharing is mainly used within the schools. Both teachers and pupils have personal accounts. They are hosted on servers provided within the school or within cloud storage. Public access allows the exchanges of documents

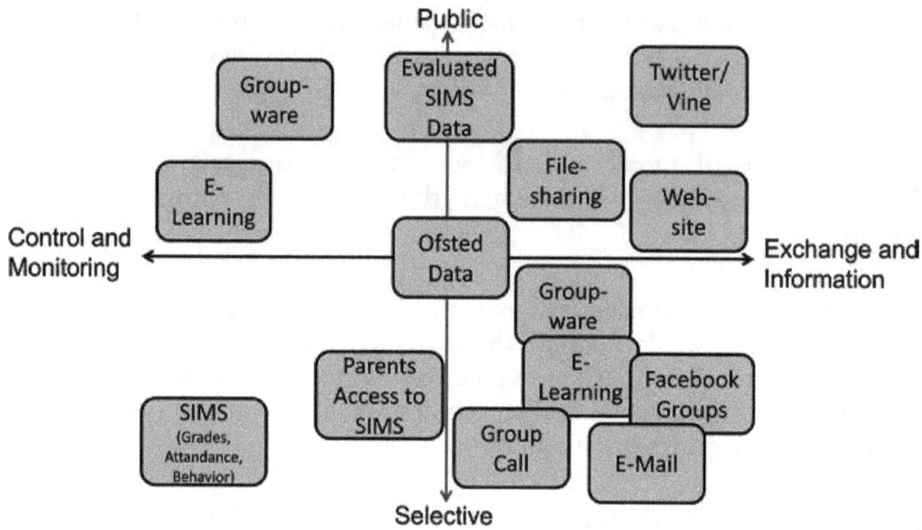

Fig. 13.1 Relation of communicative practices and media ensemble in English schools

Table 13.3 Media ensemble and actor constellation in English schools

From/to	Teacher	Pupils	Parents	Officials
Teacher	SIMS email File Sharing Pigeon Holes	LMS email File Sharing Social Media	email SIMS (LMS) Social Media Group Call Pen & Paper	SIMS email
Pupils	LMS email File Sharing Social Media Pigeon Holes	LMS File Sharing email		
Parents	email Telephone Pen & Paper Social Media			
Officials	email Telephone Pen & Paper			

Main communication form underlined; hatched cells: unknown

Table 13.4 Media ensemble and actor constellation in German schools

From/to	Teacher	Pupils	Parents	Officials
Teacher	email (private) Pen & paper SIS LMS File Sharing	email (private) Social Media LMS	email (private) Pen & paper	email (official)
Pupils	email (private) Social Media LMS			
Parents	email (private)			
Officials	Pen & paper			

Main communication form underlined; hatched cells: unknown

and media files with selected others (course, class, special groups or school-wide). The number and variety of accounts is limited by the administrators according to the school's policy. In SIMS and LMS, depending on the visited school, grades and behavioural notes concerning the pupils are accessible by parents. Additionally, general information can be spread through the systems. Registered accounts assure that especially grades and behavioural notes are only accessible by the responsible parents. LMS allow teacher–pupil communication (both ways), including the exchange of materials, which makes them a substitute for file sharing. SIMS are the second main source for communication between teachers as they cover different areas of within-school organization (decision support, budget, grades, behaviour) with connection to the group call systems. Parents and officials get in touch with teachers mostly via email, but parents especially also use phones to contact the school or selected teachers. There is also a regular paper exchange between schools/parents and officials (Table 13.4).

The same matrix was developed for the German schools. The variety of used media is significantly lower. The most used tools are private email addresses and pen and paper. Email is used in all sender–receiver combinations. Both visited schools use a SIS for the communication purposes between teachers. SIS contain many components of the SIMS in English schools, with the exclusion of some management applications like budgeting and facility management. Only one of the two SIS includes a pupil management (grades and attendance) with a link to the state-wide pupil database. Both schools use the system for communication among teachers about everyday school life, to organize a subject or help the principal to distribute certain information and directives (e.g. changes in the curriculum) among the teachers. Some teachers also use an LMS to distribute information among each other. File sharing is another important means of communication, but not that relevant as in English schools. Many teachers use email to exchange files. Some network drives can only be accessed within the school network. Some teachers use cloud storage (e.g. Dropbox) for file sharing. Teachers also use social media (mainly Facebook) to communicate with pupils. The fragmentary ICT equipment in both schools may be the reason for the less intense use of LMS as they also offer the possibility to use them from home.

The two matrices show similarities and differences among the cross-national comparison. Email has a much stronger official character in England than in Germany. In Germany, non-digital media is still very widespread, especially in combination with pigeon holes. Communication in England is more mediatized and standardized.

13.4.4 The Relation Between Communicative Practices and the School's Media Ensemble

After mapping the actor constellation and the media ensemble into a matrix, it became clear that the cross-national differences also lead to different communicative practices. We began to find an aggregated description of communicative practices in relation to the existing media, by characterizing it as either selective or public. Public information or communication can be accessed by almost everyone. On the other hand, selective communication can only be accessed by formerly chosen receivers (teachers, pupils, groups). Additionally, it became obvious that the media ensemble affords communicative practices in different situations and for different purposes. The main differentiation was between control and monitoring and exchange and information. The former is used for school management like grades, attendance or other topics concerning pupils. The latter is information about school life, dates and other announcements. In Fig. 13.1, both the selectivity and the purposes are displayed in a coordinate system for English schools only. This allows us to map the two subjects precisely. Some media may serve multiple communicative practices and may be mapped multiple times.

Communication via social media must be split up into sub-groups. Three providers were mentioned during the group discussions. Facebook groups are mainly used for the communication between teachers and pupils. The groups establish a restricted communication area which is usually limited to classes or courses. The main focus is on questions about homework or class-related topics. The closed user group makes the communication selective. The other two mentioned providers are Twitter and Vine. Both services are used by teachers for sharing information with parents. Vine especially is used regularly at Beaumonde Academy. The teachers upload small videos during class trips, which allows parents at home to stay informed. Twitter is used to publish information and results. Both services are focused on the public sphere and offer information:

> The first time we used it was on a (.) school trip that we run, erm it's a sports (out) sports trip (.) erm as part of (.) erm the PE department run but it's an open sports trip (.) and the initial usage of was about communicating with the parents a little bit more openly (.) so that they can see what the kids are up to, they know that we've arrived safely (.) things like that (.) and it was just a more instantaneous way of us doing it (…) I also use erm (.) an accompaniment to Twitter (.) erm is Vine (.) which is three-seco- er six-second videos (.) erm (.) and this one we use (.) this one we use to give snippets of what we're up to in the department (.) so parents and students can see little snippets of their work, of their kids' work (…) (teacher group discussion at Beaumonde Academy)

The communication and exchange within an LMS can be seen as similar as those within Facebook groups. LMS also offer testing and feedback options within internal groups. The focus is on control and monitoring. The test can be done within computer labs, at home or any other situation where pupils have access to the LMS. The feedback can be individual (selective) or public to the other members of the group. The main purpose of SIMS is to monitor pupils' performance and to control their learning process. This information is strictly selective and can usually only be accessed by the teachers, other teachers of that class and teachers in superior positions. The pupil-related data can be uploaded in an aggregated form to OFSTED and are later publicly available via the OFSTED homepage. Pupil-related data can also be accessed by parents. In cases of non-attendance or other incidents, parents can be informed via short message service (SMS) or a predefined voice message. Both communication media are strictly selective but more focused on information. The LMS of the Whitefall Secondary School also offers a login for parents to access pupils' grades and homework.

Besides email, SIMS and LMS, groupware systems are the fourth main group that support teachers' communication. The systems offer extended collaboration detached from time and space. The main focus in schools was on communication and coordination and the main services were shared calendars and the possibility to invite other teachers and organize events. Shared calendars and the organization of events are seen more selectively than public ones (owing to restricted access) and focus on exchange and information.

File sharing between teachers and pupils is also organized via shared hard drives within the school network or by cloud storage. It is regarded as more public than selective as the access to these data may be restricted to classes, courses or groups but access may only be granted by administrators. The uploaded data has informative content. Teachers share more sensitive and selective information via SIMS and email among each other. Sensitive data between pupils and teachers (homework, tests) is handled via email or LMS. Sensitive content between teachers (grades, behaviour, etc.) is handled via SIMS, sensitive digital communication between teachers and pupils is handled via LMS and via face-to-face communication.

All the schools we visited had websites to improve their public image. As websites are public, they do not contain sensitive information. The focus is not totally public as only interested persons (e.g. parents) access the site. In the social networks Twitter and Vine, uninvolved persons may receive the information by simply clicking through tweets or videos or because someone 'retweeted' a tweet of a school account. This makes them more public than websites, although tweets and videos are sorted by an algorithm. The published OSTED data is freely available. It offers aggregated school data and is also only visited by interested persons. Nevertheless, schools use this data to promote themselves and their success (Fig. 13.2).

German schools have some similarities but are actually quite different. First, the media ensemble has fewer varieties. Second, the control and monitoring processes can be neglected. One reason might be the less reliable ICT infrastructure. But more relevant are communicative practices as well as organizational structures and policies. German teachers organize their lessons individually and independently. Only aggregated grades have to be reported at the end of the school term. During parent visits, grades might be discussed with parents. The LMS of the Bergschule includes a grade module; but only a few teachers use it regularly. The majority log on a month before the end of school term to type

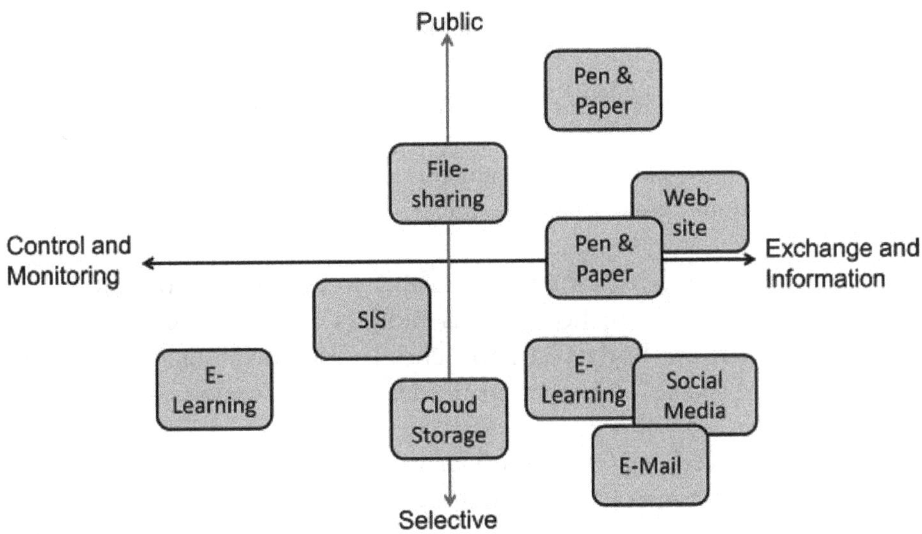

Fig. 13.2 Relation of communicative practices and media ensemble in German schools

in the final grades. Teachers do not have the possibility nor responsibility to enter data during or after each lesson as there is no computer available. Attendances and other occurrences are entered into a paper-based class register.

Paper-based communication media are used more extensively than in English schools—first because of the relevance of pigeon holes, as described above. Postal letters are still important to communicate with parents. Teachers usually do not send emails to parents but use printed letters with information about school dates (tours, parents' evenings, etc.) for the pupils to hand over at home.

Private emails and social media are used selectively and mainly for sharing information. Owing to legal constraints, the usage of private email addresses is unacknowledged, but this is sometimes the only way to reach other teachers in bigger schools. Although illegal, Facebook is used to inform pupils about urgent matters:

> (…) it was about a changed date and she [other teacher, note] said, she will post that information in Facebook that all pupils can see that (.) (teacher interview at Bergschule)

This also applies to cloud storage, which is used very selectively among smaller groups of teachers. The Waldschule uses the LMS as an official shared storage. The usability and overview of the available data is limited:

> The whole thing [LMS, note] is not intuitive. – (…) it's tricky. (teacher group discussion 'Lärche' at Waldschule)

The network in the Bergschule is accessible from every computer within the school, but not from home. This hinders teachers and pupils from actively using it. In both German schools, the main fact is that the incomplete and old ICT equipment hinders a more intense usage.

The main difference between Germany and England is the more intense usage of control and monitoring purposes in English schools. SIMS fit this purpose very well. The strong focus of control and monitoring is strongly determined by the educational governance of England. In both countries, digital media allow teachers and staff to be very selective as regards who should be the receivers of their communication. This shows that choosing the right media out of the available media ensemble that relates to the communicative practices is a key competence for teachers.

13.5 Conclusion

Our empirical study in two German and three English schools show some interesting similarities as well as large differences. If we assume that the frame of relevance of any school in a state school system is to provide good education and equal opportunities, the underlying administrative processes might vary according to the governance structures. The actor constellation is similar, although administrative staff in English schools have different responsibilities compared with their German counterparts. The media environment in both countries is comparable, although there are differences in the appropriation of social media. This applies especially to the usage of Twitter, which is much more common in the UK than in Germany. Communicative practices vary significantly and especially regarding the media ensemble of the school. As we show, the core system of communication in English schools comprises management information systems such as SIMS. Although we selected schools in Germany with an existing LMS in place, the role of this medium within the media ensemble is rather low. What are the reasons for such different developments? As indicated in the beginning, the role of governance structures is often underestimated in the appropriation of media and its related communicative practices. There is significantly more pressure within the English system owing to decentralization and, as a necessary side effect, accountability. Management principles such as new public management are far more widespread and at the centre of the English school system than so far in Germany. There is a kind of 'data culture' that embraces school rankings and data-based decision-making and the legal framework conditions alike. In all schools, the most challenging decision for teachers is to use the best suitable communication tool in the currently given context and based on the opposite communication partner(s). All schools offer a wide media ensemble for addressing colleagues. Parents expect public data and a higher degree of transparency. This is represented in the school's media ensemble. Furthermore, the right form (formal versus informal, selective versus open) has to be chosen. This applies especially to German schools, as privacy laws and policies usually prohibit a number of media-related communication practices. All in all, this is reflected in different communicative figurations which construct the school as an organization.

Notes

1. Part of the DFG Priority Program 1505 "Mediatized Worlds" (funding number: BR 2273/10-1).
2. http://www.education.gov.uk/schools/performance/. Accessed: 28 May 2015.
3. http://www.education.gov.uk/schools/performance/about/index.html. Accessed: 28 May 2015.
4. http://www.legislation.gov.uk/ukpga/2010/32/contents. Accessed: 30 March 2017.
5. http://www.naace.co.uk/ictmark. Accessed: 30 March 2017.
6. http://www.naace.co.uk/about. Accessed: 30 March 2017.
7. Strickley et al. (2014) combine four measures (expected progress in maths and writing, main threshold level, average point score, value-added) into one National Single Indicator (NSI), which ranges from A to E.

References

Academies Act 2010. 2010. http://www.legislation.gov.uk/ukpga/2010/32/contents. Accessed 30 Mar 2017.

Altrichter, Herbert. 2010. Theory and evidence on governance: Conceptual and empirical strategies of research on governance in education. *European Educational Research Journal* 9 (2): 147–158.

Anagnostopoulos, Dorothea, Stacey A. Rutledge, and Rebecca Jacobsen. 2013. *The infrastructure of accountability: Data use and the transformation of American education*. Cambridge, MA: Harvard Education Press.

Arnott, Margaret A., and Charles D. Raab. 2000. *The governance of schooling. Comparative studies of devolved management*. London and New York: Macmillan.

Avgeriou, Paris, Andreas Papasalouros, Symeon Retalis, and Manolis Skordalakis. 2003. Towards a pattern language for learning management systems. *Educational Technology & Society* 6 (2): 11–24.

Ball, Stephen. 2007. *Education Plc: Understanding private sector participation in public sector education*. London: Routledge.

Berg, Bruce L. 2009. *Qualitative research methods for the social sciences*. Boston, MA: Allyn & Bacon.

Blumberg, Arthur, and William Greenfield. 1986. *The effective principal. Perspectives on school leadership*. Boston, MA: Allyn & Bacon.

Breiter, Andreas. 2001. Digitale Medien im Schulsystem: Organisatorische Einbettung in Deutschland, den USA und Großbritannien. *Zeitschrift für Erziehungswissenschaft* 4 (4): 625–639.

Burch, Patricia E. 2006. The new educational privatization: Educational contracting and high stakes accountability. *Teachers College Record* 108 (12): 2582–2610.

Cuban, Larry. 2001. *Oversold and underused: Computers in classrooms*. Cambridge, MA: Harvard University Press.

De Smet, C., J. Bourgonjon, B. De Wever, T. Schellens, and M. Valcke. 2012. Researching instructional use and the technology acceptation of learning management systems by secondary school teachers. *Computers & Education* 58 (2): 688–696. https://doi.org/10.1016/j.compedu.2011.09.013.

DuFour, Richard. 2002. The leading-centered principal. *Educational Leadership* 59 (8): 12–15.

Elias, Norbert. 1978. *The history of manners. The civilizing process*. New York: Pantheon.

Fauske, Janice R., and Rebecca Raybold. 2005. Organizational learning theory in schools. *Journal of Educational Administration* 43 (1): 22–40.

Flick, Uwe. 2014. *An introduction to qualitative research*. London: Sage.

Fraillon, Julian, John Ainley, Wolfram Schulz, Tim Friedman, and Eveline Gebhardt. 2014. *Preparing for life in a digital age. The IEA international computer and information literacy study international report*. Open Access: Springer Online.

Fullan, Michael G. 2001. *The new meaning of educational change*, 3rd ed. New York: Teachers College Press.

Green, Reginald L. 2010. *The four dimensions of principal leadership. A framework for leading 21st century schools*. Boston, MA: Allyn & Bacon.

Grek, Sotiria. 2009. Governing by numbers: The PISA "effect" in Europe. *Journal of Education Policy* 24 (1): 23–37.
Hodas, Steven. 1996. Technology refusal and the organizational culture of schools. In *Computerization and controversy. Value conflicts and social choice*, ed. Rob Kling, 197–218. San Diego, CA: Academic Press.
Huber, Stephan G., and Bettina Gördel. 2006. Quality assurance in the German school system. *European Educational Research Journal* 5 (3): 196–209.
Jacobsen, Rebecca, and Tamara V. Young. 2013. The new politics of accountability: Research in retrospect and prospect. *Educational Policy* 27 (2): 155–169.
Karbautzki, Louisa, and Andreas Breiter. 2011. Lernplattformen im Unterricht. Organisationslücken bei der Implementierung von E-Learning in Schulen. *Log In—Informatische Bildung und Computer in der Schule* 169/170: 34–39.
KMK. 2005. *Bildungsstandards der Kultusministerkonferenz.* Bonn: Sekretariat der Ständigen Konferenz der Kultusminister der Länder in der Bundesrepublik Deutschland.
Kozma, Robert B. 2003a. ICT and educational change. A global phenomenon. In *Technology, innovation, and educational change. A global perspective. A report of the second information technology in education study module 2*, ed. Robert B. Kozma, 1–18. Eugene, OR: International Society for Technology in Education (ISTE).
Kozma, Robert B. 2003b. *Technology, innovation, and educational change. A global perspective. A report of the second information technology in education study module 2.* Eugene, OR: International Society for Technology in Education (ISTE).
Leithwood, Kenneth, and Louis K. Seashore. 1998. *Organizational learning in schools.* Lisse: Swets and Zeitlinger.
Lijphart, Arend. 1971. Comparative politics and the comparative method. *American Political Science Review* 65 (3): 682–693.
Livingstone, Sonia. 2009. *Children and the internet. Great expectations, challenging realities.* Cambridge, MA: Polity Press.
Livingstone, Sonia, and Julian Sefton-Green. 2016. *The class: Living and learning in the digital age.* New York: NYU Press.
March, James G., and Johan P. Olsen. 1986. Garbage can models of decision making in organizations. In *Ambiguity and command*, ed. James March, and Roger Weissinger-Baylon, 11–35. Marshfield, MA: Pitman.
Martens, Kerstin, Alexander-Kenneth Nagel, Michael Windzio, and Ansgar Weymann. 2010. *Transformation of education policy.* Basingstoke: Palgrave.
Martens, Kerstin, Alessandra Rusconi, and Kathrin Leuze. 2007. *New arenas of education governance—The impact of international organizations and markets on educational policymaking.* Houndmills and Basingstoke: Palgrave.
Mayer-Schönberger, Viktor, and Kenneth Cukier. 2013. *Big data: A revolution that will transform how we live, work, and think.* London: John Murray.

OECD. 2001. *What works in innovation in education: New school management approaches.* Paris: Organization of Economic Development and Co-operation.

Pelgrum, Willem J. 2001. Obstacles to the integration of ICT in education: Results from a world-wide educational assessment. *Computers & Education* 37: 163–178.

Petko, Dominik, and Thomas Moser. 2009. Bedingungen der Nutzung von Lernplattformen in Schulen. Empirische Befunde zu einem nationalen Modellprojekt aus der Schweiz. *Zeitschrift für E-Learning* 4 (3): 20–31.

Plomp, Tjeerd, Ronald E. Anderson, Nancy Law, and Andreas Quale. 2003. *Cross-national information and communication technology policies and practices in education.* Greenwich, CT: Information Age Publishing.

Pollitt, Christopher, and Geert Bouckaert. 2000. *Public management reform: A comparative analysis.* Oxford: Oxford University Press.

Putnam, Linda, and Anne M. Nicotera. 2009. *Building theories of organization: The constitutive role of communication.* New York: Routledge.

Schulz, Arne H., and Andreas Breiter. 2013. Monitoring user patterns in school information systems using logfile analysis. In *Next generation of information technology in educational management.* 10th IFIP WG 3.7 Conference, ITEM 2012. Bremen, Germany, August 2012. Revised selected papers, ed. Don Passey, Andreas Breiter, and Adrie Visscher, 94–103. Heidelberg: Springer.

Selwyn, Neil. 2011. *Schools and schooling in the digital age: A critical analysis.* London: Routledge.

Selwyn, Neil. 2013. *Education in a digital world: Global perspectives on technology and education.* New York: Routledge.

Sergiovanni, Thomas J., Martin Burlingame, Fred S. Coombs, and P. Thurston. 1987. *Educational governance and administration.* Englewood Cliffs, NJ: Prentice-Hall.

Spector, J., M.David Michael, Jan Elen Merrill, and M.J. Bishop. 2014. *Handbook of research on educational communications and technology.* Boston, MA: Springer.

Strickley, Alan, John Bertram, Dave Chapman, Michael Hart, Roy Hicks, Derek Kennedy, and Mark Phillips. 2014. A national single indicator for schools in England: Helping parents make informed decisions. In *Key competencies in ICT and informatics. Implications and issues for educational professionals and management*, ed. Don Passey and Arthur Tatnall, 331–345. Berlin and Heidelberg: Springer.

Taylor, James R., and Elizabeth J. van Every. 2011. *The situated organization: Case studies in the pragmatics of communication research.* New York: Routledge.

Volkoff, Olga, Diane M. Strong, and Michael B. Elmes. 2007. Technological embeddedness and organizational change. *Organization Science* 18 (5): 832–848.

Voogt, Joke, and Gerald Knezek. 2008. The importance of information technology attitudes and competencies in primary and secondary education. In *International handbook of information technology in primary and secondary education*, ed. Joke Voogt, and Gerald Knezek, 321–332. Boston, MA: Springer Science.

Weick, Karl E. 1969. *The social psychology of organizing*. Reading, MA: Addison Wesley.

Weick, Karl E. 1976. Educational organizations as loosely coupled systems. *Administrative Science Quarterly* 21: 1–19.

Weick, Karl E. 1982. Administering education in loosely coupled schools. *Phi Delta Kappan* 63 (10): 673–676.

Weick, Karl E., Kathleen M. Sutcliffe, and David Obstfeld. 2005. Organizing and the process of sense making. *Organization Science* 16 (4): 409–421.

Welling, Stefan, Andreas Breiter, and Arne H. Schulz. 2014. *Mediatisierte Organisationswelten in Schulen: Wie der Medienwandel die Kommunikation in den Schulen verändert.* Wiesbaden: Springer VS.

Wissinger, Jochen. 2002. Schulleitung im internationalen Vergleich—Ergebnisse der TIMSS-Schulleiterbefragung. In *Schulleitungs-Forschung und -Qualifizierung*, ed. Jochen Wissinger, and Stephan G. Huber, 45–61. Opladen: Leske + Budrich.

Wong, Kenneth K. 2013. Politics and governance: Evolving systems of school accountability. *Educational Policy* 27 (2): 410–421.

PART IV

Approaches and Methods

14

Empirical Research and Communicative Figurations

Christine Lohmeier and Rieke Böhling

14.1 Introduction

What is the best way to research a communicative figuration? How can we approach a communicative figuration as a cross-media phenomenon? And who belongs to a communicative figuration and who does not? To answer such broad and general questions, it is helpful to discuss them by considering specific examples such as cultural communities. In a past research project, one of the authors of this chapter investigated the media of the Cuban American community in Miami (Lohmeier 2014). The main questions guiding the investigation were how different

C. Lohmeier (✉) · R. Böhling
ZeMKI, Centre for Media, Communication and Information Research, University of Bremen, Bremen, Germany
e-mail: christine.lohmeier@uni-bremen.de

R. Böhling
e-mail: rieke.boehling@uni-bremen.de

media contributed to creating a sense of belonging or fragmentation, and which actors were in charge of media as institutions and in terms of media content. Questions about the meaning of community and belonging, such as the ones mentioned above, arose again and again during processes of data gathering and analyses. At the time of research, the Cuban American community was fragmented, heterogeneous, dispersed into several locations within the USA with strong ties to a diasporic community spread across the world. Making decisions on which groups within the Cuban American community to focus on, which newspaper articles and posts to read and whose words to listen to was not an easy task. No doubt querying the choices one makes in the research process is in fact an essential part of the process. One might even argue that researchers need questions such as these in order to produce valuable and critical work.

When considering this research project as a whole, employing the approach of communicative figurations as a tool for data gathering as well as for analyses and findings of the research might have proven useful for a number of reasons: First, the concept of community is highly abstract. Even if we can agree on a definition of what a community is, working with this understanding on the ground is another matter. Because, second, the realities of a community are complex, diverse, even messy, we could say. Returning to the example of the Cuban Americans in Miami, the community was fragmented by generational differences and distinct experiences of migration; there were segments of the community with a lot more financial muscle and political ambitions than others. Some did not feel represented or welcome at all, while others were living the American dream. Were all these individuals and sub-groups part of the same community? Third, communities are in a constant state of flux. Some individuals purposefully decided to leave Miami and the Cuban American community behind. Does this end their belonging to the community as a whole?

The concept of communicative figurations as we outline it in this volume could have mitigated some of the described problems. For one, it helps to operationalize our understanding of community and thereby makes it more easily 'workable'. Furthermore, owing to its scalability, it leaves room to account for the complexity and diversity of communities. Relatedly, and finally, communicative figurations are never static but always have the potential to change, and can be thought of as fluid.

That said, approaching communities as figurations is a helpful starting point. But at the same time, working with a figurational approach brings its own set of methodological requirements and challenges. There are two necessities and challenges in particular of this approach we want to discuss here: first, conducting cross-media research as a necessity and challenge and, second, defining the boundaries of a communicative figuration as a necessity and challenge. In the final section of this chapter, we will consider a specific example to illustrate how a figurational approach can be employed. Again, we are taking into account the necessity of such an approach and possible challenges that (can) come with it. For all of these themes, our line of argument will address both the requirements as well as the challenges.

14.2 Cross-Media as a Necessity and Challenge

Communicative figurations are characterized by their actor constellations, frames of relevance and communicative practices, entangled with a media ensemble. In order to understand communicative figurations and their interdependencies on one another, it is essential to reconstruct the figuration by gathering data on the actors involved, the themes that are of significance to these actors and the practices that are shared and simultaneously constitute the figuration. Returning to the example of the Cuban American community in Miami, the task thus would be to gather information on the different actors who are part of the community as a communicative figuration, their frames of relevance and their communicative practices. As Hepp and Hasebrink explain in Chap. 1, the constellation of actors within a communicative figuration forms the 'structural basis' for the communicative figuration. In the example, this includes a broad variety of actors who can be considered as making up part of the Cuban American community in relation to the city of Miami and its media, at first notwithstanding the generational differences, different experiences of the migration process, financial situations, diverse political ambitions and so on. These factors do not determine whether actors are part of a communicative figuration in the first place, but they do play into the relationship of the constellation of the actors to each other, and are thus an important factor when determining how the network within a communicative figuration is interrelated and how the different actors communicate with each other. The second dimension of the communicative figuration concerns the frames of relevance which define the 'topic' and therefore character of a communicative figuration as a social domain. In our example, the Miami media, including radio, TV, blogs, social networks, and their interrelations and interactions with different segments of the community, would construct (be it as reader, listener, viewer, journalist, producer) frames that are of particular importance. Lastly, the communicative practices that are interwoven with other social practices in this specific case are very closely related to the second dimension: the frames of relevance. The question here would be how the different actors engage with Cuban American Miami media, while also taking into account the entire media ensemble of the communicative figuration.

One of the key methodological advantages of conceptualizing social sites through a figurational approach lies in its constitutive parts: the three distinct dimensions which make up a figuration provide a framework for operationalizing research questions. In addition, the figurational framework supports a process of data gathering that is simultaneously open, on the one hand, but not arbitrary, on the other. The required balance between these two poles in the processes of data gathering is especially relevant when considering the limits of the field that is being researched or when selecting a sample. As stated in the introduction of this chapter, defining a community is difficult. The Cuban American community is fragmented, and it is difficult to define the whole spectrum of people belonging to a specific community. We will devote some more attention to the fringes of a figuration in Sect. 14.3.

However, there are certain challenges related to this kind of research, and one main challenge is its cross-media point of view. The figurational approach implies that a variety of data needs to be collected across a variety of media. To make these points more specific, let us consider Ien Ang's (1985) seminal work on television audiences in *Watching Dallas*. When Ang was working on her study in the early 1980s, she considered *Dallas* and the appropriation of the series by the people. Data was mainly gathered through encouraging audience members to write letters to the researcher about their viewing experience and their opinions of *Dallas*. While Ang's approach was at the forefront of 'new audience research', which received momentum from the mid-1980s onwards—together with work by David Morley (1980), John Fiske (1990) and Philip Schlesinger et al. (1992)—the methodology employed and the data brought together by Ien Ang leave a number of questions unanswered: In which context did audience members watch *Dallas*? With whom would they discuss the programme? In which other practices might *Dallas* and the experiences of watching *Dallas* be embedded? In which areas of daily life might the overall themes of the series and the themes of individual episodes be of relevance and relate to, contradict and oppose other relevant themes? And especially, is it possible to research the appropriation of the series without considering its relation to other kinds of media? David Morley was already pointing towards questions like this in 1992, when he called for a new type of research:

> The kind of research we need to do involves identifying and investigating all the differences behind the catch-all category of 'watching television' … we do need to focus on the complex ways in which television viewing is inextricably embedded in a whole range of everyday practices… We need to investigate television viewing … in its 'natural setting'. (Morley 1992: 177)

The 'natural setting' in which television viewing takes place has diversified over the past decades. Given the many ways in which television is consumed nowadays, considering one show in one medium through one type of methodological approach gives a limited perspective on social life, and can therefore only serve to consider one specific aspect of the life-worlds of individuals. Of course there have been methodological developments which have in some way or other answered David Morley's call for a more nuanced style of research. One such example is the volume put forward by Berker et al. (2006). Relating to and building on the domestication approach, the collection takes a wider view of the home and the interrelation between media and technologies in the home. They focus on 'the continuity of routines and patterns of everyday life, but also consider the breaking of routines and the discontinuity of some processes' (Berker et al. 2006: 3).

If we apply the figurational approach to Ang's study, we might ask how *Dallas* relates to other media consumed and appropriated, who the different actors in the family home are, how they relate to a particular programme and how they communicate with each other and with other actors about the programme, a specific episode, and the specific themes it raises. In the current state of deep mediatization, these questions should be broadened to take into account other mediated interactions that take place in relation to the viewing of a programme. If we identify the media ensembles and communication practices of different actors within a figuration, we can expect that additional actor constellations come into play in a state of deep mediatization. A one-dimensional approach would neglect these factors.

Methodological discussions of cross-media research are not new to media and communication scholarship. Kim Christian Schrøder (2011) provides a comprehensive overview of the development of cross-media research and studies employing a cross-media research design. Schrøder argues that a cross-media approach is not optional or a 'nice-to-have' when approaching audience research. He sees it as an essential part of a research design to capture what audiences or users of any kind are experiencing in their engagement with media. Says Schrøder (2011: 6):

> I shall therefore claim that a genuine audience perspective on the contemporary media culture must adopt a cross-media lens, because people in everyday life, as individuals and groups, form their identities and found their practices through being the inevitable sense-making hubs of the spokes of the mediatized culture. [...] Audiences are inherently cross-media.

Even though the final sentence of the quote might seem like stating the obvious, a cross-media approach is still not the norm for many research projects.

While the benefits of conducting research from a cross-media perspective are hard to refute, a high volume of studies in the field of media and communications work mainly with one specific type of data such as media texts (content analysis) or data gathered through interviews, to name but two examples. Our point is not to say that these studies are not of value or do not serve to answer certain types of research questions. In line with Schrøder (2011: 7): 'Some will play the game of cross-media research on the front stage of their research theatre; for others the cross-media perspective will and should remain a backstage thing.' Given the changes that have been observed in the media landscape over the past decades, it is necessary to reflect upon the validity and the meaningfulness of research focusing on a single medium or one type of data only. What we aim to emphasize is that the figurational approach allows for a holistic picture of the interrelationship between what we have traditionally thought of in different domains of study within communication and media studies: texts, audiences, uses, practices, and actors and production. By doing so, it takes questions of communication research to a broader level, positioning them in social contexts without falling into the trap of pursuing mediacentric research (Livingstone 2009).

Conducting research from a cross-media perspective gives rise to a number of challenges. For one, it forces researchers to gather data in different ways through different methods and to think of different ways of data gathering, data mining and relating diverse types of data to each other. We will present a detailed approach to how this can be achieved in the final section of this chapter. Secondly, combining data in such a way implicates ethical questions. One example is that—similar to network analysis—we might have some findings referring to people who have never agreed to take part in the research process. How can this be dealt with responsibly? The plus side promises a cross-media approach for triangulation and a richer set of data. Then again, different types of data are likely to call for different methods of analysis, meaning more time and thought will have to be devoted to the analyses.[1]

14.3 Defining Boundaries as a Necessity and Challenge

Another necessity as well as a challenge of research that we want to draw attention to is that of defining the boundaries of who and what is being researched. In other words, it is a matter of defining and deciding who belongs to a certain figuration and who does not. While the immanent characteristics of a communicative figuration (actor constellation, significant themes and practices) give the researcher indications of who is part of a communicative figuration and who is not, grey areas in which a decision has to be made are to be expected. Take as an example a company with headquarters in Berlin and subsidiaries in Amsterdam and Singapore. The data gathered so far might indicate that there are frequent meetings between staff from all locations. Similar topics are also deemed important in the three offices. However, it turns out that the work practices differ significantly between Amsterdam and Berlin, on the one hand, and Singapore, on the other. In such a case, can we still assume all three offices to be part of one figuration?

As discussed by Couldry and Hepp (2017: 72–76), figurations of figurations can be observed in different constellations. Often, media, and more recently the internet and social networking sites in particular, enable the construction of figurations of figurations—think of social movements that operate to a great extent through the use of internet platforms. In figurations of figurations, actors themselves 'can be considered as figurations' in their own right. In the example mentioned above, each team within a company can be considered a figuration which as a whole forms part of a larger figuration. For figurations of figurations to come into existence and function in a meaningful way, mediated communication and a shared media ensemble are crucial (Couldry and Hepp 2017: 73). A second principle that allows figurations of figurations to exist is a meaningful arrangement in the Weberian sense. More specifically, as Couldry and Hepp (2017: 74) explain, figurations of figurations are based upon and within 'certain discourses that connect these figurations and their meaning in the social world, and certain *larger scale relations of interdependency between domains of action* [...] that come to be associated with *assumed* relations of meaning' (emphasis in the original). Going back to the example of the transnational company with offices in Berlin, Amsterdam and Singapore, it might be useful to conceptualize this type of organization as a figuration of figurations.

In ethnographic studies, the researched is commonly referred to as 'the field' (Næss 2016). Several scholars have pointed towards the difficulties of defining where the field begins and where it ends—especially in an increasingly complex social and largely mediated world (for example Lohmeier 2014; Lohmeier in press; Mitchell 2012). Hans Erik Næss (2016: para. 2) emphasizes this point when he writes:

> In contrast to the conventional view on the field as a territorial unit, [I argue that it] should be seen as composed of several sites, processes and relations – sometimes far from each other geographically and connected with each other in different ways, on different scales and with different intensity. A field consequently, is where the phenomenon can be said to exist. Sites are localities where you can investigate the processes, actions and relations within this phenomenon ethnographically.

In a similar line of argument, Eva Nadai and Christoph Maeder (2005: para. 10) state that 'unlike traditional cultural anthropology sociological ethnography in and of complex societies rarely ever deals with a clearly bounded group in a single place'. They (Nadai and Maeder 2005: para. 24) conclude the article by arguing that the main advantage of such multi-sited ethnographies are the generalizations that can be drawn from the research: 'By using multi-sited ethnography we can enlarge the traditional "single tribe, single scribe" way of doing ethnographic research and contribute to sociological questions that cut across the boundary of a single traditional field.'

To illustrate these points, let us take research on families as an example. At first sight one might consider the family a rather straightforward and easily definable field as well as an easily definable figuration. However, under closer scrutiny, defining what makes a family is not an easy task. As pointed out in *The Blackwell companion to the sociology of families* (Scott et al. 2004) we can observe a pluralization from family to *families*. The editors state: 'Our title acknowledges the plurality of family forms and, by implication, the dynamic process of family formation and dissolution across time' (Scott et al. 2004: xvii). Recent research on families (see for example Jamieson et al. 2014) has acknowledged the complexities of families. Transnational family networks, as they have been researched by Madianou and Miller (2012) and Beck-Gernsheim (2014), are but one example of the growing diversity of families. In addition, these studies have shown that the complexities increase with the recent development in media change. In line with the broader definition of family in academia, research participants might similarly have shifting understandings of who belongs to their family, depending on circumstances. In a recent action research project with teenage refugees based in Bremen (Volmerg et al. 2016), participants were creating family-like relations with each other as well as with at least one of the researchers involved.

Definitions of the family are certainly dependent on historical and cultural contexts. As Morgan (2014) points out, the changing definition of family is partly thanks to changing circumstances and the fluidity of social life, and partly to the changing perceptions of what *can* constitute a family. From a methodological point of view, the difficulty of defining families at the point of data gathering might seriously limit the data gathering process by imposing a set definition of families from the outside. By conceptualizing families as figurations, researchers can consider their actor constellations, relevance frames and practices and thereby construct families through a multi-perspective lens. The concept of communicative figurations can therefore be used to sharpen the understanding of what 'the field' one wants to research is, by not neglecting fluidities within a figuration but by illuminating them.

Another requirement when applying a figurational approach to a field of study is that it allows for scalability. As Couldry and Hepp (2017: 70) point out:

> Certain types of figuration—associated with distinctive ensembles of media technologies—generate obligations and dependencies not just between individuals, but also between individuals and communication systems, obligations that are distinctive features of how we live within the media manifold, but which also characterize *new types* of figuration.

To this end, it is also crucial to pay attention to various interrelations between figurations. Couldry and Hepp (2017) provide an example in which they situate the figuration of the family within its web of figurations. In the context of raising and educating children, a family 'interacts over many years with organizations (schools, adult education centres, universities) that are regarded as having certain responsibilities for education' (Couldry and Hepp 2017: 75). These children, in turn, grow up and form part of various figurations themselves while probably staying connected to the communicative figuration of the family. Hence, Couldry and Hepp (2017: 75) speak of an 'ever-expanding, indeed changing, set of other figurations (and figurations of figurations)'. Some of these external figurations might consist of other human actors, while others might come into being through techno-human interaction. An example for these techno-human actors might be dating sites, whose algorithms suggest people with similar interests and supposedly matching character traits as potential future partners.

From an empirical perspective, researching figurations and figurations of figurations provides a whole new set of challenges. One is to gain an understanding of the figuration as a whole and to understand how it functions with others who might not be based in the same location. For one, this might call for mobile methods (Büscher and Urry 2009), a methodological approach that we will return to in Sect. 14.4. Depending on the research project, it might secondly call for developing new kinds of methodologies. Building up expertise in digital methods, including working with so-called 'big data', is without doubt a significant development in this area (Rogers 2013). However, even though we might find ourselves in a land of plenty when it comes to digital traces and digital data in general, it does not mean that all questions are easily answered (Lohmeier 2014). One of the current challenges is to combine and bring together data gained through digital traces with data stemming from the (material) context in a meaningful way (Hine 2015). This requires learning new skills, and developing new programmes and apps that allow for and support such data gathering (Hasebrink and Hepp 2017;

Hepp et al. 2016). For some types of research question, this could also mean working in interdisciplinary and transnational teams, which in turn comes with its own advantages and hurdles.[2]

So far, we have considered some of the necessities and challenges when approaching research with a figurational approach in mind. In particular, we have focused on cross-media research and how the fringes of a field and the periphery of a figuration can be defined. In the remainder of this chapter we aim to integrate what we have elaborated on by outlining a specific research project.

14.4 Researching Mediated Family Memory

The arguments we provided for conducting cross-media research as well as for defining boundaries of the research field as necessities when researching today's media environment and the challenges we have identified for these two necessities is rather abstract. We will now move on from the methodological considerations and present an ideal research project that addresses and illustrates in more detail some of the advantages and challenges we have outlined so far by means of this specific project. The overall theme of the project is family memory; that is, we ask how memory is constructed in the context of the family in times of deep mediatization. Taking both cross-media research as well as the issue of defining boundaries seriously, the methodology of this project is designed to gain a diverse set of data by involving ethnographic miniatures and collected mediated memory objects. Furthermore, we involve participants in the research process by asking them to take an active role in the process of data gathering.

14.4.1 Researching Mediated Family Memory: Cross-Media and the Boundaries of the Figuration

Two key features of today's media environment are that the practices of a given figuration are mediated through a media-manifold and related to non-mediated practices as well. From a methodological point of view, this calls for a cross-media perspective which also takes non-mediated objects, places and other sites of the social into account. According to Büscher and Urry (2009):

> Methods also need to be able to follow around objects, what Marcus calls 'follow the thing' (1995). This is because objects move as part of world trade which increasingly involves complex products; objects move in order to be combined into other objects (such as the components of a computer that travel the equivalent of a journey to the moon); some objects travel and lose their value (cheap souvenirs) while others enhance their value through movement (an 'old master': Lury 1997); and as objects travel, their cultural significance can grow as they accrete material and symbolic elements (107).

A figurational perspective can encompass the material aspects of life and the social as it unfolds while at the same time recognizing the current state of deep mediatization. On a methodological level, this means accepting a wider and possibly explorative approach when reconstructing a figuration in a first instance. This is not to imply that more standardized approaches to researching communicative figurations are not possible. It does, however, mean that a figuration is considered with an appropriate degree of openness in the first instance. Methodological approaches such as so-called 'mobile methods' (Büscher and Urry 2009) can provide a good way into this approach. Mobile methods is a way into the empirical where a researcher is 'trying to move with, and to be moved by, the fleeting, distributed, multiple, non-causal, sensory, emotional and kinaesthetic' (Büscher et al. 2011: 1).

In this 'ideal' project, we investigate the communicative construction of memories and mnemonic practices in the context of families in a state of deep mediatization. We distinguish between group, public and personal memories and work with a diverse sample of families: locally situated and with a migrant background, as well as traditional, blended and alternative.[3] As an overall framework, we view the family as a communicative figuration in order to understand the different ways in which memories are constructed by taking into account actor constellations, frames of relevance and communicative practices.

14.4.2 A Concrete Example: Reconstructing Communicative Figurations Through Interviews and a Multi-Situated Ethnographic Approach

To gain insights into families as communicative figurations and in order to understand the communicative construction of memories within locally situated and migrant families, this project employs a mixed-method design that includes interviews and a multi-situated, online and offline ethnography. Second, we employ a qualitative content analysis and sorting techniques that allow us to categorize digital and material memory objects relevant for the researched families. Third, throughout the whole process research participants are encouraged to get involved and support the process of data gathering. This means that they can contribute relevant (mediated) memory objects and share them with the researchers.

Drawing on Larsen (2005, 2008), Büscher and Urry (2009: 107) explain the required openness and mobility in the most literal sense for the case of researching memories:

> [m]uch mobility involves the active development and performances of 'memory' that 'haunt' people, places and especially meetings. Recovering such memories necessitates empirical methods that qualitatively investigate how photographs, letters, images, souvenirs and objects are deployed within large social groupings or within family and friendship groups.

They also point towards the "'atmosphere' of place or places" (2009: 106)—especially of the home. However, depending on the research questions and the figuration in focus, this might equally apply to an office building, a community hall, a school or university building or a public square where meetings and gatherings take place.

To reconstruct the communicative figurations of families—that is the actor constellations, communicative practices and frames of relevance—we embark on a multi-situated ethnographic approach (Beneito-Montagut 2011). This means participating in family gatherings, accompanying families on outings or spending time with them collectively or individually during regular activities. The combination of interviews and ethnographic encounters allows for a holistic picture of families as communicative figurations and their practices of communication with regard to the construction of memories. This view is central in our approach to families, as communicative figurations might or might not function as a collectivity to communicatively construct, share, exchange and negotiate family and public memories. The guiding questions are therefore as follows: Who is involved in the communicative practices of the family as a figuration? Who participates in relation to which themes, and what are the frames of relevance for the family? More broadly, how is a sense of group identity and a sense of belonging created through communication practices and a shared media ensemble? Who is constructed as part of the family by whom? Which actors dominate or have a central role in constructing the family? As part of these extended multi-situated ethnographic miniatures (Bachmann and Wittel 2006), we conduct interviews with members of each family. In these semi-structured interviews, we assess first the communicative practices within the family. In addition, we gather data on the mnemonic practices of the family. To embed the data gathered through interviews in a wider context, we employ a multi-situated, online and offline ethnographic approach. In particular, this involves spending time with the family in their home, on outings, befriending members of the family on networking sites, and participating as much as possible in their everyday lives.

Secondly, we focus on digital and material memory objects that are of relevance to research participants. The guiding questions for this part of the research process are as follows: How are memories communicatively constructed within different types of families? How do different lifestyles and other circumstances (such as mobility and flight) impact on families' memory practices? What is considered valuable in such situations? How do different families approach the construction of memories? By asking these types of questions, researchers can ensure to conduct people- rather than media-centred research (Hepp 2010). Moreover, researchers will gain access to an extensive collection of memory objects through the interviews and the ethnographic fieldwork conducted. Through this step, we will first gain insights into the different types of digital and material memory objects, the interplay between digital and material memory objects and their relevance within the communicative construction of the family. Second, the focus moves on to what types of memories the objects point to. Are they related to group memory (including family celebrations and commemorations, such as christenings, weddings and remembrances of deceased family members), public memory (such as national holidays and remembrance days, visits to a museum), and more personal, private and intimate family memories (such as favourite meals, hiding places in the house or names of dolls and teddy bears).

Finally, within this methodological approach, participants are encouraged to gather additional data relevant for the research projects. This could be pictures of material memory objects that they would like to tell us about or pictures taken at family gatherings. While the pictures are memory objects in and of themselves, they allow for a continued conversation between researchers and research participants that will bring deeper insights into the nature of the communicative and mnemonic practices. In an ideal scenario, participants will also record conversations at family gatherings or at the dinner table, similar to the data analyzed by Keppler (1994). Data gathered in this way will be analyzed by drawing on a conversation analysis (Keppler 1994; Bergmann and Luckmann 1995).

What becomes apparent with this methodology is that by focusing on actors and practices, we are required to take a cross-media approach, as these are the circumstances in which the communicative construction of memories takes place. Moreover, focusing on actors and thereby taking a people-centred perspective assists us in understanding the figuration and its limits. This type of methodology serves to understand in greater depth the various aspects of research participants' lifeworld experiences when it comes to family memory.

14.5 Conclusion

In this chapter, we have addressed some underlying questions related to approaching a research project with the notion of communicative figurations. We have done so by considering both the requirements as well as the challenges when it comes to doing cross-media research and to defining the field and its limits.

In particular, we have addressed what doing cross-media research entails. There are still only a relatively small number of projects that take the call for a cross-media approach seriously. This is not entirely surprising, as cross-media research does come with a number of challenges, some of which we have outlined above. Moreover, cross-media research does take time, effort and deviation from well-known methodological paths. The concept of communicative figurations provides a useful tool that assists researchers in thinking through their research process and how to go about it with a cross-media perspective. Gathering data on actors involved, frames of relevance and communicative practices is highly likely to include various media. Thus, the concept itself assists by focusing on more than one kind of media. This does not mean that the data are spread equally across all media sustained or used by the actors of the communicative figuration, but the approach does open up a wider perspective. On the other hand, this is not to say that a study whose main bulk of data analyses tweets, for example, cannot be of value or be based on a communicative figuration.

The second challenge we addressed was defining the boundaries of the field. We have illustrated how the concept of communicative figurations can be utilized to assess how researchers might be able to define the boundaries of the researched field without neglecting its inherent complexities and open-ended character. The concept of communicative figurations proves useful in this regard for a number of reasons. By allowing the researcher to focus on a specific set of characteristics, namely, actor constellations, frames of relevance and communicative practices, the process of de-marking a figuration is relatively clear cut and applicable for a variety of research topics. Nonetheless, as the approach also allows for the characterization of figurations of figurations, the complexities of a figuration are also taken into account.

In the latter part of the chapter, we have given a detailed example of how a broad research question regarding the communicative construction of family memory can be operationalized. Our project, on family memory, asks broadly how memory is constructed in the context of the family. Our approach takes into account the cross-media reality of families' lifeworlds by its methodological approach, and our field's boundaries are defined by taking the figuration of the family and considering its interdependencies with other figurations, as well as possible figurations of the figuration. All in all, the design of the project is reconstructing closely the (communicative) realities of today's lifeworlds in a time of deep mediatization.

Notes

1. Given the academic environments many scholars work in, however, spending more time on one particular study is not encouraged. On the contrary, from the strategic point of view of one's career, emerging scholars might be well advised to publish several papers (ideally peer-reviewed journal articles) from the set of data that was gathered quickly—Averbeck-Lietz and Sanko (2016) on the issue of time in academia. Perhaps this is part of the reason why developing cross-media research skills has not received the attention it deserves.
2. See for example Scheel et al. (2016) for a discussion of challenges and possible solutions when conducting a collaborative ethnography with researchers from various backgrounds.
3. Families consisting of two parents (mother and father) and a child or children are referred to as traditional. Blended families are those with two heterosexual partners with children from a previous marriage or partnership.

Finally, alternative families consist of homosexual partners with adopted children or single parents. Other families—such as grandparents acting as main caregivers for children owing to the death of the parents—would also be included in the category of alternative families. We are keen to emphasize that we are not looking at different families from a normative point of view but value all forms of families and their members equally. We distinguish between the different types of families in order to recognize the diversity of the social world.

References

Ang, Ien. 1985. *Watching Dallas. Soap opera and the melodramatic imagination.* London: Methuen.

Averbeck-Lietz, Stefanie, and Christina Sanko. 2016. Wissenschafts- und Forschungsethik in der Kommunikationswissenschaft. In *Handbuch nicht standardisierte Methoden in der Kommunikationswissenschaft*, eds. Stefanie Averbeck-Lietz and Michael Meyen, 125–136. Wiesbaden: Springer VS.

Bachmann, Götz, and Andreas Wittel. 2006. Medienethnographie [Media ethnography]. In *Qualitative Methoden der Medienforschung* [Qualitative methods of media research], eds. Ruth Ayaß, and Jörg R. Bergmann, 183–219. Reinbek: Rowohlt.

Beck-Gernsheim, Elisabeth. 2014. Transnationale Familien: Lebens- und Liebesformen in einer globalisierten Welt [Transnational families: Life and love forms in a globalized world]. In *Die vergessenen Kinder der Globalisierung: Psychosoziale Folgen von Migration* [The forgotten children of globalization: Psychosocial consequences of migration], eds. Elisabeth Rohr, Mechthild M. Jansen, and Jamila Adamou, 11–24. Giessen: Psychosozial-Verlag.

Beneito-Montagut, Roser. 2011. Ethnography goes online. *Qualitative Research* 11 (6): 716–735.

Bergmann, Jörg R., and Thomas Luckmann. 1995. Reconstructive genres of everyday communication. In *Aspects of oral communication*, ed. Uta Quasthoff, 68–86. Berlin, New York: de Gruyter.

Berker, Thomas, Maren Hartmann, Yves Punie, and Katie Ward. 2006. *Domestication of media and technology.* Maidenhead: Open University Press.

Büscher, Monika, and John Urry. 2009. Mobile methods and the empirical. *European Journal of Social Theory* 12 (1): 99–116.

Büscher, Monika, John Urry, and Katian Witschger. 2011. *Mobile methods.* Abingdon, New York: Routledge.

Couldry, Nick, and Andreas Hepp. 2017. *The mediated construction of reality.* Cambridge, Malden, MA: Polity Press.

Fiske, John. 1990. Women and quiz shows: Consumerism, patriarchy and resisting pleasures. In *Television and women's culture: The politics of the popular*, ed. Mary E. Brown, 134–143. London, Newbury Park, CA: Sage.

Hasebrink, Uwe, and Andreas Hepp. 2017. How to research cross-media practices? Investigating media repertoires and media ensembles. *Convergence*, online first.

Hepp, Andreas. 2010. Researching 'mediatized worlds': Non-mediacentric media and communication research as a challenge. In *Media and communication studies. Interventions and intersections*, eds. Nico Carpentier, Ilija Tomanić Trivundža, Pille Pruulmann-Vengerfeldt, Ebba Sundin, Tobias Olsson, Richard Kilborn, Hannu Nieminen, and Bart Cammaerts, 37–48. Tartu: Tartu University Press.

Hepp, Andreas, Cindy Roitsch, and Matthias Berg. 2016. Investigating communication networks contextually. Qualitative network analysis as cross-media research. *MedieKultur* 32 (60): 87–106.

Hine, Christine. 2015. *Ethnography for the internet*. London: Bloomsbury.

Jamieson, Lynn, Ruth Lewis, and Roona Simpson. 2014. *Researching families and relationships. Reflections on process*. New York: Palgrave Macmillan.

Keppler, Angela. 1994. *Tischgespräche [Dinner conversations]*. Frankfurt am Main: Suhrkamp.

Larsen, Jonas. 2005. Families seen photographing: The performativity of family photography in tourism. *Space and Culture* 8: 416–434.

Larsen, Jonas. 2008. Practices and flows of digital photography: An ethnographic framework. *Mobilities* 3: 140–160.

Livingstone, Sonia. 2009. On the mediation of everything: ICA presidential address 2008. *Journal of Communication* 59 (1): 1–18.

Lohmeier, Christine. 2014. *Cuban Americans and the Miami media*. Jefferson, NC: McFarland.

Lohmeier, Christine. in press. Zwischen "gone native" und "eine von uns": Reflektionen zu etischer und emischer Positionierung zum Forschungsfeld. In *Auswertung qualitativer Daten in der Kommunikationswissenschaft*, ed. Andreas Scheu. Wiesbaden: Springer VS Verlag.

Lury, Celia. 1997. The objects of travel. In *Touring cultures: Transformations of travel and theory*, eds. Chris Rojek, and John Urry, 75–95. London: Routledge.

Madianou, Mirca, and Daniel Miller. 2012. *Migration and new media: Transnational families and polymedia*. Abingdon, New York: Routledge.

Marcus, George E. 1995. Ethnography in/of the World System: The emergence of multi-sited ethnography. *Annual Review of Anthropology* 24: 95–117.

Mitchell, Jon P. 2012. Introduction. In *Ethnographic practice in the present*, eds. Marit Melhuus, Jon P. Mitchell, and Helena Wulff, 1–16. New York: Berghahn Books.

Morgan, David H.J. 2014. Framing relationships and families. In *Researching families and relationships. Reflections on process*, eds. Lynn Jamieson, Ruth Lewis, and Roona Simpson, 19–45. New York: Palgrave Macmillan.

Morley, David. 1980. *The 'nationwide' audience: Structure and decoding*. London: BFI.

Morley, David. 1992. *Television, audiences and cultural studies*. London: Routledge.

Nadai, Eva, and Christoph Maeder. 2005. Fuzzy fields. Multi-sited ethnography in sociological research. *Forum: Qualitative Sozialforschung* 6 (3): Art. 28.

Næss, Hans E. 2016. Creating "the field": Glocality, relationality and transformativity. *Forum: Qualitative Sozialforschung* 17 (3): Art. 15.

Rogers, Richard. 2013. *Digital methods*. Cambridge, MA: MIT Press.

Scheel, Stephan, Baki Cakici, Francisca Grommé, Evelyn Ruppert, Ville Takala, and Funda Ustek-Spilda. 2016. Transcending methodological nationalism through transversal methods? On the stakes and challenges of collaboration. ARITHMUS Working Paper Series, Paper No. 1. doi:10.13140/RG.2.2.33901.79842. http://arithmus.eu/wp-content/uploads/2015/02/Scheel-et-al-2016-Transcending-method-nationalism_ARITHMUS-Working-paper-1.pdf. Accessed 15 May 2017.

Schlesinger, Philip, Rebecca E. Dobash, Russell P. Dobash, and C. Kay Weaver. 1992. *Women viewing violence*. London: British Film Institute.

Schrøder, Kim C. 2011. Audiences are inherently cross-media: Audience studies and the cross-media challenge. *Communication Management Quarterly* 18: 5–27.

Scott, Jacqueline, Judith Treas, and Martin Richards. 2004. *The Blackwell companion to the sociology of families*. Oxford: Wiley-Blackwell.

Volmerg, B. et al. 2016. *Videoprojekt mit jungen Flüchtlingen als Gegenstand methodischer Herangehensweisen der Aktionsforschung* [Video project with young refugees as subject of methodical approaches to action research]. Presentation at the University of Bremen on 28 June.

15

Qualitative Media Research and Interviewing Strategies

Juliane Klein, Michael Walter and Uwe Schimank

15.1 Introduction

Against the backdrop of a changing media environment, the practices individuals apply on a daily basis and in different life spheres have altered dramatically. In 'times of deep mediatization' (Hepp and Hasebrink 2017/in print), most individuals' media repertoires are increasingly infusing nearly every aspect of their everyday lives. However, it is an open question whether and to what extent individuals are aware of this interrelatedness, since the use of different media might be inherent to their daily routine. This potential lack of

J. Klein (✉) · M. Walter · U. Schimank
SOCIUM—Research Center on Inequality and Social Policy,
University of Bremen, Mary-Somerville-Straße 9, 28359 Bremen, Germany
e-mail: juliane.klein@posteo.de

M. Walter
e-mail: mkwalter@uni-bremen.de

U. Schimank
e-mail: uwe.schimank@uni-bremen.de

awareness makes it difficult to research the role these transforming communications play in the individual's conduct of life.

Therefore, the purpose of this methodical chapter is to identify a qualitative interviewing strategy that meets the requirement of openness—as a core principle of qualitative research—so as to ensure the respondents' freedom to set their own relevance structures, while at the same time maintaining the thematic focus on the interviewees' media repertoire. In the same vein, we aim to reconstruct the relevance individuals attach to their media repertoires and to media change in their conduct of life with respect to disturbances and coping.

To this end, we consider different interviewing strategies representing varying degrees of explicitness when stating our media-related research interest, different levels of detail in interview questions targeted at the individuals' changing media repertoires, and different points in the course of the interview when we state the respective questions. We explored four different strategies in a pretest based on ten semi-structured interviews with members of the middle class—nine couples and one single person. The interviews were conducted within the thematic scope of investigating the communicative figurations of German middle-class couples in respect to media-related disturbances and coping practices. We included the life spheres of work, intimate relations, parenthood, long-term asset building and civil society engagement. Our main research question is to analyze how the individuals' media repertoires and the changes thereof shape both the disturbances experienced and the applied coping strategies in the five life spheres. Based on these pilot interviews, we will eventually examine which of these interviewing strategies is most suitable to the research interest of our project.

Even though we developed this approach in order to deal with a specific problem of our research project, the scope of this chapter is a far more general one. We aim to make a methodological contribution to handling the problem of the inherent tension between openness und thematic focus that emerges in qualitative interviews. In particular, we will argue that our findings can deliver profound insights for the ongoing discussion in the so-called 'non-mediacentric' media studies (e.g. Morley 2009; Tosoni and Ridell 2016).

Following this introduction, we first locate our study in the wider realm of qualitative social research and previous discussions concerning the problem of openness in qualitative interviews in methodical standard works, as well as the handling of the phenomenon of media change and media use in empirical studies focusing on the impact of media in individuals' everyday life. Afterwards we describe the different interviewing strategies we considered for researching the role of transforming communications for disturbances and coping of members of the middle classes before presenting our findings and drawing conclusions.

15.2 Qualitative (Media) Research and the Challenging Tension Between Openness and Thematic Focus

Our research project is committed to a qualitative research perspective. Thus, it centres on the principle of openness and focuses on the interviewees' subjective relevance system. We translate this orientation into our research questions by asking, firstly, which role does the interviewees' media repertoire play in their conduct of life with respect to disturbances and coping, and secondly, how does the individual experience media change.

An interviewing strategy which explicitly stresses media repertoires and media use would impose the researcher's 'thematic relevance' (Schütz and Luckmann 1973: 186ff.). Articulating our research interest in media, we would probably urge the interviewees to talk only about media-related topics. Such a 'mediacentric' approach (Deacon and Stanyer 2014, 2015; Hepp et al. 2015; Lunt and Livingstone 2016) does not allow us to find out which role media repertoires play in the individuals' general daily conduct of life.

Nevertheless, an open approach faces an evident problem. Without a thematic stimulus the interviewees might not talk at all about their media repertoire and if and how they perceive a media change related to their conduct of life. A main problem in this context is the routine character of practices in general. According to Schütz und Luckmann, a large part of our daily practices are routinized and based on 'habitual knowledge' (Schütz and Luckmann 1973: 107ff.). These more or less 'automatically' conducted practices are primarily a 'means to an end'. Such habitual knowledge has a paradoxical structure of relevance:

> It is of the greatest relevance and yet of, so to speak, subordinate relevance. It is a determining characteristic of routine that it can be performed without it coming to one's attention, therefore without it becoming thematic in the cores of experience. Routine is continually ready to be grasped without coming into the distinct grasp of consciousness proper. Habitual knowledge is continually, yet marginally relevant. (Schütz and Luckmann 1973: 109)

In view of these remarks, media use can be regarded as a special routine practice, because media, as the word literally implies, are often used as 'means' and not as 'ends'. For example, using a telephone is usually not an end but a means to get in touch with someone. Therefore, media use as a form of habitual knowledge can be highly relevant for individuals' conduct of life, but not as part of their conscious minds. This implies that an 'activating' thematic stimulus set by the interviewer is necessary in order to reconstruct this habitual knowledge of the interviewees.

The principle of openness is discussed in most of the methodical literature as the core principle of qualitative empirical research. It is the main factor that distinguishes qualitative from quantitative social research, ensuring the respondents' freedom to set their own relevance structures during the interview (e.g. Przyborski and Wohlrab-Sahr 2009: 140; Gläser and Laudel 2010: 31; Helfferich 2011: 114). If interview questions reveal the concrete research interest, this directs the interviewees' response behaviour and interviewees are not able to freely state their opinions and experiences, but answer according to the relevance structures set by the interviewer. As a result, the conditions for understanding from an outsider perspective are not given and biases occur, distorting the meaning and interpretation patterns we aim to retrieve from the respondent's interview account (Przyborski and Wohlrab-Sahr 2009: 31).

In order to avoid such biases but, at the same time, to ensure gaining the desired knowledge, scholars suggest different interview forms. Przyborski and Wohlrab-Sahr (2009), for instance, and Nohl (2012) advocate narrative interviewing strategies with open ended questions in the beginning and more precise ones in the end. Similarily, Froschauer and Lueger (2003) suggest dividing the interview into an initial narrative phase for exploration followed by a second phase of enquiry for clarification (69ff.). According to them, the thematic focus can thus be ensured by enquiring more precisely about the topic of interest as the interview proceeds and when the risk of influencing the respondents' answers is less severe. Although when using these narrative interviewing strategies researchers can adhere to the principle of openness, Nohl (2012) argues that even with this interviewing form, habitual knowledge as the aspect we are interested in cannot be retrieved as interviewees cannot reflect this kind of knowledge at all. According to Nohl, as an advocate of the Documentary Method, researchers uncover this implicit knowledge in a heuristic analysis of the interview data.

As opposed to Nohl (2012), Witzel and Reiter (2012) argue that the respondents are indeed able to reflect upon implicit phenomena. In order to stimulate this reflection, they aim at producing a most natural, everyday conversation (see also Helfferich 2011: 115). Thus, authentic statements are generated that provide the condition for interpretation through others. Nevertheless, in spite of this common awareness of the difficulty of balancing openness and thematic guidance, neither Witzel and Reiter (2012), nor Nohl (2012), nor Przyborski and Wohlrab-Sahr (2009) describe how to concretely introduce the researcher's thematic interest in the interview—whether during the course of the interview or towards its end. They do not discuss the fact that by stating their research interest in their interview question they might steer the interviewees' response behaviour.

In the same vein, authors of empirical studies on media use neglect the problem of influencing their respondents by introducing their research interest to them. As Röser states, the thematic focus on media use is openly revealed in most of the studies (2016: 491). Hence, there is hardly any problem awareness for the implicit character of media use and, although in communication studies qualitative interviewing is a well-established (Loosen 2016) and according to Röser (2016: 490) the most often used method for researching media use, the difficulty of studying media use without imposing one's own relevance structures on the respondent is hardly reflected on in respective empirical studies. Most commonly, researchers dedicate whole sets of questions in their interview guides and specific enquiries to the use of certain media such as communication media (see e.g. Döring and Dietmar 2003; Ling 2005; Linke 2010; Kirchner 2014). Others do not specify how they introduced the media topic in their interviews, nor give any information on the concrete interview topics. Examples include Clark (2013), who conducted in-depth and focus group interviews as well as observations to research how individuals negotiate the introduction of new media in their home lives, Röser and Peil (2012), who investigated the domestication of the internet with the help of joint partner interviews and representative data on internet use, and Voß (1999), who looked at work and everyday practices of individuals working in autonomous work arrangements. This neglect of precise information about the questions posed during the interview again shows a lack of awareness of the problems around the balance between thematic guidance and the principle of openness.

With regard to implicit knowledge, von Streit (2011) stresses the difficulty in asking individuals about their routine practices. In order to yield this kind of knowledge, she therefore employed an open interview question to start the interview and subsequently asked the interviewees to describe typical days, for instance, in their work life. With the help of these 'experience questions' (Patton 2002: 350), she managed to retrieve implicit knowledge that the interviewees were unlikely to reflect upon otherwise. Through this, she intended the respondents to re-live their daily routines and thus recollect activities that they were usually not aware of, such as media use. However, von Streit is not the first researcher who called attention to the implicit character of media use. Kübler (1987) earlier highlighted this phenomenon. When discussing the enquiry of media use in biographic interviews, he stated that in biographical reconstruction media play only a marginal role. According to him, respondents are not conscious of media use and do not readily recollect media use. Media have become a natural part of their daily routine, but have not reached the deep, biographical dimension of remembrance. Whereas events that have changed, for example, time structures or leisure activities (such as the purchase of a TV) are remembered more easily, slow changes remain unnoticed (1987: 56f.). Therefore, he perceives questions targeted at the share of media reception in the constitution of daily life as the production of a scientific artefact, since this methodical procedure predetermines the meaning media have for the individual (1987: 57). The stimuli effect of, for instance, associations connected with characters and idols prominent from TV could be used by the interviewer to trigger memories of and experiences with media. However, these should only be used to locate or enrich a statement, and not in order to provoke a certain response. Therefore, again, the question of how to precisely introduce the topic of interest and, hence, to maintain the thematic focus remains unclear.

For the international 'non-mediacentric' media studies which emerged in the 1980s, the methodological problem of how to reconstruct media repertoires and relevance frames of media use as integral part of everyday practices is a main focus (Morley and Silverstone 1991; Berker et al. 2006; Morley 2007, 2009; Tosoni and Ridell 2016). Paradigmatically, David Morley states in opposition to mediacentric approaches that 'we need to "decentre" the media, in our analytical framework, so as to better understand the ways in which media processes and everyday life are interwoven with each other' (Morley 2007: 200). Most studies prefer open-ended interviews as an adequate method to enable respondents to articulate their individual relevance frames (Gray 1992: 21; Krajina 2014: 51–57). Most empirical studies following this approach apply an ethnographic oriented 'methodic triangulation', and use different forms of data collection such as observation, media diaries and also qualitative interviews. The latter is attributed a 'pivotal role' (Livingstone 2010: 566) to reconstruct how individuals use media in a broader cultural and social context. There are methodological reflections about the problems that the artificial interview situations and the interviewer's interventions have the effect of limiting the possibility that respondents will tell their own 'stories'. Furthermore, there is obviously a more or less explicit awareness of the structural tension between an open-ended interview approach and the media-related research question in mind (Morley and Silverstone 1991: 155). But as far as we see, so far no *systematic* method has been worked out to address this problem. As a typical example, in his study about individuals' 'everyday encounters with public screens' in cities, Krajina characterizes his interview method as 'in-depth, unstructured conversation, loosely anchored around themes such as routines and interaction with screens' (Krajina 2014: 57). Nevertheless, the discussion explicitly poses questions of how to 'unlock' implicit or prereflective practices and knowledge in a phenomenological perspective; implicit media use which is discussed above as a special routine practice is hardly reflected in the ongoing discussion.

To summarize, we can conclude that problem awareness in the methodological literature and the media studies exists with regard to the balancing act between adhering to the principle of openness, on the one hand, and maintaining the thematic focus, on the other. What is less discussed is the implicit nature of media use as a routine practice as was outlined by Kübler in 1987, but which has been neglected subsequently. Although scholars found ways of enquiring about such routine practices with the help of experience questions that encourage respondents to reflect upon their daily routines, in most of the empirical studies researchers do not reflect upon the risk of influencing the interviewees' response behaviour by openly stating their topic of interest in the interviews. We address this research gap with considerations of alternative interviewing strategies that come into question, and an exploration of a selection of those.

15.3 Interviewing Strategies

We developed different strategies to research the role of changing media repertoires as a source for disturbances and as potential coping strategies in the middle classes' conduct of life with the help of semi-structured interviews. These strategies differ in two respects: firstly, with regard to the way of naming media repertoires and media change as a research interest; and secondly, with regard to the way of enquiring about the respondents' media use and the relevance media have in their daily routines.

On the first variable, the options are: to explicitly name the respondents' media repertoire as our research interest; to implicitly state this as being of interest; or not to mention it at all. The advantage of the first option is that the respondents are fully aware of the purpose of the study, and thus have the opportunity to reflect upon the role that media play in their conduct of life. However, at the same time, explicitly mentioning this research interest limits the interviewees in independently setting the relevance of media to their conduct of life. They might address the topic merely in order to satisfy the researcher. Analogous to the bias of 'social desirability', this response behaviour could be labelled as 'researcher's desirability'. The second option, of only implicitly mentioning media change as one research interest among others, slightly diminishes the risk of this bias by dispersing the focal point. Nevertheless, only the third option of not mentioning the media-related research interest at all allows fully unimpaired assessment of whether or not the middle-class couples perceive their media repertoires as relevant to their conduct of life. At the same time, however, media could play a crucial role in their daily practices even though the couples are not aware of it, or simply do not conceive it as significant for the study and therefore make no mention of it.

Consequently, the second variable for the enquiry method is another important factor. Again, there are three different options to be considered. The first option is to pose media-related questions after each set of questions dealing with one of the previously identified life spheres, targeting the media repertoires in the respective domain. In this way, the topic can be taken up for each of the life spheres if it was not mentioned and elaborated upon sufficiently by the interviewees before. Thus, the relevance of media set by the respondents can be controlled for, while at the same time there is no risk of fully omitting it in cases where the couples do not bring up the subject themselves. However, to the detriment of this approach, questions focusing on the respondents' media repertoires after the first set of questions could influence the relevance interviewees attach to media in the subsequently discussed life spheres, resulting in biased response behaviour. Consequently, the relevance the interviewee attaches to the role of media repertoire is distorted. The second option is to ask for media repertoires only at the end of the interview and after all the different life spheres have been addressed. These questions would encompass all domains and would make the respondent reflect upon the media impact in a comparative way without disturbing the flow of the interview for those who do not mention by themselves media as relevant to their conduct of life. Nonetheless, a disadvantage of this strategy could be the detachment of these media-related questions from the respective life spheres, requiring each interviewee to recollect them themselves. A third option is, again, not to ask for the middle-class couples' media repertoires at all. On the one hand, this strategy bears the advantage of leaving it solely to the interviewees to determine the media's relevance to their conduct of life. On the other hand, this approach runs the risk that media repertoires are not mentioned by the respondents at all.

Based on these two variables with three different options each, nine different strategies arise to investigate the role of media repertoires and media change as both sources of disturbances and as strategies of how to cope with them (see Table 15.1). These are neither to state the research interest, nor to ask questions targeting media, or not to state the media-related research interest, but to ask such questions either at the end of the entire interview or after each set of questions. Other strategies are to explicitly state the media-related research interest, not to further enquire unless the respondents address the topic themselves, or to again ask corresponding questions at the end of the interview or after each set of questions dealing with one of the identified life spheres. Finally, media change can be stated implicitly as one research interest among others, and then again, questions dealing with this area can be asked not at all, at the end of the interview or after each set of questions.

From these options we decided against the strategies of not stating our interest in media use and media change. Nevertheless, asking focused questions on the topic either at the end of the interview or after each

Table 15.1 The four implemented strategies to research the role of changing media repertoires in a pretest

	Questions related to media ensemble		
Research interest stated	Not at all	At the end of the entire interview	After each set of questions
Not at all	1		
Explicitly			2
Implicitly		3	4

set of questions appeared illogical and would have confused the interviewees. In the same vein, we dismissed the reverse strategies of explicitly or implicitly stating media change as the research interest (thus raising awareness) but then not at all or hardly following up on the topic, since we deemed this to be inconsistent. Consequently, four strategies remained. Strategy 1 involves neither stating media change as the research interest, nor following up on the topic by asking questions on it. This represents the most open interview form as it leaves it completely to the respondents whether or not they address the topic of media change and media repertoires. Strategy 2 means explicitly stating the media focus and enquiring about this after each set of questions with regard to the respective life sphere. This represents the least open interview form and has a strong focus on media repertoires. Strategy 3 involves implicitly stating the media interest and posing corresponding questions at the end of the interview. This is a looser form, giving more space for the couples to set their relevance structure. Strategy 4 implicitly states the interest in the respondents' media repertoires and follows up on this with the help of related enquiries after each set of questions on one of the chosen life spheres. This provides both orientation towards changing media repertoires as well as room for the respondents' own relevance structures.

In order to explore these different interview forms, we conducted ten semi-structured interviews between June 2015 and January 2016. One of these interviews was conducted with a single person, whereas the others were joint partner interviews.[1] All interviewees were living in a shared household with their partners in Bremen and its surroundings and were between 34 and 64 years old. Moreover, they were biological parents or caregivers of children between the age of five and 19, of whom at least one attended school. Three of the interviews were conducted in university offices and the others took place in the interviewees' private homes. All interviews were conducted in German and transcribed verbatim.

Having conducted ten interviews, we explored interviewing strategy 1 three times, strategies 2 and 3 twice each, and strategy 4 three times. Strategy 1 was conducted three times owing to practical reasons that followed from the research process, while strategy 4 was conducted three times because it turned out to be the preferred option. Although ten interviews constitute only a small sample, they provide a sufficient basis for our purpose of exploring a topic that researchers have hitherto not explicitly reflected on.

15.4 Empirical Findings: How to Figure Out a Proper Interview Strategy for a Non-mediacentric Media Study

Interviewing strategy 1

neither stating media-related research interest, nor following up on the topic during the course of the interview

With the first interviewing strategy, we neither mentioned media change as the research interest, nor posed corresponding questions during the course of the interview. Thus, we left it entirely to the respondents to address the topic if they perceived it as relevant for their conduct of life, and introduced the topic of our project as follows:

> We are interested in how this conduct of life has changed in your personal perception and your experience,[2] but also in practical questions of how you arrange your everyday life against this backdrop, and how you deal with changes and challenges.

Two remarkable cases demonstrate the ambivalent outcome of this interviewing strategy. In the case of a middle-aged couple with both partners working in information technology (IT), media use was mentioned as both disturbances and coping strategies in several of the identified life spheres without being asked. This applied, for instance, to both the domains of work and family:

IP01: That [i.e. work] interferes strongly with private life or family life. Because we're so well connected and own several smartphones which are always somewhere nearby, it actually always

> happens to me that I also read work-related emails. Partly I do this on purpose. So it happens that I'm standing on a football field attending a match or picking up a child and then reply to an (...) email if these are things for which a quick reply is required or something like that. (P1: 90–97)

Apart from the fact that their media repertoire increased the blurring of boundaries between work and family, the couple also made use of media in order to manage both life spheres:

IP01: Well, sometimes you have to be [at your workplace] on another or a second day, so then I have to make sure that this same day I don't have any appointments in the afternoon and say, '[IP02], you have to pick up the children' or something, so this is very much about communication.

IP02: Mm, well good, we have [figured out] this already to some extent with the joint calendar and so on, that's already a lot, yes. These organizational tricks, all these organizational tricks are of course already [something]; many others don't do that (...).

IP01: Yes, here come all our cool IT tools. (...) Well, we have a Google calendar, so really online, which we have on our smartphones and our computers that we're mostly using at work. (...) There is my calendar in which I have my private appointments or everything in one, my private appointments, and work appointments. [IP02] can see all of this and reversed, I can also see that. That means, if a colleague asks me, 'Can we make an appointment for 17 July?' I say, 'Oops, [IP02] has a meeting [at work] that day, that's going to be difficult in case one of the kids is sick or something.' That means, I can already consider this and I don't have to write an email or call first in order to ask whether I can schedule an appointment for this day or not. (P1: 938–968)

As these quotations illustrate, the media environment and the couple's media repertoire play a crucial role both in their work lives, as well as in how they reconcile family and work. Accordingly, the issue of media use came up naturally without any incentive being required.

However, this did not apply to another interview that was conducted employing the same interviewing strategy. Hence, one respondent interviewed individually did not mention media in any respect throughout the entire course of the interview(P4). This was the case, in spite of her being a medical professional working in her surgery in the third generation. Based on this long tradition of running the practice in her family, we can assume that she must have witnessed major media-related changes and developments, at least at her workplace. Not having been informed about our interest in media environments and repertoires, and hence, not having been encouraged to reflect upon respective changes, she did not consider these in her account. Therefore, it is likely that a stimulus drawing her attention to media change would have stimulated her to reflect upon the topic and led to a different, more yielding outcome for our purposes—despite the apparently low relevance she attaches to media in her conduct of life. As a consequence, the risk of media change not being mentioned at all seems to be too high when conducting interviews according to this first interviewing strategy.

Interviewing strategy 2

explicitly stating the media-related research interest plus enquiries after each set of questions dealing with one of the life spheres

Conducting the interviews according to the second interviewing strategy, we explicitly stated media change as the main research interest using the following formulation:

> We are interested in how this conduct of life has changed in your personal perception and your experience, but also in practical questions of how you arrange your everyday life against this backdrop, and how you deal with changes and challenges. We are particularly interested in the role that media change, i.e. increasing mediatization, e.g. in the form of an increase of digital media, such as email, or SMS impacting the individual's everyday life, plays for these changes as well as for dealing with these changes.

Subsequently, we enquired about the respondents' media repertoire after each set of questions dealing with one of the identified life spheres. The interviews conducted in this way showed that highlighting the interest in the respondents' media repertoires and their change over time when introducing the topic led to the respondents strongly focusing on the media aspect, particularly for the first set of questions.

Interviewer: All right, I would like to start with the life sphere of occupation and career, and in the media it's always discussed that there are many changes: they talk about acceleration, more mobility, more flexibility are discussed and I'm first of all interested in how you experience this in your everyday working life?

IP03: Do you want to start, yes?
IP04: Well, there is constant accessibility, right? Just through the mobile phone you're always available or at least contactable and reachable. And through email contact, well that's all much faster and, yes, graspable. (P2: 1–11)

The example shows that although the initial question was not clearly targeted at media, the respondent focused on media use which had been explicitly stated as the main research interest in the introduction to the interview. Although this choice could also reflect the relevance the respondent attaches to media in this specific domain, it seems unlikely since other interviewees chose a broader start when discussing this life sphere, or talked about further disturbances later on. In the present case, the media focus tended to limit both interviewees' responses to the topic of media, leading them to neglect other factors that might have changed and caused disturbances in their work life, and likely overshadowing their own relevance structure. Although this constraint dissolved or was less prominent with regard to domains discussed later, the narrow concentration initially limited the respondents in their reflections and response behaviour.

This initial focus on the explicitly stated research interest in media repertoires is particularly evident, since the couple in this interview did not bring up the media topic in other life spheres again unless specifically asked for it. Thus, enquiring about their media use after each set of questions discussing one life sphere proved to be useful.

Interviewer: How about media communication in the family? Do you use new media there?
IP03: Oh, we have a lot of media ((laughing)).
IP04: What do we have?
IP03: We have a lot of media ((laughing)), the two of us, don't we? Well, so that we can also communicate through email, we'll organize family issues through email. Especially if it's external, like the choir is writing, or what the violin instructor [wrote], that I can [forward this to you.
IP04: [Yes, yes, yes. Or also through telephone and SMS. (P2: 550–563)

Here another enquiry was necessary to again stimulate reflection upon media use in the life sphere of parenthood and family life, although the partners widely used media to organize their daily life. In spite of this substantial and daily presence, the media focus faded into the background over the course of the interview, showing that these enquiries are beneficial to remind the respondents and assure continuation of this thematic priority.

Interviewing strategy 3

implicitly stating the media-related research interest plus enquiries at the end of the entire interview

Following the third interviewing strategy, we mentioned media change implicitly as the research interest applying the following formulation:

> We are interested in how this conduct of life has changed in your personal perception and your experience, but also in practical questions of how you arrange your everyday life against this backdrop, and how you deal with changes and challenges, and also which role the increasing mediatization of everyday life might play for this.

We followed up on the topic only at the end of the entire interview. In some cases, this implicit stimulus and the lack of frequent enquiries on the media subject led to the respondents forgetting about this research interest over the course of the interview. Neglecting the topic might or might not reflect the relevance the respondents attach to media in their conduct of life, but could also indicate that this focus fades into the background if not taken up occasionally on the part of the interviewer, as discussed above. However, in other cases respondents interviewed with this third interviewing strategy actually did talk about the impact of a changing media repertoire on their conduct of life, referring to the implicit stimulus set in the introduction to the interview topic.

IP05: I think this topic of flexibility, mobility and so on has many qualities that I appreciate, but one real burden is that the possibilities are SO gigantic. You used to have a phone from Telekom, it wasn't called Telekom, it was called the Post. Usually it worked, but if it didn't, you called somewhere and someone came, tightened a bolt and left again. Or you didn't have a phone, then you had different problems. But NOW. Oh God! Which provider? Which call rate? With a mobile phone there are three million call rates and I realize, basically,

> this is too much for me. I don't have time for that. And then I realize—and this was an aspect you also mentioned at the beginning: digital world. I believe everything we accelerate: transcribing, typing with the computer and so on. All this always returns as a problem in the form of this flood of possibilities. (P3: 1712–1721)

Possibly, the interviewee would have mentioned this irritation in her conduct of life irrespective of the impulse to reflect upon a changing media environment and her own media repertoire. However, there are indicators that the implicitly stated research interest stimulated the consideration of this. The reference to the impulse given in the introduction to the interview implies that this inspired the respondent to make the connection between her reflections and the changing media environment. At the same time, the implicitly set stimulus did not overshadow her own relevance structure, which is supported by the fact that the topic came up in the course of her statement and was not triggered by a direct enquiry. Consequently, the implicit naming of the media-related research interest can produce an adequate balance.

With this third interviewing strategy, we further observed that the enquiry about media-related topics only at the end of the interview came as a surprise for the interviewees, who were attuned to the announced five sets of questions, and tended to be tired by the end of the interview. Thus, it is likely that they answered the respective questions in a less elaborate and committed way than previous ones. Moreover, it can be assumed that at the end, the respondents were no longer aware of, or were not able to recollect, all aspects of the previously discussed life spheres and, hence, responded in a way that does not allow for separate conclusions for the different life spheres under study. Consequently, the interviewees might neglect crucial aspects, meaning that the retrospective questions yield less detail.

Interviewing strategy 4

implicitly stating the media-related research interest plus enquiries after each set of questions dealing with one of the life spheres

Applying the fourth interviewing strategy, we stated our interest in the role of changing media environments and repertoires for the respondents' conduct of life only implicitly using the same formulation as in strategy 3 (see above).

We enquired about the respondents' media use after each set of questions dealing with one of the previously identified life spheres. The implicit statement that media was one among other research interests led some respondents to take up the topic in their narrative. Others did not talk about their media use spontaneously. This differing response behaviour implies that the stimulus was not so strong that it overshadowed their own relevance structures, but that it left room for them to discuss individual chances and disturbances. When respondents mentioned media use in the depictions of their everyday life, these statements provided the interviewer with links to further enquiry on the topic, thus enabling natural conversation.

IP17: (...) The new media enable me to do a lot of coordination work of my job myself—independent of space and time. Therefore, I'm more flexible, but therefore I'm also more out and about, and out and about in shorter intervals. I would say there are many more..., or basically it applies to me that the options of doing several things increases, with it the problem of choice increases—what I am doing is rather becoming too much. But the coordination work necessary for doing these things has all become much easier owing to the new media.

Interviewer: Could you describe again what are, or which are, these media that play a role for you? (P9: 22–32)

However, also for those who did not initially mention media during the interviews, media-related enquiries did not come as a surprise. In such cases, asking for media repertoires was not perceived as unnatural and did not disturb the course of the interview, since these questions were not posed before the topic was raised by the interviewees themselves or at the end of each section of interview questions. Consequently, the media focus did not artificially create supposedly desired responses.

Interviewer: (...) You've mentioned before that sometimes there are business trips. Do you use something like Skype or any...

IP19: No.

Interviewer: ... other media?

IP18: No. We're, I, well, ((laughing)), a friend of mine recently said that I'm a media dinosaur.

Interviewer: OK. ((laughing))
IP18: So in the sense of, that actually already distinct, doesn't exist any more. I'd also be so difficult to get hold of and so on. (P10: 856–869)

Another reason for the lack of this 'interviewer's desirability' could be the fact that media use was initially mentioned only as one among other research interests. Hence, interviewees might have perceived it as more legitimate and might have felt more comfortable about not being able to extensively talk about media. At the same time, enquiring about media use with regard to every life sphere ensured that respondents who did not attribute high relevance to media did not drop the subject entirely, as was sometimes the case with strategy 3, when such questions were posed only at the end of the interview.

Consequently, this fourth interviewing strategy allowed interviewees to express their individual relevance structures. Illustrative evidence for this claim is the interview account of a couple in which one partner is to a much higher degree involved with media and media use than the other. They readily stated their different weighting of media for their daily routines in the different interview sections. This can be shown in relation to the life sphere of work. Asked about the changes in his everyday work life, the husband, an employee of an internationally operating industrial enterprise, immediately identifies changed media repertoires as a driver for changed working practices:

IP15: Yes, OK. Yes, I'm working for [...] here in the factory in Bremen and there very, very much happens at a very, very high pace regarding the topic of change. Everything is getting more and more centralized. Areas get pooled together; you work ..., before you maybe worked only for the [main] factory, by now Germany-wide. It even stretches to, to world-wide and because of technology, like for example IT, computers, smartphones and so on, it is becoming ..., it is a lot what we as employees are facing, in my opinion. (P8: 45–51)

(...)

IP15: What has also changed, is very strongly that the technology in the environment ..., well, we work a lot, a lot now with video conferences, telephone conferences, a lot is done via internet; you activate your computer screen, and then, so to speak, you

> work in a room-spanning way on documents and you more and more, let's say, collect information instead of developing and researching it. (P8: 79–84)

This interviewee's description reveals that media change and media use are highly relevant aspects of his everyday work life. In the course of the interview, this corresponds with his strong attention to media technology and media change:

IP15:	We are only end users via smartphone or computer and type something, but in the background also very, very much happens digitally. Current control is largely ..., companies all work digitally, information gets exchanged. In my opinion, all this is also part of the topic of digitalization. (–) I believe this digitalization changes society very, very much. But it's, I think it's no longer stoppable. (P8: 3126–3131)

In contrast, his wife who works part-time as a freelancer in children's education and the care sector, does not mention media in respect to her work at all. Only after explicitly being asked about media use does she mention WhatsApp as part of her everyday work life:

IP14:	Yes, that's also such a topic. WhatsApp, right, is this, do you know this?
Interviewer:	Yes.
IP14:	Yes. At some point [during work], the women started saying: Oh, don't we want to open a WhatsApp group, like for us? Otherwise I don't need it professionally, but then, so I can cancel; if one of the children is sick, I have to call eight women, not all of them pick up, I'm stressed whether one is now waiting in front of the door and I'm not there and she doesn't know what's going on. So I gratefully accepted. But there is ..., all this nonsense that somehow gets posted. And now, I directly mute it. And in this respect, I use it a little bit in the work context, but when the group has finished, I kindly say goodbye and delete it and am gone. But otherwise I use it for work only to call. (P8: 641–650)

In contrast to her husband, for her, media use is not a crucial part of her everyday work life. She explicitly describes media usage as marginal and of minor relevance (*'I use it a little bit'*). In comparison with her husband, her media use corresponds with a generally lower subjective attention to media-related topics during the interview.

The reconstruction of the couple's different relevance structures shows that strategy 4 is well balanced between openness and thematic focus: on the one hand, it provides the interviewees with room to express their own relevance structures and, on the other hand, it allows the researcher to carefully examine the role of media use and media change. Thus, it is possible to reconstruct the degree to which mediatization and media change shape the individuals' lifeworld.

After having explored four different interviewing strategies, one of them, namely strategy 4, can be identified as the most suitable for our purposes.

Strategy 1 was successful in one, but not in the other two interviews conducted in this way. Depending on the respondents' involvement with media, without stating the media-related research request at all they attached more or less relevance to the changing media environment and their own media repertoire. However, the risk that media are not mentioned at all is too high for our project targeted at researching media-related changing communicative figurations in middle-class couples' conduct of life.

Strategy 2 proved to be ambivalent. While prominently highlighting the media focus led to an initial bias towards media-related disturbances and overshadowed the respondents' own relevance structure, the frequent enquiry about media environment and repertoires ensured recollection of the topic.

Strategy 3 again had advantages and disadvantages. On the one hand, the implicit impetus provided orientation without impairing interviewees' own relevance structures; on the other hand, some interviewees forgot about this focus in the course of the interview. This neglect was further induced by the lack of follow-up questions during the interview. Additionally, the occurrence of the media-related questions only after having discussed all the different life spheres was perceived as tiresome on the part of the respondents, who had been attuned to the announced five sets of questions.

Consequently, strategy 4 appears to be the one that best suits the purposes of our project. The set stimulus is subtle and thus does not dominate the interviewees' response behaviour; yet it is strong enough to contain the presence of the media topic throughout the interview. Most importantly, this interviewing strategy allows the respondents' individual relevance structures with respect to media and media use as part of their daily routines to be captured.

15.5 Conclusion

Studying media use in middle-class individuals' conduct of life as routine practice, we were confronted with the difficulty of how to retrieve habitual knowledge through interviewing without imposing our relevance structure onto the respondents. Therefore, we were looking for an interviewing strategy that meets both the requirement of openness as the main principle of qualitative research and of thematic guidance throughout the interview. We explored four different interviewing strategies with the help of ten semi-structured interviews covering different life spheres, namely work, intimate relations, parenthood, long-term asset building as well as civil society engagement, and found one strategy that meets our purposes. By naming media use as one research interest among others and enquiring into it only after the respondents had brought up the topic themselves or at the end of each set of questions, this strategy allows for the interviewees' habitual knowledge to be addressed and at the same time provides room for the individuals' own relevance structures.

As stated in the introduction, our findings do not only deal with a specific problem solution for our particular research project but in general can provide significant methodological insights and impulses for qualitative research approaches applying interview methods. First of all, our findings address in a pragmatical perspective a basic question of qualitative research, that is, how to 'unlock' individuals' routine practices by retrospectively asking them about it. This is, as we discussed (see Chap. 2), of particular importance for media studies because of the highly implicit character of media use as a routine practice. Furthermore, we argue that this chapter—representing a media-centred approach—can contribute to the ongoing discussion of 'media-centric' versus 'media-centred' approaches in media and communication research (Deacon and Stanyer 2014, 2015; Hepp et al. 2015; Lunt and Livingstone 2016). Our findings can provide a systematic interview guide for the examination of relevance structures that media repertoires have in individuals' everyday life from a subjective perspective. By finding the right balance between open-ended interview questions and thematic focus imposed by the researcher, our approach promotes 'a nuanced and critical grasp of the reciprocity of media and everyday life' (Tosoni and Ridell 2016: 1286). Up to now this challenge has been largely delegated to the individual researcher's improvisation skills in concrete interview situations. Finally, the interview strategy we developed here could be especially useful for the examination of *cross*-media practices because, as our empirical discussion made clear, our approach is able to highlight the relevance and diversity of media use and media technologies in certain life spheres such as work, family or civic engagement as well as in these spheres' interconnections.

Notes

1. We opted for joint partner interviews instead of separate interviews based on the assumption that there is some kind of division of labour among partners with regard to the life spheres. Thus, interviewing them together provides us with a maximum expertise for each life sphere.
2. The concept of 'conduct of life' (*Lebensführung*) was previously explained to the interviewees.

References

Berker, Thomas, Maren Hartmann, Yves Punie, and Katie J. Ward. 2006. *Domestication of media and technology*. London: Open University Press.

Clark, Lynn S. 2013. *The parent app. Understanding families in the digital age*. Oxford: Oxford University Press.

Deacon, David, and James Stanyer. 2014. Mediatization: Key concept or conceptual bandwagon? *Media, Culture and Society* 36 (7): 1032–1044.

Deacon, David, and James Stanyer. 2015. 'Mediatization *and*' or 'mediatization *of*'? A response to Hepp et al. *Media, Culture & Society* 37 (3): 655–657.

Döring, Nicola, and Christine Dietmar. 2003. Mediatisierte Paarkommunikation: Ansätze zur theoretischen Modellierung und erste qualitative Befunde. *Forum Qualitative Sozialforschung* 4 (3). http://www.qualitative-research.net/index.php/fqs/article/view/676. Accessed 30 Mar 2017.

Froschauer, Ulrike, and Manfred Lueger. 2003. *Das qualitative Interview: zur Praxis interpretativer Analyse sozialer Systeme*. Wien: UTB.

Gläser, Jochen, and Grit Laudel. 2010. *Experteninterviews und qualitative Inhaltsanalyse*. Wiesbaden: VS.

Gray, Anne. 1992. *Video playtime. The gendering of a leisure technology*. London, New York: Routledge.

Helfferich, Cornelia. 2011. *Die Qualität qualitativer Daten. Manual für die Durchführung qualitativer Interviews.* Wiesbaden: VS.

Hepp, Andreas, Stig Hjarvard, and Knut Lundby. 2015. Mediatization: Theorizing the interplay between media, culture and society. *Media, Culture and Society* 37 (2): 314–324.

Hepp, Andreas, and Uwe Hasebrink. in print, 2017. How to research cross-media practices? Investigating media repertoires and media ensembles. *Convergence.*

Kirchner, Juliane. 2014. 'Schatz, ich hab dich gegruschelt!' Nutzung von Social Network Sites in Fernbeziehungen. In *Medienkommunikation in Bewegung. Medien – Kultur – Kommunikation*, eds. Jeffrey Wimmer and Maren Hartmann, 155–169. Wiesbaden: Springer VS.

Krajina, Zlatan. 2014. *Negotiating the mediated city: Everyday encounters with public screens.* London: Routledge.

Kübler, Hans-Dieter. 1987. Medienbiographien–ein neuer Ansatz der Rezeptionsforschung? In *Medien- und Kommunikationsgeschichte. Ein Textbuch zur Einführung*, eds. Manfred Bobrowsky, Wolfgang Duchkowitsch, and Hannes Haas, 53–65. Wien: Braumüller.

Ling, Rich. 2005. *Flexible coordination in the Nomos: Stress, emotional maintenance and coordination via the mobile telephone in intact families.* https://blog.itu.dk/DMKS-E2008/files/2008/09/ling-flexible-coordination-in-the-nomos.pdf.

Linke, Christine. 2010. *Medien im Alltag von Paaren. Eine Studie zur Mediatisierung der Kommunikation in Paarbeziehungen.* Wiesbaden: VS.

Livingstone, Sonia. 2010. Giving people a voice: On the critical role of the interview in the history of audience research. *Communication, Culture & Critique* 3 (4): 566–571.

Loosen, Wiebke. 2016. Das Leitfadeninterview – eine unterschätzte Methode. In *Handbuch nicht standardisierte Methoden in der Kommunikationswissenschaft*, eds. Stefanie Averbeck-Lietz and Michael Meyen, 139–155. Wiesbaden: Springer VS.

Lunt, Peter, and Sonia Livingstone. 2016. Is 'mediatization' the new paradigm for our field? A commentary on Deacon and Stanyer (2014, 2015) and Hepp, Hjarvard and Lundby (2015). *Media, Culture and Society* 38 (3): 462–470.

Morley, David. 2007. *Media, modernity and technology. The geography of the new.* New York: Routledge.

Morley, David. 2009. For a materialist, non-media-centric media studies. *Television & New Media* 10 (1): 114–116.

Morley, David, and Roger Silverstone. 1991. Communication and context: Ethnographic perspectives on the media audience. In *Qualitative methodologies for mass communication research*, eds. Klaus B. Jensen and Nicholas W. Jankowski, 149–162. London, New York: Routledge.

Nohl, Arnd-Michael. 2012. *Interview und dokumentarische Methode. Anleitungen für die Forschungspraxis.* Wiesbaden: VS.

Patton, Michael Q. 2002. *Qualitative research and evaluation methods.* Thousand Oaks, CA: Sage.

Przyborski, Aglaja, and Monika Wohlrab-Sahr. 2009. *Qualitative Sozialforschung. Ein Arbeitsbuch.* München: Oldenburg.

Röser, Jutta. 2016. Nichtstandardisierte Methoden in der Medienrezeptionsforschung. In *Handbuch nicht standardisierte Methoden in der Kommunikationswissenschaft*, eds. Stefanie Averbeck-Lietz and Michael Meyen, 481–497. Wiesbaden: Springer VS.

Röser, Jutta, and Corinna Peil. 2012. Das Zuhause als mediatisierte Welt im Wandel. Fallstudien und Befunde zur Domestizierung des Internets als Mediatisierungsprozess. In *Mediatisierte Welten*, eds. Friedrich Krotz and Andreas Hepp, 137–163. Wiesbaden: VS.

Schütz, Alfred, and Thomas Luckmann. 1973. *Structures of the life-world*, vol. 1. Evanston, IL: Northwestern University Press.

Tosoni, Simone, and Seija Ridell. 2016. Decentering media studies, verbing the audience: Methodological considerations concerning people's uses of media in urban space. *International Journal of Communication* 10: 1277–1293.

von Streit, Anne. 2011. *Entgrenzter Alltag – Arbeiten ohne Grenzen? Das Internet und die raum-zeitlichen Organisationsstrategien von Wissensarbeitern.* Bielefeld: Transcript.

Voß, Gerd-Günter. 1999. Neue Arbeits- und Alltagspraktiken bei medienvermittelten autonomisierten Arbeitsformen. In *Neue Medien im Alltag. Von individueller Nutzung zu soziokulturellem Wandel*, eds. Klaus Boehnke, Werner Dilger, Stephan Habscheid, Werner Holly, Evelyn Keitel, Josef Kresm, Thomas Münch, Josef Schmied, Martin Stegu, and Gerd-Günter Voß, 245–287. Lengerich: Pabst.

Witzel, Andreas, and Herwig Reiter. 2012. *The problem-centred Interview.* Los Angeles, CA: Sage.

16

Deep Mediatization and Datafication

Andreas Breiter and Andreas Hepp

16.1 Introduction

A prominent characteristic of deep mediatization is an ongoing datafication. This means that in a moment when more and more media become digital they are not only means of communication but increasingly also of generating data. These data can be used for very different purposes. The basis of this datafication are 'digital traces'. Whatever users do, as soon as they live in this highly mediatized social world they leave 'footprints' of their digital media use that build 'digital traces'. Partly, users do this consciously, for example by uploading photographs or writing comments on the 'time lines' of digital platforms. But often users are not aware of it and it 'happens' as an (unintended) side effect of our media-related

A. Breiter (✉) · A. Hepp
ZeMKI, Centre for Media, Communication and Information Research, University of Bremen, Bremen, Germany
e-mail: abreiter@uni-bremen.de

A. Hepp
e-mail: ahepp@uni-bremen.de

activities. This is, for example, the case when using a search engine or when reading newspapers online, where only a limited group of users are aware of the scope of related traces and their further use, for example in the advertizing industry (Turow 2011). But digital traces go even further: they are not just made by the users themselves but also by others when they interact online with reference to them, for example by synchronizing their address books with our digital addresses, by tagging pictures, texts or other digital artefacts with the names of other users. Digital traces nowadays even begin before the date of birth and beyond death. One example for this is the 'mediatization of parenthood' (Damkjær 2015), which results in processes of constructing 'parenthood' before birth, as pregnancy is accompanied with an ongoing flow of communication via apps and platforms that produces digital traces of a 'forthcoming child'. Then the question '*who* is allowed to leave these traces of an even unborn?' becomes an issue in a kind of family communication policy. In such a sense, as individuals, collectivities or organizations 'we cannot not leave digital traces' (Merzeau 2009: 4) in times of deep mediatization. Therefore, datafication reflects an increasing complexity of the social world by adding a new level of social construction that is delegated to algorithms and software.

Methodologically speaking, the emergence of such kinds of digital traces is a problem for empirical media and communication research. Existing research on datafication shows that one problem is the access to such kinds of data. In many cases, the application program interfaces (APIs) which open access to this kind of data are controlled by companies in outstanding power positions, such as Apple, Twitter, Facebook or Google. However, even if such an access is given, yet another problem arises. How can this data be put into context in a way that one is able to analyze it in a socially meaningful way?

In this chapter, we want to deepen the discussion of this second problem of contextualizing digital traces. First, we will reflect on digital traces as a phenomenon of complexity more generally. Then we will take the example of data from learning management systems to discuss possible strategies of how to put such automatically generated data into context by the use of qualitative methods that become triangulated. On such a basis, we finally want to draw some conclusions about the future challenges of this kind of research. Overall, this chapter can only argue in an exemplary way, taking a specific and thus limited case of analysis. But we hope that our more detailed discussion makes it possible to outline different options for future methodological developments in media and communication research.

16.2 Digital Traces as a Phenomenon of Complexity

Understanding digital traces as the sequence of 'digital footprints' which are left by the use of digital media and services represents quite a new area of media and communication research. At the same time, we can refer this back to more prolonged discussions about whether 'new' media also require 'new' methods of research (see for example Golding and Splichal 2013; Hutchinson 2016), and have to contextualize it in the much more far-reaching discussion surrounding 'digital humanities' and its methods (Baum and Stäcker 2015; Gardiner and Musto 2015). As a phenomenon, digital traces have evoked a sophisticated but also controversial methodological discussion (Kitchin 2014). In this respect, we can notice a multiple complexity of the phenomenon.

First of all, it is important to be aware that they are more than just (big) data. As 'big data' is used as 'a catch-all, amorphous phrase' (Kitchin and McArdle 2016), it provokes substantial discussions about its capacity. Heavily criticized by one group of scholars (boyd and Crawford 2012; Andrejevic 2014), it is regarded as the future of empirical research by others (Mayer-Schönberger and Cukier 2013; Townsend 2013). Hence, we follow a different direction while discussing some questions of big data later more in detail. Digital traces are a kind of digital data which become meaningful because this sequence of 'digital footprints' is in a technical procedure of construction related to a certain actor or action, typically an individual but in principle also a collectivity or an organization. By such procedures of connecting data with entities of the social world they become meaningful information, and this is the reason why companies and other organizations of data processing are highly interested in this kind of data aggregation in relation to 'real' people. For the purpose of empirical research, a good starting point is to define digital traces as numerically produced correlations of disparate kinds of data that are generated by practices of individual, collective and corporative actors in a digitalized media environment.[1] The complexity of digital traces is reasoned by the variety of their production, but also the variety of possible correlations.

Recently, digital traces and related possibilities of data generation became an issue of fundamental critique of social science methods; one that we do not share in detail but have to be aware of. The argument at this point is that with increasing datafication, methods of social sciences increasingly entered a 'crisis' as digital traces seem to be a much more proper data source than the kinds of data typically used in social sciences (Savage and Burrows 2007). While the sample survey and the in-depth interview once represented innovative contributions to a methodologically informed description and understanding of the social world, nowadays because of datafication—and hence accessible data sources—they would produce a much more limited access to the procedures of how society is constructed. Its main governing organizations—companies, administrations, educational and government institutions—get much of their information via an ongoing observation and analysis of the various digital traces left by the people. Against such sources, any proposition academic research can produce based on surveys and interviews seems to be flawed. Many established methods would come under pressure with recent datafication as they cannot deliver proper answers to the problems under question, something that is described as the 'social life of methods' (Savage 2013: 5). Therefore, we would need to 'reassemble social science methods' (Ruppert et al. 2013: 22). A widely discussed conclusion from this is to think about new forms of data collection and analysis that are based on 'digital methods' (Rogers 2013: 1, 13). Methods such as crawling, scraping or data mining take digital traces as sources for empirical research. They do not use special procedures for data collection to produce data that is then analyzed; but rather they are methods of using digital traces as a source for analysis.

Some proponents even go one step further, arguing that digital traces would allow for the first time a direct access to ongoing processes of social construction. Maybe the most prominent example is Bruno Latour's integration of digital traces investigation into his overall approach to social analysis (see Latour 2007). A 'digital traceability' (Venturini and Latour 2010: 6) then becomes a possibility for analyzing processes of social construction in situ: 'Being interested in the construction of social phenomena implies tracking each of the actors involved and each of the interactions between them' (Venturini and Latour 2010: 5). With digital traces, so the argument, we might have such a direct access, as they would allow us to witness processes of assembling in the moment they take place (see Latour et al. 2012; Venturini 2012).

From our point of view, this move largely misunderstands the main points of digital traces and the complexity of their analysis. First of all, there remains the fundamental problem of misinterpreting the social world as 'flat' and therefore as reconstructable solely by an analysis of correlated 'footprints' in digital media. This is one point of access which is non-responsive, but one that reduces the present complexity of the datafied social world to the ontology of a flat society.[2] Second, and even more fundamentally, such an approach misunderstands digital traces as something 'neutral', offering us a 'direct access' to society. However, digital traces are not 'neutral phenomena'; rather, they rely on the technical procedures of governing institutions: the companies, administrations and agencies that produce this kind of data. With governing we mean that these institutions are organizations that are in a powerful position to define the character and structure of data and metadata as well as its possible purposes of use. Actors can access this purposefully constructed and not objective data as individuals (independent workers, civic hackers), collectivities or organizations only in a controlled way. Therefore, as in any established method of social science, digital traces as indicators of social reality have to be critically reflected with regard to their particular perspective and the underlying biases in which they are produced.

Concluding from this, our approach to digital traces refers back to a critique of any naïve understanding of 'big data' (cf. Puschmann and Burgess 2014). Especially beyond academic research, there is high hope of the promise of new forms of analysis with reference to a so-called 'revolution of big data'. The core argument of this hope is that huge amounts of data-based information can be related and analyzed with automated procedures without predefining theoretical assumptions, and at the same time can lay the ground to predict future developments. This would make a new, purely data-oriented knowledge production possible that is partly positioned against theoretically informed forms of academic research. As prominent representatives of big data analysis put it, 'no longer do we necessarily require a valid substantive hypothesis about a phenomenon to begin to understand our world' (Mayer-Schönberger and Cukier 2013: 55). Or, as formulated in the sub-title of a best-selling practical guide (Marr 2015), it is about 'using smart big data, analytics and metrics to make better decisions and improve performance'. In education, 'learning analytics' (Ferguson 2012; Papamitsiou and Economides 2014) based on big data become the new vision to control and manage individual learning processes purely by algorithms. Similarly, student assessment data based on psychometric tests are used by administrators to rank schools, incentivize teachers and to create their accountability systems (Anagnostopoulos et al. 2013). But as Perrotta and Williamson (2016) clearly point out, the production of the underlying data structures and algorithms and their construction power in social life are often neglected.

Such an approach reduces the complexity of the phenomenon of digital traces to a 'big data paradigm' that is about 'managing data and transforming it into usable and sellable knowledge' (Elmer et al. 2015: 3). From the point of view of empirical research methods in social sciences, such hopes are partly based on what we can call a 'mythology of big data', that is 'large data sets offer a higher form of intelligence and knowledge that can generate insights that were previously impossible, with the aura of truth, objectivity, and accuracy' (boyd and Crawford 2012: 2). This kind of 'social analytics' (Couldry et al. 2015) refers back to the 'gradual normalisation of datafication' (van Dijck 2014: 198) as a new paradigm in science and society. This is exactly the point where we have to be careful: researchers of big data 'tend to echo these claims concerning the nature of social media data as natural traces and of platforms as neutral facilitators' (van Dijck 2014: 199). The idea is that once the easy work of gathering data is completed, the 'data will speak for itself' (Mosco 2014: 180). The hope becoming articulated in such a discourse is that big data would offer a possibility to reduce the complexity of analyzing the social. Or put another way: big data is constructed as an easy way to handle the complexity of our datafied social world by datafication.

As we know in the meantime, (meta)data cannot be considered as 'raw resources' that offer any direct access to a complex datafied social world (Gitelman and Jackson 2013, 7: Bowker 2014: 1797; van Dijck 2014: 201; Borgman 2015). In contrast, the main methodological task for empirical research on digital traces is to make them meaningful in a social sense, that is to explain the causalities and relations that go beyond pure aggregations and correlations as they are put up by automated collections of data. As a consequence, the methodological challenge for researching transforming communications is less than just an automated analysis of big data, as often postulated: rather, the methodological challenge lies in how to relate digital traces to further sources of data by means of which such traces become validated as well as interpretable and can subsequently be referred to in more sophisticated explanations and procedures of theory building (see Crampton et al. 2013; Lohmeier 2014). We must be very careful to avoid possible misunderstandings at this point. We share the position that competences in new forms of 'digital methods' (Rogers 2013) and 'automatized analysis' (Neuendorf 2017) are a necessity for media and communication research that endeavours to be up to date, and we subscribe to this discussion about datafication (Hepp 2016: 234–237). This said, we are critical of any approaches that understand data purely as a direct source for describing the society. We need the combination with further information about the figuration under investigation. Following the semiotic theory, information is data in context referring to its semantics (O'Connor et al. 2001).

16.3 School Learning Management Systems as an Example: Analyzing Digital Traces as Putting Them into Context

If we follow the line of argument up to this point, the main challenge is how we can analyze digital traces in a way that we can contextualize them within the figurations of humans that produce these sequences of 'digital footprints' but also *use* them as a means for social construction. From such a point of view, we have to think about how to relate the 'information' of digital traces to specific actor constellations, frames of relevance, and practices of communication in and by which they are produced. The main examples on which we want to discuss this challenge are data systems as they are nowadays widespread in schools, originally especially in the USA and the UK, but increasingly also in Germany.

School learning management systems as a software define the 'space' in which data are produced as 'digital traces' which, however, are also used by others to subsequently construct social reality. Or put differently: the school information systems are not only the means to 'collect' data; they are also means for powerful processes of construction, typically on the part of their providers who do 'data analysis'. The way in which data are embedded into communicative practices in schools plays an important role: for example, the use of grades for decision-making, the use of upload and download traces to define student involvement or teacher or parent engagement.

Learning management systems (Ifenthaler 2012) in schools and higher education institutions are supposed to support the learning process of students and the management processes of teachers. Most studies reflect the forms of instructional use, teachers' and learners' attitudes, and the impact on learning (e.g. De Smet et al. 2012). But the organizational processes of schools, that is interactions between students, teachers and parents and within their groups, between school management and staff, school district and school board, are often neglected (see Breiter 2014). In an empirical study of German secondary schools headed by one of the authors,[3] the goal was to reconstruct the school as a social organization by analyzing communicative practices of key stakeholders. Hence, online, face-to-face as well as paper-based forms were studied. A subset of our research addressed the interdependence of communication networks between teachers in the world of the school building and in the world of the learning management system. The underlying hypothesis assumed a very similar activity structure inside and outside the technical system: those who interact regularly and intensively will do so online. For this purpose, we collected digital traces that teachers left in the learning management system. As in most server-based systems, the paths of users can be traced back by using log-files. Log-files provide information, problems or errors pertaining to the system and its applications (Markov and Larose 2007; Suneetha and Krishnamoorthi 2009; Liu 2011; Oliner et al. 2012), often in the Extended Common Log-file Format:

Looking at these log-files from a webserver as in Fig. 16.1—here in an anonymized and therefore fictive form—it is possible to identify the user by her internet protocol (IP) (1.2.3.4) and additionally the Browser Operating System combination if multiple users use the same internet connection. Once a user is identified, one can track the movement within the site because the second last entry contains the page the user came from, the so-called referrer. In the example given here, the user enters the site at index.php, stays on the site for 14 seconds and moves on to page2.php by using a hyperlink. These 'clicks' are called actions. Using this information, we can track all movements from all users separately. There are mainly five ways to conduct a log-file analysis: (1) display which pages of a website are accessed more than others and how many users selected a specific function; (2) show paths from visitors through the site; (3) cluster visitors into groups, the clusters being based on movements or paths through the system; (4) social network analysis to identify connections between users and/or websites based on the 'clickstream' data; and (5) other statistical methods and algorithms (e.g. multi-level analysis).

Logfile analyses are non-reactive. All information is gathered on the application layer or server layer and not actively put in by the user. Furthermore, data are stored in a machine-readable format and can be used in real time. But there is a main disadvantage of such a strategy for collecting data: the lack of any information about the user's practices. Furthermore, there is usually no information about socio-demographic data of the user. Additionally, log-files can cause high privacy concerns.

```
1.2.3.4 - - [25/Aug/2011:12:15:33 +0100] "GET /index.php HTTP/1.1" 200 23578 - "Webbrowser
(System etc.)"
1.2.3.4 - - [25/Aug/2011:12:15:47 +0100] "GET /page2.php HTTP/1.1" 200
15789"http://www.domain.com/index.php" "Webbrowser (System etc.)"
```

Fig. 16.1 Example for log-file entries

The users normally have no control over the log-files that are produced by the server or application. As the IP address is stored, the users are easy to identify. Therefore, log-files must be made anonymous by the researchers. But while this is necessary from the point of view of research ethics, it additionally limits the interpretation of such data.

We gathered anonymous data from a learning management system in a larger German secondary school (>100 teachers and >1000 students). The system is mainly used by the staff for coordination and communication. As it is hosted by an external company it can be accessed from inside the school's network and from home. The learning management system offers the following features: announcements, calendar, file exchange and discussion groups.

The log-files investigated by us span over a period of 12 months, including holiday breaks. In the log-files we analyzed, 120,000 hits from 138 users are recorded. After the deletion of all irrelevant data (e.g. by bots) and by using path completion algorithms, the sum of hits is approximately 62,000. The 138 unique users had a total of 4451 visits.[4] In Fig. 16.2, a network graph of this data is shown.[5] Such a visualization makes it possible to identify three main groups in the upper part of the graph, which are connected to the categories 'miscellaneous', 'reports' and 'conferences'. All are mainly linked to dates, some to announcements and materials. Announcements and materials are more likely accessed than dates. This is no surprise as dates can be viewed in a calendar-like overview. The items themselves are mainly linked to the category and not linked among themselves.

In the bottom left are many materials closely connected to each other. Above these materials are two subjects—one bigger and one smaller. In contrast to the representation of the former three categories, the nodes are overlapping each other and are not only linked to the subject itself but also to each other. This indicates that the items are closely linked together and due to the force-driven representation. The relative big node size is another indicator for the intensive material exchange within these two subjects.

To deepen such an analysis, we can do a scatter plot of this data. Scatter plots are mathematical diagrams with two coordinates to visualize values of variables. As the points have different sizes, they represent a third variable (in this case uploader). The scatter plot in Fig. 16.3 compares the number of materials per subject and the sum of hits to these materials. The size of each subject shows the number of different contributors. English has the most hits (2300) and the most materials (23). That is no surprise and was already assumed if we refer to the previous data set. Spanish, on the other hand, is more interesting. It has the second most materials (15), but only around 500 hits and only three contributors. Based on the log-files, we can only speculate about the reasons.

As we can see in this example of digital traces in a school information system, the interpretation of so-called big data is only possible with context-specific knowledge. Log-files can give researchers a broad view into an information system and its usage. They do not allow to identify 'significant behaviour'. Our analyzed data had a time span of about 300 days. There may be the possibility to overlook significant behaviour as the amount of data is large, and significant behaviour must not be the most common behaviour. But statistical methods such as sequential pattern or cluster analysis try to find a common and frequent pattern, not a rare or unique pattern which is potentially more relevant. This may lead to an opposition of available methods and research aims. Additionally, patterns which can be identified statistically need to be embedded in the physical world of classrooms, different staff rooms, subject- and/or grade-related rooms and 'water coolers' (Earl 2001).[6] To understand schools as communicative figurations, we need to identify the actor constellation which will only partly be mapped in the log-files—non-active members of staff and their communicative practices are neglected, even if they might have a media ensemble which allows data exchange.

In our case, we accompanied our quantitative analysis with in-depth qualitative studies based on participant observations and interviews (Welling et al. 2015). Over a period of one school year, we observed teachers in their staff room as well as in subject-specific rooms. Based on an observation protocol, the use of the information system as well as situations and locations for exchange about administrative and organizational issues were recorded and later analyzed with an open coding scheme. The interviews with different groups of

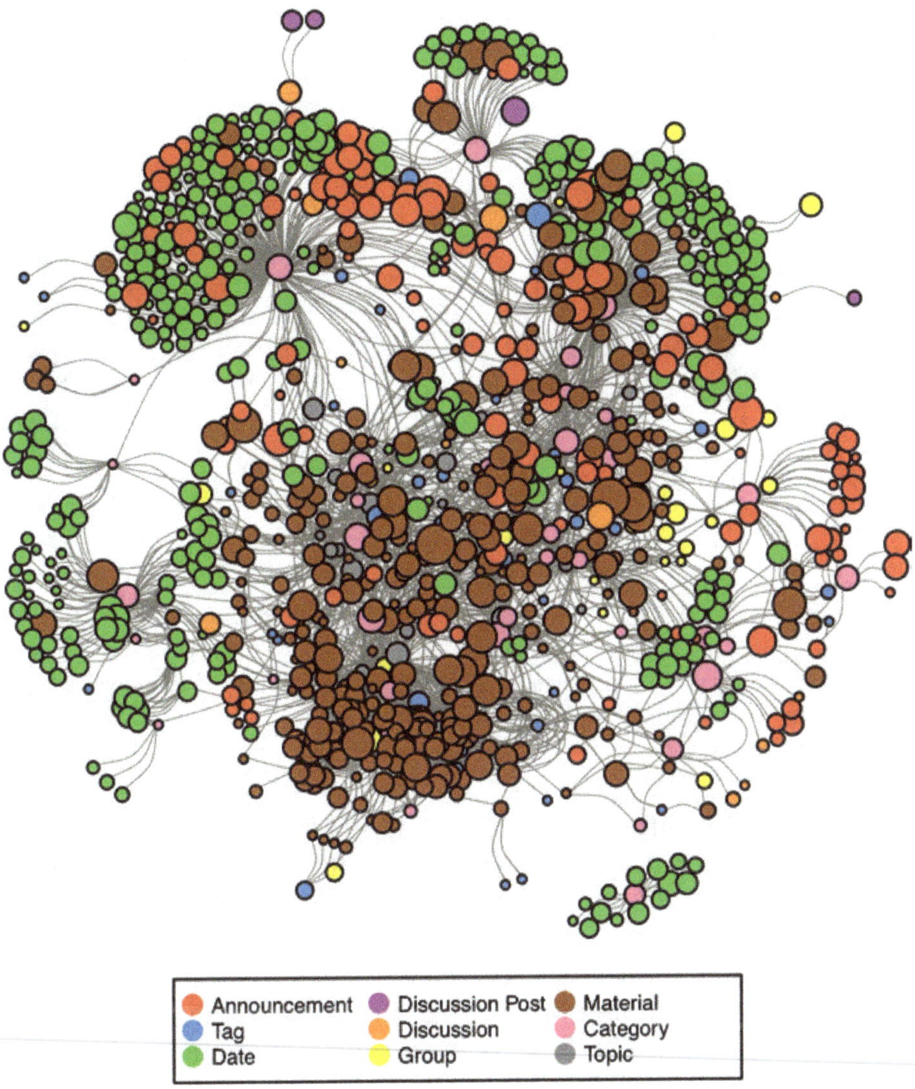

Fig. 16.2 Data from learning management system as network graph. *Source* Schulz and Breiter (2013)

teachers were recorded and coded according to standards of qualitative data analysis. Based on both data sources, we could find clusters of activities as well as subject-specific communicative practices. In both cases, the usage of the school information system was an integral part of the data collection. This helped us to identify patterns which could be reconstructed in the log-file analysis.

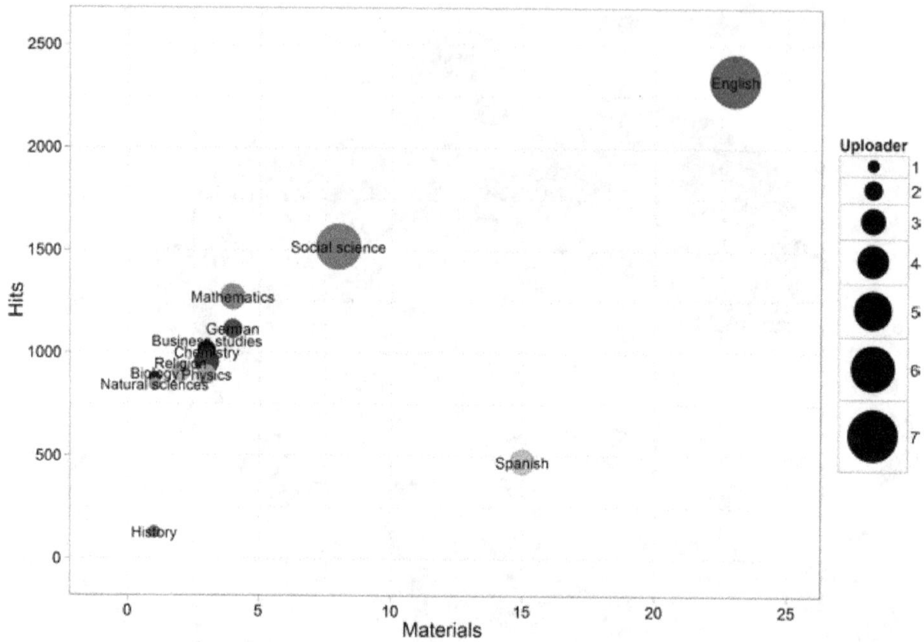

Fig. 16.3 Materials and hits by subject. Data from log-files of learning management system. *Source* Schulz and Breiter (2013)

This offered a different and more detailed view on the organizational processes of a school beyond the data in the system. Spanish is a small subject; the teachers usually teach at different schools and need to be virtually present at different locations. Time management is difficult and the learning management system with calendar function allows the scheduling of meetings and book resources online any time and anywhere. The link to their subject community is mainly organized through web-based systems. The English subject group has a long-standing tradition of exchanging classroom materials. Years before the introduction of the learning management system, they arranged their exchange via paper folders in their subject-related staff room.

This example of digital traces in school data systems highlights the relevance of digital traces in context, which can be very rich empirical data if analyzed interdependently. Dealing with log-files entails additional concerns about research ethics and privacy. Users cannot give their consent a priori.

16.4 Conclusion: Challenges Putting Digital Traces in Context

Taking the example of school data systems, we could demonstrate what it means to put digital traces in context: the data collected by the respective systems have to be linked with further, detailed information to make them socially meaningful. Only in this way do such data become a source of describing our present complex social world of datafication. For empirical analysis, this is related to three challenges which we consider as fundamental for any social science analysis of digital traces.

The first challenge is to find a way to grasp digital traces with reference to a defined social entity. Very often, digital traces are understood as a phenomenon of a single actor, an individual who left the traces through the use of digital media and services. While this is correct for a basic definition of digital traces as well as for many procedures of data generation (it is the single user of an online system who leaves the footprints that are collected by this system—often because the individual is of interest as a customer), our example demonstrates that we rather have to consider these individuals as social actors whose practices are located and embedded in the figurations of further institutional contexts and groups of people (in the case of our example the organization of the school and the different groups of teachers). Only by reflecting this does the data become meaningful. Therefore, we have to have the whole communicative figurations in mind in which the individual who is the 'originator' of the respective traces acts. The challenge here is to find a way to link the data being automatically generated with a social analysis of such a figuration. To achieve this, it seems to be appropriate to start the research with the frame of relevance of this figuration and locate the analysis of the digital traces. By so doing, there is a chance of finding helpful ways of contextualizing.

As a second challenge, we are confronted with the triangulation of quantitative 'digital methods' (in the case of our example the log-file analysis) with forms of qualitative analysis that offer the context information which is needed. As we have seen, combining automatized collected and processed data, on the one hand, with various forms of qualitative interviews or focus groups, on the other, is a promising method. But this again refers back to the first challenge: only if the actor constellation of the figuration under consideration is known does it become possible to conduct such interviews and focus groups. This offers rich data, which because of their richness at the same time might become critical from a research ethics point of view.

Therefore, research ethics are the third challenge. Any approach which puts digital traces in context in such a way entails linking digital data that are left (partly without any detailed knowledge of this on the part of the persons concerned) with further information about certain persons. The knowledge being gathered in this way can be very far reaching—at many times much more far reaching than the knowledge a person has about him or herself. For research ethics, one consequence of this is the necessity to inform the investigated persons in detail about such possibilities of data collection and analysis (and to offer them, for example, the opportunity to have such unknown information communicated back to them). Another consequence is that as researchers we must be very careful of how we publish such results because the publication of data on digital traces in triangulation with further information about individuals might offer others the chance to isolate these persons. Anonymization becomes an important and complicated task.

With respect to these three challenges, it becomes obvious how far the meaningful analysis of digital traces is more than just a new field for media and communication research. As a new field, it is necessary not only to reflect in a new way about the relations of qualitative and quantitative data but also about our (digital) research ethics. This is essential if we want to conduct a form of media and communication research that addresses the complexity of the present social world, which is increasingly characterized by datafication. We hope that this chapter offers some stimulation for further steps in such a direction.

Notes

1. The term 'trace' collects numerous meanings and appendices (to trace, track, traceable, traceability, tracing, etc.) and seems to connote an isolated object as well as an action or a process (Serres 2002: 1; Reigeluth 2014: 249). Because of this semantic richness of 'trace' in general, there is some ambiguity determining 'digital traces' in a proper way, which we want to clarify with the definition above.
2. Here the general problem of the idea of the social world as the sum of assemblages becomes replicated (for a critique of such an approach see Couldry and Hepp 2016: 57–78).

3. Funded by the Deutsche Forschungsgemeinschaft (BR-2273/10-1). Acknowledgements to Arne Hendrik Ruhe for data processing and producing the figures in this project, which we quote in the following.
4. A visit is defined as a sequence of hits from a unique user. A visit ends after 30 minutes of inactivity.
5. The network visualization represents the links within the SIS. Edges are (bi-directional) links, nodes are single entries (dates, appointments, etc.). The linking was done by hand by the teachers. The arrangement was done by a 'force-driven' algorithm (Fruchterman-Reingold), based on which closely related (linked) nodes were grouped.
6. Research on knowledge management often describes informal communicative practices at the workplace with the 'water cooler'. Usually located at a central place in a US office, staff gather spontaneously to chat (e.g. Earl 2001).

References

Anagnostopoulos, Dorothea, Stacy A. Rutledge, and Rebecca Jacobsen. 2013. *The infrastructure of accountability: Data use and the transformation of American education.* Cambridge, MA: Harvard Education Press.

Andrejevic, Mark. 2014. The big data divide. *International Journal of Communication* 8: 17.

Baum, Constanze, and Thomas Stäcker. 2015. Die Digital Humanities im deutschsprachigen Raum. Methoden – Theorien – Projekte. *Sonderband der Zeitschrift für digitale Geisteswissenschaften* 1. doi:10.17175/sb001_023.

Borgman, Christine L. 2015. *Big data, little data, no data: Scholarship in the networked world.* Cambridge, MA: MIT Press.

Bowker, Geoffrey C. 2014. The theory/data thing. *International Journal of Communication* 8: 1795–1799.

danah, boyd, and Kate Crawford. 2012. Critical questions for big data: Provocations for a cultural, technological, and scholarly phenomenon. *Information, Communication & Society* 15: 662–679.

Breiter, Andreas. 2014. Schools as mediatized organizations from a cross-cultural perspective. In *Mediatized worlds*, ed. Andreas Hepp and Friedrich Krotz, 288–303. London: Palgrave.

Couldry, Nick, and Andreas Hepp. 2016. *The mediated construction of reality.* Cambridge: Polity Press.

Couldry, Nick, Aristea Fotopoulou, and Luke Dickens. 2015. Real social analytics: A contribution towards a phenomenology of a digital world. *British Journal of Sociology* 67 (1): 118–137.

Crampton, Jeremy W., Mark Graham, Ate Poorthuis, Taylor Shelton, Monica Stephens, Matthew W. Wilson, and Matthew Zook. 2013. Beyond the geotag: Situating 'big data' and leveraging the potential of the geoweb. *Cartography and Geographic Information Science* 40: 130–139.

Damkjær, Maja S. 2015. Becoming a parent in a digitized age: Facebook as an agent of change?—Performative, dialogical, and preservative Facebook strategies in the transition to parenthood. Paper presented at Nordmedia 2015, Copenhagen, Denmark, 13 August 2015.

De Smet, C., J. Bourgonjon, B. De Wever, T. Schellens, and M. Valcke. 2012. Researching instructional use and the technology acceptation of learning management systems by secondary school teachers. *Computers & Education* 58 (2): 688–696. https://doi.org/10.1016/j.compedu.2011.09.013.

Earl, Michael J. 2001. Knowledge management strategies: Towards a taxonomy. *Journal of Management Information Systems* 18: 215–233.

Elmer, Greg, Ganaele Langlois, and Joanna Redden. 2015. Introduction: Compromised data—from social media to big data. In *Compromised data: From social media to big data*, 1st ed, ed. Greg Elmer, Ganaele Langlois, and Joanna Redden, 1–14. London: Bloomsbury Academic.

Ferguson, Rebecca. 2012. Learning analytics: Drivers, developments and challenges. *International Journal of Technology Enhanced Learning* 4: 304–317.

Gardiner, Eileen, and Ronald G. Musto. 2015. *The digital humanities*. Cambridge: Cambridge University Press.

Gitelman, Lisa, and Virginia Jackson. 2013. Introduction. In *"Raw data" is an oxymoron*, ed. Lisa Gitelman, 1–14. Cambridge, MA: MIT Press.

Golding, Peter, and Slavko Splichal. 2013. New media, new research challenges. An Introduction. *Javnost—The Public* 22: 5–10.

Hepp, Andreas. 2016. Kommunikations- und Medienwissenschaft in datengetriebenen Zeiten. *Publizistik* 61 (3): 225–246.

Hutchinson, Jonathon. 2016. An introduction to digital media research methods: How to research and the implications of new media data. *Communication Research and Practice* 2: 1–6.

Ifenthaler, Dirk. 2012. Learning management systems. In *Encyclopedia of the sciences of learning*, vol. 11, ed. Norbert M. Seel, 1689–1692. Boston, MA: Springer.

Kitchin, Rob. 2014. *The data revolution: Big data, open data, data infrastructures and their consequences*. London: Sage.

Kitchin, Rob, and Gavin McArdle. 2016. What makes big data, big data? Exploring the ontological characteristics of 26 datasets. *Big Data & Society* 3: 1–10.

Latour, Bruno. 2007. Beware, your imagination leaves digital traces. *Times Higher Literary Supplement* 6. http://www.bruno-latour.fr/sites/default/files/P-129-THES-GB.pdf. Accessed 27 Apr 2017.

Latour, Bruno, Pablo Jensen, Tommaso Venturini, Sébastian Grauwin, and Dominique Boullier. 2012. The whole is always smaller than its parts:

A digital test of Gabriel Tarde's monads. *British Journal of Sociology* 63: 590–615.

Liu, Bing. 2011. *Web data mining: Exploring hyperlinks, contents, and usage data*. Berlin: Springer.

Lohmeier, Christine. 2014. The researcher and the never-ending field: Reconsidering big data and digital ethnography. In *Studies in qualitative methodology*, ed. Martin Hand and Sam Hillyard, 75–89. Bingley: Emerald Group Publishing.

Markov, Zdravko, and Daniel T. Larose. 2007. *Data mining the web: Uncovering patterns in web content, structure and usage*. Hoboken, NJ: Wiley.

Marr, Bernard. 2015. *Big data: Using smart big data, analytics and metrics to make better decisions and improve performance*. Chichester: Wiley.

Mayer-Schönberger, Viktor, and Kenneth Cukier. 2013. *Big data: A revolution that will transform how we live, work and think*. New York: John Murray.

Merzeau, Louise. 2009. Présence numérique: Les médiations de l'identité. *Les Enjeux de l'information et de la communication* 1: 79–91.

Mosco, Vincent. 2014. *To the cloud: Big data in a turbulent world*. St Paul, MN: Paradigm Publishers.

Neuendorf, Kimberly A. 2017. *The Content Analysis Guide*. Los Angeles, CA: Sage.

O'Connor, Daniel, Rob Shields, Suzan Ilcan, and Edwina Taborsky. 2001. Data, information, and knowledge. In *Organizational semiotics. Evolving a science of information systems*, ed. Kecheng Liu, Rodney J. Clarke, Peter Bøgh Andersen, Ronald K. Stamper, and El-Sayed Abou-Zeid, 21–40. Boston: Kluwer.

Oliner, Adam, Archana Ganapathi, and Wei Xu. 2012. Advances and challenges in log analysis. *Communications of the ACM* 55: 55–61.

Papamitsiou, Zacharoula, and Anastasios A. Economides. 2014. Learning analytics and educational data mining in practice: A systematic literature review of empirical evidence. *Educational Technology & Society* 17: 49–64.

Perrotta, Carlo, and Ben Williamson. 2016. The social life of learning analytics: Cluster analysis and the 'performance' of algorithmic education. *Learning, Media and Technology*: 1–14. doi:10.1080/17439884.2016.1182927.

Puschmann, Cornelius, and Jean Burgess. 2014. Metaphors of big data. *International Journal of Communication* 8: 20.

Reigeluth, Tyler B. 2014. Why data is not enough: Digital traces as control of self and self-control. *Surveillance & Society* 12: 243–254.

Rogers, Richard. 2013. *Digital methods*. Cambridge, MA: MIT Press.

Ruppert, Evelyn, John Law, and Mike Savage. 2013. Reassembling social science methods: The challenge of digital devices. *Theory, Culture & Society* 30: 22–46.

Savage, Mike. 2013. The 'social life of methods': A critical introduction. *Theory, Culture & Society* 30: 3–21.

Savage, Mike, and Roger Burrows. 2007. The coming crisis of empirical sociology. *Sociology* 41: 885–899.

Schulz, Arne H., and Andreas Breiter. 2013. Monitoring user patterns in school information systems using logfile analysis. In *Next generation of IT in educational management*, ed. Don Passey, Andreas Breiter, and Adrie J. Visscher, 94–103. Berlin: Springer.

Serres, Alexandre. 2002. Quelle(s) problématique(s) de la trace? Texte d'une communication prononcée lors du séminaire du CERCOR (actuellement CERSIC), 13 December 2002.

Suneetha, K.R., and R. Krishnamoorthi. 2009. Identifying user behavior by analyzing web server access log file. *International Journal of Computer Science and Network Security* 9: 327–332.

Townsend, Anthony M. 2013. *Smart cities: Big data, civic hackers, and the quest for a new utopia*. New York: WW Norton.

Turow, Joseph. 2011. *The daily you: How the new advertising industry is defining your identity and your worth*. New Haven, CT and London: Yale University Press.

van Dijck, José. 2014. Datafication, dataism and dataveillance: Big data between scientific paradigm and ideology. *Surveillance & Society* 12: 197–208.

Venturini, Tommaso. 2012. Building on faults: How to represent controversies with digital methods. *Public Understanding of Science* 21: 796–812.

Venturini, Tommaso, and Bruno Latour. 2010. The social fabric: Digital traces and quali-quantitative methods. In *Proceedings of Future En Seine*, 15–30.

Welling, Stefan, Andreas Breiter, and Arne H. Schulz. 2015. *Mediatisierte Organisationswelten in Schulen: Wie der Medienwandel die Kommunikation in den Schulen verändert*. Wiesbaden: VS.

17

A Cross-Media Perspective on Communicative Figurations Research

Kim Christian Schrøder

17.1 Introduction

What do urban young people's media-anchored communities, a national hacker non-governmental organization (NGO), repair cafés, DIY maker networks, a city's media ensemble, secondary classes in a local school, national news publics, a financial blogging community, the Roman Catholic Church in Germany, political decision meetings and secondary school administrations have in common?

Well, according to this edited volume what all these mediated collectivities have in common is their status as 'communicative figurations', which should be analyzed empirically in a cross-media perspective for the common purpose of better understanding how communications landscapes are transforming in times of deep mediatization, and how they influence wider social and cultural processes.

It is great that a concept which has been theoretically described and analytically exemplified frequently but sporadically in the mediatization

---

K.C. Schrøder (✉)
Department of Communication and Arts, Roskilde University,
Roskilde, Denmark
e-mail: kimsc@ruc.dk

literature in recent years has been given a full volume that is dedicated to showing its potential, not just as a helpful heuristic but as a mature theoretical construct which can be operationalized to orchestrate many kinds of empirical research in the mediatized culture. Perhaps, as the insights provided by the contributions to this volume make their impact on scholarly debates about mediatization, the time will come to start reflecting on ways to further sharpen the concept of communicative figuration, when operationalizing its conceptual inventory for empirical research, as media technologies and contents continue to play pivotal influential roles in the wider processes of cultural, political and social transformation.

This postscript is intended to reflect on the accomplishments of figurational media research so far, and to discuss some of the paths along which such clarification and development may occur, in the service of further developing an evidently very useful heuristic lens into an even more rigorous analytical concept.

17.2 Communicative Figurations as Constitutive of Mediatization

In a research seminar three or four years ago I was applauding the merits of mediatization theory as a promising way, not contaminated by 'effects research', to conceptualize the influence of media on the ongoing transformations of culture and society. An experienced news media researcher, a trifle condescendingly, then remarked: 'I am not a member of that congregation!'. The beauty of the concept of communicative figuration as I see it is that you don't have to be a member of 'the mediatization congregation' in order to embrace it theoretically and to apply it to orchestrate a wide range of different research endeavours about cross-media practices.

Of course, as laid out by Andreas Hepp and Uwe Hasebrink in the book's foundational Chap. 2 (and in numerous earlier publications, for instance Hepp 2013, 2014), the concept 'communicative configuration' does have its origins within what has been termed the constructionist variety of mediatization research, where the concept has a particular role to play in the empirical investigation of 'deep' mediatization processes.

In their theoretical introduction to this volume, Hepp and Hasebrink argue that the study of how media influence social processes has become more complicated as a result of the rapidly evolving media manifold (Couldry 2012: 44), life with polymedia (Madianou 2014) and so on.

As a result of the intensifying processes of digitization and datafication, media are changing communication in historically unprecedented ways, with profound implications for the 'communicative construction of reality' under conditions of deep mediatization (Couldry and Hepp 2016). In order to understand the mediatized culture, our research efforts should be directed towards the specific 'domains' in which social transformations are played out, as a consequence of complex social forces, one of which is coming from the communications media.

Incidentally, this insistence on domain specificity also serves to demarcate Hepp and Hasebrink's 'constructivist' brand of mediatization theory from so-called 'institutionalist' mediatization theory, which sees the media as an independent societal institution (Strömbäck 2008; Hjarvard 2013): Hepp and Hasebrink see it as less helpful to understand (mass) media as a domain of its own, because under conditions of deep mediatization 'digital media permeate the various domains of society', making it less appropriate 'to see them as a domain of their own' (Hepp and Hasebrink, Chap. 2). In other words, because 'the media' are inherently a cross-domain phenomenon, they should not be conceptualized as one institution to be studied in order to understand the stage of deep mediatization. Instead we must look at domains not defined in media terms and see how cross-media ensembles function in these domains, with agency and social practice in the foreground.

This is where communicative figurations become relevant: the relevant domains can be analyzed empirically through the heuristic lens of communicative figurations: "This means a perspective that moves the figurations of human actors into the foreground and at the same time takes into account how far these figurations are entangled with media as contents and technologies, which on a deeper level refers both to media organizations and infrastructures" (Hepp and Hasebrink, Chap. 2). Communicative figurations can thus be understood as a domain-specific recipe for researching mediatization processes empirically—they are a conceptual tool for describing "*in detail* how the transformation that we relate to the term mediatization actually takes place" (Hepp and Hasebrink, Chap. 2).

Chapter 2 thus paves the way for the dozen case studies in the following chapters, by brilliantly unfolding in an accessible way (see for instance the model in Fig. 2.1: 31) how the complex conceptual territory of mediatization theory can be encapsulated in a model of how the defining *trends* of deep mediatization (differentiation, connectivity, omnipresence, pace of innovation, datafication) are played out in *social domains.*

These domains are then conceptualized as *communicative figurations*, with possible internal and external *consequences*, such as changing hierarchies of authority, modes of participation, blurring boundaries between media producers and recipients, social surveillance, social inclusions and exclusions, and so on.

Within this overall matrix for understanding mediatization, communicative figurations are defined, with inspiration from Norbert Elias, in terms of their *constellation of actors*, their *frames of relevance* and their *communicative practices*. In addition to their non-mediated face-to-face communicative practices, communicative figurations are heavily populated with media. Again, the media aspect is rigorously conceptualized on three levels: as the entire *media environment*, available at a given point in time, as the *media ensemble* which is the subset of media used in a particular social domain, and as the *media repertoire* appropriated by the individual across the relevant social domains of his/her everyday life. Communicative figurations thus provide a bridge between research that defines media repertoires according to social domains such as the workplace, the family, commuter transport and so on (Taneja et al. 2012) and those who analyze the media repertoires of individuals (Helles et al. 2015; Kobbernagel and Schrøder 2016). And—like media audiences—they are inherently a cross-media phenomenon (Schrøder 2011).

A further definitional characteristic of communicative figurations is their scalability, from the smallest everyday grouping, such as a family or a municipal committee, to the largest (supra)national collectivity, such as a country's public sphere, or the global financial market (Couldry and Hepp 2016). This has the advantage of providing analytical flexibility to the application of communicative figurations (any social grouping or area can be nominated for analysis as a communicative figuration), but it also comes with a blurriness that risks diluting the concept (Hepp and Hasebrink, Chap. 2). I shall return to this issue later.

Another challenge for research into communicative figurations stems from the inherent porousness of the boundaries between communicative figurations, both within the micro, meso- and macro-levels and between these levels. This is not so much a theoretical challenge as a methodological and empirical challenge: one can easily grasp theoretically that 'figurations of social domains are interrelated in various ways' (Hepp and Hasebrink, Chap. 2), for instance in terms of their overlapping actor constellations. Similarly, 'figurations of collectivities and organizations can become "supra-individual actors" [...] that are part of the actor constellation of other figurations and thus build "figurations of figurations"' (Hepp and Hasebrink, Chap. 2). However, with one or two exceptions, the case studies in the volume do not attempt to systematically operationalize such figurational embeddedness for empirical investigation, which would probably also be quite staggering in methodological terms. However, even without empirical anchoring of this added level of complexity, the volume collectively represents a major step forward in the pursuit of analytical insights about our increasingly and excitingly mediatized culture.

17.3 A Selection from the Buffet of Communicative Figurations

The 12 empirical chapters demonstrate through their extremely varied choice of social domains and communicative figurations how the concept of communicative figurations can be applied as a heuristic framework for producing insights about the ways in which 'our social domains are moulded by media' (Hepp and Hasebrink, Chap. 2), or rather—if we adhere to a strict practice theoretical perspective—how these social domains are moulded by the practices in which social actors *are using media* to achieve their mundane, professional and political ends: 'The concept of figurations links a micro-analysis of individual practices with a meso-analysis of certain social domains and thus offers us various possibilities to contextualize this with macro questions about society' (Hepp and Hasebrink, Chap. 2). The study in Chap. 13 by Andreas Breiter and Arne Hendrik Ruhe is a case in point: Applying the core concepts of figurational theory, their chapter shows how the figurational framework can be used to rigorously map the mediated managerial governance structures of German and English schools. The analysis focuses on the meso (organizational) level, its media ensemble and the role of management information systems, but in order to do so analyzes the media repertoires of individual teachers and administrators,[1] and also anchors the communicative practices discovered in the macro national educational governance systems in the two countries: "The school's media ensemble is a moulding force for changes in communicative practices within the actor constellation of schools, among staff, students and administrators as well as in contact with parents" (Breiter and Ruhe, Chap. 13).

It is striking how all chapters are very explicit about their adherence to the theoretical framework laid out by the editors' introduction (for an exceptionally elaborate and graphic use of the full conceptual inventory of cross-media practices and actor constellations, see the comparative case study of online gamers and DIY groups by Wolf and Wudarski, Chap. 6; see also Friemel and Bixler, Chap. 8). Because the chapters apply the conceptual framework so literally, one could say that collectively they really serve as a variegated and successful test bed for the ability of the concept of communicative figurations to serve as an eye-opening descriptive and explanatory lens through which we can see how our social reality is constructed in and through such communicative figurations.

Andreas Hepp, Piet Simon and Monika Sowinska's chapter about young people's urban communities (Chap. 3) may serve as an illustration of the way the figurational approach can illuminate the communicative practices of small-scale cross-media collectivities (groups of friends). Asking what extensive mediatization means to young people in their daily urban sense of community, and defining media as both technologies and content, the authors studied young people's cross-media urban communities in two mediated cities (Leipzig, Bremen). The methodological design consisted of qualitative interviews with 60 youths and ethnographic observation of selected urban locations. These communities were studied as three interrelated communicative figurations: friendship groups, urban locations (shopping mall, cinema, Hackerspace) and the level of imagined communities (i.e. how the young people feel attached to their city). Faced with the paradox that 'not every young person for whom the city is an important space of opportunity for community thinks the city as imagined community to be very important' (73), the analysis identified four 'horizons of communitization': localists, centrists, multi-localists and pluralists (73). Interestingly, irrespective of their degree of allegiance to the city, '[a]ll of those we interviewed ranked their group of friends very much above the city' (75). Overall the chapter shows how the theoretical framework of communicative figurations and mediatization can be used productively to study how young people make sense of their cross-media lives in the mediated city: it demonstrates 'the degree to which for young urban dwellers—besides family, acquaintances and colleagues—it is their network of friends that remains the primary figuration of their experience of community construction. And this has become to a very great degree a mediatized phenomenon'

(52) It is an interesting insight that the full cross-media potential of the young people's available media ensemble is almost neutralized by the normative pressure within the group to use one form of media: Facebook.

Chapter 4 by Sebastian Kubitschko takes figurational analysis into the area of civil society organizations, as he analyzes the German national hacker organization The Chaos Computer Club as a communicative figuration. The research question, how does the Chaos Computer Club communicatively construct media technologies and infrastructures as a political category in its own right, aims to understand how one of the world's oldest and largest hacker organization's 'political engagement today relies on a wide range of practices related to media technologies and infrastructures and, at the same time, continues to be oriented towards larger publics as well as "traditional" centres of political power' (82). The methodological design takes the form of an extended case study that brings together data from 40 face-to-face interviews with Club members and participant observation of internal and public gatherings, contextualizing these with insights from a wide range of media discourses (such as the Club magazine, its official Twitter account, mainstream media coverage of prominent hacks). The analysis uses the figurational lens to create historical insights about the organizations changing actor constellations, communicative practices and political frames of relevance, showing how the organization has been a transformative force, achieving and maintaining socio-political influence through its media ensemble and its cross-media communicative practices. More generally, the analysis shows how communicative figurations can be a useful sensitizing concept for structuring an empirical analysis that maps the communicative context around a politically oriented organization.

Chapter 9 by Leif Kramp and Wiebke Loosen takes us into the realm of the national public sphere, as they use the figurational mindset in the service of substantiating media-related cultural transformations in a diverse, cross-media news ecology. The complete figurational mindset is encapsulated in a visual model (208), as they explore how journalistic role conceptions are being adapted to a transforming news landscape. Here journalists are struggling to find their professional feet on the continuum from traditional legacy news media ideals of gatekeeper and watchdog, to the more participatory, dialogic ideals of a platform-diverse news universe increasingly colonized by social media and the 'omnipresence of audience feedback' (206). Drawing on previously conducted empirical research,[2] their comparative study of the actor constellation of news producers and news audiences shows how the emerging new role orientations (conceptualized as the figuration's frame of relevance) are the outcome of complex mutual expectations among journalists and citizen audiences. The study thus shows how the figurational approach is not just suitable for analyzing actor constellations characterized by the proximity of actors in small groups or organizations, but how the producer/recipient nexus of mass-mediated communication across a spatio-temporal distance can be conceptualized and operationalized as a communicative figuration on a national scale.

17.4 When is Something (Not) a Communicative Figuration?

There are a couple of studies in this volume which are insightful in their own terms, but which I have some difficulty in seeing as entirely felicitous analyses of communicative figurations. Perhaps there is a risk at this point that communicative figuration research is encountering a 'bandwagon effect': the terminological inventory that comes with communicative figurations offers a systematic, heuristic vocabulary that many are tempted to associate their research with, although strictly speaking the theoretical and analytical tools of the figurational approach are not fully compatible with the research question.

For instance, in their interesting study of the attempts in the 1950s of Hamburg and Leipzig to brand themselves as urban spaces of identity, in a process of 'urban collectivity building', in Chap. 7, Yvonne Robel and Inge Marszolek recognize that '[...] the concept of figuration exhibits a strong bias to the investigation of communicative practices. However, not only individuals are involved in these communicative practices but also collectivities and organizations.' On this basis, they argue that it is justified to ask about the role of the cities' media organization for the 'collective processes of identity building', and their analysis accordingly applies a cross-media critical discourse analysis of the two cities' broadcasting and electronic media content, considering significant metaphors which position the cities in different ways as a 'bridge to the world' (Leipzig) and 'gateway to the world' (Hamburg). However, my problem is that we are not presented with an actor constellation whose negotiations, contestations and concerted efforts can be said to have resulted in the 'communicative practices' (or simply 'contents') disseminated by the media. Moreover, the analysis is framed by references to 'deep mediatization', in spite of the fact that this era is a phenomenon of the twenty-first century. In other words, maybe the figurational framework is here grafted onto a fairly straightforward discourse analysis of the media representation of cities?

Similarly, in their insightful discourse analysis of how deliberative and moralizing norms and values around the causes and consequences of the financial crisis are communicatively constructed on four financial blogs, in Chap. 10, Rebecca Venema and Stephanie Averbeck-Lietz position their analysis within the figurational approach: 'The figurational approach [...] offered the chance for an integrative, cross-media analysis of crisis-related normative controversies, while reflecting on the specific interplay of actors, practices and structures characterizing and moulding these processes' (256). They analyze a 'media ensemble' of four blogs populated by an 'actor constellation' of three prominent bloggers and a multi-author group, some of whom are specialized journalists while others are financial experts. This actor constellation is characterized as 'a specific and dynamic collectivity of debate emerging in cross-media debates on the crisis' (247). However, it is not clear in what sense these three types of actors, who write for four selected blogs, can be seen as a 'collectivity' or an actor constellation. Is it not rather that they have been sampled to *represent* a much larger communicative figuration, or domain, of financial reporting and debate, with a much larger actor constellation, which should have been considered analytically in order to justify the claim of having analyzed a communicative figuration?

A related objection could be raised against the claim that the analyzed debates 'are primarily situated in a specific media ensemble: the aforementioned blogs' (249). It is not evident in what sense the four selected blogs constitute a media ensemble, apart from having been selected by the authors for analytical scrutiny. The authors describe how the blog debates 'are related to the figurations of other publics [...], including for example expert journals or newspapers and television coverage about the crisis' (249), and state that one blog in particular 'connects to other blogs as well as national and international mass and specialist media' (249). In order to qualify as an analysis of a 'communicative figuration', it could be said that the analysis should have encompassed (at least parts of) the interdiscursive media ensemble, and not just the four blogs. It is thus not evident to me how this discourse analysis of a sample of blog debates about the 2008 financial crisis qualifies as an example of the application of the figurational framework.

I was also puzzled by the way in which the study by Tanja Pritzlaff-Scheele and Frank Nullmeier, Chap. 12, analyzed its communicative figuration of political decision-making meetings by proxy, projecting the findings from an experimental laboratory on to the real-life setting of political decision-making. The aim of the study was to explore why politicians continue to prefer face-to-face settings for their decision meetings, at a time when most other areas of political communication are becoming mediatized. Instead of analyzing genuine communicative figuration of decision-making, Pritzlaff-Scheele and Nullmeier conducted micro-ethnographic analysis comparing, on the one hand, face-to-face group experiments in which participants communicated naturally with speech–body acts, and, on the other hand, computer-mediated chat experiments that were purely text-based. The groups' decision topics were taken from public news topics and everyday personal matters. Unsurprisingly, they found that in the text-based chat groups 'participants find it difficult to build trust in this environment' (298). As I understand the experiment, the differences between the experimental setting and the real-life situation of political decision-making seem so evident that the study can hardly count as a study of any communicative figuration, other than that of the laboratory: For instance, the chat-based decision groups used cumbersome text-based computer-mediated communication (CMC) only, and did not include video conferencing, and the experimental participants, presumably with no prior collaborative relations, seem to have little at stake compared with the participants in real-life decision meetings.

Another problematizing discussion (already hinted at above) has to do with the scalability of communicative figurations, and the risk of diluting the concept if the scalability is infinite.

In principle, the scalability of communicative figurations, from the smallest grouping (such as a meeting of a handful of people in a company) to the most complex networked entity (such as the global financial market), follows logically from the definition of the concept. Any entity that can be said to have an actor constellation, a frame of relevance, and a set of communicative practices (with a media ensemble) is a communicative figuration. But, speaking from a position of conceptual formalism, one unintended consequence of the scalability may be that the concept of communicative figuration verges on being empty—if anything can be nominated as a communicative figuration? Perhaps it is worth discussing whether a boundary can be pragmatically set up between rigorously defined, yet flexible communicative figurations, and other forms of social collectivities that are not communicative figurations.

This said, it is obviously not possible to police the proper use of 'communicative figurations' for analytical purposes; however, it can be suggested that however helpful this conceptual framework may be as a heuristic lens for researching almost any communicative phenomenon, it should perhaps be used more discriminatingly. Maybe a consensus could be reached about what does and what does not constitute a felicitous communicative figuration.

One such core operational area for communicative figurations research could be research which aims to *map* the cross-media practices in a social domain, in the form of a mapping and explaining their interrelations with media ensembles and repertoires. Many of the case studies in the present volume, ranging from the mapping of the communicative practices of small collectivities (such as groups of friends or institutionally defined groups), over larger community groups and organizations (such as NGOs and educational institutions), to entire country-wide communicative landscapes (such as the news ecology or a national grassroots organization), would fulfil this criterion of carrying out a descriptive and explanatory mapping of a communicative figuration with a definable constellation of actors, common frames of relevance and a set of communicative practices entangled with a media ensemble.

17.5 Methodological Media-Centrism and Non-Media-Centrism in Figurational Research

Looking over the analytical methods used in the dozen case studies of communicative figurations in this volume, it is clear there are no prescribed methods in the figurational research community, although a clear preponderance of qualitative methods stands out, especially qualitative interviews in naturalistic settings, but also varieties of ethnographic observation and discourse analysis, often in mixed-method combinations: the reader encounters qualitative interviews (sometimes with photo elicitation or card sorting), participant observation, discourse analysis, quantitative social network analysis, quantitative surveys, quantitative content analysis and qualitative analysis of laboratory experiments. One therefore cannot but applaud the diversity of the methodological toolbox applied by figurational researchers.

Considering that two defining features of deep mediatization are digitization and datafication, it is remarkable there are no full case studies that exploit the tracking capability of online communication, and only one study which uses netnography to understand the online communication of actor constellations (Wolf and Wudarski, Chap. 6).

However, in the interesting and reflective Chap. 16, Andreas Breiter and Andreas Hepp discuss digital traces as a controversial methodological challenge for the social sciences in general and for figurational research in particular. The crucial question is 'how we can analyze digital traces in a way that we can contextualize them with the figurations of humans that *produce* these sequences of "digital footprints" but also *use* them as a means for social construction' (393). The chapter uses the example of school information systems to discuss in a preliminary way how automatically generated data can be combined with qualitative methods in a mixed-method strategy for the illumination of the given social domain.

To this we may add that as long as society's media ensembles and most people's media repertoires are hybrid constellations of both legacy media and online media, exclusive reliance on the tracking of media users' digital footprints would make the use of all non-digital media disappear from view. Therefore, either researchers will have to overcome the practical technological difficulties of aggregate measurement of individuals' offline and online media use, or a holistic record of people's complete media repertoires will have to be established through quantitative and qualitative forms of self-report methods (Schrøder 2016).

Chapter 15, by Juliane Klein, Michael Walter and Uwe Schimank, is devoted to an immensely inspiring systematic in-depth inquiry into the strengths and weakness of different forms of qualitative interviews for constructing people's cross-media repertoires from the available media ensemble. The general interest of their exploration, beyond optimization of the knowledge interest of their own figurational project, has to do with finding a best practice for the non-mediacentric understanding of media use in the life-world. Following the call for non-mediacentric media research of David Morley (2009); Zlatan Krajina et al. (2014) and others, their study is essentially devoted to the solving of the age-old so-called Observer's Paradox; that is, the fact that the aim of ethnographic research is to find out how people are behaving when they are not being systematically observed—yet this can only be done by observing them systematically (Labov 1972: 209). Therefore, all research that engages people in the collection of data is intrusive and subject to bias.

The research interest of Klein et al. lies in establishing how media play a part in five life spheres: work, intimate relations, parenthood, asset building, and civil society engagement: 'which role does the interviewees' media repertoires play in their conduct of life with respect to disturbances and coping' (364). In pursuing this aim they are concerned with exploring how the participants' own horizon of relevance can be given priority: what method can ensure a large measure of openness while retaining the researcher's thematic focus on media? The obvious problem faced by many qualitative researchers is that if researchers state their media-focused research interest in their initial framing of the interview and frequently during the course of the interview, 'they might steer the interviewees' response behaviour' (366) and impose a media-centric focus which may not accurately reflect how the interviewees perceive media in the different life spheres.

In order to find a solution to this problem, Klein et al. devise an impressively systematic research design, which takes into account that media-centrism is a continuum. They set up a taxonomic methodological system of media-centrism, which enables researchers to choose the degree of media-centrism that best serves the knowledge interest of their project (Table 15.1: 372). Out of the taxonomy's nine possible interview strategies they select four for experimental testing, with an increasing order of media-centrism:

- Strategy 1: The least mediacentric interview strategy, in which the researcher does not mention media at all, waiting for interviewees to spontaneously bring media into the talk.
- Strategy 3: Media are mentioned in a non-conspicuous way at the beginning of the interview, and are only brought in at the very end after having dealt with the life spheres.
- Strategy 4: Media are mentioned in a non-conspicuous way at the beginning of the interview, and are brought in explicitly after each of the life spheres has been dealt with.
- Strategy 2: Media are emphatically mentioned at the beginning of the interview, and are also brought in explicitly after each of the life spheres has been dealt with.

The analysis of these four interviewing strategies then looked for the prominence that media repertoires displayed in the participants' accounts of how they coped with changes in the different life spheres. On this basis, Klein et al. opted for Strategy 4 as the one which best fulfilled their research interest in studying first people's life spheres and secondly the media ensembles drawn into them:

> [...]strategy 4 appears to be the one that best suits the purposes of our project. The set stimulus is subtle and thus does not dominate the interviewees' response behaviour, yet it is strong enough to contain the presence of the media topic throughout the interview. Most importantly, this interviewing strategy allows the respondents' individual relevance structures with respect to media and media use as part of their daily routines to be captured. (382–383)

However, other researchers may ask themselves whether Strategy 4 should necessarily be seen as the universal solution to the methodological conundrums of non-mediacentric media research—whether this strategy would be the appropriate one for contributing to *their* knowledge interest.

For other kinds of figurational research, in which media practices are a more central concern, it can be necessary to be more mediacentric, and still succeed in not being overly mediacentric. For instance, if one is interested in mapping repertoires of cross-media news consumption at the national level, I would think that news media must play a relatively explicit role throughout the interview in order not to risk letting lesser used news sources disappear from view. Moreover, other factors than the interviewer's explicitness in verbalizing media may cause the interviewee to feel at ease or not, and hence affect the extent to which they speak authentically about the role of media in their lifeworld: in general it is of paramount importance to establish a high degree of rapport with the interviewee; more concretely the choice of a domestic versus a more formal (such as a university) location for the interview can affect whether the interview mobilizes undesirable filters on their account of lifeworld-with-the-media experiences.

In my own research, I have opted for something like Strategy 2, because my knowledge interest was somewhat less non-mediacentric (in other words *more* mediacentric) than that of Klein et al. My knowledge interest was to build insights about people's individual appropriation of the news media ensemble in the national public sphere: how, across the many communicative figurations of their lifeworld, deliberately and routinely, they assembled the personal media repertoires which best served their various objectives of democratic and everyday public connection (Couldry et al. 2007), diversion and entertainment, specific instrumental knowledge, and so on (Kobbernagel and Schrøder 2016).

Briefly, therefore, we started our interviews with a solid day-in-the-life conversation in which we pursued in an open manner the sequence of communicative figurations traversed by the interviewee during the course of a day, asking which media were used in them. The interviewee's relevance structures were catered to by adhering to a framework that subtly explored along seven dimensions how the various news media used were experienced as 'worthwhile' by the interviewee. This open stage of the interview was followed by a card-sorting stage, in which interviewees sorted 36 cards representing what we deemed to be the relevant national news media ensemble at the time, according to the role they played in the interviewee's lifeworld. The card sorts were then factor-analyzed using Q-methodological procedure, which resulted in the creation of six news media repertoires, which were further substantiated by excerpts from the interview transcripts.

This is not to say that one interview strategy is inherently better than another. In planning new research into young people's news consumption repertoires under deep mediatization, I could easily imagine adopting, for instance, a narrower interest in online news consumption only, for which a more open methodological approach may be superior. For instance, one could combine the record from the tracking of the participants' digital footprints with qualitative interviews that inquire into the blending of news and other media experiences across communicative figurations in daily life. An additional component could be an open observation of the participants' on-screen navigation with a think-aloud plus interview component.

As I hope to have shown in the comments above, the dozen case studies described in this volume contribute significantly to the understanding of an interesting mosaic of communicative figurations across German society, from the small-scale repair cafés, through the intermediate level of NGOs and public institutions schools, to the national level of the public sphere. They are rich in descriptive details, often demonstrate interesting connections and consequences, and sometimes discover surprising insights about the role of communication media in ongoing socio-cultural transformations. As a whole, therefore, the volume is an enriching and innovative contribution to our knowledge about the ways in which communication media make a difference in ongoing cross-domain and cross-media transformations of culture and society.

Notes

1. Breiter and Ruhe state that 'the micro level of classroom management will be excluded from the analysis' (317). However, the administrative practices of individual teachers, including their use of mobile phones, are traced in group discussions (321).
2. Just as Kramp and Loosen repurpose and reinterpret their previous research to create new insights in a figurational study, it is striking how some classical studies of media practices can retrospectively be seen as analyses of communicative figurations. For instance, James Lull's seminal ethnographic study of the social uses of television can be seen as an analysis of the communicative figuration of the (American) family (Lull 1980); and even more so Janice Radway's similarly ground-breaking study of women's reading of romance novels can be seen as an analysis of the ways in which these media-based collectivities were incrementally transforming gender roles in the early 1980s (Radway 1984). A significant difference, though, is that these two studies did not analyze cross-media repertoires.

References

Couldry, Nick. 2012. *Media, society, world: Social theory and digital media practices.* Cambridge: Polity Press.

Couldry, Nick, and Andreas Hepp. 2016. *The mediated construction of reality.* Cambridge: Polity Press.

Couldry, Nick, Sonia Livingstone, and Tim Markham. 2007. *Media consumption and public engagement. Beyond the presumption of attention.* Basingstoke: Palgrave Macmillan.

Helles, Rasmus, Jacob Ørmen, Casper Radil, and Klaus B. Jensen. 2015. The media landscapes of European audiences. *International Journal of Communication* 9: 299–320.

Hepp, Andreas. 2013. The communicative figurations of mediatized worlds: Mediatization research in times of the 'mediation of everything'. *European Journal of Communication* 28 (6): 615–629.

Hepp, Andreas. 2014. Communicative figurations. In *Media practice and everyday agency in Europe*, ed. Leif Kramp, Nico Carpentier, Andreas Hepp, Ilija Tomanić Trivundža, Hannu Nieminen, Risto Kunelius, Tobias Olsson, Ebba Sundin, and Richard Kilborn, 83–99. Bremen: Edition Lumière.

Hepp, Andreas, and Uwe Hasebrink. 2017. How to research cross-media practices? Investigating media repertoires and media ensembles. *Convergence: The International Journal of Research into New Media Technologies*. First published date: 7 April 2017. doi:10.1177/1354856517700384.

Hjarvard, Stig. 2013. *The mediatization of culture and society*. New York: Routledge.

Kobbernagel, Christian, and Kim C. Schrøder. 2016. From everyday communicative figurations to rigorous audience news repertoires. A mixed method approach to cross-media news consumption. *Mediekultur* 32(60): 6–31.

Krajina, Zlatan, Shaun Moores, and David Morley. 2014. Non-media-centric media studies: A cross-generational conversation. *European Journal of Cultural Studies* 17 (6): 682–700.

Labov, William. 1972. *Sociolinguistic patterns*. Philadelphia: University of Pennsylvania Press.

Lull, James. 1980. The social uses of television. *Human communication research* 6: 197–209.

Madianou, Mirca. 2014. Polymedia: Communication and mediatized migration: An ethnographic approach. In *Mediatization of communication*, ed. Knut Lundby, 323–346. Berlin and Boston: De Gruyter/Mouton.

Morley, David. 2009. For a materialist, non-media-centric media studies. *Television and New Media* 10 (1): 114–116.

Radway, Janice A. 1984. *Reading the romance: Women, patriarchy and popular literature*. Chapel Hill: University of North Carolina Press.

Schrøder, Kim C. 2011. Audiences are inherently cross-media: Audience studies and the cross-media challenge. *Communication management quarterly* 18 (6): 5–27.

Schrøder, Kim C. 2016. Q-method and news audience research. In *The SAGE handbook of digital journalism*, ed. Tamara Witschge, C.W. Anderson, David Domingo, and Alfred Hermida, 528–546. Los Angeles, CA: Sage.

Strömbäck, Jesper. 2008. Four phases of mediatization: An analysis of the mediatization of politics. *The International Journal of Press/Politics* 13 (3): 228–246.

Taneja, Harsh, James G. Webster, Edward C. Malthouse, and Thomas B. Ksiazek. 2012. Media consumption across platforms: Identifying user-defined repertoires. *New Media and Society* 14 (6): 951–968.

18

Conclusion

Giselinde Kuipers

18.1 Introduction: Figurations and Mediations

In *What is Sociology?* Norbert Elias introduces the concept 'figuration' with a metaphor: a game of cards. He writes:

> When four people are sitting around a table and play cards together, they form a figuration. Their actions are interdependent. Indeed, common [...] usage allows us to speak in this case of "game" as if it had some existence in itself. One can say "the game moves slowly." But despite all objectifying expressions, it is in this case quite clear that the course of the game springs from the interweaving of the actions of a group of interdependent individuals. (Elias 2006[1970]: 172; author's translation).

As Elias discusses these four people and their actions, he gradually unfolds the rationale of the figuration concept. This concept aims to overcome the distinction between 'the individual' and 'the social'. To show how social life is always a process. To show that there are shifting balances of power, rather than fixed positions of power and subordination. Finally, this concept aims to

G. Kuipers (✉)
Sociology Department, University of Amsterdam, Amsterdam, Netherlands
e-mail: g.m.m.kuipers@uva.nl

show that 'the game'—and thus, any social interaction—has a reality and a logic of its own that cannot be reduced to the intentions of individual players.

But can one understand the game by just looking at the players? Elias mentions the role of the table, which should please Latourians. But what about the deck of cards? Without taking into account the cards—are they thrown or held onto, in one person's hand, another's, or on the table, isolated or in specific combinations?—the actions of the human players make little sense. The cards are part of the figuration. Not as actors, however. But what, then?

Reading this volume, it occurred to me that the cards are a *medium*. The cards relay information between the players, mediating their relations and interactions. They have content (numbers, colours), technology (print) and a material basis (cardboard, plastic coating). They can be recombined to convey different messages. They encompass different genres, ranging from sophisticated (bridge) to simple (old maid), from global (poker) to local (*Skat*). They even can work on different 'platforms'. Today, many card games are played on the 'meta-medium' (see Hepp and Hasebrink, this volume) of the computer.

All human figurations are mediated. Elias, in the late 1960s, was fighting different battles: against Parsonian functionalism, behaviourism and anti-historicism (Elias 2006 [1970]; Elias and Scotson 2008 [1965]). Thus, he was not concerned with issues of mediation and mediatization.[1] But in the twenty-first century, increasing mediatization is reshaping social life at a high pace. The role of media in human interaction has taken centre stage. This volume, and the larger research programme into Communicative Figurations that most of its authors are involved in, successfully revives Elias's notion of figuration to make sense of the current age of 'deep mediatization'.

Reading the various chapters, I was struck to see how well the concept of figuration worked to understand the way people organize themselves in fluctuating groups, organized through and around a wide range of media. The figurational approach allows researchers to bridge social life and media life, as well as social theory and media theory. This is an important and timely intervention. Neither social science nor media studies has, in my view, been able to successfully conceptualize the increasing interweaving of media and social life.[2] The new figurational approach of the 'Bremen School' is an ambitious, potentially fruitful step towards thinking about media and social life as integrated and co-constitutive.

My reading of this volume was guided by three questions. First, does this figurational approach work? Does it allow us to see things that we previously did not? Do we see relations or patterns that we previously missed? Second, how does the new figurational approach relate to the figurational approach as developed by Elias and his followers? What does it add or improve? Third, is this, or can this be, the beginning of a new paradigm that bridges media and social theory?

18.2 Does the Figurational Approach Allow Us to See New Things?

The true test of any theoretical approach is its usefulness: does it allow us to see or understand things that we previously did not? In this volume, the figurational approach is employed to analyze a wide variety of topics: from (non)tweeting clerics to instant-messaging adolescents, and from political decision-making to hacker collectives. Methods vary too: content analysis, surveys, interviews, ethnography. Throughout, the chapters refer to the figurational approach as outlined in the introductory chapter by Hepp and Hasebrink (Chap. 2). This gives the volume coherence and shows the merits of the approach.

All chapters show, in various ways, how people and media come together to create fluctuating figurations. Various forms of media, or 'media ensembles', are central to these figurations. As all authors show, the workings of these figurations cannot be understood without taking into account the diverse media practices of the actors involved. This is as true for adolescent friendship groups as it is for journalists, clerics, social activists or school principals. Moreover, these figurations are not fixed: they change, and they look different from different perspectives. Typically, the authors use the term 'network' (always with the same Elias quote) to describe these shifting figurations. The approach also comes with a clear methodological logic: in most chapters, looking for these networks of actors is the first step of the analysis. The second step is the connection of these networks with their media ensembles. Thus, the analytical steps automatically lead the authors to consider people and media in conjunction.

Many chapters highlight the nested nature of these figurations of people and media. All figurations are embedded in larger 'figurations of figurations'. Thus, organizations and institutions also form networks, which operate by the same mediated, fluctuating logic. This nesting is evident in the chapters in the second part, which deal with institutions and organizations such as journalism, blogging, schools and the Church. The nested view is most effective, however, when applied to more fluid domains. The interweaving of different figurations helps us understand bottom-up social action, such as the repair cafés discussed by Kannengießer (Chap. 5) or the hacker collectives discussed by Kubitschko (Chap. 4). Furthermore, the analysis of everyday mediated and unmediated interactions, such as the social life in cities as analyzed by Hepp et al. (Chap. 3), is much enlightened by this layered approach. Finally, this interweaving sheds light on the interconnectedness of global and local, as shown by Robel and Marszolek (Chap. 7).

This nested nature of figurations can also be extended downwards, to everyday interactions or even to individual or intra-individual level: the formation of self and identity, the expression of emotions, the regulation of bodies. The theoretical agenda certainly allows for this. However, the focus seems to be more on the upwards connection, from micro- towards meso- and macro-levels, rather than across micro-levels. Every now and then, the chapters offer tantalizing glimpses of an extension towards the shaping of selves and the role of emotions in these figurations. For instance, Wolf and Wudarski discuss the emergence of new, informal ways of learning, and new forms of expertise in online gaming (Chap. 6). Friemel and Bixler show how adolescents bond while communicating through media, about media (Chap. 8). Pritzlaff-Scheele and Nullmeier show that people (sadly) have more trouble reaching decisions in online settings (Chap. 12). In these cases, the figurations expand upwards, towards wider societal networks, but also downwards, towards the shaping of emotions and identities.

Throughout the volume, authors show how people and media come together in figurations through *practice*. The practice-based approach captures people's simultaneous engagement with various media and other people, highlighting not only the interweaving, but also the co-constitution[3] of figurations through people and media. The focus on practice means that media and people are seen simultaneously, without one having analytical or causal precedence over the other. In some chapters, the analytical focus on practice is combined with the nesting of figurations on different levels—especially Hepp et al. (Chap. 3); Kubitschko (Chap. 4), Kramp and Loosen (Chap. 9); Breiter and Ruhe (Chap. 13); Friemel and Bixler (Chap. 8). In these cases, the new figurational approach to me seemed the most productive theoretically: new connections between media, human action and social groupings became visible that would have been difficult to see with other perspectives.

This volume also shows—maybe inadvertently—how difficult it is to show the interweaving of people and media without looking at practices. Not all methods and topics are equally suited to a practice theory. As is explained in an insightful chapter on methods at the end of the book (Chap. 17), capturing practices is difficult in general. Sometimes, authors in this volume attempt to infer practices from media texts or survey responses. In these cases, the focus on practices becomes somewhat strained, and the simultaneous focus on people and media more tenuous.

Finally, all chapters see figurations are linked by shared 'frames of relevance'. This is a true innovation as compared with the original Eliasian concept. The focus on shared frames of relevance enables researchers to analytically separate figurations. The recurring problem in the study of (informal) networks is that they have no clear boundaries: in the end, everybody is connected to everybody, and everything is connected to everything. Too easily, scholars then fall back on conventional institutional delineations. However, as the chapters in Part II on institutions and organizations show, in this era of deep mediatization organizations often have fuzzy boundaries and many outward connections, while internally they may be fragmented and scattered. The figurational approach allows us to see how 'hard' institutions such as schools, news organizations and even the Church are made up of various communicative figurations, with different linkages to the outside world. Indeed, institutions and organizations in this perspective form the meeting point of many figurations, each held together by shared 'frames of relevance'.

Again, the usefulness of the figurational approach is both theoretical and empirical. The 'frame of relevance' helps to identify and delineate the unit(s) of analysis, and it yields interesting empirical results. Like the focus on practice, not all contributors manage to make optimal use of this concept. Sometimes, authors do not need it because the figuration is rather easy to delineate. More often, the question where figurations end, of how to identify a figuration, is simply not posed. But when applied, as for instance in the contribution of Friemel and Bixler (Chap. 8), Robel and Marszolek (Chap. 7) and Venema and Averbeck-Lietz (Chap. 10), the notion of frame of relevance seems a powerful tool for dealing with the fluidity, unboundedness and interconnectedness of communicative figurations.

The figurational approach clearly has added value as a theoretical perspective. Throughout the volume, it works as a clear methodological guideline. The chapters consistently connect people with media practices and ensembles. In the majority of the chapters, the figurational approach works well to highlight issues and relations that would otherwise remain unseen. However, in some chapters the figurational approach was more integral to the analysis than in others. The perspective works best when the various elements of the Hepp–Hasebrink three-step programme (constellation of actors, frame of relevance, media practices) are integrated with each other, and inform both theory and empirical approach. A truly fruitful use of this perspective, however, implies the adoption of a number of assumptions that to me appear to underlie the communicative figurations approach. As I see it, these assumptions are: (1) social life is relational; (2) social life is processual; (3) meaning is constitutive of, and emerging from, interaction. I will return to these assumptions at the end of this chapter.

18.3 Does the New Figurational Approach Improve the Old Figurational Approach?

The second question that occupied me during the reading of this volume was its relation to the original figurational approach, and 'figurational sociology' as I have come to know it. Reading the volume, I sometimes felt like Darwin on the Galapagos Islands. During a period of separation, two different species have evolved from the same finch. The figurational finch that I am most familiar with was developed by Elias's students and their students, in the Netherlands, Germany and the UK (cf. Mennell 1994; Wouters 2007; Dunning and Hughes 2013). The communicative figurations finch seems to me a uniquely German species, adapted to a habitat of media scholars and German social theorists.

Two innovations of the Bremen finch recur throughout the book: the focus on media and the explicit connection with practice theory. The latter, it seems to me, follows developments in social science as a whole. The specific inspiration in the communicative figurational finch seems to be the work of Nick Couldry (Couldry 2004, 2012). The figurational finch I am more familiar with has evolved in a similar direction, but mostly in interaction with the work of Pierre Bourdieu (1977, 1984). Both approaches have been concerned with the relation between figurations of different levels. The figurational sociologists, following the younger

Elias of *The Civilising Process*, have focused on the relation between societal change, state formation and 'personality make-up' or 'habitus'. This has led to an engagement with the sociology of emotions and the body on the one hand; and with historical–comparative sociology on the other.

The communicative figurational scholars, maybe influenced by systems theory, have analyzed 'figurations of figurations', mainly focusing on the interactions of systems and organizations within one society. Interestingly, the different approaches have sometimes come up with similar solutions. In this volume, the analysis of 'figurations of figurations' leads Kubitschko to use the metaphor of the spiral (Chap. 4), which is exactly the metaphor chosen by Cas Wouters in his study of informalization (Wouters 2007). In this respect, the two schools seem nicely complementary.

What strikes me most in the communicative figurations finch is its cross-breeding with phenomenology. As noted above, I consider the focus on 'frames of relevance' an important, though not completely developed, theoretical innovation. This concept reflects a deeper engagement with meaning-making as the basis of social life that seems inspired by phenomenology. This comes out clearly in the theoretical companion to this volume, *The mediated construction of reality* (Couldry and Hepp 2016). The title says it all: Berger and Luckman for the media age.

There are also some characteristics that this finch has lost, or maybe that are still there but atrophied. I have already mentioned the absence of emotions and bodies, and the relative lack of attention to the figurational shaping of selves—all classical themes of the younger Elias of court society and the civilizing process. Most notable is the near-disappearance of Elias's core concept of the power balance. The figuration concept was originally developed in a study of urban inequality and conflict (Elias and Scotson 2008). Power balances are also at the heart of the game metaphor. The players in a game are, as Elias notes, both allies (*Verbündete*, or people tied together) and adversaries. In the course of the game, power relations shift, but these balances are supported by all players, the weak and the strong. Power is therefore strongly related to Elias's other central concept: interdependencies.

I am inclined to connect the disappearance of power in the Bremen school with the phenomenological slant. Add power to the social construction of reality, and the result easily becomes rather paranoid, or at least deeply Gramscian: the social construction merely a projection of the powerful. However, several of the contributions in this volume could have done with the relational power concept as developed in figurational sociology. To name some obvious examples: the relations between people with different levels of expertise in games (Wolf and Wudarski, Chap. 6); the shifting balance of power between journalists and their audiences (Kramp and Loosen, Chap. 9); the power structures limiting the media use of clerics (Radde-Antweiler et al., Chap. 11), and the varying impacts of national states on urban identity (Robel and Marszolek Chap. 7) or media use in schools (Breiter and Ruhe, Chap. 13). Moreover, the relative absence of power in the analysis makes it difficult to grasp the balances of dependence and power between people, media and media producers and organizations. In all case studies in this book, this is an invisible, but all-important figuration: between people and their media, between 'users' and producers'. Interestingly, in these media figurations power balances are often fluid, nested and complex—ideally suited to figurational analysis.

18.4 Towards a New Paradigm?

The final question: do we see here the beginning of a new paradigm that bridges social and media theory? As I have argued here, this book presents a novel, potentially very productive approach. The combination of figurational with practice theory is particularly good at simultaneously capturing people and their media, or media and their people. Certainly, from the perspective of social science, this is a great step forward. Despite considerable, I would say fundamental, changes to social life, the toolbox of sociologists has remained fundamentally unchanged since the 1990s (or maybe even since the 1800s). In general, media theory has done better in conceptualizing the two-way relationship between media and persons. Additionally, the communicative figurations approach offers a clear methodological recipe that works well across a range of topics, methodologies and even theoretical traditions.

As I noted above, the communicative figurations approach seems to hinge on three basic assumptions: (1) social life is relational; (2) social life is processual; (3) meaning is constitutive of, and emerging from, interaction. Not all chapters in this book embrace these assumptions, but the editors clearly do. These assumptions link this approach not only to figurational sociology, but to a wider category of theories, many of which are discussed in the theoretical introduction (Chap. 1).

The communicative figurations approach is a member of the family of 'relational theories', which generally is said to include Elias, Bourdieu, present-day practice theory, network theory and new institutional theory (cf. Emirbayer 1997; Uitermark et al. 2016). What connects these theories is a focus on relations rather than individuals, and on meaning, value and power as emerging from relations between people. To my knowledge, media in any form are not central to these approaches. The chapters in this book show that media can be included seamlessly in a relational analysis. Here, we have maybe not a new paradigm, but surely the fruitful expansion of an existing paradigm.

The second assumption is the basic processual character of (mediated) social life. Communicative figurations, and the figurations of these figurations, are constantly shifting because of the fluctuating nature of human and human–media relations. The backdrop of every interaction is formed by several longer-term processes, each moving at its own pace. As people are living their mediated lives, they are engulfed by processes of media diversification, growing connectivity and media omnipresence, rapid innovation and datafication (see Hepp and Hasebrink in this volume; Couldry and Hepp 2016). Inherent in the figurational approach, therefore, is the realization that things are always in flux. Moreover, different processes move at different speeds (Elias 2006 [1970]; cf. Abbott 2001). Many authors embraced this processual approach in their framework, but in their analysis reverted to more static approaches. I sympathize with these authors. In fact, the main reason that I am at best a part-time Eliasian is the immense difficulty of being consistently processual in empirical research. However, in an era of fast and deep mediatization, static approaches seem increasingly insufficient. This, then, is a paradigm shift that is difficult, but might be called for. Maybe here, a further integration of media and social theory might help. Media scholars have been developing new tools to study their elusive, fragmented and flighty topic. Other scholars could use their innovation to try anew to capture change.

The third assumption is related to the blending of phenomenological and figurational perspectives in the communicative figurations approach: the centrality of meaning to (mediated) social life. This assumption translates directly into the concept of the 'frames of relevance', which conceptualizes figurations as connections of people through shared meanings and orientations. In other words: what makes a figuration is a sharing of meaning, no matter how fleeting and temporary. This sharing may lead to the construction of new meanings, which can be 'carried' towards yet other figurations. This solves a number of issues related to the original concept of figuration. What is the boundary of a figuration? What separates one figuration from another? How do people switch from one figuration to another? Can they be part of several figurations at the same time, and how does this work? These questions were difficult enough to answer before deep mediatization. Today, the ramifications are almost impossible. The concept of a frame of relevance offers us a way to understand the increasingly complex linkages between people, in a way that no paradigm I am aware of can do.

Let us return to the game of cards. The four players share a frame of relevance: the game. However, they may be playing their game in a place—say, a bar—with other people. Presumably, they also share a frame of relevance, though less intensely, with these people. Possibly, their relations with the people in the room vary. Maybe the husband of one of the players is there. Marriage is typically a two-person figuration. The other players may have other shared frames of relevance with this person: family, friend, neighbour. These nested and overlapping figurations can all be captured and analyzed with the concept of the 'frames of relevance', which can be expanded endlessly upward, downward and outward.

Now imagine a game of cards that is played online. Maybe all four players are in different corners of the world. One may be home alone, one in a train, one in a bar, one surreptitiously playing a game at work. In a mediated situation, the permutations are endless. To make up a figuration, physical co-presence is not necessary at all. Especially in such complex mediated cases, thinking of figurations as delineated by shared frames of relevance is a fruitful innovation. The consequence, of course, is that everybody is always part of many figurations at the same time, spread across different locations. But this 'complex and also contradictory' situation, as Hepp, Simon and Sowinska observe (Chap. 3), is the normal state of affairs for most people today.

With this budding new paradigm, we at least have the words to describe it.

Notes

1. See however, Elias 2010 [1991] and Elias 2011 [1989].
2. As a sociologist, I am sad to admit that media scholars have done a much better job at this than social scientists (see for instance Livingstone 2009; Couldry 2012; van Dijck 2013). Social scientists, when they consider

media at all, tend to conceptualize them either as a continuation of existing interaction patterns by other means, or as a 'cause' that has 'effects' on individuals and interactions.

3. On co-constitution, (see Breiger 2000; Mohr 2000; Friedland et al. 2014).

References

Abbott, Andrew. 2001. *Time matters: On theory and method.* Chicago: Chicago University Press.

Breiger, Ronald. 2000. A tool kit for practice theory. *Poetics* 27 (2–3): 91–115.

Bourdieu, Pierre. 1977. *Outline of a theory of practice.* Cambridge: Cambridge University Press.

Bourdieu, Pierre. 1984. *Distinction: A social critique of the judgment of taste.* London: Routledge.

Couldry, Nick. 2004. Theorizing media as practice. *Social semiotics* 14 (2): 115–132.

Couldry, Nick. 2012. *Media, society, world. Social theory and digital media practice.* Cambridge: Polity Press.

Couldry, Nick, and Andreas Hepp. 2016. *The mediated construction of reality.* Cambridge: Polity Press.

Dunning, Eric, and Jason Hughes. 2013. *Norbert Elias and modern sociology. Knowledge, interdependence, power, process.* London: Bloomsbury.

Elias, Norbert. 2006 [1970]. *Was ist Soziologie?* Berlin: Suhrkamp Verlag.

Elias, Norbert. 2010 [1991]. *The society of individuals.* Dublin: University College Dublin Press.

Elias, Norbert. 2011 [1989]. *The symbol theory.* Dublin: University College Dublin Press.

Elias, Norbert, and John Scotson. 2008 [1965]. *The established and the outsiders.* Dublin: University College Dublin Press.

Emirbayer, Mustafa. 1997. Manifesto for a relational sociology. *American Journal of Sociology* 103 (2): 281–317.

Friedland, Roger, John Mohr, Henk Roose, and Paolo Gardinali. 2014. The institutional logics of love: measuring intimate life. *Theory and society* 43: 333–370.

Livingstone, Sonia M. 2009. On the mediation of everything. *Journal of Communication* 59 (1): 1–18.

Mennell, Stephen. 1994. The formation of we-images: A process theory. In *Social theory and the politics of identity*, ed. Craig Calhoun, 174–197. Cambridge: Blackwell.

Mohr, John. 2000. Introduction: Structures, institutions and cultural analysis. *Poetics* 27 (2–3): 57–68.

Uitermark, Justus, Vincent A. Traag, and Jeroen Bruggeman. 2016. Dissecting discursive contention: A relational analysis of the Dutch debate on minority integration, 1990–2006. *Social Networks* 47: 107–115.

van Dijck, José. 2013. *The culture of connectivity. A critical history of social media.* Oxford: Oxford University Press.

Permissions

All chapters in this book were first published in CFTCTDM, by Springer; hereby published with permission under the Creative Commons Attribution License or equivalent. Every chapter published in this book has been scrutinized by our experts. Their significance has been extensively debated. The topics covered herein carry significant information for a comprehensive understanding. They may even be implemented as practical applications or may be referred to as a beginning point for further studies.

The contributors of this book come from diverse backgrounds, making this book a truly international effort. We would like to thank all the contributing authors for lending their expertise to make the book truly unique. They have played a crucial role in the development of this book. Without their invaluable contributions this book wouldn't have been possible. They have made vital efforts to compile up to date information on the varied aspects of this subject to make this book a valuable addition to the collection of many professionals and students.

This book was conceptualized with the vision of imparting up-to-date and integrated information in this field. To ensure the same, a matchless editorial board was set up. Every individual on the board went through rigorous rounds of assessment to prove their worth. After which they invested a large part of their time researching and compiling the most relevant data for our readers.

The editorial board has been involved in producing this book since its inception. They have spent rigorous hours researching and exploring the diverse topics which have resulted in the successful publishing of this book. They have passed on their knowledge of decades through this book. To expedite this challenging task, the publisher supported the team at every step. A small team of assistant editors was also appointed to further simplify the editing procedure and attain best results for the readers.

Apart from the editorial board, the designing team has also invested a significant amount of their time in understanding the subject and creating the most relevant covers. They scrutinized every image to scout for the most suitable representation of the subject and create an appropriate cover for the book.

The publishing team has been an ardent support to the editorial, designing and production team. Their endless efforts to recruit the best for this project, has resulted in the accomplishment of this book. They are a veteran in the field of academics and their pool of knowledge is as vast as their experience in printing. Their expertise and guidance has proved useful at every step. Their uncompromising quality standards have made this book an exceptional effort. Their encouragement from time to time has been an inspiration for everyone.

The publisher and the editorial board hope that this book will prove to be a valuable piece of knowledge for students, practitioners and scholars across the globe.

Index

www.ingramcontent.com/pod-product-compliance
Lightning Source LLC
LaVergne TN
LVHW080643210926
848485LV00003B/316